SUBVERSION AS FOREIGN POLICY

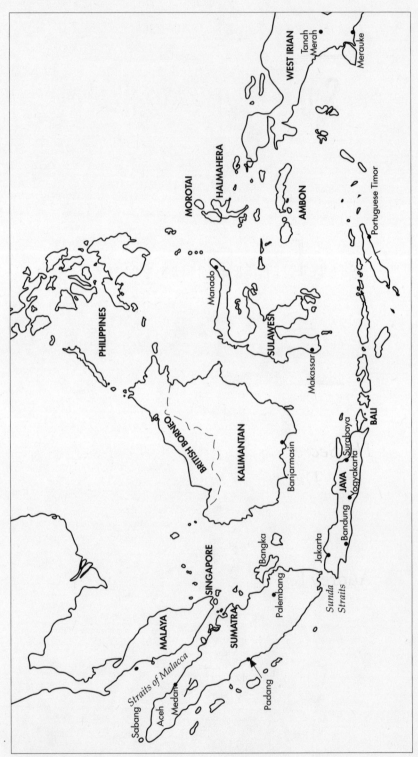

Map 1: The Indonesian Archipelago

SUBVERSION

AS

FOREIGN

POLICY

The Secret Eisenhower and Dulles
Debacle in Indonesia

Audrey R. & George McT. Kahin

THE NEW PRESS
New York

ISBN 1-56584-244-8
Library of Congress Catalog Card Number 95-67153

Published in the United States by The New Press, New York
Distributed by W. W. Norton & Company, Inc., New York

Established in 1990 as a major alternative to the large, commercial
publishing houses, The New Press is the first full-scale nonprofit American
book publisher outside of the university presses. The Press is operated
editorially in the public interest, rather than for private gain; it is
committed to publishing in innovative ways works of educational,
cultural, and community value that, despite their intellectual merits,
might not normally be commercially viable. The New Press's
editorial offices are located at the City University of New York.

Production management by Kim Waymer

Book design by Ann Antoshak

Printed in the United States of America

95 96 97 98   9 8 7 6 5 4 3 2 1

To Ange and Owen

CONTENTS

Maps

A Note on Spelling

In general, spelling of Indonesian words follows the new system introduced on August 17, 1972, with the exception of quotations from documents. (The most important of the changes were that dj became j [thus Jakarta, not Djakarta]; j became y; and tj became c.)

Personal names have been spelled according to individual preferences so far as this can be determined, and organizations that ceased to exist before the introduction of the new system retain their old spelling.

SUBVERSION AS FOREIGN POLICY

INTRODUCTION

DURING THE LATE 1950s the Eisenhower administration provoked and strongly abetted a major rebellion and then civil war in Indonesia that tore the country apart. Aiming to replace and transform its political leadership, the administration launched what was then the largest U.S. covert operation since World War II, involving not only the Central Intelligence Agency (CIA) but also the U.S. Navy and a camouflaged American air force. It was not only larger but also lasted considerably longer and involved a much greater loss of life than the now-well-known Bay of Pigs fiasco in Cuba. But while the latter occurred within 90 miles of Florida and was, in its broad outline at least, almost immediately well publicized, the American public and nearly all of its Congress never saw more than the well-shrouded tip of the iceberg of the earlier U.S. Indonesian intervention athwart the equator on the other side of the world. And it has remained one of the most zealously guarded secrets in the history of U.S. covert overseas operations.

Although the Indonesian intervention was not divulged to the public or to Congress, within the tight inner circle at the top of the American government it was bracketed with the Bay of Pigs as a foreign policy debacle. Thus, in the board of inquiry established by President Kennedy to investigate the Bay of Pigs catastrophe, Robert Lovett (who held posts of under secretary of state and secretary of defense under Eisenhower) drew a parallel between the U.S. action in Cuba and what he termed the "dismal failure" of "an almost similar incident which occurred in Indonesia" three years earlier.[1] Both fiascos were partly attributable to a considerable measure of presidential prejudice and spleen directed against the leaders of these two countries, Sukarno and Castro, as well as a consequence of the CIA's appallingly poor intelligence and political naïveté in assessing it. Of the two, the intervention in Indonesia was by far the most destructive in human terms, had a heavier and more lasting political impact, and, with respect to U.S. objectives, was the most counterproductive.

Why, nearly four decades after the event, has this Indonesian intervention remained so secret? What was the nature of this massive undertaking? How was it conceived and under what circumstances? Did it meet the objectives of the Eisenhower administration? What were its consequences —both immediate and long-range—for the Indonesian people? What effect did this intervention have on the emergence and character of Indonesia's present government and its relation with Indonesian society? Did it affect the nature and scope of subsequent American policy toward Indonesia? What can this experience tell us about presidential use of the CIA as an instrument of foreign policy? Are there any insights to be drawn from it as to Eisenhower's and John Foster Dulles's approach to the Third World? Is the nature and outcome of this episode germane to arguments about legislative oversight of the CIA and other covert arms of the American government? We believe that our study is relevant to all these questions.

• • • • •

Concern over the potential spread of communism was clearly the fundamental stratum on which the Eisenhower administration's global policies rested. The potency of this factor during the 1950s (and well after) was greatly enhanced by the contemporary cast of American domestic politics. Although the foreign policies of all American administrations have been sensitive to domestic political considerations, Eisenhower's was especially so. The temper of the times and particularly the circumstances of its election ensured this. Already powerful in the immediate postwar years under the Truman administration, the issue of communism had gained much greater influence on the American political stage with the appearance of Senator Joseph McCarthy and his supporters. Its impact on American policy in Asia grew especially heavy when it became intertwined with and nourished by the specious but politically potent "loss-of-China" issue. The spurious charge that the Democrats' incompetence, and even betrayal, had been responsible for the Chinese Communist victory over Chiang Kai-shek's Kuomintang was used effectively by the Republicans against the Truman administration in the elections of 1950 and 1952. And that lesson was very much on the minds of the senior leaders of the Eisenhower administration, who found themselves enthralled by a dynamic they had helped to create, from which they had profited, and which could easily be extended to the rest of Asia. They were aware that if the American public could be persuaded that the Truman administration had possessed the capacity to halt the march of communism in China and was responsible for its "loss" to the "Free World," then surely successor administrations might well be held responsible if any further areas of Asia were lost to Communist control. Preoccupation with this corollary and its potential impact on Republican domestic political fortunes weighed heavily in the Eisenhower administration's approach to Southeast Asia and was of central importance in the calculations that led to its covert militarized interventions there.

Brandishing the "loss-of-China" club with particular force and recklessness after as well as during the election campaign of 1952, McCarthy and his allies in the Senate, enthusiastically supported by the pro-Chiang Kai-shek China Lobby, found a receptive audience among many Americans. The Senator's power in the early 1950s undoubtedly influenced the Eisenhower administration's foreign policy toward the countries of Southeast

Asia. Especially damaging was Dulles's and Eisenhower's yielding to the appointment of McCarthy's stout ally, Scott McLeod, as the State Department's chief security officer, charged with vetting the department's personnel—whether stationed in Washington, D.C., or overseas—as to their "positive loyalty" to the United States. Although Dulles soon realized that appointing McLeod encouraged rather than mollified McCarthy in his attacks against the State Department and its Asian policies, neither the secretary of state nor the president dared dismiss this zealous bigot or restrain him from his and McCarthy's vicious and unfounded charges that led to the firing of most of the department's best experts on China.[2] That example, and McLeod's continuing immunity from criticism by his superiors in the administration, was not lost on the department's Washington employees and members of the Foreign Service stationed overseas. It sent a chill through their ranks that disposed many of them to keep McCarthy's prejudices firmly in mind when dealing with matters relating to communism and its potential in Asia. They surely wished to avoid conduct and recommendations that might be construed as improving the chances for the expansion of communism into additional areas of Asia—a politically potent charge they knew the administration much wanted to avoid. Such consideration powerfully affected Eisenhower's and Dulles's approach to all of Southeast Asia.

Over the years the pendulum has swung back and forth as to whether Eisenhower or his secretary of state, John Foster Dulles, took the lead in fashioning their administration's foreign policy. Over the last decade, however, as more and more records have become available, a fairly broad consensus has emerged among historians that Eisenhower's role was most important and that, at least at the most fundamental level, he left more of an imprint on policy than did Dulles. On the basis of the newly available data, one of Eisenhower's major biographers, Stephen Ambrose, has concluded: "The truth was that Eisenhower, not Dulles, made the policy, as anyone who knew anything about the inner workings of the Eisenhower Administrations realized." By the nature of their jobs Dulles, of course, had more time to spend on the actual execution of foreign policy than did Eisenhower, and the same was true for Allen Dulles, the CIA head to whom the two often delegated a substantial implementing role. The fact that Dulles sometimes got more credit for policies than did Eisenhower, was, Ambrose believes, because "it was easier, more convenient, more profitable to blame Dulles, rather than Eisenhower, for specific failures."[3] And indeed Dulles often served as something of a lightning rod for the president, and as another biographer of Eisenhower observes, drew "hostile fire away from the president himself."[4] A balanced evaluation of this discourse has been provided by Richard Immerman, who more recently observed: "The president did retain control of policy—and decision making. But Dulles was an integral actor in the sphere of formulation as well as implementation. . . . Moreover, because their levels of interest and expertise differed, their contributions to different policy issues and areas varied. On some occasions Dulles took the lead; on others it was Eisenhower. They were in a real sense a team."[5] That seems to have been the case in their approach to the Third World, and certainly Southeast Asia, where the president and his secretary of state appear to have consistently worked in a harmonious and mutually reinforcing way.

In their conduct of foreign policy Eisenhower and Dulles relied much more heavily on the CIA than had the previous administration. Under Truman, who had established it in 1947, the agency had been largely concerned with gathering and evaluating intelligence from other countries, and it had limited its interventions into their political life primarily to funding newspapers and political parties. But as Ambrose has written: "Eisenhower believed the Agency could by used more effectively, indeed could become one of America's chief weapons in the Cold War. . . . Under Eisenhower's leadership and Allen Dulles' direction the size and scope of the CIA's activities increased dramatically during the 1950's."[6] Note the distinction: Eisenhower's leadership and Allen Dulles's direction. The CIA is an instrument of presidential policy; the president decides what it is to do, and he is responsible for its actions. Efforts to shield a president from responsibility for evident failures of covert policies carried out by the CIA at his direction, or simply to discredit the agency, have tended to promote the "rogue elephant" myth—that the CIA is a willful beast, acting on its own, independent of the president. Roguish the actions of the CIA sometimes are, but the elephant's mahout, the driver who sits on top and steers it, is always the president. He may give the elephant some leeway, it may well nudge him a bit, and occasionally it may stray a little from the path he wants it to follow, but it is he who decides the basic direction. And so when one observes the tremendous upsurge in activist, intrusive CIA activities under Eisenhower—when the agency "helped to overthrow governments in the Middle East and Latin America, tried to do so in Central and Eastern Europe . . . and hatched assassination plots against foreign leaders"[7]—one must bear in mind that these were the president's policies.

But this does not mean that the CIA cannot bring to bear considerable influence in the genesis and shaping of such decisions and the way they are carried out. For these, of course, reflect not only the a priori inclinations and personal prejudices of the president and his top advisers but also the intelligence available to them—or, more accurately, those elements they choose to rely on from what they have been able to assimilate from the vast body of information that has been collected. The pattern of selection has varied with presidents, but in Eisenhower's case, at least where clandestine operations in the Third World were concerned, this proclivity to rely heavily on the CIA for intelligence was clear. This was particularly marked in the case of Indonesia when, during the crucial period from mid-1957 to mid-1958, the reporting of the American Embassy in Jakarta, as well as that of foreign service officers on the State Department's Indonesia desk was of distinctly marginal influence. Undoubtedly this partiality for the CIA's intelligence was partly attributable to the generally harmonious working relationship between Eisenhower and John Foster Dulles and the unusual circumstance that the latter's own brother, Allen, was director of the CIA.

In his heavy reliance on the CIA Eisenhower was especially attracted to its capacity for covert operations. The official rationale for such secrecy was argued then, and has been so ever since, in terms of American security and protecting from foreign scrutiny the actions taken to secure that objective. But in fact, for both Eisenhower and his successors, the secrecy in the planning and execution of these actions has been primarily to shield them from the *American* public and its Congress rather than from the inhabitants of the country involved—who usually learn about them soon enough, and generally long before most Americans. For American presidents the principal attraction of covert operations has been, of course, that they provide a means for carrying out foreign policy that finesses the normal constraints of checks and balances from the legislative branch of government. Such secret operations could be planned and executed speedily without hindrance from a potentially recalcitrant Congress or the probings of the press and the public debate that might ensue. (At the most a few predictably approving congressmen were made privy to them, and even then only after the plan had been made and usually after its implementation was already actually under way.) Eisenhower regarded it as imperative that as president he have unimpeded use of covert foreign policy; he bridled at any attempts to establish congressional oversight of his role in this and was more successful than at least most of his successors in successfully resisting attempts to introduce any such constraints. In shielding his covert foreign policies from public scrutiny Eisenhower, like his successors, was able to rely on the formula of *plausible denial*, which was regularly built into all major secret overseas operations. Although calculated primarily to protect the reputation of the president (and the United States)—especially when the effort went awry— this procedure, of course, has militated seriously against presidential accountability. In the words of Loch K. Johnson in his recent highly regarded study.[8]

> The objective of plausible denial was to brush away footprints in a covert operation to prevent anyone from following the tracks back to the Oval Office. Above all, the virtue of the nation was to be protected by shielding the reputation of the president. His office was to be disassociated—in memoranda, minutes, or other records—from any dirty deeds that might be necessary in the rough-and-tumble world outside the U.S. Should the CIA or other agencies have to discuss an "extralegal" or unsavory operation with the president to obtain his approval, euphemisms and doubletalk were to be used: this would leave the chief executive free to deny, plausibly, that he had granted authority for its execution. It was decision-making by "a wink and a nod."

Consequently, even if the CIA were willing to declassify all pertinent documents bearing on a clandestine operation it still might be very difficult to establish clearly the president's role.

The shroud of secrecy can, of course, be most easily drawn over covert operations where the country involved is little known to Americans. This has usually been the case where Third World countries are concerned, and during the Eisenhower era was especially evident in its relations with the newly emerged ex-colonial countries. It was, understandably, generally more difficult to conduct such operations in European countries from which Americans or their forebears had emigrated and in which, consequently, events were sufficiently followed to make it relatively difficult for those fashioning foreign policy to keep the public in ignorance. The disparity was, of course, reinforced because American media coverage of most Third World countries was so meager.

In cases in which the Eisenhower administration perceived its clandestine effort to have been successful, particularly in its opposition to neutralists in the cold war or to socioeconomic radicals, whether or not they were Communists, it often arranged for calculated leaks to reach the public regarding the American "success." This was the case following the covert U.S. interventions in Iran in 1953 and Guatemala in 1954. But even with these two now-well-known examples the publicly cited "success" was short-lived. Having been instrumental in overthrowing Guatemala's elected non-Communist government, the administration was left there with a succession of brutal military leaders who have remained in power to this day. And in Iran, where it helped oust another non-Communist government and install the authoritarian regime of the Shah, the United States ultimately reaped the whirlwind when his heavy repression provoked a popular uprising that resulted in the installation of the regime of the Ayatollah Khomeini. Certainly in the long run, even by the standards of the Eisenhower period, these two cases must now be regarded as disastrous failures.

· · · · ·

Probably at no time since World War II has violence—especially on a militarized level—in the execution of covert American foreign policy been so widespread as during the Eisenhower administration. Especially was this so with respect to U.S. relations with Third World countries, where the importance of such operations often overshadowed the overt official level of policy. In none of these interventions were the consequences ephemeral. The more the record has been disclosed, the clearer it has become that they were failures, especially in their long-term, often unintended, results. Indeed, it is now clear that their impact has been seriously harmful to the peoples of the countries targeted. Moreover, the ongoing effects of these failures have often tended to constrain severely the scope and flexibility for the wisest exercise of subsequent American policy.

In no part of the Third World were the Eisenhower administration's *militarized* interventions—whether direct or by proxy—so extensive (or have they been so little chronicled) as in the newly emerged ex-colonial states of Southeast Asia. They encompassed Burma, Cambodia, Indonesia, and Laos, as well as Vietnam. There was also extensive covert American intervention in the Philippines, involving U.S. military and CIA advisers, military equipment, and financing, which resulted in the temporary defeat of a peasant rebellion and the election of a pro-American president, but this did not involve the injection of U.S. military power as such. (Although this is still often touted as having been a great success, lack of follow-through with respect to promised agrarian reform left peasant discontent smoldering and soon to flare up again.)

These secret interventions in Southeast Asia must to some extent be seen against the background of the skepticism of many officials of the Eisenhower administration as to the capacity of the newly independent former colonies to govern themselves sensibly (usually meaning in accordance with fundamental U.S. interests). An even more important liability was Washington's inability to understand the powerful thrust of nationalism in the ex-colonial states of this area and its great influence on their foreign policies. Indeed, this pulsing force was the principal root of their dedication to neutralist international policies and their determination to adopt an independent international stance unaligned with any great power. In the context of the cold war that, of course, meant alignment neither with the United States and its allies nor with what was then seen as a Sino-Soviet bloc. On the other hand, a dogged opposition to neutralism constituted one of the defining features in the Eisenhower administration's approach to Southeast Asia—second in importance only to its dedication to halting the growth of Communist power in the region. In the Manichaean worldview of President Eisenhower, John Foster Dulles, and Allen Dulles, the pursuit of a neutralist policy was regarded as politically naive and likely only to benefit the Sino-Soviet bloc. In effect, then, in the context of the cold war, those who would not stand with the United States were viewed as standing against it.

A common denominator in the approach of Eisenhower and Dulles to all the countries of Southeast Asia was their private assessment of the reasons for the "loss of China" to Communist control. They shared a somewhat more informed and sophisticated evaluation than the McCarthyites, attributing the Communist success in large part to what they believed was the Truman administration's overemphasis on maintaining China's full territorial integrity in the face of great Chinese Communist power. They argued that the United States should have been more realistic and been willing to give up the most vulnerable areas of the country temporarily, while husbanding the strength of Chiang Kai-shek's forces in more easily defended territory, pending a rollback after the Communists had, as they believed would inevitably be the case, alienated populations in the areas they had occupied. As Dulles put it to Hugh S. Cumming, Jr., on the eve of his departure in 1953 to take up the position of ambassador in Indonesia: "The territorial integrity of China became a shibboleth. We finally got a territorially integrated China—for whose benefit? The Communists."[9] Unwilling to make this mistake again, in their determination to prevent areas of Southeast Asia falling under Communist control, Eisenhower and Dulles were willing to see countries temporarily break up into "racial and geographic units," which could provide bases for moving against Communist power in other parts of their territory.[10]

Indonesia was the locus of by far the largest, and to this day the least known, of the Eisenhower administration's covert militarized interventions. That episode was, however, not unique, and the nature of the American policy that lay behind it can be more easily comprehended if it is viewed in the context of administration involvements elsewhere in Southeast Asia.

Burma provides a striking example of the Eisenhower administration's opposition to both neutralism and to the Chinese Communist government, as well as its willingness to subvert the sovereignty of a friendly state to achieve its ends. During the last year of the Korean War, Eisenhower took over and reinforced Truman's policy of trying to open up a second front based in northeastern Burma, designed to relieve military pressure against American forces in Korea by drawing Chinese troops from that front to guard against invasion across China's southern frontier. Organized, financed, and armed by the CIA, the approximately 15,000 Chinese Nationalist troops used in this covert operation were primarily remnants of Chiang Kai-shek's armies that had fled to Burma toward the end of China's civil war. Resisting Burmese attempts to disarm them, they were soon encadred by CIA advisers and periodically augmented during the 1950s by Chiang's elite troops flown in from Taiwan, a final increment of 1,200 of these men being added during the last year of the Eisenhower administration.

Burma, led at the time by one of the few elected governments of Southeast Asia, had from the outset been committed to a neutralist foreign policy, a prudent stance in view of its 1,000-mile-plus frontier with China. The government in Rangoon protested repeatedly to both the United States and Taiwan over their blatant violation of Burma's sovereignty, one which Burma was powerless to stop but which could easily provoke an equally disastrous riposte by Mao Tse-tung's army into Burma. The United States disclaimed any knowledge of the operations against China, even to its own ambassador in Rangoon, who finally resigned when he discovered the nature of this covert American involvement and that he had been completely bypassed by both the CIA and his own superiors at the State Department.[11]

After the travesty of a few short, ineffective probes into China's southern Yunnan province in which they were utterly routed, Chiang Kai-shek's troops moved further south into Burma, pillaging and plundering as they went. The poorly equipped Burmese army already had its hands full in putting down a major rebellion by Burmese Communists and smaller insurrections by some of the country's ethnic minorities. It was able to marshal enough troops to stop Chiang Kai-shek's forces from moving even deeper into the country only by drawing heavily on those of its own army already committed to battle against the Burmese Communists.[12] And soon in Burma's northeast some of Chiang's units began to dragoon local inhabitants into working for their rapidly expanding production and trade in opium, ultimately emerging as the world's major source of heroin by far, a position they and their successors hold until this day.

The end of the Korean War did not bring a halt to the American intervention in Burma. This was continued to the end of the Eisenhower administration, with CIA and Taiwan air-force planes still shuttling back and forth between Taiwan and Chiang's major redoubt in northeastern Burma, either directly or via Thailand. But the administration now had a new rationale, equally secret and just as dangerous for Burma as its effort to use it as a base in the Korean War. Insofar as the new policy had an official face, it was to maintain Chiang's troops in northeastern Burma as an obstacle should Mao Tse-tung's generals decide to strike south through Burma and into Thailand. But in the Burmese view this little occupation army was so closely tied to Peking's major enemies—the United States and Taiwan—as to risk provoking China into sending its army over the border to chastize Chiang and in the process devastating even more of their country. This prospect, the *New York Times* speculated and the Burmese leadership firmly believed, was part of an American plan to push Burma off its neutralist perch by obliging it to "turn to the United States for protection."[13]

The counterproductivity of the American strategy was dramatically evident when, after the final buildup of Chiang's force in Burma in 1960, desperate Burmese military leaders invited Chinese Communist regiments to cross the border and join with them in a pincers movement that dealt a devastating blow to most of Chiang's army.

The firm dedication of the Burmese to a neutralist policy was unshaken by these events, but an inadvertent consequence of the American intervention was to upset severely the structure of Burma's civilian government. Oversupplied with modern American weapons, Chiang's forces sold many of them to the country's insurgent minorities and in a few cases even concluded brief tactical alliances with some of the minorities against Rangoon. Facing both the Kuomintang troops and the now much better armed Burmese insurgents, Burma's civilian government was obliged during the last Eisenhower years to devolve increasingly greater administrative authority to its own armed forces in or near contested areas. The Burmese military, having materially benefited from this role, was unwilling to relinquish it. Finally charging that the civilian government was prepared to go too far in arriving at a compromise settlement with the insurgent ethnic minorities, in 1962 army leaders mounted a coup that put into power a military dictatorship that has remained in the saddle to this day. Although neither this nor Burma's emergence as the world's major producer of heroin had been the purpose of American policy, it had inadvertently contributed to these outcomes.

Opposition to neutralism was also paramount in the Eisenhower administration's dealings with Cambodia and its leader, Prince Norodom Sihanouk, a man dedicated to the proposition that his country's survival depended on maintaining a strict neutrality in the cold war. The administration was angered when Sihanouk spurned its offer to include Cambodia under the mantle of the anti-Communist Southeast Asia Treaty Organization (SEATO) set up in the fall of 1954 after France's defeat in Vietnam. It was further alienated by his insistence during the next few years that Cambodia match diplomatic relations with the United States and its allies—including South Vietnam and Thailand—by opening them with the Soviet Union, China, and North Vietnam.

Beginning in 1958 the Eisenhower administration launched a sustained campaign against Sihanouk that was widely understood to be aimed at either ousting him from office or at least making him tractable enough to abandon his neutralist stance. To that end a proxy military effort was begun by the CIA (one that did not end until well into the Johnson administration) of organizing, financing, and arming the Khmer Serei (Free Cambodians), an anti-Sihanouk force led by his long-standing rival, Son Ngoc Thanh. These rebel troops, recruited from the Cambodian minorities of southwestern South Vietnam and Thailand's Surin province, mounted recurring attacks for almost a decade across the western and eastern borders of Cambodia, inflicting considerable damage and tying up most of the small Cambodian army. In view of U.S. objectives, however, these actions were distinctly counterproductive, leading to a nationalist backlash wherein Cambodians rallied all the more strongly to Sihanouk, who was himself even more resolute in his determination not to align his country's foreign policy with that of the United States.

There was an adjunct of this policy which more directly reflected the Eisenhower-Dulles determination not to let the "shibboleth" of territorial integrity impede pursuit of anti-Communist or even antineutralist goals. This was their administration's encouragement of Thailand and South Vietnam in early 1959 to back the Khmer Serei in supporting an attempt led by the governor of Cambodia's Siem Riep province to detach his and an adjacent province to form an autonomous regime. The attempt was quickly put down, but the incident left Sihanouk even more distrustful of the United States. Since the Khmer Serei were supported by the CIA, and Sihanouk, with some justification, regarded South Vietnam and Thailand as client states of the United States, he had reason to believe that this was an American-sanctioned effort.[14]

For almost another decade Sihanouk managed to remain in power and to keep his country out of any serious involvement in the Vietnam War. But in 1970 Henry Kissinger and Richard Nixon, together with Son Ngoc Thanh's resuscitated Khmer Serei, helped engineer Sihanouk's overthrow by General Lon Nol, and within a month found it necessary to send thousands of American and South Vietnamese troops into Cambodia in an attempt to rescue the general's tottering regime.[15] From the wreckage wrought by this invasion, the reaction to it of Vietnamese Communist forces (that now left their border enclaves to penetrate more deeply into Cambodia), and the enormous weight of American bombing, there soon arose Pol Pot and his Khmer Rouge. Twenty-four years after Sihanouk's ouster, the Clinton administration was desperately hoping that this now seriously ill leader could cling long enough to life to keep Cambodia's fragile government coalition sufficiently intact and operationally alive to deal effectively with a now smaller but still seriously threatening Khmer Rouge.

In Laos, too, American policy during the Eisenhower years was a reflection of his and Dulles's reading of the lesson to be drawn from the Communists' victory in China. In addition to being strongly hostile to Laotian attempts to follow a neutralist foreign policy, it called for keeping at least most of the country free from the pro-Communist Pathet Lao. To this end, the administration ordered a doubling of the size of the Royal Laotian Army, paying the entire costs of the country's military establishment, despite strong opposition from the Pentagon, which was convinced that the effort would be futile since there was nothing solid to build on. An enormous economic aid program (with the highest per capita disbursement of any U.S. economic assistance program in the world) was introduced, aimed at winning the support of the Laotian people, but its benefits for the most part passed well over their heads and into the pockets of one of Southeast Asia's most corrupt bureaucracies. Efforts to overcome the corruption were for the most part grossly ineffective, even though the number of American officials deployed in Laos soon exceeded the highest number of personnel the French had posted there when the country was a French colony. These Americans did, however, manage to be so conspicuously involved in the blatant stage management of Laotian elections as to produce a strong nationalistic anti-American backlash.[16]

The British, French, and Indian governments all clearly recognized that the only real prospect for containing the growth of the Pathet Lao lay in supporting the government led by the relatively popular but avowedly neutralist prime minister, Prince Souvanna Phouma. Throughout the mid- and late 1950s, however, the Eisenhower administration made a continuous and intermittently successful effort to keep him out of office in favor of someone—almost any Laotian—who would both outlaw the Pathet Lao and abandon neutralism in favor of full alignment with the United States. Finally, in Eisenhower's last year in office, more than a year after severe illness and then death had removed John Foster Dulles from the State Department, the United States, while still officially recognizing Souvanna Phouma's government and maintaining the U.S. embassy in his capital at Vientiane, made its strongest effort to bring him to heel. First it cut off all economic aid to his government and then, in collaboration with the Thai dictator, Marshal Sarit Thanarat, instituted a tight economic blockade calculated to topple Souvanna Phouma and open the way for the replacement of his government with a right-wing Lao general of appallingly little political or military competence. Souvanna Phouma, with his capital running dangerously short of food, finally saw no option but to turn to the Soviet Union for help. And so, ironically, U.S. pressure now pushed him to open diplomatic relations with Moscow and accept its offer of a major airlift of food and other supplies, which quickly got underway at the beginning of December 1960. When the United States protested to the Soviet Union, it firmly, and presumably gleefully, responded that it had every right to provide relief for the government that the United States still officially recognized.

Then, in his last six weeks in office, Eisenhower launched a major escalation of his confrontation with Souvanna Phouma and Laotian neutralism. In the face of a large Lao military force, with American advisers and modern U.S. equipment, advancing from the south while Thai artillery pounded Vientiane from just across the Mekong River, Souvanna Phouma and his supporting neutralist forces were forced to flee the capital. His troops, who had so recently been fighting the Pathet Lao, now felt compelled to arrive at a truce with them and effect a tactical alliance against what they both saw as a puppet American government occupying the capital. American policy, then, could be credited with having pushed the neutralist middle of the Lao political spectrum together with the Pathet Lao, leaving Laos more dangerously politically polarized than ever. The eroded neutralist middle sector of Laotian politics never recovered, and the American-financed army continued to discredit itself by its self-seeking corruption. These were clearly important elements in the Pathet Lao's ultimate success in 1975 and its ability to establish a Communist government for the whole country.

After France's defeat in Vietnam in 1954 the policies pursued by Eisenhower and Dulles for halting the spread of communism there conformed closely to the lessons they believed should be drawn from their analysis of the "loss of China" to Communist rule, when they settled, at least temporarily, for the establishment of a separate anti-Communist state in just half of Vietnam, confined to the area south of the 17th parallel.[17] Previously, like the Truman administration, they had lavishly supported the French and their puppet administration headed by Emperor Bao Dai with its claim to authority over *all* Vietnam.

The southern half of the country was the territory designated by the 1954 Geneva agreements as the regroupment zone for all French troops, with France responsible for its administration pending internationally supervised elections scheduled to be held throughout Vietnam in 1956, which were to provide the basis for reuniting it. With the United States abruptly ending its role as paymaster to French troops in Vietnam and France needing them as reinforcements to cope with nationalist rebellions in its North African colonies, the last French military units left Vietnam well before these elections could be held. This opened the way for the Eisenhower administration, in defiance of the terms of the Geneva agreements, to transform the regroupment boundary at the 17th parallel into a political border and embark on a program of political engineering aimed at building a firmly anti-Communist American-dependent state in the south. Constituting the most fundamental decision taken by the United States in its long Vietnam involvement, this was a basically political move, but one with inescapable military implications, and a critical prerequisite in the increased interventions of subsequent administrations.

From the base it was establishing in the south the Eisenhower administration planned to mount a "rollback" of the control of Ho Chi Minh's Vietminh government in the north, ultimately absorbing that area into a single anti-Communist state. Although this plan was not revealed to the American public, it remained a presidentially endorsed objective until at least the end of 1958. Consistent with this plan, the National Security Council, again in secret session, also called for the United States to "conduct covert operations on a large and effective scale" in order to "exploit available means to make more difficult the control by the Vietminh of North Vietnam."[18] One of the main reasons the administration picked Ngo Dinh Diem rather than the much abler Prince Buu Hoi to head its Saigon regime was that the prince was dedicated to honoring the provision of the Geneva agreements calling for internationally supervised reunification elections, while it knew that Diem was opposed. Both the U.S. government and Diem were against holding them for the same reason: They knew he could not outpoll Ho Chi Minh. But to the American public the administration maintained that it was Ho who refused these elections, and it obscured the fundamental fact that a firm promise to hold them had been of central importance in the Vietminh's agreement to a military armistice.

It was primarily to provide a protective border for this new United States-backed political entity in what became popularly referred to as the

"State of South Vietnam" that Secretary Dulles crafted SEATO (or Manila Pact). The treaty's central purpose, as he described it to the U.S. Senate, was to protect South Vietnam from cross-border invasion by Ho's government in the north or by China. Only after Dulles had explicitly assured the wary senators that the treaty was in no sense a commitment for the United States to put down a rebellion or subversive movement in South Vietnam did they agree to support it.

And, as is better known, the Eisenhower administration provided Diem with an army by taking over from the French the role of paymaster of the Vietnamese mercenary component of what had been the French colonial army and then adding to this nucleus the now American-salaried remnants of the militias of the Cao Dai and Hoa Hao religious sects that had previously been subsidized and utilized by France. It was this United States-funded and armed conglomerate that was presented to the American public as the "national army" of the Republic of South Vietnam.

Seen against against the background of the Eisenhower administration's efforts at political engineering elsewhere in Southeast Asia, its relatively little known covert intervention in Indonesia should be more easily understood. In many ways the political and economic importance of Indonesia far exceeded that of any other Southeast Asian country. An archipelago of more than 3,000 islands stretching a distance as great as that from New York City to the coast of Ireland, economically rich and strategically important, it was the largest Islamic country in the world and had the fifth largest population. To a striking degree the massive involvement of the United States in Indonesia was part of a piece with the composite pattern of anticommunism, loss-of-China prescription, and opposition to neutralism that was so prominent in its relations with other Southeast Asian countries.

The intervention began at a time when U.S. government confidence in its ability to shape the polities of the Third World had been reinforced by what it construed as its successes in ousting the leaders of Iran and Guatemala, building a separate, anti-Communist state in South Vietnam, and establishing Ramon Magsaysay in power in the Philippines. Belief that these recent, heavily covert operations had been skillfully managed triumphs of political engineering produced a heady elixir in the upper reaches of the administration that undoubtedly encouraged it to make a much larger and more sustained effort in Indonesia.

By mid-1957 President Eisenhower, Secretary of State John Foster Dulles, and CIA Director Allen Dulles had become deeply worried that the Indonesian government, that major part of its armed forces stationed on Java, and especially its president, Sukarno, were under growing Communist influence and drifting dangerously to the left. This anxiety was reinforced by that government's continuing insistence on adhering to a neutralist foreign policy and by gains made by the Communist party in the midyear elections, which moved it from fourth to third place.

In September senior administration officials concluded that discontent in some of the islands outside Java provided an opening they could exploit to reverse this process, change the character of the Indonesian government, and move the country into an anti-Communist alignment with the United States. To accomplish this task they sought to shape this disaffection—especially in Sumatra and Sulawesi—into a fulcrum on which American power could be applied to effect these changes. The immediate objective was to eliminate the Communist party, weaken the army's strength on Java, and drastically clip the wings of, if not fully remove, President Sukarno.

In its substantial and prolonged effort to achieve these goals the Eisenhower administration ultimately enlisted not only the CIA and large supplies of modern U.S. military equipment but also substantial components of the U.S. Seventh Fleet and American planes and pilots together with supporting military personnel, facilities, and supplies from the Chinese Nationalist government on Taiwan and the government of the Philippines, with more modest but significant help from Britain and Australia. As noted, the approach to Indonesia taken by Eisenhower and Dulles strongly reflected the same political considerations in operation in their relations with the rest of Southeast Asia. But their policies were also heavily affected by the credence they gave to the CIA's frequently tendentious and often badly flawed reporting—information and interpretations of it that accorded well with their known prejudices—rather than their relying on the generally more sober and reliable dispatches from their ambassadors to Jakarta and their staffs, including their military attachés.

The administration's failure to understand the true situation in Indonesia was clearly exacerbated by the fact that the CIA's influence, as against that of the United States' Jakarta embassy, was enhanced because its director was the brother of the secretary of state and because the man appointed by the secretary to be liaison officer between the State Department and the CIA was Hugh S. Cumming, Jr., an ex-ambassador to Indonesia who had developed a bitter personal animus against Sukarno. That Secretary Dulles found Cumming's views on Indonesia congenial was evident in his appointing him to head the task force charged in mid-1957 with fashioning a new, covert interventionist policy toward Indonesia. Nothing more clearly reflects the unbridgable disparity between the CIA-Cumming strand of reporting and assessment and that of the Jakarta embassy than Secretary Dulles's peremptory firing of Ambassador John Allison, at that time probably the senior Foreign Service officer in Asia, and his exile to Prague after serving less than eleven months in Indonesia.

The biased selectivity of senior administration leaders in their utilization of available intelligence sources must be appreciated if one is to understand why their policies so poorly accorded with political realities in Indonesia and why they had such sanguine expectations as to the prospects of American intervention there. More specifically, it helps account for how pejoratively they viewed the central government's army and the country's paramount political leader, President Sukarno, and why they regarded the strength and potential of the Indonesian Communist party in such alarmist and apocalyptic terms. And it does much to explain their exaggerated assessments of the military prowess and popular backing of dissident regional colonels.

By mid-1958 the Eisenhower administration had been forced to acknowledge that its Indonesian intervention had failed; it then decided to cut its losses, concluding that the wisest course was now to make concessions to and try to get along as best it could with the government it had just been trying to overthrow. It could manage this opportunistic switch, and escape public humiliation for its failure, because its policies had been so largely covert and unknown to the American audience. The rebels, however, did not have the luxury of cutting their losses; they simply lost and lost so heavily that they never recovered.

Only well after the rebellion had turned to civil war did senior American officials, relying now more on the intelligence supplied by the U.S. embassy than on the CIA and ex-Ambassador Cumming's interagency task force, turn their old estimate on its head and finally conclude that Jakarta's army was in fact fundamentally anti-Communist and a potent and reliable ally in opposing the increase of Communist strength in Indonesia. But this switch occurred only after continuing rebel military defeats had seriously undermined the credibility of the intelligence on which the administration had relied in launching its intervention.

An appreciation of this divergence between American policy and Indonesian reality requires that we describe the conditions that actually existed in Indonesia during the period on which this study focuses. But the backdrop of Indonesia's experience under colonialism and early independence must first be sketched and brief mention made of the interaction of the Truman administration and Indonesia's first post-World War II governments, for to a significant degree this history helped set the stage for and conditioned the course of relations during the Eisenhower era.

As we describe in this book the unfolding of events in Indonesia and the United States that brought about this interventionist American policy, with its impact on the lives of Indonesians and on their country's immediate and long-term political development, it should be evident what an abysmal failure this essentially covert operation was and why the American government has been so reluctant to release the most important documents that bear on it. Presumably the CIA and other involved components of the U.S. government have concluded they would lose face and diminish public support for further covert activities if Americans were to be come aware of their egregious debacle in Indonesia. And so for American citizens the CIA still treats this episode of thirty-seven years ago as just as "covert" as if it were occurring today, persistently refusing to release relevant documents that would impugn its reputation and that of leaders in the Eisenhower administration with which it worked. The fact that not a single American pilot, sailor, or CIA agent appears to have lost his life in this massive Indonesian operation has undoubtedly made it much easier to hide it from the American public. But what was covert for Americans was anything but secret for those many Indonesians who directly experienced the impact of American power. Certainly for the families of those thousands of them—military and civilian—who were killed, the nature of this ultimately very heavy intrusion could hardly be disguised.

1. Colonial Rule, Revolution, and the Beginnings of American Involvement

Colonial Rule

On the eve of World War II the Netherlands East Indies—precursor to the state known after 1949 as Indonesia—was probably the world's richest colony. At the very least it ranked just after India in the wealth it brought to a colonial power, and it was certainly more important to the Dutch economy than India was to Britain's. Dutch authority over this vast archipelago, though beginning with the wresting of a small foothold on Java in 1619, was not completed until the conquests of Aceh (northernmost Sumatra) and Bali in 1909, and its impact varied widely. But on fertile Java, with two thirds of the country's population, and in most of Sumatra and Sulawesi (formerly the Celebes)—rich in rubber, oil, tin, and copra—Dutch power, consolidated by the middle of the nineteenth century, was heavily administered.

Accompanying this relatively effective system of Dutch political control was an extraction of wealth whose efficiency was the envy of other colonial powers. But it was not until well into the second decade of the twentieth century that a still-embryonic group of Indonesian nationalists began to comprehend just how advantageous these economic arrangements were to the Netherlands and how inequitable they were for the Indonesian people. The figures that the excellent Dutch statistical offices supplied could hardly have led to a different conclusion, and in themselves they gave a sharper edge to the movement for independence. Although some economists might dispute the weight to be attached to export-import figures in arriving at conclusions as to social equity, for politically conscious Indonesians the fact that these showed exports running at more than twice imports spelled stark exploitation.[1]

Income tax figures assembled by the colonial authorities reinforced considerably this conclusion. In 1940 the population of the Netherlands East Indies was officially estimated at 69,700,000 ethnic Indonesians, and there were in addition approximately 1,300,000 Chinese, 130,000 "other foreign Asiatics" (more than half of them Arab and most of the remainder Indian), and 270,000 Europeans (well over 90 percent of whom were Dutch and Dutch Eurasians).[2] In the nonagrarian sectors of the economy, 22,854 Europeans had an income assessed at 5,000 guilders (approximately U.S. $2,500) or more, with 3,799 Chinese and "other foreign Asiatics" in this category and only 1,239 Indonesians. Although most Indonesians earned their living from agriculture and paid a land tax rather than an income tax, these figures eloquently demonstrate how little Indonesians participated in the upper and middle reaches of the colonial economy. (It should be noted that, in contrast with India, the Philippines, or even Vietnam, in Indonesia there were few large native landholdings.)

These statistics also help indicate how small was the indigenous middle class in colonial Indonesia. Indeed, insofar as it existed it was largely drawn from the colonial bureaucracy rather than the entrepreneurial sector, the upper reaches of which were almost entirely European and Chinese, with the middle sector overwhelmingly Chinese. With respect to the bureaucracy, Indonesians felt a keen sense of grievance, for they were heavily discriminated against, with most middle-rank and almost all senior-level positions being reserved for the Dutch. As late as 1940, of 3,039 higher-ranking civil service positions only 221 were held by Indonesians. There was, then, no counterpart to the Indian civil service, wherein a considerable number of talented native officials could have their abilities recognized and advance to the higher strata of the administrative bureaucracy. Indonesian nationalists were equally envious of the upward mobility of Filipinos in the administrative system run by the United States in its Southeast Asian colony.

Indonesian nationalists who voiced their dissatisfaction with this discrimination were admonished that "function must be equivalent to education," yet the secondary and tertiary education opened to Indonesians by the Dutch colonial authorities made a travesty of that proposition. Although such facilities in the colony were of generally very high quality, they were largely reserved for the Dutch themselves. Thus, for the school year 1938-39, official government statistics reported a total of 777 students graduating from high school, of whom 457 were Europeans (nearly all Dutch), 116 were "foreign Orientals" (mostly Chinese), and just 204 were Indonesians (of a native population then of at least 67 million).[3] Moreover, even those Indonesians who managed to receive a Western education from the schools open to them encountered heavy discrimination whether they sought positions in the bureaucracy or in the Dutch-controlled business sector. Even in the year just before the great depression of 1930-31, a government commission determined that 25 percent of the Indonesians who had graduated from Western schools in the country were unable to find jobs in which their education could be utilized. It concluded that these Indonesians found their diplomas "devalued" and were only able to get "jobs that were on the periphery of economic life." In that last year before the depression the commission found that as a consequence of a recent expansion of the still-meager educational facilities "about twice as many pupils graduated with Western education as jobs can be found for," and it envisaged the situation as growing much worse.[4]

But even more important in kindling the rancor of Indonesian national-ists against Dutch rule was its heavy repression of those who had the audac-ity to speak out about such discrimination and who advocated at least ulti-mate independence from colonial authority. In the last two prewar decades this repression increased significantly, and the most outspoken of the nationalists were jailed, exiled to remote areas of Indonesia, or in most cases packed off to the notorious Boven Digul concentration camp deep in the jungle of central Dutch New Guinea. Most nationalist leaders of any stature went through these experiences, with some of the most promi-nent—including Sukarno, Mohammad Hatta, and Sutan Sjahrir—being released after seven to nine years of detention only with the Japanese inva-sion early in 1942.

The Japanese Occupation

Against this background it is understandable why so many Indonesians welcomed the Japanese and were at first disposed to accept their anti-West-ern propaganda and believe in their intimations of ultimate independence. Contributing to this sentiment was the rapidity with which the invaders overwhelmed the Dutch armed forces, many of whom were already dispir-ited by the speed and effectiveness of the Japanese in their preceding con-quest of Malaya and Singapore. Indonesians did not witness the coura-geous, if futile, stand made by the small naval and air units of the Netherlands against the invading forces, but they did directly observe the lack of fight of most Dutch army units and the hasty capitulation of Lieu-tenant General Ter Poorten, the Dutch commander-in-chief of Allied forces on Java. Dutch prestige suffered a further blow when Indonesians learned that the general had surrendered all Allied forces on Java without consult-ing the British, Australian, and American officers under his command, who allegedly had informed him of their desire to fight on with their 8,000 troops.[5] Moreover, the colonial authorities had refused both training and weapons to the small group of Western-oriented Indonesians who had vol-unteered to help in resisting an invasion—leading them to accuse the Dutch of having neither defended Indonesia nor given Indonesians the means of defending themselves against the invaders. Given the increasing harshness Indonesians experienced during the course of three and a half years of Japanese occupation, this accusation became more entrenched in the minds of a great many of them and reinforced their determination to resist any reassertion of Dutch authority after the end of the war.

Whereas in their occupation of Indochina the Japanese could rely on the mostly pro-Vichy French police, armed forces, and civil service to adminis-ter these colonies under their direct supervision, with little need for Japan-ese troops or civil administrators, such was not the case in Indonesia. The

Japanese could hardly expect that, after their ally Hitler had overrun and so savagely treated the Netherlands, they would receive reliable cooperation from such colonial elements in Indonesia, so they promptly confined Dutch officials in concentration camps. The Japanese had in the first place trained an insufficient number of military-government personnel for Indonesia, and of those who had been prepared for this work probably at least half had been drowned when Allied submarines sank the vessel carrying them to Indonesia. Thus, to an even greater degree than they had anticipated, Japan's occupation authorities had to rely on Indonesians to flesh out their administration. Sheer expediency, then, obliged them to elevate a great many Indonesian civil servants one, two, and even three steps up the administrative ladder into positions to which they could not have aspired under the Dutch. Many of these Indonesians found that they could fill the positions with a considerable degree of competence, and they came increasingly to conclude that they could perform as well as the Dutch officials whom for so long they had been taught to regard as endowed with superior abilities. This fostered self-confidence and increased their belief that Indonesians in general were quite capable of governing themselves. It also, of course, created for the Indonesians a vested interest that they perceived as incompatible with a return of Dutch authority. All these factors increased their nationalist feelings and naturally turned them to look expectantly toward those who had won greatest stature as nationalist leaders in the early 1930s before being arrested and removed from the scene by the colonial authorities.

Paramount among these mostly Western-educated leaders was the forty-one-year-old Sukarno, half Javanese and half Balinese, trained in engineering, without peer then or later as an orator. He was released by the Japanese after having been jailed and then spending nine years of enforced exile in Flores and later Benkulen. The next most prominent was the forty-year-old Sumatra-born Mohammad Hatta, one of a few Netherlands-trained Indonesian economists, who after his arrest in 1934 had initially been sent by the Dutch to Boven Digul and then interned on the small, remote island of Banda before being released by the Dutch as Japanese armed forces were approaching Indonesia. Both these leaders were Muslim (Hatta clearly the more devout of the two); both regarded themselves as social democrats and espoused some variant of socialism, and both were ardent nationalists strongly opposed to the return of Dutch rule. Neither could be regarded as pro-Japanese, but both were politically pragmatic enough to believe that they had to make some degree of accommodation to Japanese interests if the forces of Indonesian nationalism were to be given scope for advancement.

The Japanese also had a pragmatic calculus and realized they had to make concessions to these two widely respected and influential leaders if Japanese interests were to be served. That conviction became even firmer after a series of American naval victories had by mid-1943 begun to raise fears in Tokyo of a prospective threat to its sea communications with Indonesia. A sort of tacit trade-off developed under which, in return for help from these two Indonesian leaders—particularly Sukarno—in mobilizing forced labor (most laborers were harshly treated and some sent to other parts of Southeast Asia) and compulsory deliveries of rice, the Japanese provided them with access to the radio network and considerable freedom of movement in the countryside (such as the Dutch had never permitted). While Sukarno's speeches were clearly anti-Western in tone, their antiimperialist thrust was often sufficiently generic to undermine for many listeners the legitimacy of Japanese as well as Dutch authority. And of great importance, Sukarno's addresses aroused the spirit of nationalism among a broad audience, rural as well as urban, which he and other nationalist leaders had never been able to contact under the constraints of Dutch rule.

Spokesmen for the Dutch government during the war and for several years thereafter denounced Sukarno as an unprincipled, pro-Japanese collaborator (with Soviet sources applying the same charge against both him and Hatta). But after the Japanese occupation, the Dutch governor general himself observed: "From documents later discovered it is very clear that in all his objectionable activities he (Soekarno) was always governed by the objective of an independent Indonesia."[6] And Sutan Sjahrir, the most prominent of the noncollaborating nationalists and probably the most articulate critic of those who collaborated for their own personal ends, wrote that Sukarno, like Hatta, regarded the Japanese "as pure fascists, and felt that we must use the most subtle countermethods to get around them." Nevertheless, the Dutch were quite successful in painting Sukarno as a "quisling," and many of their officials did not cease to do so until, after the onset of the cold war, they shifted to depicting him as a political radical strongly influenced by communism and willing to open up all Indonesia to Communist penetration. However absurd these charges appear in retrospect, they had a serious impact on postwar public opinion in the Netherlands and significantly affected American policy.

When by October 1943 the Japanese began to worry about the possibility of Allied landings on Java and Sumatra, they took a step that was to have important consequences for the ability of Indonesians to contest the reimposition of Dutch rule and one that would also have an enduring effect on Indonesian domestic politics once independence had been achieved. With their limited forces thinly spread across Java and the enormous California-sized island of Sumatra—where they believed an Allied attack most likely—the Japanese commanders on those two islands felt it prudent to augment their forces by training an auxiliary Indonesian militia, ultimately totaling about 20,000 on Sumatra and 37,000 on Java. And whereas the Dutch had feared giving arms to the Muslim Sumatrans and Javanese and reserved them almost exclusively for the country's Christian minority (elements of which they had incorporated into their colonial army) from such distant outlying areas as Ambon, Flores, and northeastern Sulawesi, the Japanese followed exactly the opposite course.

The war ended without the Japanese having to test the loyalty of their Indonesian militia in the face of any Allied landing. They had some reason to worry about this, however, for the weight of Japanese economic exactions and the harshness of their rule had mounted so considerably during the last year of the war that several intense small-scale armed revolts had broken out in Java, some involving units of this militia. But, of long-term importance, these two militias were to form the main core of the Indonesian armed forces that would contest the return of Dutch power to Indonesia. That surely was one of the most important of the tangible legacies of Japan's occupation.

The Coming of Independence

By the time the Japanese surrendered to the Allies on August 15, 1945, American forces had occupied northwestern New Guinea and the adjacent islands of Halmahera and Morotai, and Australian troops had taken over many other points in the eastern part of the Indonesian archipelago. The Japanese were, however, still solidly in control of the rest of Indonesia. Until late in the war the East Indies had been an American area of responsibility. But as plans developed for an Allied assault on Japan itself, it was decided that as many U.S. troops as possible should be husbanded for that purpose, and so at the Potsdam Conference of the Allies in June 1945 it was decided that General Douglas A. MacArthur should turn over responsibility for operations in Indonesia to Britain's Admiral Louis Mountbatten. The United States thereby avoided a difficult problem. And, with only a few months' warning, Britain was assigned responsibility for accepting the Japanese surrender in Indonesia, for disarming and repatriating all their troops, and for releasing some 85,000 Allied prisoners of war and civilian internees. It was not, however, until seven weeks after Japan's surrender that the first unit of regular British troops arrived in Java.

In the meantime in Jakarta (the renamed old Dutch East Indies capital of Batavia), Sukarno and Hatta, pressed by impatient youth groups, had jointly proclaimed their country's independence on August 17. Without any real resistance from most Japanese and with clear encouragement from a few, they then set about establishing an independent government, the Republic of Indonesia. To the acclaim of nearly all other prominent nationalists, Sukarno and Hatta took their places as president and vice president, respectively, of the republic's nascent government. Within less than three months, however, although continuing to hold these offices, they turned over most of their power to two other eminent nationalist leaders who were widely regarded as the most prominent noncollaborators with the Japanese—Sutan Sjahrir and Amir Sjarifuddin. These two successively held the new office of prime minister over the next two and a half years. The reason for this shift testifies to the pragmatism of all four of these leaders. Correctly regarding Indonesia as being in the Anglo-American sphere of power, they concluded that, because of the success of the drumbeat of Dutch charges that Sukarno and Hatta were unreliable quislings, the republic would fare better in dealing with the Allied powers if it were led by men who even the Dutch acknowledged had not collaborated with the Japanese.[7]

The Japanese troops, disheartened by their emperor's unexpected proclamation of surrender and in many cases sympathetic to the Indonesians' aspirations for independence, only sporadically resisted efforts by Indonesian youths and former militia members to seize arms from Japanese arsenals; in a few cases they actually encouraged them to do so. Japanese commanders, however, feared Allied reprisals if they failed to carry out their orders to maintain law and order until relieved by British troops. In some cases they sought to withdraw from cities and concentrate their forces in less provocative positions, but nevertheless bitter fighting often erupted as Indonesians sought to occupy all public buildings.

The incoming British, whose commanders, it should be noted, had been denied full information by both Dutch and American intelligence concerning conditions in Indonesia, were astonished to find that an already-functioning, if rudimentary, Indonesian government was already in place and with such strong popular backing that they were obliged to deal with it. British forces were soon substantially increased. Initially, with their troops mostly confined to a few major port cities, the British had reasonably smooth relations with the newly launched republic. However, when Indonesians learned that (contrary to the judgment of the local British commander) the British government had given the Dutch official assurances of British recognition of continued Dutch sovereignty over Indonesia, and with the now-augmented British forces having begun to shoehorn in small Dutch military units, there was an explosion of outrage from the Indonesian side.

The British, largely dependent on troops from their Indian army, most of whom had little stomach for fighting fellow victims of colonialism, were stunned by the fierceness of the Indonesian reaction. During the first half of November 1945 in the battle for Java's second largest city, the port of Surabaya, a brigade of British and Indian troops lost two generals—one killed and one captured (until released by Sukarno's personal intervention)—and was nearly overwhelmed by much more numerous, though poorly armed, Indonesian forces before British air and naval reinforcements finally drove off the attackers. Fighting spread to many other cities and towns, and in desperation the British rearmed whole regiments of Japanese troops to fight on their side.[8]

All this was much more than the British had bargained for. They had grave financial problems at home and mutinies in India and had sustained in Indonesia some 2,400 casualties. So, less than a year after their arrival they informed the Dutch that they would no longer provide military support to their effort at reconquest and would withdraw British troops by the end of November 1946. When they did so more than 91,000 Dutch troops had been brought in, a considerably larger force than the British had mustered at their peak strength. Although continuing to enjoy logistical support from Britain, and more discreetly from the United States, it was the Dutch armed forces alone that now faced those of the Indonesian republic. Their military effort would last another three years, with often bitter fighting throughout wide areas of Java and Sumatra.

• • • • •

During the course of this long military struggle the government of the Republic of Indonesia sank progressively deeper roots into all strata of the population. The Dutch were able to conquer considerable territory, especially on Java, as a consequence of the fighting, but they did not win the allegiance of the people of these areas. The preponderant majority of the populations of Java and Sumatra remained loyal to the republic and its president and vice president, Sukarno and Hatta. And even in other areas of Indonesia that, thanks to Australian military power, the Netherlands force had occupied without the necessity of any serious fighting—Dutch Borneo, Sulawesi, and the smaller islands further east—most politically conscious elements of the population tended to look with pride on the republic and its leaders, regarding them as symbols of resistance against the Dutch efforts to reestablish control.

Insofar as the newly born republic had an articulated political philosophy, this had been presented by Sukarno in an off-the-cuff speech he had given in June 1945 to prominent nationalist leaders, constituting an Independence Preparatory Committee, established by the Japanese after they had explicitly promised Indonesian independence and only a few months before they capitulated to the Allies. Sukarno's address, an avowed effort to reconcile the divergent views among the members of this committee, particularly on the contentious subject of religion, became enshrined as the official state philosophy, the *Panca Sila* (Five Principles). These five fundamental principles were, in the order then presented by Sukarno: nationalism, internationalism (also called humanitarianism), representative government, social justice, and belief in God in a context of religious freedom.

There was a geopolitical element in the *Panca Sila* concept of nationalism, for the Indonesian nation was defined as including the whole of the former Dutch colony of the East Indies—that is, including West Irian (the western half of the huge island known by the Australians as New Guinea that four and a half years later the Netherlands, after yielding sovereignty over the rest of their colony, refused to relinquish). Indonesian nationalism was not to be chauvinistic and should harmonize with other nationalisms so that the world would become "one family of nations," in which each member would retain its national identity. Then, partly to mollify Islamic critics on the committee, Sukarno argued that the envisaged representative government would incorporate the Islamic principle of consultation, with a house of representatives providing Muslims with ample opportunity to work toward an Islamic political order while simultaneously giving followers of other religions an equal opportunity to advance their own ideas.

But representative government would mean little if not undergirded by social justice. In America and the countries of Western Europe, Sukarno argued, "the capitalists are in control," and in them political democracy is unaccompanied by economic democracy. "Political democracy," he stated, citing Jean Jaurès, does not ensure "economic democracy." If social justice was to be secured for the Indonesian people, both kinds of democracy were needed; "if we are seeking democracy, the need is not for the democracy of the West, but for . . . politico-economic democracy."

It was also under the chairmanship of Sukarno that a group of sixty prominent Indonesian nationalists drafted Indonesia's first constitution during the last month of the war.[9] The document that emerged from these tense discussions was both a positive statement of fundamental tenets of political philosophy consistent with the *Panca Sila* and a reflection of an intense effort by Sukarno, generally strongly supported by Hatta, to ensure that the new Indonesia would be a secular state with equality of religion rather than an "Islamic state" as advocated by a large number of the committee members. (It should be noted that, although 85 to 90 percent of Indonesia's population is Muslim, the degree of adherence to the tenets of that religion varies considerably among those who regard themselves as such.)

Although himself more devout a Muslim than Sukarno, Hatta shared his opposition to any attempt to establish an Islamic state in Indonesia. Given the size and importance of the country's Catholic, Protestant, and Hindu-Buddhist (on Bali) minorities—amounting collectively to 10 to 15 percent of the population—he shared Sukarno's conviction that such an effort would tear the country apart. And, like Sukarno, he realized that about half of the Muslims living on Java were *abangan*—who incorporated in their religion elements of the Buddhism, Hinduism, or animism that preceded the introduction of Islam and who were rather easygoing in their adherence to Islamic strictures—hardly the most reliable candidates for an Islamic state.

The final compromise that emerged—with the most grudging consent from some of the more doctrinaire Islamic leaders—was a major, if hard-fought victory for both Sukarno and Hatta, but it bore primarily the imprimatur of Sukarno.

American Policy during the First Years of the Revolution

Despite a fairly widespread anticolonial sentiment prevailing in the United States, sometimes mirrored in the public rhetoric of its officials, the actions of the Truman administration during the first postwar years were not supportive of the Indonesian struggle for independence. The administration's actions, while discreet and largely indirect, were in fact heavily beneficial to the Dutch effort for reconquest. American policymakers' fear of communism overrode their often genuine, though much weaker, opposition to colonialism. But during these first postwar years, their preoccupation with the potential of communism focused on *Europe* rather than on the areas of Southeast Asia still claimed by the European colonial powers. Indeed, the strategic, political, and economic priorities of the United States in Europe were then the central determinants behind its policies toward the independence movements in both Indonesia and Vietnam. The danger that the Communist parties in France and the Netherlands would become stronger, with the consequent prospect of an expansion of Soviet influence there, was regarded by American policymakers as much too great to brook "quixotic" anticolonial American policies in support of independence movements in their colonies.

The existing French and Dutch governments were dominated by anti-Communists (even though Communists held a minority of posts in the French cabinet), but American policymakers believed that, if these non-Communist governments were to be protected against the growth of local Communist power, the United States had to work in harmony with them. Key foreign-policy officials in Washington believed that the nationalist sensitivities of both French and Dutch citizens, smarting from the cruelty and humiliation of the long Nazi occupation, would be outraged, and their precarious governments destabilized, if the United States pressured them to give up their colonial empires.

The Truman administration assessed the postwar internal political balance in the Netherlands as less favorable for the Dutch Communist party than the prospects for the Communist party in France. Nevertheless, it regarded the potential for the growth of Communist influence in the Netherlands as dangerous because of the magnitude and intensity of Holland's economic problems, the devastation visited on that country during the war having been far worse than in France. Some of the most influential American policymakers regarded the Netherlands East Indies as the cork on which much of the Dutch economy had floated—providing some 20 percent of national income—which, if regained, could again buoy that economy. They believed that, without continuing Dutch control over the archipelago's oil, tin, rubber, and copra, even major infusions of American dollars into the Netherlands home economy would not strengthen it sufficiently to undercut the growth of radical political forces there. Also influencing American policy, although of considerably less importance, were the significant American investments in Indonesia (particularly Sumatra), especially in oil and rubber.

Closely tied to this anxiety over the internal political balance in France and the Netherlands was the U.S. government's overarching preoccupation with the need to ensure these countries' cooperation in building a joint military shield to contain the threat of Soviet power against Western Europe. So high was the priority assigned to achieving this objective that the Truman administration soon concluded that a denial of American backing to Dutch and French efforts to reassert control over Indonesia and Indochina would provoke reactions in the Netherlands and France sufficiently adverse as to jeopardize their effective cooperation in the United States' containment policy in Europe.

Thus, in the first postwar years considerations lying preponderantly in Europe—and not in Asia—brought the United States to back the major military expeditions launched by both the Dutch and French in Southeast Asia. The magnitude of American support of these efforts was extensive—whether measured in terms of financial subventions, transfers of modern arms, or the transport of troops—and was absolutely critical to the ability of the European metropoles to mount their expeditions against the independence movements led by militant nationalists in Vietnam and Indonesia. Indeed, as the Marshall Plan went into full gear the amount of American dollars being pumped into France and the Netherlands was approximately equaled by the funds being siphoned from their treasuries to finance their expeditionary forces in Southeast Asia.[10]

It was evident to the Indonesians that the United States was providing crucial support to the Netherlands. Any peasant could see that the Dutch were using weapons supplied by the United States, for many of the tanks, trucks, and planes still bore U.S. insignia, and, at least as late as January 1949, some members of the Netherlands' crack Marine Brigade wore combat fatigues clearly marked (above the breast pocket) "U.S. Marines."[11] It was widely believed, too, that the United States was also financially underwriting the Netherlands' effort at reconquest. Thus, a CIA report of November 14, 1947, noted: "Already in Indonesia and Indochina the native population tends to regard Dutch and French efforts to reestablish their control as having been made with U.S. support. To the extent that the European Recovery Program [Marshall Plan] enhances Dutch and French capabilities in Southeast Asia, native resentment will increase."[12]

By late 1947, when the Dutch and French economies were beginning to recover, the potential of communism in those two countries had appreciably receded. But by that time it appeared that the Communists might soon triumph in China, and with that prospect the United States became much more concerned over the threat of communism's spread in Asia—not only Japan but also the areas of anticolonial insurgency—notably Indonesia and Vietnam. The Truman administration now more readily accepted the colonial powers' contention that their conflicts were fundamentally aimed at containment of the spread of communism rather than reestablishment of colonial rule. It was thus now much easier for the French to convince most American officials that Ho Chi Minh's nationalism was simply an expedient handmaiden of his communism and that the emergence of an Asian Tito in Vietnam was out of the question. And, as noted above, it was only a little more difficult for the Netherlands officials to convince key American policymakers that in Indonesia Sukarno, Hatta, and other top leaders of the Indonesian Republic, whom the Dutch had initially described as pro-Japanese quislings, were irresponsible opportunists dangerously susceptible to Communist influence, who, if successful in withstanding the Netherlands expeditionary force, would permit Communists to operate freely throughout the entire archipelago and open it up to Soviet penetration.

Change in American Policy: 1948-49

The striking parallel between the essential features of U.S. policy toward Vietnam and Indonesia for some three and a half years after Japan's capitulation might well have continued considerably longer if it had not been for two unexpected episodes that in combination brought the United States to alter dramatically its attitude toward the Dutch-Indonesian dispute and finally tilt in favor of the Indonesian republic rather than the Netherlands. The first and most influential of these was the Madiun rebellion, a revolt in Central Java from September to November 1948 by a disorganized group of Soviet-oriented Indonesian Communists against the leadership of Sukarno and Hatta, which the republic's army put down through some bitter fighting and the execution of the top Communist leaders.[13] After the suppression of this rebellion it was no longer possible for the Dutch to continue their propaganda that the republic was but a bridge to communism.

The clearest indication of the sudden emergence of a new U.S. policy option was reflected in actions by the CIA. Once it had become evident that the forces loyal to Sukarno and Hatta clearly had the upper hand against the rebelling Communists and were certain to prevail, the CIA sent a senior agent to Yogyakarta, the capital of the republic, on a mission which before this event would have been unthinkable. He soon began interviewing young officers of the Police Mobile Brigade, selecting the most promising and making arrangements to fly them out through the Dutch blockade to American military facilities for special training.[14] The displeasure of the Dutch, whose own airpower was impotent to stop this exodus, is not difficult to imagine.

Presumably the rationale for this covert policy was that, if the republic should ultimately prevail against the Dutch, these American-trained officers could be counted on to throw their weight not only against any resurgence of Soviet-oriented communism but also against the supporters of the nationalist Communist leader, Tan Malaka, who had long since broken with the Soviet Union and whose adherents had just joined the republic's army in fighting the pro-Soviet Communists in the Madiun rebellion. The socioeconomic program of these nationalist Communists was even more hostile to Western economic interests in Indonesia than that of their now subdued pro-Soviet rivals. If the fighting against the Dutch were to continue their numbers could be expected to grow, as would support for the scorched-earth tactics they advocated against both American and Dutch properties.

But a decisive change in American policy required the addition of a second element beyond the demonstration by the leaders of the Indonesian republic of their solid anti-Communist credentials. This element was the threat the Dutch were seen as posing to the future of the United Nations. For, in mounting their heaviest attack against the republic at the end of 1948, they refused to heed the United Nations' call to halt their military operations and at least withdraw from the republic's capital and release Sukarno, Hatta, and other political leaders they had captured. If the nascent and as-yet little-tested United Nations could not enforce its writ against a minor power like the Netherlands, it seemed likely it would soon end up just as impotent and discredited as the League of Nations.[15]

Counting on a blitzkrieg that would present the world with a fait accompli, the Dutch on December 19, 1948, launched their final military campaign against the republic, a scant six weeks after it had defeated the Communist uprising at Madiun and when, as a consequence of that operation, the republic's forces facing the Dutch lines were weakened and disorganized. However, Dutch troops ran into much more tenacious military resistance and civilian noncooperation than they had expected and by late March were largely on the defensive in what became a bitter guerrilla war.[16] Having unleashed their 140,000 man army in the face of a United Nations-sponsored truce they had signed less than a year before, the Dutch found they had stirred up a hornet's nest in the United Nations, where even most of their former supporters, including the United States, now lined up against them.[17] (The French, it should be noted, suffered from no such disability in carrying out their equally militant policies in Vietnam, for France—unlike the Netherlands—was a permanent member of the Security Council and was thereby armed with a veto power that kept its dispute with the Vietminh off the Security Council's agenda.)

Although the Soviet-oriented Indonesian Communists had now been crushed, some influential American officials became increasingly worried that the anti-Stalinist, strongly nationalist Communists led by Tan Malaka were benefiting from the military stalemate between Dutch forces and the republic. These officials now saw Tan Malaka's followers and other socio-

economic radicals as likely to win more adherents because of the frustration of the nationalist drive for independence that many Indonesians now
believed was blocked because the United States and other Western powers
with an economic stake in Indonesia continued to back the Dutch. Indeed,
with a long guerrilla war now a prospect, it seemed reasonable to assume
that increasing numbers of Indonesians would look to more radical leaders
than the still-popular but now-impotent Sukarno and Hatta, who remained
under Dutch arrest.[18] Added to this possibility was the pragmatic consideration that the guerrilla resistance was accelerating a scorched-earth campaign against Dutch plantations and other properties that threatened soon
to destroy most of the economic assets the Netherlands government sought
to protect. Thus, the self-interest of Dutch businessmen induced defections
from their ranks to join Dutch liberals who had long opposed the war. The
perceived self-interest of Americans with investments in Indonesia encouraged a comparable shift in their attitudes, and this undoubtedly had some
influence on American policy.

All these factors combined to bring many American congressmen and
senior government officials, who had earlier taken little interest in the
Dutch-Indonesian dispute or had been inclined to support the Netherlands,
to exert pressures that Secretary of State Dean Acheson, despite his own
continuing partiality to the Dutch position, was unable to resist. During
the spring of 1949 American policy changed and swung behind the Indonesians' cause, speeding the resolution of their struggle against the Netherlands, which finally yielded sovereignty at the end of December.

Indonesia's Nonalignment

It should not be assumed that this eleventh-hour change in American policy
resulted in such gratitude among victorious Indonesian nationalists as to
align them with the United States in the now well-developed cold war.
There were several reasons for the newly independent state's insistence on
following a foreign policy of nonalignment—a stance that, of course, was
not unusual among ex-colonial countries. Distrust of the Soviet Union born
of the belief (although direct evidence was lacking) that it had encouraged
the Madiun rebellion by no means canceled out the distrust of the United
States, which stemmed from its long period of support to the Dutch. Moreover, at The Hague conference in November and December 1949, at which
the Netherlands transferred sovereignty to the republic, the American representative, Merle Cochran, in exercising his role as moderator, sided with
the Dutch in exacting two major concessions from the Indonesians that significantly detracted from their broader success. With the United States still
concerned over the economic viability of the Netherlands, Cochran insisted
that the republic shoulder $1.13 billion of the Netherlands East Indies debt.

Approximately 70 percent of this amount constituted the entire internal debt of the colonial government, of which the Indonesians calculated that 42 percent had been incurred by Dutch military operations against the republic. Given the fact that they had agreed that all Dutch (and other foreign) investments in Indonesia would be fully protected, this condition struck Indonesians of all political persuasions as grossly unfair.[19] Cochran's private assurance to Indonesian negotiators that they could count on substantial U.S. economic assistance to help compensate for this debt burden soon sounded hollow when what was actually provided was only $100 million in export-import credits, which had to be repaid.

But in political terms, the most important concession Cochran insisted on was that the western half of New Guinea (West Irian), geographically a major component of the Dutch East Indies, be withheld from Indonesian control, with its future to be negotiated bilaterally within a year's time between the Netherlands and Indonesia. The temporary withholding of this part of the old colony was seen—probably correctly—as necessary to placate the nationalism of chauvinistic elements in Holland whose support was regarded as crucial to winning the necessary backing for the overall agreement in the Dutch Parliament.

And, thus, although at the end of December 1949 a fully independent Indonesia entered the international arena still harboring considerable good will toward the United States, the Truman administration's Washington's backing of Cochran's stand on the debt issue and the status of West Irian had significantly reinforced the country's previously existing preference for a foreign policy aligned with neither superpower.

· · · · ·

The first U.S. ambassador to Indonesia was the same Merle Cochran who had served as chairman of the United Nations-sponsored conference at The Hague that had in the last months of 1949 negotiated the transfer of Dutch authority to the Republic of Indonesia. In the McCarthyist ambience of Washington, D.C., in the early 1950s he apparently believed he would advance his career if he could induce the Indonesian government to abandon its policy of nonalignment in favor of joining the American camp.[20] Disregarding the advice of Indonesia specialists in the State Department, he mounted a devious attempt in January 1952 to bring the Indonesian cabinet to sign an agreement for economic assistance from the United States on terms, which he falsely claimed congressional legislation required, that clearly implied alignment of Indonesian foreign policy with that of the United States. Not knowing that Cochran had been instructed that such a concession was unnecessary, the Indonesian government finally signed on the ambassador's terms. When the Indonesian press learned that other nonaligned countries, such as Burma and India, had been given aid under the same congressional legislation without any such strings of alignment attached, there was an explosion of indignation all across the Indonesian political spectrum. Cochran was roundly scolded by the chair of the U.S. Senate's Foreign Relations Committee for having taken an unwarranted and unauthorized initiative, and he never received another foreign-policy assignment, but the damage to Indonesian-American relations had been done.

The most pro-American Indonesian cabinet to emerge in the decade after independence collapsed over the public outcry at this departure from nonalignment and a perception that an American ambassador was seeking to manipulate the country's foreign policy. As Robert J. McMahon observes: "This incident would serve as a forceful reminder to future Indonesian cabinets of the risks inherent in identifying themselves too closely with Washington."[21]

However, soon overshadowing the relatively ephemeral dispute over economic aid was the increasing bitterness among Indonesian leaders over what they saw as a continuing American collusion with the Dutch to keep the West Irian issue off the United Nations' agenda, thereby continuing in effect to deprive them of what they regarded as a legitimate part of their heritage. Even the most pro-American Indonesians were keenly disappointed that the United States was unwilling to permit the West Irian issue even to be discussed in the United Nations, and they fully realized that it was primarily the United States' influence—not Holland's—that made it impossible to muster a sufficient majority of votes to place the question on the agenda.[22]

Those American officials who were most ardent in supporting Dutch retention of West Irian acknowledged that administration of this huge, economically backward area was a drain on the Netherlands' resources, but they held that Dutch nationalism would be outraged if their country's flag did not continue to wave over this last major outpost of empire. They argued that, if the United States were to support a United Nations debate on West Irian, it risked undermining the loyalty of an important component of the North-Atlantic Treaty Organization (NATO). Why run that risk for the benefit of a country that refused to align with the American camp?

The Netherlands' retention of New Guinea was to impair Indonesia's relations with the United States as well as with the Netherlands until 1962, when the issue was resolved through the United Nations, following a Kennedy administration initiative. But until then Indonesian efforts at the United Nations were blocked by the Dutch—strongly backed by Australia—who continued to enjoy tacit support from an officially neutral United States. That stance was in itself sufficient to ensure Jakarta's continuing resolve to adhere to an independent nonaligned foreign policy.

2. POSTREVOLUTIONARY REALITIES

The Fruits of Independence

FOUR AND A half years of revolution had greatly increased the political and national consciousness of Indonesia's people and raised their hopes regarding the future rewards of independence. Indonesians now looked forward to enjoying as their own legitimate right the economic, social, and political benefits formerly considered the preserves of the Dutch. But the new Indonesia was immensely poorer in developed economic resources than the prewar Netherlands East Indies; the exactions of the Japanese occupation, the bombing raids of World War II, long and bitter fighting during the revolution, and frequent recourse to scorched-earth policies both on the eve of the Japanese occupation and during the revolution had resulted in wide-scale devastation. Most transportation and communication facilities, oil installations, plantation equipment, and the few industrial enterprises that the prewar economy had supported had been extensively damaged or totally destroyed. In addition, under the United Nations-sponsored agreement of December 1949 in which the Dutch formally relinquished sovereignty over Indonesia, the country had been saddled with a heavy indebtedness to the Netherlands, one that from the outset was a significant drain upon its economy.

Moreover, as a consequence of the destruction of prewar industrial and processing enterprises, Indonesia's economy was now even more lopsided, even more preponderantly dependent than before the war on the export of a few generally unprocessed raw materials (rubber, tin, oil, and copra) that were largely concentrated in the islands outside Java. And the prices of most of these exports on the world market fluctuated widely, making long-term planning difficult. With the government dependent primarily on export and import taxes for its revenue, this problem was to become critical.

The impact of World War II, the Japanese occupation, and Indonesia's revolution against the Dutch had thus seriously eroded the economic base of the country. This meant that, during these years of hardship, although Indonesia's population had not increased so rapidly as before, the number of its inhabitants, particularly those on Java, still far exceeded the capacity of its developed resources to sustain them adequately.[1] The disparity in population in the mid-1950s as between Java, with some two-thirds of Indonesia's 82 million people but less than one twelfth its area of some 600,000 square miles (740,000 square miles if West Irian, claimed by

Indonesia but still occupied by the Dutch, were included) and the other islands was matched by a substantial discrepancy in export earnings, most of which came from the Outer Islands. There Sumatra alone, the largest earner of foreign exchange, brought in considerably more than Java. The highly uneven concentration of population and resources across an ethnically diverse archipelago broader than the continental United States would in any case have generated problems for the country's political system — but these had been rendered more intractable by the unwillingness of Indonesia's leaders to embrace a federal system and the degree of local autonomy that it could have accommodated. They were reluctant to advocate such an arrangement primarily because the Dutch had badly discredited it by using federalism as a means of divide and rule in their efforts from 1946 to 1949 to control the thrust of the Indonesian revolution.

Indonesia's postwar economy above the village level was still capitalistic in character and still preponderantly in the hands of non-Indonesians, primarily Netherlanders and locally domiciled Chinese. Much Western capital was still invested (Dutch investments, despite destruction suffered during the revolution, still stood in the neighborhood of a billion dollars), but its political leverage was infinitely less than that of the colonial period. The similar educational background and common colonial and revolutionary conditioning of the small educated Indonesian elite had tended to promote considerable homogeneity in their approach to socioeconomic problems, and most of them espoused some variant of socialism. Thus, Western economic enterprise now had to deal with a government in which most leaders were unsympathetic to an increase of foreign capital and dedicated to the idea of its eventual displacement by a predominantly socialist economic order (with only modest scope for cooperatives and small-scale private entrepreneurs).

In most of Java and Sumatra, village-level society was more democratic than before the revolution, and the village leaders — a majority of them now elected — were often obliged to come to terms with a more politically conscious village populace and new and sometimes aggressive unofficial local leaders. But in the central and provincial governments, until the elections of 1955 Indonesia's national governmental leaders generally exercised power without significant interaction with the mass of the population.

One striking difference between postrevolutionary and colonial Indonesian society lay in the bureaucracy. Before the revolution few Western-educated Indonesians had been given access to its middle and upper ranks, but now these positions were their exclusive preserve. As had traditionally been the case, the Javanese in particular still regarded government service as a profession of great prestige, but its economic rewards were disappointing because of the poverty of the postrevolutionary government and the enormous inflation in the number of government officials. Nor did the bureaucrats comprise a harmonious and unified group. By the early 1950s, the national civil service—obliged to absorb officials of both the revolutionary republic and the Dutch colonial regime—had become four times as great as before the war (more than 600,000 as against approximately 150,000). Their loss of morale was soon exacerbated as competition among political parties resulted in the growing politicization of the bureaucracy, where appointments were now frequently made more in terms of political patronage than of merit.

Sukarno and Hatta

During the four-and-a-half-year anticolonial struggle and for several years after the Dutch yielded sovereignty, Sukarno was content to share power, initially with Hatta and later with a series of prime ministers of a parliament whose members had for the most part been appointed.[2] During the early 1950s, however, he became increasingly frustrated with the ineffectiveness of the parliamentary system, and after the national elections of 1955, he, along with a good many other Indonesians, was disillusioned and discontented with the parliament that had been elected, a parliament whose stewardship seemed to be no better than the preceding one. Thereafter he began to assert a much more active role in government, and by the end of 1956 he and the Indonesian army, now increasingly his major rival, were shouldering aside Parliament as the major repository of power.

Sukarno's political strength in the 1950s derived not only from his historical role as a leader of the nationalist movement and the revolution. His personal attributes ensured his continuing prominence. A handsome man with a warm and engaging personality, he exuded a powerful charisma. This quality infused his oratory and helped ensure that his speeches were extraordinarily effective—unmatched by those of any other Indonesian. He could always excite, often electrify, and generally convince the large crowds he addressed. He had enormous rapport with the masses, especially on Java. At the same time, speaking good English as well as Dutch and reasonably well read in Western history and political thought, in private discussions he could, and often did, impress and sometimes charm Western diplomats—even some who were initially among the most critical and skeptical. He was certainly not a modest man, but politically he was extremely sensitive and shrewd. He lived comfortably but was not wealthy and was known to be one of the few Southeast Asian heads of state who refrained from siphoning off public funds for deposit in bank accounts abroad.

With a degree in architectural engineering, Sukarno not only maintained a lively interest in and support of Indonesia's artists, but, as Hatta shrewdly noted, his artistic temperament seemed to be reflected in his political orientation. Thus, in 1957, Hatta observed to the American ambassador that, just as Sukarno was upset when he saw a building or picture that was "incomplete or lacking in symmetry," he had "emotionally similar reactions when he saw the country lacking in unity and one element pulling against another to [the] detriment of [the] well being of [the] people as a whole."[3]

Sukarno's major preoccupation was national unity — a daunting objective in a country so ethnically and linguistically diverse and geographically fragmented and far flung as Indonesia. The country had succeeded in winning its independence. But achieving real unity after the Dutch withdrawal, Sukarno believed, would take a full decade. He worked hard during the 1950s, traveling extensively throughout the archipelago, to achieve this unity.

It was not only geographical unity that commanded his concern. He also sought peaceful coexistence among the country's religious communities and the maximum possible ideological harmony at the political level. The system of multiparty parliamentary democracy patterned on the Dutch model, which had been taken over with little forethought or discussion, was clearly ill-suited to Indonesia's needs. Indeed, the Netherlands' multiparty system was one of the least appropriate of Western models, and, as applied to Indonesia, almost ensured that cabinets would usually be coalitions of divergently oriented individuals. And Sukarno persistently argued that a system in which decisions were made by as little as 51 percent of parliamentary representatives was not conducive to consensus and certainly not to political harmony. His country's unhappy experience with the system contributed to Sukarno's increasing tendency to generalize negatively about "Western-style democracy." Especially after the mid-1950s, when the continuing difficulty in reaching a consensus hobbled the parliament's ability to perform effectively, he concluded that Western-style democracy was unsuited for Indonesian conditions.

National unity, Sukarno believed, was not only a matter of geography but also ideology. An ideological eclectic, he regarded himself as a socialist — and never a proponent of communism. Among those political thinkers to whom he was especially drawn were the French revisionist socialist Jean Jaurès and Thomas Jefferson. In his own mind he had brought together a somewhat-shifting synthesis of elements of Javanese mysticism, Islam, and Western political thought — including components of revisionist Marxism (specifically excluding the concepts of class struggle and proletarian dictatorship, which he felt quite unsuited to Indonesia). He had intermittently attempted to develop a national ideology, dubbed *Marhaenism* for a peasant with whom Sukarno had lengthy discussions in the 1930s, but this only partially reflected his own cast of mind, and he lacked the commitment to work these rather limited and inchoate ideas into a coherent and meaningful political prescription.

Although Marhaenism was, in fact, officially adopted by the country's largest secular political party, the Indonesian National party (PNI), it had scant influence either on the party or on the Indonesian public in general and was soon largely forgotten, eventually it seemed even by Sukarno himself. But the much more narrowly focused ideological effort, the *Panca Sila*, did have some lasting effect. While Sukarno did not believe it was realistic in postindependence Indonesia to try to go beyond the *Panca Sila*'s fundamental principles in achieving an ideological consensus, he did believe it was important to strive for ideological harmony. Good government, he held, should reflect a harmonious coexistence between the most prominent streams of Indonesian ideology and a sufficient mutual respect among their proponents, to open the way for their effective cooperation. To extrapolate from Benedict Anderson's classic study, "The Idea of Power in Javanese Culture," just as a leader's claim to power rested on his "ability to contain opposites and to absorb his adversaries," so a powerful and effective government needed to contain and absorb a state's major political currents.[4]

It was this conviction that led Sukarno, beginning in 1956, to urge that all four major political parties form part of the government, including the Indonesian Communist party (PKI), which by winning 18 percent of the vote in the 1955 elections had emerged as the fourth largest. To exclude the PKI would, he argued, push the Communists into an irresponsible opposition. Having the PKI represented in the government would oblige them to share responsibility and block them from benefiting as the main channel for the public's discontent with the shortcomings and mistakes of government. (Controlling by far the largest and best organized of Indonesia's labor organizations [SOBSI], the PKI was in a position through strikes alone to inflict considerable damage on the country's fragile economy.) Political harmony, and thus governmental effectiveness, would be best served by its participation in the cabinet, even if it was excluded from major ministries, as was Sukarno's inclination.

To those who cited the Communist party's maneuvering into power in Czechoslovakia in 1948 and argued that, once inside the cabinet, the PKI would similarly soon take over the government, Sukarno could point to the postwar histories of France and Italy, where Communist party participation in their cabinets was followed by a decrease in their votes, and he observed that, unlike Czechoslovakia, these two countries, as with Indonesia, were not occupied by Soviet troops.

Sukarno correctly perceived the PKI as an essentially nationalist Communist party, and one that he was confident he could, in his words, "domesticate." He admired independent nationalist Communists such as Tito and Ho Chi Minh (and in Ho's struggle against France he saw a parallel to Indonesia's fight against the Dutch). After a visit to China in mid-1956, he developed a favorable opinion of Mao Tse-tung, and especially Chou En-lai. But he evidenced no such regard for Stalin. He perceived the PKI of the 1950s and 1960s as independent of the Soviet Union and China, but, if it could not be domesticated and it resorted to violence, he was prepared to move against it with force, such as he had authorized in the crushing of the Communist Madiun rebellion in 1948 and in supporting the arrest and temporary detention of Communist leaders in August 1951.[5] And, like Mohammad Hatta, from the outset Sukarno insisted that Indonesia should align itself with neither the United States nor the Soviet Union and should pursue a nonaligned but "independent and active" foreign policy.

Sukarno thus did not perceive the PKI as the bugbear and threat that in the climate of the cold war most of those Western diplomats who dealt with his country did. He, along with the PNI—by a slight margin the largest of the major parties and the one whose political leadership identified most strongly with him—saw the main threat to a democratic political system coming from the right wings of the Masjumi and Nahdatul Ulama, the two largest Islamic political parties (ranking second and third, respectively, in the 1955 elections). In short, they saw the threat of a doctrinaire Islamic state as overshadowing the threat of communism. (Not until the PKI markedly increased its vote in the 1957 provincial elections did the PNI depart from this judgment.)

Probably Sukarno's greatest weakness was his lack of understanding of economic problems and how to deal with them. He did not have the patience to accord them sufficient study, and though he continued to regard himself as a socialist he had no clear idea as to how to apply socialist prescriptions to his country's economy. And it was partly a consequence of his shallowness in understanding Indonesia's economic situation that he sometimes showed a lack of sensitivity to the economic grievances of the areas outside Java. Although the exports of raw materials from these other islands earned Indonesia approximately three quarters of its foreign exchange, Jakarta allocated to them only about a quarter of this amount for imports from abroad, the rest going to Java. While aware of this disparity, Sukarno never seemed to realize sufficiently its political implications and the extent to which it reinforced regional feelings of resentment toward Jakarta and what were perceived as its Javacentric policies. Consequently he did not fully appreciate the strength of the desire in the regions for greater administrative and economic autonomy.

For these two major weaknesses of Sukarno, Mohammad Hatta, the country's first and, until then, sole vice president, significantly—though not sufficiently—compensated. Indeed, in several ways he was a fitting complement to the Javanese Sukarno. Hailing from the Minangkabau area of Central Sumatra, he was regarded by most Sumatrans as their chief representative in the central government. And being a much more devout Muslim than Sukarno, his presence in the vice-presidential office tended to relieve the anxieties of Islamic leaders.

Like Sukarno, Hatta was a socialist, but he was much better grounded in the tenets of socialism and indeed was one of a handful of Indonesians with a really profound knowledge of Marxism. He was also one of the few

Indonesians who was a trained economist, not only having read widely in
that discipline but also having studied in the late 1920s at the Rotterdam
School of Economics. Hatta found Islam and socialism to be fully compatible, and in this respect his perspective was close to the "religious socialists"
who led the progressive wing of the major Islamic political party, the
Masjumi. More specifically, he advocated a mixed economy, in which
socialism would be the largest component, closely followed by a large
cooperative sector. He regarded himself as a social democrat as well as a
religious socialist and saw nothing incompatible between the two.

Hatta's stature derived not only from the leading role he had played in
the prewar nationalist movement but also from his preeminent political
role during the second half of the revolution (1948-49) and first critical
postrevolutionary year (December 1949-September 5, 1950). In both periods he served concurrently as prime minister and vice president. (During
the revolutionary years—except for a few times of acute crisis—Sukarno
generally took something of a back seat to the republican government's
prime ministers and to Hatta in the year immediately after the revolution.)

Apart from Hatta's frequent exasperation over Sukarno's lack of understanding of and concern over economic matters, there were two other issues
over which—by the mid-1950s—the two men had come strongly to dis-
agree. Hatta advocated an administratively decentralized, quasi-federal
state, believing that local needs could best be understood and addressed
by the people of the regions themselves. He felt that the local people would
be more strongly motivated to carry out programs beneficial to their areas
if they themselves ran these programs and had access to funds more com-
mensurate with the foreign exchange their areas' exports earned than if
most senior local administrative personnel continued to be Javanese and
disbursement of finances remained largely at the discretion of bureaucrats
in Jakarta.

While Sukarno recognized this argument, he feared that such autonomy
might abet centrifugal forces and lead to separatist movements that would
sunder the national fabric. Moreover, he argued that as a practical matter
there had to be considerable reliance on Javanese bureaucrats in the Outer
Islands because, as a consequence of Dutch colonial administrative prac-
tice, the overwhelming majority of experienced senior administrative civil
servants were Javanese.

But by the mid-1950s the sharpest issue dividing the two men was over
PKI representation in the cabinet. While Sukarno, for the reasons above
cited, believed its inclusion would yield greater interparty harmony and
PKI responsibility, Hatta was adamantly opposed. Rather than promote
harmony and political stability, PKI inclusion in the cabinet would, he
argued, introduce a dangerously disruptive element, since the Communists
were dedicated to different objectives from the other parties and aimed at
ultimate political dominance.

"If cooperation with the Communists were imposed on the other parties, the existing antagonisms would be heightened," he contended, "and the prospect for national unity would become more remote." Moreover, if the PKI were represented in the cabinet, it would no longer be possible for Indonesia to hold to an independent foreign policy since that party would work to subordinate Indonesia's interests to those of the Soviet Union. To include the Communists in the cabinet would be as futile as "to try and mix water and oil"; their proper place was in the parliamentary opposition.

As Sukarno became more assertive on the political scene in the mid-1950s, Hatta retreated into the background. In contrast to the active role he had played in government during the revolution and the first year thereafter, Hatta's position after September 1950 was primarily symbolic, symbolic particularly of national unity. He and Sukarno increasingly diverged in their views regarding the basis for solving salient national problems and in their attitudes toward the Communist and Islamic political parties. Their estrangement, noticeable as early as 1952, over these issues, in particular Hatta's advocacy of a greater autonomy for the regions and Sukarno's desire to include Communists in the cabinet, became increasingly serious. Sukarno became less and less receptive to Hatta's advice, and Hatta ultimately resigned as vice president in December 1956.

Islam in the Republic

One of Sukarno's major political preoccupations, one shared to a significant degree by Vice President Hatta, as noted above, was with what he conceived as the very real threat from proponents of an Islamic political order and his fear that, if successful, they might so antagonize non-Islamic and nominally Islamic elements as to risk national disintegration.

Until 1952, the political party that generally represented most Indonesian Muslims was the Masjumi (Madjelis Sjuro Muslimin Indonesia — Indonesian Muslim Consultative Council), a loose federation of semiautonomous Islamic social and educational organizations, such as the modernist Muhammadiyah and the more conservative Nahdatul Ulama. But in mid-1952 the Nahdatul Ulama withdrew from the federation, emerging as a separate party and removing much of the Masjumi's base in East and Central Java. In 1952, too, the influence of Isa Anshary, chairman of the Masjumi's West Java branch, further strained party unity. Dogmatic in his approach and intolerant of what he considered the backsliding of many Indonesian Muslims, Anshary openly advocated establishment of an Islamic state. The less dogmatic Masjumi leaders, including the group of "religious socialists" led by the party's chairman, Mohammad Natsir, viewed the concept of an Islamic state as more of an ideal than an immediately realizable goal. But there was no firm assurance that the moderate leaders of the Masjumi would continue to be able to withstand pressures from the zealots within the party, led by Anshary, whom Natsir privately referred to as "our Joe McCarthy."[6] Concern over the threat posed by proponents of an Islamic state was a major factor during the 1950s in inducing Sukarno and the largest secular nationalist party, the PNI, to move toward a tacit ad hoc common front with the PKI against the growth of Masjumi power.

In his concern over the political potential of Islam Sukarno had strong and consistent support across a wide range of political opinion, including leaders of the Catholic and Christian parties and the Indonesian Socialist party (PSI), as well as those of the PNI and the PKI. Most of the non-Communists among them considered an Islamic state to be a more immediate danger than a Communist regime. Together with Sukarno and Hatta they were especially worried over the threat to Indonesian unity posed by attempts to introduce such an Islamic state, fearing that it would provoke efforts at secession by areas with Christian majorities—such as Ambon, Flores, Indonesian West Timor, North Sulawesi, and Tapanuli and adjacent Christian Batak areas of North Sumatra—as well as Hindu-Buddhist Bali.

This widespread fear of radical Islam stemmed in no small measure from the activities of the Darul Islam (House of Islam), the insurgent group led by Sekarmadji Maridjan Kartosuwirjo, whose armed forces had held control since 1948 of substantial areas of the mountainous districts of central West Java, in an effort to realize by force "the ideals of a *Negara Islam Indonesia*, or Islamic State of Indonesia."[7] After waging an anti-Dutch guerrilla war in West Java, its forces mounted a fierce resistance in much of the area against the republic's efforts to impose its authority. With the transfer of sovereignty from the Dutch to the newly independent Indonesian government, the Darul Islam still controlled about a third of the countryside in West Java,[8] and for most of the next decade kept Jakarta's authority at bay in large areas of that province.

The Jakarta government faced armed challenges from dissidents in the other parts of the archipelago during the early 1950s that prevented it from concentrating its forces against those of Kartosuwirjo. Some of these rebellious movements, including those of Kahar Muzakkar in South Sulawesi and Daud Beureu'eh in Aceh, were in varying degrees Islamic in character and loosely allied with the Darul Islam to form a so-called government of the Islamic State of Indonesia. There was, however, little substance to this government and no real coordination among its regional components.

Nevertheless, throughout the 1950s the Darul Islam constituted an ominous cloud on Jakarta's political horizon, with many of the government's best battalions tied down in combatting its forces in West Java. Masjumi reluctance to condemn the Darul Islam unequivocally, and the party's general contention that government policies and the heavy-handedness of army troops were responsible for the continuing militancy of the Darul

Islam, served to nourish the suspicion that some Masjumi leaders did in fact maintain friendly relations with the Islamic rebels.

Persistence of the West Irian Issue

There was one major issue on which Sukarno and Hatta and indeed the whole spectrum of Indonesia's leadership were united: the Indonesian claim to West Irian (West New Guinea), the 140,000 square-mile part of the Indonesian archipelago the Dutch had refused to relinquish. This claim was a strongly emotional one, in part because in the swamps of the southeastern part of West New Guinea near Merauke had been located the notorious colonial prison camp of Tanah Merah (Boven Digul), where the Dutch had interned so many Indonesian nationalists, including Mohammad Hatta, in the final decades of colonial rule. In his study of nationalism, Benedict Anderson observes that "the internment and often interment there of nationalist martyrs gave West New Guinea a central place in the folklore of the anticolonial struggle and made it a sacred site in the national imagining."[9] Indeed, during the struggle for independence West Irian had always been regarded as an intrinsic part of the envisaged independent nation, with "Indonesia Free—from Sabang [off the northern tip of Sumatra] to Merauke" a popular revolutionary slogan.

As noted above, the discussions between the Dutch and Indonesians in December 1950 and January 1952 ended in deadlock—both sides still claiming complete sovereignty over the territory. For the Dutch, compromise was out of the question, and on February 15, 1952, at the very time negotiations were underway with Indonesia over the territory's status, the Netherlands Parliament voted to incorporate the area into the realm of the Netherlands. After this vote the Dutch refused further negotiation on the question of sovereignty and "considered the issue as closed."[10]

But for the Indonesians, the West Irian dispute was anything but closed. It remained pivotal in Indonesian domestic politics, emerging by 1953 as a central, consuming concern—with all political parties from across the political spectrum united in support for President Sukarno's persistent championing of the territory's incorporation in the republic. It was to a major extent because of its articulate support of this national claim that the PKI, resoundingly crushed only five years before, was able to pull its remnants together and regain political respectability. Now distancing itself from both the Soviet Union and China, the PKI was able to establish itself as a nationalistic Communist party that purported to back Sukarno fully. Its skillful espousal of the West Irian issue and its ability thereby to reinsert itself in the mainstream of a still-vibrant Indonesian nationalism were clearly of importance in reestablishing its position as a significant political party.

The Postrevolutionary Army

Critical to the survival of Indonesia's several cabinets in the decade after independence were the role and attitude of its armed forces. In the early 1950s Indonesia's army was a highly heterogeneous force, incorporating two broad components poorly suited to working harmoniously together: first, the semiguerrilla revolutionary republican army, Tentara National Indonesia (TNI) made up of both regular and irregular forces; and second, sizable elements of the disbanded Dutch colonial army, Koninklijk Nederlands Indisch Leger (KNIL). Even the TNI itself was anything but homogeneous. Built around a core of demobilized Japanese-trained auxiliary militias and headed primarily by a few Dutch-trained Indonesian officers who had fought on the side of the republic, the TNI incorporated numerous independent bands of young people and militias of several of the political parties. In the final years of the revolution (1948-49) and in 1950, Army Chief of Staff Colonel Abdul Haris Nasution and Vice President Hatta (then serving as prime minister), attempted to impose a structure on these bands and reduce a largely undisciplined array of about half a million regular and irregular forces into a streamlined mobile, well-trained army of ideally only about 57,000 troops. Among the irregulars least willing to be incorporated within the TNI had been the Islamic militias, many of whose units succeeded in retaining their autonomy from the regular army throughout the revolution, with some of those in West Java forming the nucleus of the DI.

According to the Round Table Agreement under which the Dutch transferred sovereignty to the republic, Royal Netherlands Army troops, numbering about 80,000, were to be withdrawn from Indonesia as rapidly as possible, while the KNIL—a predominantly Christian Indonesian and Eurasian force of some 65,000 men—was to be demobilized in Indonesia and dissolved by July 26, 1950. The dissolution of the KNIL was not in fact completed until June 1951, with about half of this ex-colonial force being absorbed into the new Indonesian army. The fate of some 100,000 republican guerrilla soldiers in Java, Sumatra, Sulawesi, and Kalimantan, who had belonged to the many irregular prorepublican militias and not to the official TNI, was equally uncertain. Clearly, if they were not incorporated into the new army, provision had to be made for placing them in civilian life—a task that was hard enough as a psychological problem but even more difficult thanks to the economic and administrative weakness of the government.

Prospects for the viability of this conglomerate postindependence national army were threatened by the government leadership's decision to liquidate the federal Republic of the United States of Indonesia (RUSI), set up under the agreements at the conference in The Hague, in favor of a unitary state. The generally accepted rationale for this action was the fact that, in terms of actual population, the federal states deriving from Dutch efforts at divide-and-rule held grossly disproportionate power in the RUSI House of Representatives, with 100 of its 150 members coming from the fifteen Dutch-created "states" despite the fact that the republic as a component had well over half of Indonesia's population. But many non-Javanese saw the movement toward a unitary state as an attempt by the Javanese majority to impose its hegemony. As a consequence, violent opposition to the dissolution of the RUSI erupted in several regions of the country—notably Ambon, Sulawesi, West Kalimantan, and parts of West Java where the KNIL had not been fully demobilized. Although these movements enjoyed little support, in some areas the military suppression of this regional opposition in the first year after the transfer of sovereignty already led to the cry: "Gone is Dutch colonialism, coming is Javanese colonialism."[11]

Even within the regular detachments of the TNI, there were many serious impediments to unity, for it incorporated ideologically diverse elements, frequently with different levels of training and military experience. Only a tiny handful of men had been trained during the last years of the colonial regime as noncommissioned officers in the KNIL, and even fewer as commissioned officers. But men from this group assumed the top positions in the hierarchy of the armed forces after the death of Commander-in-Chief Sudirman on January 19, 1950.[12]

Most of the army's other officers were drawn from two major elements—those who had been trained by the Japanese and had subsequently fought for the republic in the revolution, and those who had not had any previous military training but had received all their experience during the struggle against the Dutch. A significant proportion of the Japanese-trained and indoctrinated group felt that the army should have a major voice in politics, and they often tended to have a sympathetic view of authoritarian political organization, with little regard for democratic government. Most of those officers trained exclusively during the revolution, many of whom had formerly been teachers and students, were, however, initially inclined to view politics as something that an army officer should eschew.

Another important factor hindering unity was the regional divisions within the army. Most soldiers had been recruited in the areas where they fought, and to conduct successful guerrilla warfare the revolutionary army had had to develop close and sympathetic rapport with the local populations. As a result, local army units tended to identify with the inhabitants of the regions in which they operated, regarding themselves as representatives of the civilian society. Although in the postrevolutionary period some units were transferred from stable to unstable regions in an effort to enforce the new republican government's writ, in many areas, particularly in Sumatra, most of the army was still made up of soldiers who had fought there against the Dutch and had strong roots among the local population. During the revolution, moreover, in some parts of the country, officers had become so accustomed to carrying out a wide range of political and administrative functions in their areas that they were often reluctant to relinquish these extramilitary roles when the fighting ended. In the early years of independence they grudgingly did so, but as the ineffectiveness of civilian government grew increasingly evident, many army officers began to be drawn into the political arena.[13]

Army-Civilian Clashes

The postrevolutionary civilian government was weakened by the large number of political parties competing for power. In the still-appointed parliament that existed from August 1950 until early 1956 no party ever held more than fifty-two of 237 seats, necessitating a sharing of power within coalition governments mainly comprising two or three of the largest parties. From September 1950 to April 1957 Indonesia had six parliament-based cabinets, their short lives dependent in large part on the competing interests of the changing coalition of party partners. Their weakness stemmed not only from the interparty rivalries but also from the increasing friction between political leaders and President Sukarno over control of the armed forces. This friction was exacerbated by dissension among the military's senior officers, particularly over the continuing attempts of Army Chief of Staff Nasution to rationalize and modernize the army. During 1950, the standing army had been cut back by about 200,000 men, and he planned to reduce it by at least a further 50,000 over the next three to four years.[14] The projected dismissals would impinge most heavily on those less educated men who had been trained initially during the Japanese period, the group that, on the whole, stood closest to Sukarno.

These tensions erupted into direct confrontation in 1952, when officers of the former Japanese-sponsored Java-based militia, Peta, tried to enlist President Sukarno's help in challenging Nasution and his policies.[15] Civilian politicians capitalized on the issue to join in criticism of the top army leadership, which then largely rallied to the side of the chief of staff. This support emboldened Nasution to confront President Sukarno. On October 17, 1952, together with a group of senior officers, he met with the president and presented him with a request that Parliament be dissolved and elections held. Meanwhile, about 30,000 of their supporters were demonstrating outside the palace. Sukarno played for time, calming the demonstration and not challenging the army delegation. He reassured the officers that he understood the difficulty of their position and that he would discuss the issues with the government and urge it to hold a general election as soon as possible. These moves were successful. Although Parliament went into recess and the army enforced emergency restrictions in the capital for several days, a sufficient number of officers opposing Nasution's rationalization policies sided with the president for him to reject the army leaders' demands.

Nasution has strongly denied that the events of October 17 were any form of attempted military coup, and in his memoirs he blames a document, widely circulated in subsequent weeks by his rival, Colonel Zulkifli Lubis, head of armed forces intelligence, for generating and disseminating such a perception.[16] Nevertheless, Nasution spent the weeks following after the event on enforced leave until he was finally discharged on December 18, 1952.[17]

• • • • •

Tensions within the army continued at a high pitch during the next few years as the DI stepped up its military activities in West Java, South Sulawesi, and Aceh, while local army commanders became ever more independent in conducting affairs in their regions and in their attitude toward the army's central command. In February 1955 intraarmy dissension was only cosmetically laid to rest with the "Charter of Unity" signed after a two-day conference in Yogyakarta, a solemn and impressive ceremony attended by 270 high- and middle-ranking officers, as well as leading politicians, including Sukarno, Hatta, and Prime Minister Ali Sastroamidjojo.[18]

Within three months of the signing of the Charter of Unity, however, tensions were reignited when Nasution's successor resigned, and Lubis, now deputy chief of staff, was charged with running army headquarters until a replacement was found. When the PNI-led Ali government appointed South Sumatra commander Colonel Bambang Utojo as the new chief of staff, there was widespread dissatisfaction in the officer corps, and Lubis refused to hand over his acting command. According to Lubis, he "was not against Utojo as such but against Ali's insistence on appointing him [because of his pro-PNI leanings], for the Yogyakarta agreement had stipulated certain qualifications which a chief of staff would have to meet, technical, physical, etc. and Utojo was ill."[19] (Utojo had suffered a severe wound in his hand during the revolution that had never healed.) With the support of the territorial commanders, Lubis demanded that a new chief of staff be appointed "on the basis of competence rather than political partisanship" (which the Yogyakarta charter had also proscribed). The army's moves ultimately forced Ali's cabinet to resign, leading to the formation of a coalition government under Burhanuddin Harahap, of the Masjumi, which held office from August 12, 1955, through March 26, 1956. The Masjumi cabinet rescinded Utojo's appointment and retained Lubis in his post as acting chief of staff, although it never removed his "acting" status.

Outcome of the Elections

The four main parties emerged from the nationwide elections held in September 1955 with a total of 198 of 257 seats. The PNI had fifty-seven seats (with 22.3 percent of the vote); the Masjumi also had fifty-seven (with 20.9 percent of the vote); the second-largest Muslim party, the Nahdatul Ulama, forty-five (with 18.4 percent of the vote); and the Communist PKI, thirty-nine (with 16.4 percent of the vote).[20] Noteworthy in these results was the fact that the Masjumi polled nearly 50 percent of its vote outside Java (mostly in Sumatra and South Sulawesi), a little over 25 percent in West Java and Jakarta, and only 25 percent in East and Central Java combined. It was also striking that the PKI significantly increased its stature, with its parliamentary representation growing from seventeen to thirty-nine seats. Of its votes, 88.6 percent came from Java, with 75 percent from Central and East Java alone. The PKI won much of its following, particularly on Java, because it had helped build increasingly effective labor unions and championed a socioeconomic program favoring small peasants, grossly underpaid teachers, and other disadvantaged elements in society, and it was also significantly advantaged by its strong position on West Irian.

After the elections, Burhanuddin's coalition cabinet continued temporarily in power, as the Masjumi and the center and right wing of the nationalist PNI, alarmed over the unexpectedly large vote won by the Communists, worked to reestablish sufficient cooperation to permit their joining together in a new cabinet that would exclude the PKI. At the end of March 1956, such a cabinet was formed, again under the prime ministership of the PNI's Ali Sastroamidjojo. In addition to the Masjumi and PNI, the new cabinet incorporated the Nahdatul Ulama and representatives of several small parties.

Continuing indications of bureaucratic corruption, mounting inflation, and the government's ineffectiveness in dealing with Indonesia's major economic and administrative problems brought keen disappointment to the many Indonesians who had expected that elections would provide some sort of panacea and would usher in an effective government. According to Nasution, "The elections seemed to the military officers as merely legitimizing the old system of party government, with the same people in power and with just as much corruption as ever."[21] As a consequence, disillusionment with parliamentary democracy became increasingly widespread among soldiers and civilians alike. Understandably it was the Communist PKI that benefited from this situation. As the only major party not represented in the government, it could avoid responsibility for the discouraging situation while growing in strength as a symbol of protest. In recognition of PKI success in the elections, and to make the party more accountable, Sukarno now began to advocate inclusion of some Communist representatives in the cabinet. He remained confident that he would be able to domesticate the party

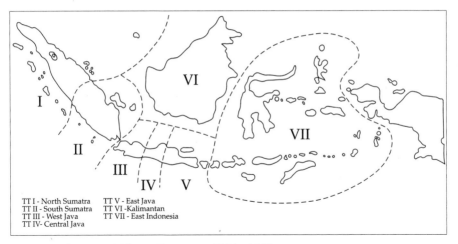

TT I - North Sumatra   TT V - East Java
TT II - South Sumatra   TT VI -Kalimantan
TT III - West Java   TT VII - East Indonesia
TT IV- Central Java

Map 2: Indonesia's Military Divisions, 1950–1958

so that its primary loyalty would be to Indonesia rather than China or the Soviet Union, and he continued in his conviction that it would be more controllable inside the government than outside, where PKI members were free of responsibility and could play on the people's discontent.

Rivalries and Dissension in the Army

After the elections, a new army chief of staff had to be selected, with the choice between the now politically rehabilitated Nasution, his chief rival Lubis, and several other senior officers, including Colonel Maludin Simbolon, territorial commander in North Sumatra, Colonel Gatot Subroto, former territorial commander of East Indonesia, and Colonel Alex E. Kawilarang, commander of West Java's Siliwangi division. Nasution received support from Burhanuddin's lame-duck cabinet and most of the officer corps and at least tacit acceptance from Sukarno.[22] On November 7, 1955, he was officially reinstated as army chief of staff after being assured he would have sufficient authority to reorganize the armed forces.

Nasution's renewed efforts to rationalize and streamline the army, however, soon made him once again the target of dissatisfaction in several quarters, particularly among those who had been his leading rivals for the position. Especially contentious were his moves in early 1956 to consolidate his position by rotating long-established regional territorial commanders. Kawilarang reluctantly accepted his replacement by a pro-Nasution Siliwangi officer and his reassignment as military attaché to Washington.[23] In eastern Indonesia, Colonel J. F. Warouw was replaced by his chief of staff, Lieutenant Colonel H. V. Sumual, and was himself to become military attaché in Peking. As part of this rotation, Nasution planned to transfer

Simbolon from his powerful and financially remunerative post of commander in North Sumatra to take up an unspecified position at army headquarters. He was to be replaced by Lubis, who was to surrender his position as
deputy chief of staff in favor of Nasution-stalwart Gatot Subroto.

Such changes were acceptable to neither Lubis nor Simbolon. On August
20 Lubis stepped down as deputy chief of staff but refused to be transferred
to North Sumatra, preferring to remain in Java near the center of his power
among elements of the Siliwangi division of West Java, and Simbolon
refused to leave his North Sumatran power base. In face of the threatened
transfers, these two colonels moved closer together in opposition to Nasution and were joined by other officers who had been slated for transfer.

On November 15, Lubis launched a coup, which was designed to oust
both Nasution and Prime Minister Ali Sastroamidjojo, as well as ostensibly
to clean up governmental corruption. The attempt failed when his plans
were disclosed before he could move certain battalions of the Siliwangi
division and paratroop units from Bandung to Jakarta. Lubis later
acknowledged his intentions and the poor planning and execution of this
abortive coup.[24]

A few days later, Nasution unsuccessfully attempted to arrest Lubis at an
anniversary meeting of the Army Staff and Command School (SSKAD) held
in Bandung from November 21-24, but he did succeed in detaining several
of Lubis's supporters. By this act, however, Nasution alienated even more
of the top army leadership, including the commandant of the SSKAD, who
had guaranteed the safety of all officers attending the anniversary celebra-
tion.[25] Lubis officially went underground, but, in fact, he spent most of his
time in a suburb of Jakarta.[26] The upheaval of the subsequent months seems
to have been as much a result of Nasution's own heavy-handed attempts to
impose his wishes on his subordinate officers as that of the conspiratorial
activities of Lubis.[27]

• • • • •

During 1956, differences among political parties and between Sukarno and
Hatta continued to grow. Although the Masjumi had emerged from the
elections as definitely the major party outside Java—particularly in Sumatra—its representatives in the cabinet held a clearly subordinate position
from which the party was unable to promote measures calculated to
assuage mounting regional restiveness. The Masjumi's central leadership
therefore found itself under great pressure from regional leaders to pull out
of the cabinet and go into opposition—pressures that its chairman,
Mohammad Natsir, resisted for the time being, arguing that such an action
would further weaken national unity and benefit only the Communists.

Sukarno, never enthusiastic about PNI leader Ali Sastroamidjojo's second cabinet (March 26, 1956-April 9, 1957), increased his criticism of it

and, eventually, the whole system of parliamentary government. After returning from a visit to the Soviet-bloc countries and China, he made a speech in late October 1956, ascribing many of the country's ills to the multiplicity of political parties and declaring "that he dreamed of the day when they would be replaced by one party." On being criticized in the press for being antidemocratic, he responded in a speech on October 30: "I don't want to be a dictator because it is contrary to my own conscience. I am a democrat, but I don't desire democratic liberalism. On the contrary I want a guided democracy . . . . I have a conception of my own which I will put at the disposal of the party leaders if required." On November 10, in his opening address to the Constituent Assembly, he returned to the theme, arguing that "the freedom to set up political parties does not constitute the only means to keep the democratic system going" and that Indonesian democracy should be unique and not a copy of imported systems.[28] He asserted that the weaker groups in Indonesian society should be protected from the stronger and that "one group should not be exploited by another." This necessitated an overhaul of Indonesia's system of democracy whereby, "for the time being, our democracy must be a guided democracy." Sukarno's call for "guided democracy" and his attacks on the system of parliamentary democracy widened the breach with Hatta, a separation that was formalized with Hatta's resignation as vice president on December 1, 1956.

3. DISSENT IN THE REGIONS

Toward Regional Autonomy

A SCANT YEAR after independence, regional dissatisfaction with the central government was already evident. The government failed to take effective action to further the economic development of the regions outside Java or even to address their most immediate economic problems; nor was it willing to grant sufficient administrative and fiscal decentralization for the local governments to meet their needs themselves. There was growing regional resentment at the preponderance of the country's foreign exchange being channeled to Java—rather than to the other islands where nearly three fourths of this income was being earned.[1]

To these economic grievances were added social and political ones. The imposition of a unitary form of government in 1950 resulted in the shifting of many of the powers exercised by local authorities during the revolution to the central government, with civilian provincial leaders now appointed by Jakarta rather than elected by the people they served. Charges that the Javanese had replaced the Dutch as colonizers were particularly potent in strongly Islamic areas, such as Aceh, the Sundanese region of West Java, South Sulawesi, South Kalimantan, and West Sumatra, with the first three of these regions being major centers of the Darul Islam insurgency.

The results of the 1955 election reflected the dichotomy between Java and the other islands, and the latter's fears that their representatives in Jakarta were losing power at the center crystalized with Vice President Hatta's resignation.[2] Long the strongest national voice arguing for greater regional autonomy, Hatta's intention to resign from the vice presidency, first expressed on July 20, 1956, was viewed particularly by the Muslim parties as a serious threat to the country's political equilibrium. His actual resignation on December 1 may well have provided the spark that ignited regional autonomy movements and may also have ensured that the first such outburst did not take place in either of the important economic exporting regions of North and South Sumatra but rather in West Sumatra, Hatta's birthplace and a strongly Islamic region that viewed him as its particular representative in the central government.

In the years after General Nasution's resignation as army chief of staff in 1952, territorial commanders had increased their power at the expense of the army's central command. By 1956, they had become the principal instruments channeling regional grievances into open defiance of the

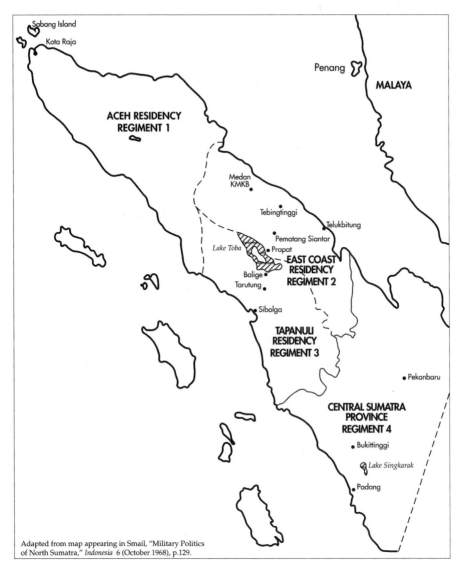

Sabang Island
Kota Raja
Penang
MALAYA
ACEH RESIDENCY
REGIMENT 1
Medan
KMKB
Tebingtinggi
Telukbitung
Lake Toba
Pematang Siantar
Prapat
EAST COAST
RESIDENCY
Balige
REGIMENT 2
Tarutung
Sibolga
TAPANULI
RESIDENCY
REGIMENT 3
Pekanbaru
CENTRAL SUMATRA
PROVINCE
REGIMENT 4
Bukittinggi
Lake Singkarak
Padang

Adapted from map appearing in Smail, "Military Politics
of North Sumatra," *Indonesia* 6 (October 1968), p.129.

Map 3: The First Military Region, North Sumatra

Jakarta government. As Ruth McVey observes, "The weakness of the center not only allowed more power to be exercised at lower levels but it aided the consolidation of power there."[3] At the same time, the central army headquarters' loss of influence vis-à-vis the civilian government had meant a reduction in the military budget, with a drastic effect on the living conditions of the ordinary soldiers.

The plight of the troops under their command led territorial commanders, particularly in Sulawesi and Sumatra, to take matters into their own hands and begin an illegal barter trade in copra and rubber to raise funds both to meet the needs of their soldiers and to fight local insurgencies. Although the government responded by taking legal measures particularly against Colonel J. F. Warouw, territorial commander in East Indonesia, the smuggling continued to increase. Colonel Simbolon, in charge of the First Territorial Command (TTI) in northern Sumatra, initiated a profitable barter trade in rubber between the North Sumatran ports and Singapore, described in December 1956 by the British consul in Medan:

> Like a rolling snowball, from small beginnings these illegal transactions have assumed bigger and bigger proportions with the years, and recent smuggling scandals in which the Colonel [Simbolon] himself has been involved have been hushed up only with great difficulty and considerable embarrassment—plus a good deal of friction with the local civilian authorities. As did Colonel Warouw, following the exposure of his copra-smuggling operations in Celebes two years ago, Simbolon has always stoutly maintained that whatever money may have been raised in deals of the kind has been used entirely to bolster up the inadequate budget of Territorium I, and that his hands are clean personally."[4]

The powerful and remunerative positions enjoyed by the local military commanders were threatened when Nasution resumed the post of army chief of staff in November 1955 and began attempts to reassert central control by reorganizing the military territories and rotating their regional commanders, many of whom by then were virtual warlords. Repercussions soon came to a head in Simbolon's TTI.

The huge island of Sumatra was divided into only two military regions, TTI in the north, with its headquarters in Medan, and TTII in the south, with its command center in Palembang. The TTI, a patchwork area created at the end of the revolution in December 1949, incorporated diverse areas and people, including the intensely Islamic regions of Aceh and West Sumatra, the several (often competing) mainly Christian Batak regions of East Sumatra and Tapanuli, and a large immigrant community of 700,000 Javanese who made up most of the labor in the plantations of East Sumatra.[5]

Although he was one of the foremost officers in the Indonesian army—and one of the leading candidates for the post of chief of staff in 1955—Maludin Simbolon was never able to take his position for granted.[6] He was himself a Christian Toba Batak and enjoyed considerable support in Tapanuli and limited additional Batak areas, but he was also an object of resentment, particularly in Aceh. Suspicions among the intensely Islamic Acehnese that Christian Bataks were trying to gain the upper hand in the North Sumatra army had been growing since the end of 1949, when the Acehnese military forces had been incorporated into TTI, headed first by a Christian Menadonese, Alex Kawilarang, and then successively by Christian Bataks Haris Sitompul and Simbolon. In fact, when, in 1955, an ethnic Acehnese, Syamaun Gaharu, was appointed to head the Aceh regiment, it was only "at Nasution's promise that Maludin Simbolon would be transferred in the near future that he accepted the position."[7]

Simbolon was reportedly popular, however, among most rank-and-file Batak soldiers, enjoying a reputation for standing up for his men and looking after their welfare.[8] His large-scale smuggling activities in North Sumatra had undermined his standing among local civilian leaders as well as in Jakarta, but, according to John Smail, they were, in fact, "an effort by Simbolon to carry his restive officers with him by uniting them in defiance of Djakarta and distributing very large sums (the bulk of the proceeds) directly to or through them."[9]

Although he had had little experience outside Indonesia, the six-foot-tall Simbolon's impressive physical mien and good knowledge of English made him popular among the foreign diplomatic community in Medan, particularly the Americans. The British consul there observed: "He possesses a sense of humour and an ease of manner which distinguish him from the great majority of his countrymen. He was perfectly 'at home' in the company of Europeans, and has for many years been on almost 'intimate' terms with the succession of American Consuls in Medan and the U.S. Consulate personnel in general."[10]

Once Kawilarang and Warouw had accepted their transfers from West Java and East Indonesia in August 1956 and departed to take up their posts as military attaché in Washington and Peking, respectively, Simbolon and Lubis became the major opposition to Chief of Staff Nasution. At the same time, other elements within the officer corps were for various reasons aligning against him and demanding changes in the military power structure. This dissatisfaction became overt at the November 1956 reunion of the Army Staff and Command School (SSKAD) in Bandung, at which the participants criticized Nasution's reorganization policies and suggested that the army's leadership needed to be changed. Several North Sumatran officers were present, and on their return to Medan they joined Simbolon in sponsoring a gathering of North Sumatran officers in early December that called for regional military commanders to free themselves from central control. They met again on December 16 and made a collective vow to attain this objective, "then drank a toast and smashed their glasses to symbolize their break with the old ways."[11]

The Colonels Take Action

Colonel Husein's Takeover in West Sumatra

Simbolon and his officers, however, had stopped short of a full break with Jakarta, and it was in the West Sumatran town of Bukittinggi that the first overt challenge to the central government was launched. West Sumatra was probably one of the regions most disillusioned with the course of events since Indonesia achieved its independence. At the end of 1949, its Minangkabau people entertained especially high hopes for their future position in the new state. Not only was their region the birthplace of Vice President Hatta, but it was also the home region of a whole cluster of the leaders heading the republic's government in Jakarta.[12] Moreover, West Sumatra had been the seat of Indonesia's emergency government during the final year of the revolution when the Dutch had occupied Yogyakarta, and Bukittinggi became known as Indonesia's second capital.

Their revolutionary record, coupled with their representation at the center, then, had led the Minangkabau to anticipate an important role for their region in postrevolutionary Indonesia. But their hopes for a favored status within the newly independent nation were almost immediately dashed. As was the case in Aceh and other regions, their military forces, too, the so-called Banteng division, were dissolved and incorporated into the North Sumatra military command (TTI), while a Javanese governor was appointed to head their region and their own representative council was deprived of power.[13] Further disillusionment set in during 1955-56, with the inconclusive elections and Hatta's threats of resignation.

In 1956, the commander of West Sumatra's forces—the residual units of the Banteng division now forming Regiment 4 of TTI—was Lieutenant Colonel Ahmad Husein.[14] Born in Padang in 1925, Husein had joined the Japanese volunteer auxiliary militia, in which he was a second lieutenant at the time of Japan's capitulation. In the early days of the revolution he commanded the Kuranji battalion, fighting on the boundaries of the town of Padang—occupied first by the British and then the Dutch—where his battalion's exploits earned him the name "Tiger of Kuranji." With the transfer of sovereignty Husein had been assigned to West Java to fight the dissident Darul Islam, but he returned to West Sumatra at the end of 1951, when he was appointed commander of the Banteng brigade.

Throughout his career Husein's ties with his men had been close and his attitude toward them protective. A flamboyant and courageous fighter, he had risen to prominence among his contemporaries while still in his early twenties. He was clearly one of the young Minangkabau soldiers whose hopes for power and prestige had been frustrated by the military retrenchment and the downgrading of the Banteng division after the transfer of sovereignty. As a fervent Muslim, he must have been further disillusioned during his stint in West Java by being called on to fight the Darul Islam. This background clearly influenced his response to the hardships faced by the soldiers in West Sumatra in the early 1950s. Like Simbolon in Medan and Warouw in Sulawesi, Husein protested to Jakarta the poor living conditions of the men under his command and led a delegation to Jakarta to seek redress. While in the capital, Husein was approached by some of his former colleagues from West Sumatra who urged him to organize a reunion of the former Banteng division, which was ultimately held in West Sumatra

November 20-24, 1956. A total of 612 veterans attended the reunion, together with North Sumatra commander Simbolon and his counterpart for South Sumatra, Lieutenant Colonel Barlian, as well as a representative of Chief of Staff Nasution.

The final session of this reunion produced the "Banteng Charter," signed by all the veterans, which demanded immediate changes in Indonesia's military and civilian leadership, broad autonomy for West Sumatra, reinstatement of the former Banteng division, and abolition of Indonesia's centralized system of government.[15] The reunion appointed seventeen West Sumatrans to the Banteng Council (Dewan Banteng), headed by Husein, that was charged with implementing the charter.

On December 20 in Bukittinggi, as head of and in the name of the Banteng Council, Husein took over power from Governor Roeslan Moeljohardjo and declared himself in charge of the government in Central Sumatra.

Colonel Simbolon's Coup Fails in Medan

Husein's actions were the opening salvo in a series of regional takeovers that plunged the Republic of Indonesia into its most severe crisis since achieving independence. Apparently taken by surprise at the timing of Husein's declaration and so as to avert his own long-pending transfer to army headquarters that he had finally agreed should take place on December 27, Simbolon launched his own coup in Medan.[16] On December 22, in an action that bore all the marks of being hurriedly and inadequately prepared, he announced that his military district had dissociated itself from the central government in Jakarta and that he himself had taken over authority from the acting governor. He then proclaimed a state of war and siege for the province of North Sumatra.

Both Simbolon and Husein stressed their continued loyalty to Sukarno while calling for a restoration of the Sukarno-Hatta *dwitunggal* (duumvirate).[17] But the central government's response differentiated between the two councils, reacting cautiously to Husein in Bukittinggi while moving swiftly against Simbolon in Medan with a two-pronged countercoup.

In Jakarta, Prime Minister Ali Sastroamidjojo's cabinet met in an emergency session on the night of December 22, 1956, and the following morning Sukarno announced the government's decision to relieve Simbolon temporarily of his position and appoint his deputy, Lieutenant Colonel Djamin Gintings, as his replacement. If for any reason Gintings was unable to assume the position, Lieutenant Colonel Wahab Macmoer, commander of the Second Regiment, should take over instead.[18] After initially hesitating, Gintings ordered his troops to surround Simbolon's home and take over army installations in Medan. Perceiving his danger, Simbolon slipped out of his Medan headquarters and took temporary asylum on the northern borders of the town. From there he began to move south, accompanied by forces loyal to him, and established himself at the Tapanuli town of Balige on the southern shore of Lake Toba.

In the meantime, both Gintings and Macmoer claimed to be commander of TTI, until Deputy Chief of Staff Gatot Subroto arrived from Jakarta to confirm Gintings's appointment and formally install him as Simbolon's successor. Gintings then remained sitting "rather uneasily in Medan," where there was suspicion that his supposedly subordinate Javanese garrison commander was actually "the real boss."[19]

In this way, the central government successfully blunted Simbolon's major challenge in Medan, exploiting the fissures in North Sumatra's mixed society and the rivalries among Simbolon's subordinate officers. This political maneuvering had taken place virtually without a shot being fired, and it had not been accompanied by any matching display of military force. In fact, the only military attack mounted by the center was a total fiasco—one so glaring as to induce both local military leaders and Western observers to underrate Jakarta's future military capabilities. This attack was a parachute operation launched by the central government on December 28 against the Medan airport in support of Gintings's maneuvers within the city. As the British consulate reported:

> Medan residents living near the airport were amazed after days of silence to hear and see a large army transport 'plane circling the area at low altitude without landing. It seemed to be in difficulty. They were even more amazed when they saw a dozen or so parachutists trailing out behind. Whether this operation had been staged by the authorities in Djakarta with a view to strengthening security at the airport in case the Air Force police unit stationed there should prove unreliable, or whether it was designed merely to impress the local population is not known, but the result was disastrous, and only by imposing a strict press censorship on military affairs has it been possible to suppress any open references to it. However, the facts have gradually leaked out and are now common gossip. It seems that, of the 30 odd men who were ordered to jump, only 17 did so. Of these, one was killed, 14 suffered broken limbs, and 2 escaped serious injury. The rest remained in the 'plane. It is said that (a) the 'plane was flying too low, and (b) the men had not received adequate training. All 17 were quietly picked up and removed to the local Military Hospital.[20]

The military territory of North Sumatra had now disintegrated into its discrete components. Immediately after Simbolon's coup Nasution withdrew Husein's regiment and the Aceh regiment, under Lieutenant Colonel Syamaun Gaharu, from the North Sumatra command, at least formally placing both directly under his own authority as army chief of staff. The commander of the Tapanuli regiment, Major Samosir, had openly supported the ousted Simbolon, and on December 31, declaring he could not recognize the authority of Jakarta's new appointee, took a middle road by also placing his regiment directly under Nasution.[21]

Stalemate in South Sumatra

Events in South Sumatra's TTII during December 1956 and January 1957 were not nearly so dramatic or decisive as in the areas to the north. In the aftermath of the takeovers by Husein and Simbolon, the South Sumatra governor took steps to forestall parallel military actions in his region and maneuvered to retain his post. In mid-January, however, Palembang did seem to be following the same pattern as Bukittinggi and Medan when Lieutenant Colonel Barlian, commander of TTII, proclaimed formation of the Garuda Council, led on a day-to-day basis by his deputy chief of staff, Major Nawawi.[22]

But Barlian moved much more cautiously than his fellow commanders, in part because of South Sumatra's proximity to Java and also because of the deep ethnic and ideological splits within his military region. Another reason may have been his own close ties with Nasution, who said he regarded Barlian as "a younger brother."[23] The Garuda Council, set up in mid-January, portrayed itself as an "advisory" group rather than a "governing" body. It unsuccessfully attempted to replace the Javanese governor with a local appointee but took no further steps when the governor refused to cede his position.

The Palembang area was strategically important to all sides in the dispute as the major center of the oil industry in Sumatra, with not only the oilfields but also the refineries of two of the principal oil companies in Indonesia—BPM (Shell) and Standard Vacuum Oil—being located there. (The refineries were situated just across and upriver from the city of Palembang at Plaju and Sungei Gerong.) The Standard Vacuum refinery at Sungei Gerong was producing about 65,000 barrels a day in early 1956, with a major expansion program underway.[24] The territory of the South Sumatra military command was, then, Indonesia's most important single region in economic terms. In 1956, it provided 63.5 percent ($143 million of $225 million) of Indonesia's oil exports and 36 percent ($317 million of $882 million) of its total exports.[25]

As a result, as with Padang, the central government at this stage was much more circumspect in dealing with Palembang than it had been with Medan. Although Jakarta had cut communications with Central Sumatra immediately after the Banteng takeover, imposing a food blockade until early January 1957, at the same time frequent central government missions were sent to Central and South Sumatra, which in January took with them Rp.150 million and Rp.370 million, respectively, to augment the central government's normal subsidy to the two regions.[26]

The government also moved to alleviate legitimate regional grievances. From mid-1956 through early 1957 legislation had passed the parliament, calculated to assuage regional discontent at Indonesia's overly centralized administration. Although few results were as yet visible, Jakarta promised to speed up implementation of these decentralization laws granting greater regional administrative and fiscal autonomy. Under this legislation, the number of Indonesia's provinces was increased from nine to fifteen; district heads were to be elected by local councils rather than appointed from Jakarta, municipalities were reestablished in Central Sumatra, and in April 1957, Prime Minister Djuanda promised an expanded public-works program for areas outside Java.[27]

The Jakarta government realized that differences existed between the dissident movements in the three areas of Sumatra, in particular with regard to the amount of local support each enjoyed. Both Barlian and Simbolon only headed factions within their respective regions and did not even have all their subordinate officers behind them. They were thus potentially vulnerable to being isolated and removed. But certainly in these early months the Banteng Council in West Sumatra enjoyed widespread backing not only from army units there but from the major social organizations, religious leaders, political parties, and even local officials of the central government's own bureaucracy. All these groups issued statements essentially supporting the actions taken by the Banteng Council.[28]

The only party that did not give the Banteng Council at least ostensible backing at this stage was the local branch of the PKI. Although small, receiving only 5.75 percent of the local vote in the 1955 elections, the Communist party was one of the most active of the nonreligious parties in Central Sumatra.[29] Not all its local members opposed the Banteng Council, and some reportedly left the party because of its position. But the party's official opposition led to Banteng Council reprisals, when three leaders from the PKI-dominated labor organization in Pekanbaru were arrested in January 1957 and imprisoned in Bukittinggi.[30]

Within a month of the proclamation of the Banteng Council, an uneasy calm had returned to center-regional relations. Despite expectations, the declarations of regional autonomy had had no decisive effect on the balance of power at the center, on Nasution's position as chief of staff, or on the fragile existence of Ali Sastroamidjojo's government. It's position was seriously weakened by the withdrawal of key members of the cabinet— mostly Masjumi—but the government did not at this stage fall.

· · · · ·

Army Chief of Staff Nasution was very conscious that his own authority was at stake. He responded swiftly and decisively in his successful moves against Simbolon. But he made a series of conciliatory moves toward the other commanders by dividing Sumatra into four military districts (Aceh, North Sumatra, Central Sumatra, and South Sumatra), rather than the existing two, and agreeing to appoint Husein as head of the new military command of Central Sumatra, thus granting him effective authority, at least in military matters, in Jambi and Riau as well as West Sumatra.

Territorial commanders in other regions of Indonesia were alert to the takeovers in Sumatra and central government reaction to them. There had been a brief flurry of activity in South Kalimantan, when a strong supporter of Zulkifli Lubis, Colonel Abimanyu, ordered the arrest in mid-November 1956 of all officials coming from Jakarta. Nasution responded quickly through a local hero from the time of the revolution and a former military governor of South Kalimantan, Hassan Basry, who had achieved striking success against a Darul Islam rebellion there. Basry marshaled support among other regiments in the region against Abimanyu's order, and Abimanyu himself, when summoned by Nasution to Jakarta, was induced to shift his allegiance from Lubis.[31]

Permesta in Sulawesi

In the army's Seventh Territorial Command — embracing all of Eastern Indonesia — the situation was different.[32] The center of the TTVII was the island of Sulawesi, which, after the transfer of sovereignty in 1950 and the dissolution of the Dutch-sponsored Federal State of East Indonesia (NIT), had been constituted as a single province, with its capital in Makassar, in the southwestern part of the island. Revenue from the copra trade in North and Central Sulawesi was the major support for the economy of the whole island. After taking over from Gatot Subroto as commander of TTVII in October 1952, Colonel Warouw, a native of the Minahasan region of Sulawesi, sanctioned and encouraged a barter trade in this copra with foreign purchasers that evaded Jakarta's export controls and denied it the major portion of the foreign exchange that it previously derived from these exports.

Many of the guerrillas in South Sulawesi who had supported the republican cause against the Dutch had gone into rebellion in 1950-51 against the government's moves to dissolve their military units. They then made common cause with Kahar Muzakkar, the Muslim leader who during the revolution had led some effective armed South Sulawesi youth forces on Java. On his return to South Sulawesi in April 1950 with many of his young soldiers, Muzakkar had been slated to become Warouw's deputy, but he was dissatisfied with the government's plans to demobilize so many of the guerrilla forces and took his struggle into the jungles.[33] On January 20, 1952, Muzakkar officially joined forces with the West Java Darul Islam movement, accepting an offer by S. M. Kartosuwirjo that his troops become the Sulawesi Command of the Islamic Army of Indonesia.

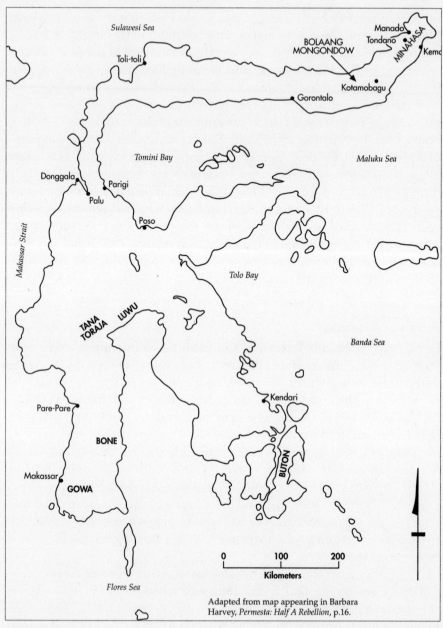

Map 4: Sulawesi

By 1956, Muzakkar's guerrillas controlled much of the South Sulawesi countryside.

When in August 1956 Nasution successfully ousted Warouw from his East Indonesia command and sent him as military attaché to Peking, he installed Lieutenant Colonel H. N. Ventje Sumual, another Christian Minahasan and Warouw's former chief of staff, as the new commander. Sumual's sympathies, however, were also with the Sulawesi's demands for autonomy. In November 1956, he participated in the SSKAD reunion in Bandung that proposed changing the army's central leadership, and he protested to Nasution at the arrests of Lubis's supporters there.[34] Over the following months Sumual maintained contact with both Husein and Simbolon.

Throughout January and February 1957 Nasution tried to dissuade military officers in Sulawesi from following their Sumatran colleagues into rebellion. After meeting on January 7 and 8 with two Islamic officers from South Sulawesi, Lieutenant Colonel Saleh Lahade and Major Andi Jusuf, to discuss the reaction on that island to the events on Sumatra, Nasution agreed to remove four of the Javanese battalions from South and Southeast Sulawesi and increase the importance of local troops and commanders. These actions, however, though they satisfied Major Jusuf, were not enough to win over Saleh Lahade and division commander Sumual.[35]

Senior officers from North and South Sulawesi held a meeting on February 25, 1957, in which Saleh Lahade played the major role. He summed up the current demands and dissatisfactions in Sulawesi and pointed out the similarities between their situation and that on Sumatra. It was agreed that Sumual should go to Jakarta to press demands for greater provincial autonomy for the regions of East Indonesia. On Java, he met with the army command and the officer corps of SSKAD and explained the steps he and his colleagues intended to take in Sulawesi. On March 2, the day after his return to Makassar, Sumual proclaimed a state of emergency in East Indonesia and instituted martial law. Saleh Lahade read a "charter of inclusive struggle," or Permesta (Piagam Perjuangan Semesta Alam), which incorporated East Indonesia's demands for greater local autonomy, economic development, and control of revenue, and nationally for the introduction of decentralization and restoration of the Sukarno-Hatta duumvirate. Sumual headed the new military government as "military administrator" with Saleh Lahade as his chief of staff, and with four military governors responsible to him.[36]

The central government feared that the South Sulawesi aristocracy might support the dissidents, but more important was the fact that this island— occupied successively by Australian and Dutch forces—had not been an integral part of the republic during the struggle for independence, fueling fears that it did not sufficiently share the affinity for Indonesian unity that characterized the western regions of the archipelago.[37]

Colonel Barlian Acts in South Sumatra

Encouraged by Sumual's example in Sulawesi, Colonel Barlian, the military commander of South Sumatra, now finally followed in the steps of his fellow officers, announcing on March 9, 1957, that he too had taken over the civil administration in his area by ousting the governor.[38] Allegedly on Sukarno's orders, the Javanese commander of one of his regiments, Djuhartono, challenged Barlian's takeover but was soon forced to flee to the airport, where he was sent about 400 paratroopers from Jakarta as reinforcements.[39]

Protesting these actions by the central government, Barlian spurned Nasution's efforts to negotiate an agreement. He now assumed an unexpectedly forceful stance, requisitioning vehicles from the oil companies, calling up and arming as many as 2,000 veterans, making it clear that he was willing to respond militarily to any attacks against him, and threatening to blow up the oil refineries if he was compelled to withdraw from Palembang. He appealed for help to the Banteng Council, which promised to send him 1,200 troops in the event of an attack by the central government.

Barlian's threats succeeded. When Nasution returned to Java, Djuhartono accompanied him, and the Javanese paratroop reinforcements were gradually withdrawn. The situation had been defused in Barlian's favor, and relative calm returned to Palembang. While Barlian consolidated his position in Palembang and Husein expanded his control in Central Sumatra, the government sent in small but steady reinforcements of Javanese troops to pro-government units in Medan, the only major center on Sumatra it still controlled.

From this series of bloodless coups, the local commanders, with the exception of Simbolon (now under Husein's protection in Padang), had emerged thus far triumphant. Nasution's attempts at negotiation and conciliation had made him appear weak and indecisive. Even Simbolon's downfall—Jakarta's one success—had resulted not from the military power of the central government but from its political ability to exploit the internal divisions in the North Sumatra command. The only military maneuvers mounted by the center—the paratroop fiasco in Medan and the reinforcements sent into Palembang airport—had been dismal failures. The stream of fact-finding delegations that the central government sent to the rebellious regions returned to Jakarta to report that the insurgent commanders—particularly in West Sumatra—enjoyed widespread local backing, and, rather than having been weakened by their severance of ties with Jakarta, were in fact strengthening their control over the local government.

Response from the Center

On February 21, 1957, Sukarno had formally advocated his *konsepsi* (conception) of a new political system, under which there should be a four-party (PNI, Masjumi, Nahdatul Ulama, and PKI) NASAKOM cabinet, advised by a National Council consisting of functional groups from all segments of

Indonesian society.[40] Although there was a strong reaction in the regions as well as in Jakarta, against the proposed inclusion of the Communist PKI in the cabinet, one of the regional dissidents' demands was met when, because of its failure to meet their challenge, the second Ali Sastroamidjojo cabinet resigned on March 14.

On the eve of his resignation Sastroamidjojo acceded to Nasution's request for a declaration of martial law and signed a decree proclaiming a national state of siege, under which "the military authority is empowered, in deviation from provisions of general regulations, to take measures of any kind whatsoever . . . when it considers them necessary in view of the immediate emergency situation." Many of the rebel commanders had proclaimed martial law in their own regions, and, through the declaration of a national state of siege, Nasution hoped to control these local moves and contain the growing splits within the armed forces. At the same time, martial law legalized the widespread entry of the armed forces into Indonesia's political life, and the division between military and civilian lines of authority became blurred. The power of the political parties was undermined, and the military leadership was able "to intervene anywhere and at any time it chose."[41]

Initially Nasution had to be cautious in trying to apply his augmented powers, lest he provoke disobedient and hostile reactions. But he did achieve one immediate success from his expanded powers in dealing with the regional dissidents—a cease-fire in mid-April between his forces and those of the Darul Islam in Aceh. This cease-fire was important, for it freed Nasution's military supporters in the Sumatran areas south of the Aceh border to deal with any revived threat from Simbolon.

But in Jakarta, after a month of infighting and maneuvering during which it seemed possible for a while that Hatta might in fact return to head a presidential cabinet, Sukarno on April 14 appointed Djuanda Kartawidjaja, a respected nonparty independent who had served in several previous cabinets, to head a new government, which the president described as a Kabinet Karya (working cabinet). Djuanda was a moderate as well as, most important, a Sundanese from West Java who had made the Haj and was thus potentially more sympathetic to non-Javanese and Islamic grievances than was the previous PNI-headed government. His prominence at the center served as something of a brake against Sundanese discontent and Zulkifli Lubis's efforts to expand his support in West Java.

The new prime minister now began a serious attempt along the road of conciliation with the regions. The first conference Djuanda sponsored was of military administrators and civilian officials, in Jakarta April 26-29, 1957. The dissident colonels, Husein, Barlian, and Sumual, all attended, Husein reportedly at Djuanda's personal urging, and Sukarno "went out of his way to thank both Col. Hussein and Col. Sumual for coming."[42] The representatives to the conference advocated cooperation between Hatta and Sukarno, increased autonomy for the provinces, and settlement of the army's internal problems.[43]

During the second half of May Hatta traveled through Sumatra. In Padang he "stressed that the regional movements which began in Central Sumatra were not movements that wished to separate themselves from the unitary state."[44] This view was echoed by Husein who, in welcoming Hatta to Padang, said, "We in Central Sumatra will further strive after achieving [a] just and prosperous Indonesia. We'll prove to those who did not want to believe us that the movement [is] directed in support [of the] unity of [the] Indonesian State."[45]

But less conciliatory voices were also being raised and were being recorded by Western journalists who began traveling to Sumatra during April to talk with the successful "rebels." In reporting to the American embassy in Jakarta about their discussions with some of the dissidents, American journalists stressed in particular what they saw as ousted-colonel Simbolon's important role in the movement. In their view, the former North Sumatra commander, now in refuge with Husein in Padang, had "in effect assumed the position of the unofficial spokesman of the Sumatran rebels" and was "the guiding hand and most important figure behind the Sumatran movement." These journalists were "uniformly impressed by his intelligence and by the importance of his position." This view was shared by a manager of the Standard Vacuum Sales Company, who reported being approached by Simbolon and Husein during a business trip to Padang. According to the manager, the day after this meeting the two army officers gave him a letter outlining Simbolon's opposition to the central government, wherein "Simbolon said he was unalterably opposed to the inclusion of Communists in the government, that if Sukarno attempted to introduce them into the government, he, Simbolon, would fight. If it came to a fight, Simbolon said he and others like him would need assistance. Acknowledging that Standard Vacuum could not openly help, Simbolon asked it to consider ways and means of covertly assisting them with money, foodstuffs, and equipment." There is no confirmation for this version of the letter, because immediately after the manager read it, he and the officers "went to the men's room in the terminal." Tearing the letter into small pieces, he "burned some of the bits and threw the others, plus the ashes of the burned portion into the toilet. The officers expressed satisfaction and took their leave."[46]

The United States Shows Interest

The advent of Djuanda and his more conciliatory approach to the regions, the growing power that Nasution and the central army command derived from the nationwide state of martial law, and the lessening of the Darul

Islam threat with the cease-fire in Aceh all led the recently arrived American ambassador, John Allison, to report to the U.S. State Department in mid-May 1957 that "calmer counsels may be prevailing" on the Indonesian scene.[47] But it was the journalists' reports and those from Standard Vacuum that caught the attention of Secretary of State John Foster Dulles, and these reports were apparently being confirmed by "another agency of the government," presumably the CIA, which cabled Washington that "events in Indonesia are moving rapidly and that country is closer to civil war than at any time since Madiun Affair."[48]

Some senior American officials were by now being attracted to the dissident colonels, viewing them as a potential alternative to what was increasingly perceived as a dangerous leftward drift of the Indonesian government. Analysts in Washington and the CIA's Jakarta station evidently took no comfort from the declaration of martial law and the consequent enhancement of the power of the military high command. They concentrated instead on Sukarno's *konsepsi* of bringing the "fourth leg" of the horse, the PKI, into the government. Although this proposal had not materialized because of the opposition from the major non-Communist parties, the three radical non-Communist leftists who did join the cabinet—all in minor positions—were portrayed as "figures who may be expected to support policies not displeasing to the Communist leadership," and the new advisory National Council was erroneously assessed as being "of predominantly leftist persuasion."[49] The visit of the Soviet president, Marshal Kliment Voroshilov, to Indonesia May 6-11 enhanced American fears of Sukarno moving to the left. It should be noted, however, that, although the Indonesian president had wanted to be evenhanded in such invitations, the White House consciously snubbed his invitations to Eisenhower and other top American officials to visit Indonesia.

What finally convinced American officials that Indonesia was on the brink of falling into the Communist camp were the local elections held in Java between June and August of 1957. In these, the PKI emerged as the only party to have increased its support since the 1955 elections, coming in first in Central Java and second in Greater Jakarta, East Java, and West Java.[50]

Divisions among the Dissidents

The differing reports and assessments reaching Washington were not merely a result of the confused situation both in the regions and in Jakarta and the disparity between the views held by Sukarno, the various political parties, the central army leadership, and the regional commanders. These differences also stemmed from the conflicting aims among the dissident colonels themselves. To some of these local commanders the major goals of their movement were no longer, if they ever had been, confined to decentralization and regional autonomy, but were also national and ideological and not without considerable concern for the advancement of their own careers.[51]

Both Husein and, to a lesser extent, Barlian were now well on their way to achieving the autonomy and additional central government development funds for their regions that they had been demanding; their own personal power had been enhanced, and their new status was recognized both by Chief of Staff Nasution and by the president. Several of their fellow officers, however, were in a different situation. Simbolon had little hope for advancement. He had lost his territorial command, and it was clear that Nasution would never willingly appoint him to any position of authority in the central army leadership. The same applied to Lubis, reportedly still spending most of his time in the Jakarta suburb of Kebayoran but also making frequent visits to the rebel colonels on Sumatra.

In June 1957, Sumual, commander of the military territory of East Indonesia (TTVII), also joined the dispossessed colonels when Nasution dissolved his command and its constituent South and Southeast Sulawesi Commands (KoDPSST) and split East Indonesia into four military regions.[52] Nasution had first proposed dividing the territory at a meeting of the regional commanders in Jakarta on March 15-22 shortly after the Permesta was proclaimed. At the time Sumual protested, warning the army chief of staff that such a division could lead to civil war. He reiterated these objections in June at another meeting with Nasution in Makassar on the eve of the dissolution, proposing at least an interregional command to coordinate the four new territories. Nasution agreed, giving Sumual the impression that he would be appointed to head the coordinating command, When the old TTVII was dissolved, however, Nasution himself took over direct responsibility for all of East Indonesia and merely appointed Sumual as a temporary chief of staff of the coordinating command.[53]

On June 19, a still-defiant Sumual transferred Permesta headquarters to Kinilow in northeastern Sulawesi, a territory under command of the Hasanuddin division headed by a Permesta sympathizer. He was joined there by most of his fellow Minahasan officers.[54] Thus, Simbolon, Lubis, and Sumual had all lost their commands, were in direct personal confrontation with Chief of Staff Nasution, and had little to gain through any form of compromise with the central government.

To these disaffected and dissident military officers was now added a notable civilian, Dr. Sumitro Djojohadikusumo, a former finance minister. In March, the army had summoned Sumitro for questioning because of his association with a Chinese businessman who had been arrested on charges of fraud, bribery, and subversion. After two interrogations regarding his financial ties with the businessman, Sumitro refused to comply with a third summons on May 8, 1957, and instead fled Jakarta. Arriving in Central Sumatra on May 13 he joined the rebel colonels, expanding his ties both with the military leaders on Sumatra and with Colonel Sumual on Sulawesi. Traveling frequently to Singapore and beyond, he and Simbolon became the rebels' major spokesmen in explaining regional aims to foreign government representatives and journalists and in attacking the central government.[55] In Singapore he was soon in contact with a senior CIA agent whom he had previously known in Jakarta.[56]

As there were fissures and conflicting aims among the dissident leaders in the regions, so too were such divisions evident among the political forces in Jakarta. It was clearly contrary to the interests of the Communist party for accommodations to be made through which some of the demands of the generally right-wing colonels could be met — officers whose anti-Communist cries were becoming louder during the second half of 1957. Nor was it in the interests of the Communist party to have the Sukarno-Hatta duumvirate restored. Similarly, for Chief of Staff Nasution it was becoming increasingly difficult to follow the path of compromise. Two essential motivations among most of the dissident regional officers had been personal animosity against him and a desire to defeat his centralization efforts and maintain power in their own hands. In the face of this attitude, his efforts to negotiate with these rebel colonels had thus far been unsuccessful and made him appear ineffective, thus undermining his own position as head of the army.

As the PKI intensified its attacks on the regionalists and as Nasution began to take stronger measures against the rebel colonels, it became increasingly difficult for those at the center who sympathized with regional demands not to take sides. Masjumi party head Mohammad Natsir publicly criticized Sukarno's moves toward "guided democracy,"[57] and Colonel Dahlan Djambek, who had for months been Nasution's major liaison with the regional dissidents, finally offered his resignation and, after a grenade exploded in the yard of his house, fled with his family to Padang, arriving there on August 24.[58] Djambek, who had been the first commander of the Banteng division in West Sumatra in 1945, was the son of one of the outstanding Muslim leaders in the region, and when he rallied to the rebel cause, he gave an added impetus to the anti-Communist character of the rebellion.

Attempts at a Settlement: The Munas Conference

The lines, then, appeared to be becoming more starkly drawn, but the forces for moderation could still muster powerful voices, among them not only that of Hatta but also those of the Sultan of Yogyakarta and Prime Minister Djuanda. It was Djuanda who in mid-August 1957 pressed for the convening of a national conference (Musyawarah National, or Munas) at which all regions were to be represented. Hatta as well as Djuanda clearly hoped that some form of compromise could be reached at this conference. Sukarno's desire for a reconciliation was indicated when shortly before the conference he agreed to release forty-one political detainees, twenty-one of whom were members of Husein's and Barlian's Banteng and Garuda councils.[59] The Djuanda cabinet opened the door for even the recently discharged commanders to participate in the national conference. As the American embassy reported, the "Cabinet decision to invite only provincial officials by name and allow them to select advisers has enabled Djuanda and other Ministers to evade responsibility for selecting or omitting dissident leaders such as Simbolon and Zulkifli Lubis, who do not now hold official positions."[60]

But even before the conference opened on September 10, the military were falling firmly into opposing camps. Nasution met with his supporters among the territorial commanders on August 29 in Bandung, while Sumual proposed that a meeting of all the rebel councils be held at Palembang on September 4.[61] Nasution forbade this projected Palembang meeting, but nevertheless, under cover of an ongoing conference of Islamic religious leaders, the dissident colonels and Dr. Sumitro met in Palembang on September 7-8. From their discussions issued a declaration, the "Palembang Charter," signed by the three commanders heading the dissident military regions, Barlian, Husein, and Sumual (although Djambek, Lubis, and Simbolon also participated). The charter included six major demands: (1) restoration of the Sukarno-Hatta duumvirate; (2) replacement of the existing central military leadership (meaning Nasution's resignation); (3) implementation of a policy of decentralization by giving extensive autonomy to the regions; (4) formation of a senate; (5) general rejuvenation and simplification of the government; and (6) banning of "internationally oriented Communism."[62]

The uncompromising nature of these demands, made only two days before the Munas conference was scheduled to begin, did not augur well for the success of that Jakarta-sponsored national reconciliation effort.[63] And as Barbara Harvey has observed, the charter incorporated the "first overt rebel demand for the banning of Communism."[64]

Of those attending the Palembang conference, Sumitro and Simbolon—and possibly Sumual and Lubis—had already been in touch for some time with American officials interested in strengthening the hands of the dissident colonels against Sukarno's government. After their Palembang discussions, Sumitro told a visiting American that, once the Munas conference was over in Jakarta, he expected to get "full powers" from Barlian and Husein, with which he would go first to Singapore to see "U.S. Consul

General Foster Collins, an old friend" (and widely regarded by Indonesian leaders as being the area's top CIA agent) and subsequently to the United States "to inform U.S. officials at [the] highest possible level of developments in dissident areas."[65]

Presumably their new American connections, as well as the degree of accord they had already reached at Palembang, stiffened the resolve of the dissident colonels who participated in the Munas conference held in Jakarta September 10-12, diminishing whatever area of compromise had previously existed.[66] The conference ended with President Sukarno and former vice president Hatta pledging to "cooperate with entire Indonesian people" for the good of the country, but with no restoration of the *dwitunggal* (their earlier co-leadership). In the official view of the American embassy, the resolutions passed on financial and administrative questions "contained nothing new," although a further conference on specifically economic matters was planned for a few weeks later.[67] The only concrete action to come out of the Munas conference was the establishment of a seven-man committee to study military questions and "recommend actions to end differences between Army Headquarters and Regional Commanders."[68] According to one of the seven, Hamengku Buwono IX, Sultan of Yogyakarta (and former minister of defense), a face-saving compromise, supported by him and Sukarno, was opposed by Nasution's staff and some of the younger territorial commanders, who insisted that army unity could not be restored unless Simbolon was dismissed from the army.[69] Nevertheless, despite the paucity of concrete results from the conference, there was a sense of relief that it had "ended on at least [a] surface note [of] national unity" and that the first tentative steps had been taken toward a rapprochement between Hatta and Sukarno and between the rebels and the central government.

As a result of long conversations with Sukarno, Hatta, and Djuanda in the weeks leading up to Munas, Ambassador Allison had become convinced that the conference offered hope for some compromise between the central government and the rebels, and he expressed this conviction in his cables to the Department of State. He was thus completely nonplussed when three weeks before the Munas conference was to open he received a cable from Secretary of State Dulles stating, "We have strong reservations from standpoint of possibility stemming Communist threat Indonesia about holding such a conference at this time," and then asserting unequivocally:

> we do not repeat not believe that a QUOTE successful UNQUOTE national conference along compromising lines apparently envisaged by Djuanda would be helpful. It would seem to be preferable at this time for anti-Communist leaders in outlying areas as well as in Java to develop further strength before attempting direct negotiations with Sukarno.[70]

To Allison, the Eisenhower administration's policy seemed to be discouraging compromise and encouraging polarization among political forces in Indonesia, and the American ambassador began to suspect that in fact the administration had two channels for dealing with the Indonesian situation, only one of which ran through the embassy in Jakarta.[71]

4. GENESIS OF EISENHOWER'S INDONESIAN POLICY

The Indonesia/China Analogue

EISENHOWER AND JOHN Foster Dulles's evaluation of the Communists' victory in China, it will be recalled, attributed their success primarily to the United States's overemphasis on maintaining the country's territorial integrity in the face of superior Communist power. The most vulnerable areas, they argued, should have been temporarily abandoned while Chiang Kai-shek's forces were husbanded in more easily defended parts of China pending an ultimate rollback of the Communists after their expected alienation of the population. This evaluation explicitly underlay the instructions given Hugh S. Cumming Jr. on the eve of his departure for Jakarta in early October 1953, where he was to replace Merle Cochran as ambassador. Referring to the oral instructions Eisenhower and Dulles separately gave him for his assignment in Indonesia, Cumming stated that he regarded these consistent directives "as really the summary—the essential—of the policy I was supposed to follow as opportunity offered." His notes record that the president told him: "The problem of unifying such a country would be a very great one, particularly since they had no tradition of self-government, that as against a unified Indonesia, which would fall to the Communists, and a break up of that country into smaller segments, he would prefer the latter."[1]

Dulles went into more detail, stating:

> As a matter of general policies, don't tie yourself irrevocably to a policy of preserving the unity of Indonesia. The important thing is that we help Indonesia, to the extent they will allow us, to resist any outside influence—especially Communism. The preservation of unification of a country can have danger. And I refer (and I can remember this almost word for word) to China. The territorial integrity of China became a shibboleth. We finally got a territorially integrated China—for whose benefit? The Communists. Now, this is something that cannot be in writing, but you should know where my mind is running. You may arrive at a different conclusion yourself, when you've been there. But this is my own feeling: As between a territorially united Indonesia which is leaning and progressing towards Communism and a break up of that country into racial and geographical units, I would prefer the latter as furnishing a fulcrum which the United States could work later to help them eliminate Communism in one place or another, and then in the end, if they so wish arrive back again at a united Indonesia.[2]

Cumming stated that his own State Department experience in dealing with Denmark during World War II reinforced his acceptance of Eisenhower's and Dulles's retrospective analysis of American policy toward China. He recalled that, after the Nazis had overrun Denmark, the United States worked successfully to keep Danish Greenland free of German control even though it lacked the capacity to keep Denmark itself from being overwhelmed by the Nazi tide. Bases in free Greenland, he held, were important in assisting the United States in rolling back German power after it began to erode in Europe. The conditions as between China and Denmark were scarcely analogous, of course, but nevertheless Cumming averred that his experience in dealing with the Danish situation predisposed him to a more positive acceptance of a prescription for Indonesia based on Dulles's and Eisenhower's assessment of the reasons for the American failure in China.[3]

But when Cumming took up his new post in Indonesia in October 1953, he did not then, or for at least another three and a half years, feel that the situation there warranted application of the Dulles and Eisenhower formula. Until then, he said, his reference to it called for an "open-ended" policy, involving "a watching brief" and "playing it by ear" as developments in Indonesia unfolded.[4] And the record now available in the U.S. National Archives and Eisenhower Library lends credence to that claim. Cumming recalled that his own concern over the potential of communism in Indonesia went back to 1926-27 when, as a businessman in Singapore, he followed the course of the abortive and rather feeble anticolonial Communist uprisings in Java and Sumatra. During his period as ambassador (October 11, 1953-March 3, 1957), however, he did not assess the prospects of communism in Indonesia to be as threatening as did Dulles. And, initially at least, he was considerably more sanguine than Dulles as to Indonesia's capacity for democratic self government.[5] Cumming displayed no antagonism toward Sukarno or other government leaders because of their attraction to socialism, some variant of which was still espoused by almost the whole range of the non-Communist political elite. Indeed, Eisenhower himself evidenced a sympathetic understanding of this penchant, remarking in a National Security Council meeting in April 1956 that Indonesia could not avoid being socialist and that there was no basis for a "free private enterprise economy such as that of the United States."[6]

Cumming did not partake of Dulles's and Eisenhower's strong opposition to neutralist foreign policies, showing a more sympathetic understanding of Indonesia's attachment to nonalignment in world politics—a sentiment that he soon realized ran across the country's political spectrum. And it is evident that he did not share Dulles's strong opposition to Indonesia's initiative in organizing and hosting an Asian-African Conference in the West Java city of Bandung in April 1955. While not all of the twenty-four countries that attended it were nonaligned, the conference did tend to strengthen the neutralist tendencies of some. And most upsetting for the

Eisenhower administration, Chou En-lai, in representing China, managed, as Jawaharlal Nehru, one of the conference's sponsors, had hoped, to overcome the suspicions and hostility of several of the Asian states represented there, putting the United States on the defensive in the eyes of many of them with respect to its China policy, especially the ongoing Formosa Straits crisis.[7]

With respect to West Irian, Cumming was less rigid than Dulles, indicating to the State Department that he was not averse to Indonesian-Dutch negotiation of the issue. But in the face of the secretary of state's almost unwavering insistence on holding to a "neutral" status quo, the ambassador was not disposed to argue with him. Moreover, he was also sensitive to the position of the United States's Dutch NATO ally, both because of the views of Dulles and Eisenhower on this matter and because of his own experience on the State Department's Northern European desk where he had responsibility for a time before World War II for Holland and the Dutch East Indies.

Although Cumming was concerned over the Communists' ability to place fourth (with 16.4 percent of the vote) in the parliamentary elections of 1955 and over their increasing strength with organized labor, he did not appear to be as alarmed at their successes as the U.S. secretary of state or his brother, Allen Dulles, director of the CIA. Cumming was strongly impressed by Sukarno's great popularity and pivotal political position and gave no indication of sharing Dulles's disapproval of Sukarno's well-known penchant for womanizing — an attribute criticized by few Indonesians.

Cumming had become much more critical of Sukarno by the conclusion of his posting to Jakarta in March 1957, but he still evidenced greater understanding and appreciation of him than did either John Foster or Allen Dulles. This was apparent in Cumming's briefing cable of February 23, 1957, to his successor, Ambassador John Allison.[8] He wrote the cable just after Sukarno had delivered a major speech declaring that Western-style democracy had failed, because with its provision of a political opposition it was incompatible with the Indonesian values of social harmony and solidarity. It was in this speech that the Indonesian president called for a cross-the-spectrum cabinet incorporating all four major political parties, the Communists (PKI) included. Cumming reported sympathetically — and accurately — that "Sukarno's rejection [of] western political democracy with political opposition and his theory he can establish special Indonesian unity is expression [of] widespread Indonesian aversion to political conflict and desire to return to unity [of] purpose [of the] Indonesian revolution." Noting that this ignored the Communist attempt in the Madiun rebellion to take over leadership of the republic by force, he observed: "One of Indonesia's biggest political puzzles [is] whether Sukarno has changed since Madiun when he ordered army [to] put down Communist rebellion with bloody success."

Ten days later, after his farewell audience with Sukarno, Cumming reported that the president had assured him that the PKI was nationalist, operating free of Soviet influence in the same way as Tito and Mao Tse-tung, and that "if at any time the PKI departed from their Indonesian nationalism he would crush them as he did at Madiun." As for "Sukarno's insistence [on the] inclusion [of the] PKI" in the cabinet, that, Cumming explained, "does not necessarily mean Sukarno [is] pro-communist but, ignoring all experience [in] other countries, indicative [of] his belief he can invite Communists in with impunity and control them thus eliminating strikes and other crippling blows which PKI outside [the cabinet] might deliver."[9] Cumming went on to observe:

> I do not think pessimistic conclusion necessarily warranted yet. Sukarno faced with situation in which political parties have failed [to] provide country with decisive leadership, is trying to find effective alternative. He alone has thus far exhibited courage and imagination [to] make this attempt. He remains open to our influence and to influence [of] better political elements here.

For his part, Sukarno found Cumming an improvement over Cochran, who had forfeited his trust as a consequence of his duplicity over economic assistance and thereby helped undermine the Indonesian president's generally positive feelings toward the United States. He did, however, think Cumming "too protocolish" and "overly official" and was impatient with what he perceived to be his lack of sufficient appreciation of the importance of the West Irian issue.[10] Generally, however, Sukarno got along reasonably well with Ambassador Cumming, as is indicated by his request in January 1957 that the State Department extend Cumming's stay, which it agreed to do for an additional six weeks.

Although in later years, after his return to Washington in 1957, Cumming worked closely with the CIA on Indonesian policy, he maintained that he did not do so while ambassador. Yet he acknowledged that initially he regarded as "a promising phenomenon" the antigovernment extremist Darul Islam movement in West Java, and he recalled that on a trip to Washington in December 1954 he was told that covert operations of some sort were about to begin in Indonesia.[11] It is difficult to accept Cumming's contention that he wanted to hear no details about covert operations, but it is possible that this operation was concerned not only with helping finance the election campaigns of legal non-Communist political parties but also with supporting the West Java Darul Islam and the kindred strongly Islamic rebellion led by Daud Beureuh in Aceh.[12] Indeed, Sukarno and numerous other knowledgeable Indonesians strongly suspected that the CIA was backing these groups.[13]

Cumming recalled that when he was called back to Washington for consultations in late January or early February 1956, "a second covert operation was discussed [with his participation] and approved."[14] He was unwilling, when interviewed, to disclose the nature of this operation.

Communists' Potential and the West Irian Issue

Indonesia's first national elections, in 1955, brought the Eisenhower administration to focus on Indonesia's domestic politics with greater concern. Although the Communist PKI emerged as only the fourth largest party, Washington regarded this development as ominous. Cumming, along with other embassy personnel, saw a major reason for this growth in the increasing salience of the West Irian issue in Indonesian politics and the skill of the PKI in championing Indonesia's claim.[15] His sensitivity to the Indonesian viewpoint on West Irian was clear in the letter he wrote on May 20, 1955, to Kenneth Young, then State Department director of the Office of Philippine and Southeast Asia Affairs. Sukarno, Cumming explained, believed that "the Indonesian revolution will be incomplete until Indonesian sovereignty is extended over Dutch New Guinea" and also believed,

> together with many other Indonesians, that this country was under such heavy pressure at the Round Table Conference in 1949 that it had no choice but to allow the Dutch to remain in control of New Guinea. They regard as a betrayal of faith the Dutch failure to agree to a determination of the status of New Guinea within one year from the time of the transfer of sovereignty and the current refusal of the Dutch even to talk about, much less transfer, sovereignty over West New Guinea. . . . The fact that some 28 nations at Bandung, including many of our allies, agreed that Dutch Indonesian negotiations should take place is going to encourage the present government to continue its agitation on the subject. . . . It is simply because we shall be plagued by the New Guinea question until it is satisfactorily settled that I see some reason to consider at this time alternatives to our present policy of neutrality.[16]

But the secretary of state did not support any such change in American policy on West Irian, at least not until a "slightly better government" emerged in Indonesia that the United States "would not want to rebuff." Adherence to the American policy of "neutrality" on the issue would still extend to abstention in any vote in the United Nations as to whether it was to be even discussed there. Privately Dulles assured the Australian government, which adamantly supported Dutch retention of West Irian, that, although "we did not feel we should jeopardize our influence with Indonesia by taking sides in the dispute, . . . if it came to a real showdown about New Guinea, then the United States [presumably in the context of the ANZUS treaty] would back Australia 'right or wrong.'"[17]

That Dulles was indeed prepared to buck his European desks and risk angering the Dutch if a "slightly better government" (i.e., clearly anti-

Communist government) emerged in Indonesia became evident during the Masjumi-led government of Burhanuddin Harahap, which held office from August 12, 1955, until March 26, 1956. After a long period of unsuccessful negotiations, the Harahap cabinet moved on February 21 more strongly against Dutch interests than had any previous government by unilaterally abrogating the economic and financial agreements arrived at with the Netherlands in The Hague Round Table Conference at the end of 1949. This meant an end to the privileged Dutch economic position and the suspension of further payment of interest or principal on the Dutch East Indies's debt that the Indonesian government had then been obliged to assume.[18]

This move strongly reflected Indonesian frustration over the Dutch refusal to discuss that other major disagreement of The Hague conference—the status of West Irian. Although Dulles expected that the successor to the Harahap government (which would soon have to be formed to reflect party strength in the recently held elections) "was not likely to be as friendly to the United States," he accepted this Masjumi-led move against the Dutch with apparent equanimity, noting that it was unlikely that American investments would suffer, despite a furious outcry by the Dutch foreign minister that the lack of Western reaction to the Indonesian move had encouraged Nasser to take the Suez Canal and had "no parallel since the repudiation of the Tsarist debts by the Soviet Communist Government." (Most of Indonesia's debt had been paid off, with only $171 million remaining.)[19] Had the elections enabled a government of similar character to the Harahap administration to be formed, it seems likely that Dulles would have been prepared to look favorably on suggestions for a policy on West Irian more supportive of the Indonesian cause.

Courting Sukarno

In any case, the makeup of the new postelection coalition government formed by the PNI's Ali Sastroamidjojo in mid-March 1956, incorporating substantial Masjumi representation, appeared to reassure the secretary of state, who visited Indonesia for twenty-four hours (March 12-13) during the period of cabinet formation. (In fact he believed his presence might have contributed to what was regarded as a reasonably favorable outcome—especially in view of the PNI's right to be selected by Sukarno as the party that would form the new cabinet, one earned thanks to its slightly outpolling the Masjumi in the election.[20]) There was no reneging on the United States's tacit support of the Indonesian actions abrogating their economic and financial agreements with the Netherlands.[21] Indeed, Dulles was apparently sufficiently well impressed with the probable composition of the new cabinet that in his meeting with Sukarno he extended an invitation from Eisenhower for the Indonesian president to visit the United States, an offer that Sukarno warmly accepted.

Although Cumming remained keenly aware of the overriding concern of Sukarno and most other Indonesian leaders with Indonesia's claim to West Irian, he understood just as clearly the limitations Dulles's "neutral" status quo position had set with respect to any change in American policy. He concluded, nevertheless, that if Washington courted Sukarno sufficiently it need not change its stance toward the West Irian issue. Exaggerating the strength of his own personal relationship with Sukarno, Cumming believed that, even without a change in American policy toward Irian, with sufficient backing from the American government he could move Sukarno into a closer relationship with the United States and a less permissive attitude toward the PKI.[22]

It was in this expectation that he had sought Eisenhower's invitation to Sukarno. The Indonesian president's trip to the United States during late May and early June 1956 did go well, with Sukarno making a favorable impression on an initially cool and skeptical Eisenhower. With his usual oratorical verve, Sukarno projected himself becomingly in an address to a joint session of the two houses of Congress on May 17, and during his visit he was appreciated for his generally favorable remarks about American democracy and his high praise of Jefferson and Lincoln, two Americans whom he in fact greatly admired.[23] Soon after his return to Indonesia he made a major public address in Semarang, in which he highly praised the United States, leading Cumming to report: "This speech alone would seem to justify whole cost of Sukarno visit since I believe Semarang remarks give assurance [of] what Sukarno really believes in his heart and represent fixed position to which he will increasingly return."[24] Cumming was delighted, believing that Sukarno, and thereby Indonesia, had been drawn closer to the United States.

But three months later, while Cumming was savoring this success, Sukarno followed up invitations from the Soviet Union and China, visiting them, together with several European countries, between late August and mid-October 1956. He paid handsome tributes to Lenin and Mao Tse-tung and was openly enthusiastic at Mao's rebuilding of China's economy. He maintained this enthusiasm after returning to Indonesia, for he felt that the economic achievements of an underdeveloped country such as China were more relevant to Indonesia than those of advanced Western economies, such as that of the United States. With Indonesia's president returning from his trips just as wed to a nonaligned foreign policy and ideology as when he departed, the Eisenhower administration's disappointment was considerable. Even though Cumming's dispatches to the United States appeared calculated to minimize this concern, he later stated privately that Sukarno's positive reaction to China was for him—as with

Dulles and Eisenhower—a major letdown and constituted "a watershed" in his own attitude toward Sukarno.[25] But in fact no such watershed was evidenced during the last six months of Cumming's tour as ambassador, during which his reporting appeared to remain about as sympathetic and understanding of Sukarno as before the China trip. It was only after Cumming's new posting to Washington in the spring of 1957 that his "watershed" appeared to be operative. There after working closely with Dulles, who indeed had become much more critical of Sukarno because of his statements about China, Cumming emerged as a strong and persistent critic of Sukarno, every bit as antagonistic toward him as Dulles had become.

For his part, Sukarno was still determined that Indonesia hew to an independent nonaligned foreign policy. But when he invited the United States and Soviet chiefs of state for reciprocal visits to Indonesia, Eisenhower spurned the invitation while Moscow accepted it, having already invited Sukarno to pay a second visit to the Soviet Union. President Voroshilov made a successful trip to Indonesia in May 1957, which probably flattered Sukarno and inevitably increased the prestige of the Indonesian Communist party. Undersecretary of State Christian Herter then refused to include Indonesia in his Far Eastern trip in early September and instead summoned the new U.S. ambassador to Jakarta, John Allison, to Bangkok, explaining that for him to have visited Indonesia would have given Sukarno greater political legitimacy.[26]

Throughout 1956 Indonesian efforts to secure any significant amount of U.S. economic assistance continued to make little headway—$15 million being the maximum offered. Increasingly disappointed at the American refusal to provide more than this token assistance, the Indonesian parliament waited nearly two years before finally accepting in the spring of 1958 $100 million in Soviet credits offered to Sukarno during his 1956 visit to Moscow. The Indonesian government was similarly frustrated at the United State's denial of General Nasution's persistent requests during 1956-57 to buy American military equipment and desperately needed spare parts for existing U.S. weaponry. Although the American army chief of staff, Maxwell Taylor, and U.S. military attachés in Jakarta, who long supported these pleas, were finally joined on November 12, 1957, by all the American service chiefs, they continued to be overruled by Dulles for what were described as political reasons. These military chiefs argued that "token shipments could be designed so as not to increase materially the ability of the Central Government either to mount a punitive expedition against the regionalist movements in the outlying islands or attempt to take over West New Guinea by force."[27] But Dulles responded that delivery of American arms would be too provocative to the Dutch (who held that the arms would encourage Indonesia to attack them in West Irian).

Ambassadorial and Policy Shifts

When Cumming's posting to Jakarta ended on March 3, 1957, the West Irian issue still loomed every bit as large on the local political horizon as when he had arrived more than three years before. Indeed, bitterness had increased among all political elements in Indonesia when the Netherlands government on August 21, 1956, formally approved its parliament's amendment of the Dutch constitution to incorporate that area as part of the territory of the Netherlands. There had been no official American acceptance of this unilateral Dutch move, but there was also no change in the United States's stance of pro-Netherlands "neutrality" on the West Irian dispute in the United Nations. There, on February 28, 1957, as had been the case three years before, a resolution in the General Assembly requesting appointment of a good offices' commission charged with assisting in negotiations between the Dutch and Indonesians "in order that a just and peaceful solution" of the Irian question might be achieved failed to gain the necessary two-thirds majority. Forty countries voted in favor, twenty-five opposed, and the United States was among the thirteen that abstained.

Ambassador Cumming, on leaving Jakarta, became director of the State Department's intelligence arm, the Bureau of Research and Intelligence. Previously of only modest importance, this new position became one of considerable influence because of Dulles's confidence in Cumming. Soon Cumming was also appointed the State Department's liaison with the CIA and additionally was given the assignment of overseeing the selection each morning of the incoming cables from U.S. diplomatic posts all over the world that Secretary Dulles was to read. Despite his global responsibilities, however, the ex-ambassador remained disproportionately preoccupied with Indonesia.[28] So much was this the case that by mid-1957 several of his State Department subordinates began privately referring to him as "the Assistant Secretary in Charge of Indonesian Affairs." Certainly they saw no indication that he discouraged Dulles's own increasing misgivings about Sukarno, which stemmed in varying degrees from the Indonesian president's desire to incorporate all parties, including a token number of Communists, in the "guided democracy" cabinet he was organizing; his continuing insistence on an unaligned foreign policy, and a sometimes promiscuous life-style repugnant to the secretary's severely moralistic Presbyterian upbringing.

But it was only with the shock from the Communists' striking gains in the mid-1957 provincial elections on Java (see below) that the Eisenhower administration became seriously alarmed about Indonesia's political prospects. And it was this development too that tended to crystallize doubts about Sukarno's capacity and willingness to contain the strength of the Indonesian Communist party. The outcome of these elections, more than any other factor, established a shift in American policy, one leading almost inevitably to a revival of the Eisenhower administration's disposition to see Indonesia in the apocalyptic vision contained in Cumming's original instructions of 1953.

· · · · ·

Consistent with government officials' misgivings were the marching orders given John Allison, Cumming's successor as ambassador, on the eve of his departure for Jakarta: "Don't let Sukarno get tied up with the Communists. Don't let him use force against the Dutch. Don't encourage his extremism . . . Above all, do what you can to make sure that Sumatra (the oil producing island) doesn't fall to the Communists."[29]

On February 21, 1957, while still ambassador to Japan, Allison had been appointed to replace Cumming in Jakarta, and he took up his new posting early the following month. Having previously served as assistant secretary for Far Eastern affairs, he had some knowledge of Indonesia, although not an extensive amount. He expected to have a close and cordial relationship with Secretary of State Dulles since the two of them had worked closely together for fifteen months during 1950-51 in fashioning the U.S. peace treaty and mutual security treaty with Japan when Allison served as director of the State Department's Office of Northeast Asian Affairs.

Allison quickly realized the importance of the West Irian issue and identified it as the touchstone to Indonesian politics and friendship with Sukarno that it undoubtedly had become. He also appreciated that the PKI's unstinting and well-organized support of the West Irian claim was both enhancing its nationalist credentials and improving its relationship with Sukarno. America's intransigent support of the Dutch position, he believed, was greatly abetting this process while driving a deeper wedge between the United States and Indonesia.[30]

Beginnings of a Covert Track

By the end of 1956 the administration had begun to grope its way toward a second, covert track of policy, augmenting its official diplomatic track still represented by its embassy in Jakarta. This reflected its now much greater concern for what it perceived to be a dangerous leftward drift in Indonesia, its desire to strengthen the anti-Communist forces there, and its effort to influence Sukarno to curtail the growth of the Indonesian Communist party and move away from his independent international stance toward closer alignment with the West.

Sensing the anxiety and impatience of his superiors, Frank G. Wisner, head of the Office of Policy Coordination (OPC), the CIA's covert action arm, responded to their cues by making clear to his subordinates that they should develop options for satisfying what he perceived to be the objectives of the top level of the administration. As recounted by one of the key middle-level players in this undertaking, Joseph Burkolder Smith of the CIA's Indonesia/Malaysia desk (FE/5), the point of departure was Wisner's statement in November 1956 to Al Ulmer, his new Far Eastern chief (a man with no previous experience in that part of the world): "I think it's time we held Sukarno's feet to the fire."[31] Smith later wrote he was sure that Wisner's metaphorical language "stemmed from some conversation between John Foster and his brother Allen Dulles." That colorful phrase, he explained, "meant that no one wanted to put any orders in writing" and that officers in CIA's FE/5 and the Jakarta station "were supposed to discover some intelligence information that would look good enough on paper to justify NSC's Special Group [the component of the National Security Council that formally authorized covert operations] approval of action to diminish or even destroy Sukarno's power in Indonesia and his influence in world affairs."[32]

In other words, before seeking formal permission for covert anti-Sukarno action, a plausible case had to be built up justifying such action while giving no hint that the information presented was being selected and prepared with the idea that its cumulative impact would provide this justification. Here then was an exciting opportunity for Smith and his colleagues, with additional impetus provided by Wisner's admonition that if they couldn't come up with a plan they might be assigned to "far worse jobs."[33] Wisner and his colleagues apparently skewed the available data to accord with their awareness that the Dulles brothers had lost patience with Sukarno's steadfast neutralism in foreign policy and his unwillingness to suppress the Communist party. Ambassador Allison ascribed the CIA's warped view of the situation in Indonesia not only to its operatives in Indonesia but also to "the head of the Far Eastern Section of the CIA" (Al Ulmer), a "young man with no experience in the Far East," who was dispatched by Allen Dulles "to look into the situation on the spot." Allison stated that he learned that when Ulmer returned to Washington he reported that "Sukarno was beyond redemption" and that Allison "seemed confused and was inclined to be soft on communism."[34] According to Smith, Ulmer had been dispatched because Allen Dulles wanted "to strengthen the case" for a "more vigorous policy" against Sukarno.[35] The agency, he states, was so keen on presenting Sukarno "in as unfavorable and unsympathetic light as possible" that in its zeal it produced a bogus "blue" film featuring an actor who slightly resembled the Indonesian president frolicking in a boudoir with a woman purported to be a blackmailing Soviet intelligence agent. The attempt presumably sought to capitalize on Secretary Dulles's known disapproval of Sukarno's womanizing, but the product was so unconvincing that it was apparently never shown to the secretary of state.[36]

Much more convincing was the agency's depiction of the government's deteriorating authority in the islands outside Java. Here there was enough actual substance to make its exaggerated reporting credible. That hyperbole may well have been more attributable to Ulmer and other senior CIA officials than to the agency's field operatives. But as Dean Almy, the top CIA officer then stationed in Sumatra, later acknowledged: "We may have got caught up in what we were doing. You get sympathetic to the people you are working with; some of our people may have sent in information that got Washington more enthusiastic about this than they should have been."[37]

In any case, Colonel Ahmad Husein's seizure of power at the head of the Banteng Council in West Sumatra, with several other military leaders in Sumatra and Sulawesi either following suit, or, as in South Kalimantan, reportedly poised to do so, together with the Jakarta government's apparent inability to deal effectively with this regional disaffection, began to stimulate fresh thinking in the Eisenhower administration consistent with Dulles's original briefing of Cumming four years before. Within it there was now a rapidly developing sentiment that the regional autonomy movements at least offered the possibility of providing a fulcrum for American political leverage on Jakarta, and the hyperbolic nature of the CIA's reporting no doubt considerably strengthened the disposition to think so.

The unreliability of the CIA's portrayal of the political situation in Indonesia became starkly evident in the meeting of the National Security Council on March 14, 1957, in which Allen Dulles gave the astonishing report that "the process of disintegration has continued in Indonesia to a point where only the island of Java remains under the control of the Central Government. The armed forces of all the outlying islands have declared their independence of the Central Government in Jakarta."[38]

Apparently even more myopic than Allen Dulles as to the realities of the Indonesian political scene was the commander in chief of U.S. Pacific Forces (CINCPAC), Admiral Felix Stump, who clearly at this time inclined toward military intervention. After the chairman of the Joint Chiefs of Staff, General Nathan F. Twining, observed that, while at present there were no American military forces in the immediate area of Indonesia, "CINCPAC had plans for military operations if such operations were required [deletion follows]," Secretary of Defense Charles E. Wilson stated that Stump had wired for guidance. This brought Eisenhower to point out that "the first thing to do was to make clear to Admiral Stump our view of what is actually happening in Indonesia, and particularly that the trouble there [in Sumatra] was essentially anti-Communist in inspiration rather than Communist." Apparently concerned at the admiral's impulsiveness, Eisenhower repeated his admonition that Stump "understand the situation the way we here in Washington see it [deletion by government censor]." The importance of disabusing the admiral of any current need for military action was reflected in the National Security Council's action memorandum following this meeting. In accordance with the president's statement, the Joint Chiefs of Staff were to "arrange consultation with CINCPAC to ensure that there is a mutual understanding of the current situation in Indonesia, which does not appear at this time to require military action (other than continued planning)."[39]

The Breakup of Indonesia?

After this March 14 National Security Council meeting, it was apparent that a powerful element of opinion existed within the administration that envisaged Indonesia's disintegration and was pressing for a policy calculated to capitalize on the expected breakup. This school of thought, which appeared to be most strongly represented in the CIA, gathered sufficient backing so that in early May the assistant secretary of state, Walter Robertson, sent the deputy director of the Office of Southwest Pacific Affairs, Gordon Mein, a specialist with previous experience in Indonesia, to Jakarta to assess "the possible break-up of Indonesia." Mein's report of May 17 was cogent, well-informed, and also generally consistent with the thinking of Ambassador Allison and his staff with whom, according to Allison, Mein worked harmoniously.[40] It was sufficiently persuasive in the State Department to put a damper on the growth in influence of the "breakup" school at least until after the returns were in from the Java provincial elections.

Mein argued against the prospect of Indonesia's disintegration, stating that the vast majority of the Indonesian people remained loyal to the ideal of a unified Indonesian nation, that the rebel colonels' initial major demand was merely the resignation of the Ali Sastroamidjojo cabinet, and that their present primary demand was for a reestablishment of the Sukarno-Hatta partnership, not for recognition of their regions' independence. He concluded that, "on balance, it would appear that a break up of the Republic of Indonesia would not serve U.S. policy objectives in the area" and that "resultant political chaos and economic dislocation would probably, in the long run, serve rather than hinder Communist efforts to win control of the archipelago."

The high quality and prescience of Mein's analysis are helpful to an understanding of the political factors in Indonesia involved in any of the breakup scenarios that were then circulating in sectors of the administration. First, he noted in his memorandum:

Arguments which might be advanced in support of the contention that the U.S. should regard with satisfaction, if not encourage discreetly, the separation of Sumatra and other of the major outlying islands from the Republic can be summarized as follows:

1. Communist strength is concentrated on the island of Java. The outer islands, on the other hand, are the strongholds of the religious parties, strongly anti-communist in orientation.

2. The central government follows a neutralist foreign policy and appears to be subject to leftist influences. The existence of anti-communist governments in the area might provide a useful counter-balance.

3. President Sukarno, because of his obsession with colonialism, his suspicion of the former colonial powers of Western Europe, and his apparent obliviousness to the internal and external communist menace, is at best a highly unreliable political influence. A reduction of the area under his control would be beneficial.

4. The outer islands of Indonesia, particularly Sumatra, account for a high percentage of Indonesia's foreign exchange revenues through the production of rubber, oil, petroleum, tin, and other strategic raw materials. It would be advantageous to have the sources of such commodities under more reliable political control.

5. Sumatra, with the Malay Peninsula, dominates the Straits of Malacca, and is of great strategic importance.

Then, turning to political factors, he effectively demolished much of the foundation consciously or unconsciously assumed by the interventionists:

The first and most important is the dubious viability of Sumatra as a political unit. Sumatra is, in effect, a group of separate communities in a sea of jungle. There are on the island at least five distinct, and in some instances mutually hostile, major ethnic and cultural groups, linked by land by a single circuitous paved road impassable in the rainy season. The principal economic centers, Medan and Palembang, are both linked closely to Djakarta but have few if any common ties. One area, Atjeh, has already been for the past four years in armed rebellion against the central government, and although it has been reported that a provisional understanding has been reached with the Central Sumatran leader Lt. Col. Hussein, it appears unlikely that the fanatically Moslem Atjehnese would make their peace with the staunchly Christian Bataks and submit to any inter-regional Sumatran authority. Therefore, once the unifying concept of "one people, one nation, one language" had been repudiated, and the disintegration of the republic begun, political fragmentation would be almost certain to continue below the major island level, and the U.S. would be confronted in Sumatra not with one authority, but with three or four semi-autonomous areas. Lt. Col. Hussein, the most resolute and intransigent of the regionalist military leaders, is reported to be strongly influenced by orthodox Moslem circles in West Sumatra, and allegedly has announced as a precondition for settlement with the central government the supression [sic] not only of the Communist Party, but also the political parties of millions of Indonesians who believe in God but also favor a separation of religion and politics. Hussein, in this regard, is closer to the fanatical Darul Islam than to the Masjumi and Nahdatul Ulama. He has not specified the manner in which this belief in God is to be expressed, but the Moslem inspiration for such a concept could hardly be reassuring to his Christian colleagues. In any case, this demand, while perhaps strengthening his position in the strongly Moslem areas around Padang, is extreme and unrealistic in the broad Indonesian political context, and tends to establish Hussein as a leader of only limited, local significance.

In his conclusions Mein also stated that a breakup of the Republic of Indonesia "could succeed only with substantial material assistance from the United States" and that

> U.S. objectives could be furthered most effectively by discouraging the dissipation of anti-communist strength in the outer islands in quixotic regional rebellions, by encouraging anti-communist elements in these areas to lend their support to their colleagues and co-religionist [sic] on Java within the framework of a single national state, and by encouraging and assisting the central government to satisfy legitimate regional demands.

Although Ambassador Allison believed it vital that the regionalist rebels not be crushed, he was hopeful that a politically healthy compromise could be worked out between them and the new nonparty cabinet led by Djuanda Kartawidjaja that Sukarno had appointed soon after the Sastroamidjojo government fell on March 17.[41] The ambassador reported on June 1 that the new cabinet was "much more realistic and constructive than its predecessor" and urged "patience and understanding" of the problems it faced and that the United States take no public action indicating lack of faith in the central government's ability to solve its problems.[42]

But the increased Communist party strength manifested in the Central and East Java provincial elections of July-August 1957 led the United States to disregard Allison's hopeful assessments. Indeed, Secretary of State Dulles ordered on July 25 that the existing National Intelligence Estimate (NIE) for Indonesia be drastically revised as a consequence of these elections and saw to it that the National Security Council, with President Eisenhower presiding, met on August 1 to discuss policy toward it.

The discussions in this National Security Council's meeting reflected the mounting concern.[43] "Mr. Cutler [Special Assistant to the President] asked whether, in light of the briefing by the Director of the Central Intelligence Agency on Indonesia [this briefing has been deleted from the record], the Joint Chiefs of Staff should be asked to study the military consequences of Java falling under Communist control. The President said he would like to have the views of the Department of State also." Undersecretary of State Christian Herter wanted to know

> the probable consequences of a division between Java and Sumatra. Such an estimate would be very helpful in enabling us to decide how much effort to devote to Indonesia in the future. . . . Mr. Cutler pointed out that

> Indonesia might fall to pieces, with Java becoming Communist and the rest of the islands remaining non-Communist. . . . The Vice President [Richard Nixon] thought that Sukarno was probably right in believing that a democratic government was not the best kind for Indonesia. He said the Communists could probably not be beaten in election campaigns because they were so well organized, and were able to play on the ignorance of the people. In his view, the United States should work through the Indonesian military organization to mobilize opposition to Communism. Admiral Radford [chairman of the Joint Chiefs of Staff] agreed that there was a good chance of working successfully with the Indonesian military. [deletions] The President asked what military strength Sukarno controlled. Mr. Dulles said he controlled the Indonesian military strength in Java.

Admiral Radford "suggested that the Departments of State and Defense make a prompt survey of the situation in Indonesia in order to be prepared for fast action if necessary."

The National Security Council then agreed that a group composed of representatives of the Department of State (as chairman), Department of Defense, the Joint Chiefs of Staff, the CIA, and the International Cooperation Administration should prepare by September 1 a report for the NSC's consideration on

a. The implications for U.S. security of recent developments in Indonesia, especially Communist political gains in Java.
b. Possible actions which the United States might take with respect to the situation in Indonesia pursuant to NSC 5518 [presumably the existing security council memorandum governing U.S. policy toward Indonesia], including possible actions in the event of imminent or actual Communist control of Java.

The crucial decision was taken that "because of the adverse repercussions within the U.N. and S.E.A.T.O. and in Asia in general the employment of U.S. armed forces [in Indonesia] was neither feasible nor appropriate while the Indonesian situation remains one of political fluidity." For the time being, then, the use of American military force was not authorized. Recommendations as to what actions would be pursued—overt as well as covert—were to be made by a newly appointed Ad Hoc Interdepartmental Committee with representation from the Departments of State and Defense and the CIA and chaired by Hugh S. Cumming, who had by then become Secretary Dulles's most influential State Department adviser on Indonesia.[44] The core working group of this committee included Admiral Arleigh Burke, chief of Naval Operations, and Howard Jones, deputy assistant secretary of state for the Far East. Deputy Assistant Secretary of Defense Karl G. Herr, Jr. was appointed to represent the Department of Defense, and Colonel Joseph Harrison of the Joint Chiefs of Staff Joint Strategic Plans Group was that body's representative. The committee and its work were so secret that the Indonesia desk officer for the State Department, Francis Underhill, learned of its existence only several years later, and he was kept completely "out of the loop" so far as the covert level of operations was concerned. "Every bar girl in Singapore and Manila knew more about these operations than the Indonesian desk officer," he later recalled. His first real clue came by accident when at a dinner party in the spring of 1958 an officer working in naval operations drew him aside and said: "Francis, what are you guys in State up to in Indonesia? We've had submarines for two weeks off the coast of Sumatra near Padang unloading tons of ammunition."[45]

During the balance of 1957 there was a growing belief within the Eisenhower administration that Communist control of Java was indeed "imminent." An illustration of this was the cable that Assistant Secretary of State Robertson sent Allison the day after the August 1 National Security Council meeting. Although some of the message remains sanitized, its tone presaged the heightened anxiety that was beginning to permeate the upper reaches of the administration:

> 1. . . . Dept . . . at high level [has] been devoting considerable attention over a period of months to what appears to us to be a steadily deteriorating situation in Indonesia . . . and the prospect that through inadequate action on our part Communists may soon be in a position to play a determinant role in the organized political life of that country. It seems clear that the net effect of the course of action Sukarno is (deliberately or unwittingly) taking is to greatly bolster PKI. We also feel that Djuanda does not have the political strength and backing to stem the tide of what appears from here to be a snowballing Communist trend, or to prevent the ascendancy of the National Council over the Cabinet. Communist infiltration of Indonesian Govt and society bears some unpleasant similarities to situation which pertained in Guatemala under Arbenz.[46]

(It will be recalled that fears that Arbenz, an elected president, was drifting leftward resulted in a major CIA action that ousted him.)

The Eisenhower Administration Bypasses Its Own Embassy

Allison was deeply upset that he was apprised of the formation of the Ad Hoc Interdepartmental Committee only well after it had been authorized and that he had not been consulted as to its creation.[47] On finally being informed of the recommendations of the National Security Council's August 1 meeting, he cabled Assistant Secretary Robertson on August 12 that, given the complexity of the situation, it was "unrealistic to suppose that by September 1 the interagency group should be able to produce any valid estimate on course of events in Indonesia upon which government decisions can be made as to courses of action we should follow here. . . . I am concerned that interagency group is making what may be most significant long range recommendations on policy toward Indonesia without benefit of first hand discussion with those who have had recent experience here." He "strongly believed" he himself should be present at its meetings.[48] Later that day, with Cumming serving as chairman, the Inter-Agency Committee on Indonesia held the first meeting of its core working group in Cumming's office, with no representative of the American embassy in Jakarta present.[49]

Assistant Secretary Robertson's response to Allison's August 12 cable was hardly conciliatory and made abundantly clear the widening rift between the department's thinking and that of its ambassador. Robertson rebuffed the ambassador's request to come to Washington to participate in the discussions of the interagency group and pointed out that Allison's recommended courses of action were essentially "along the lines which we have attempted in the past and found wanting." The situation in Indonesia, Robertson said, "transcends both in quality and intensity any of the crises of the past. . . . [W]e must be skeptical whether Sukarno, even if he had the will, would be able to appreciably curb" the Communists' power. "On the contrary, we would expect, all other things being equal, continued growth of Communist strength on Java to the point that ultimately they may have the capability to take power through legal or quasi-legal means."[50]

In his cable Allison had once more strongly emphasized the importance of the American administration at least agreeing that the West Irian issue be discussed in the United Nations if the United States were to retain any influence with Sukarno and the position of the PKI to be weakened. But Secretary Dulles soon afterward suggested a very different course: that the United States should move away from its tacitly pro-Dutch "neutrality" toward an unambiguous support of the Netherlands. In a memorandum on August 21 he stated: "I think we should carefully reconsider our UN policy. It seems to me that in view of the pro-Communist trend of Sukarno, the fact that their own government is now extra-constitutional, and the unrest in their own country—it is almost absurd to be neutral toward the extending of the Indonesian authority to a new area."[51] Although Dulles never in fact moved closer to the Dutch position on West Irian and continued to hew to the tacitly pro-Dutch "neutral" position, this memorandum shows Dulles's leanings and how fruitless it was for Allison to attempt to induce him to move toward the actually neutral position that supporting a discussion of the issue in the United Nations would have constituted.

If Allison had any further doubts over the divergence of his own views from those of the secretary of state they were probably laid to rest with Dulles's August 24 cable (see chap. 3), in which he objected to the proposed Munas conference and discounted the value of any political compromise between the Djuanda government and the regional dissidents. To Dulles's admonition that the conference "would not in reality provide a means through which [the] anti-Communism of dissident leaders could exert a definitive influence over Sukarno and his associates, which would compel them to assume an anti-Communist posture," Allison sent him an unambiguously critical rejoinder.[52]

> I do not understand how dissident leaders are to exercise definitive influence over Sukarno without contact with him. I also think it is grossest self-deception to believe that any Indonesian government, even one headed by Hatta with Sukarno completely eliminated, is going to adopt an "anti-Communist Posture". We can look forward, if our policies are wise to a non-Communist Government which is truly independent and natural [sic, neutral] but to expect anything more in the foreseeable future is unrealistic. For us to attempt to bring about an "anti-Communist posture" could very easily bring about the very thing we wish to avoid — a definite switch into the Communist camp.
>
> Djuanda and Hatta are non-Communist. To think that they will be influenced in [an]other direction and that they cannot themselves in company with dissident regional leaders, exercise influence is [in] my opinion defeatist.

Dulles was clearly not pleased with this lecture and responded accordingly:

> Department appreciates considerations raised you #505, but your statement that Department's position reflects quote completely defeatist attitude unquote is gross misrepresentation of Department's thinking. Our concern is 1) that advantage may be taken of conference by Communists or army to arrest or eliminate leading anti-Communist elements present [in] Djakarta, and 2) that for a lack of adequate preparation conference may not succeed which would only strengthen hand of Sukarno and lead to further disintegration of Indonesia to advantage of Communists. You shall seek and report as much information as possible concerning conference.[53]

On September 3, 1957, Cumming's Ad Hoc Interdepartmental Committee on Indonesia after seven formal meetings submitted its "Special Report on Indonesia" to the National Security Council, a report based on the assumption that American security interests throughout Southeast Asia, the Western Pacific, and Australia would be seriously affected should the Communists gain political control of the Jakarta government or at least the island of Java.[54] It laid the foundation for a concurrent two-track American policy: one overt, calling for maintaining "official diplomatic relations" with Indonesia "as near as possible to what they have been in the recent past"; the other covert, which was to "contribute to the establishment of a government able and willing to pursue vigorous anti-Communist domestic policies and actions."

The attainment of American objectives via this covert track was to be furthered by "exploiting the not inconsiderable potential political resources

and economic leverage available in the outer islands, particularly in Sumatra and Sulawesi (Celebes)." This required that the U. S.:

a. . . . strengthen the determination, will and cohesion of the anti-
   Communist forces in the outer islands, particularly in Sumatra and
   Sulawesi, in order through their strength to affect favorably the situation in Java, and to provide a rallying point if the Communists should
   take over Java.
b. [entire paragraph deleted from text released]
c. Utilize such leverage as is available and may be built up by the anti-
   Communist forces in the outer islands to continue our efforts to try to
   unify and stimulate into action, singly or in unison, non- and anti-
   Communist elements on Java against the Communists.

Growth of "the military potential of the government military forces on
Java" was to be prevented because they might "ultimately fall under Communist influence and be used to reduce the anti-Communist forces in the
outer islands." However, support should be given to "the non- and anti-
Communist elements in the military and paramilitary forces on Java and in
the Central Government."

There was to be no official indication that the United States was recon-
sidering its policies, but "unless and until" Communist strength on Java
declined, American technical assistance and economic development programs were to be "oriented toward the outer islands." Any Indonesian
application for PL 480 Commodities [US surplus agricultural products—
mostly rice] was to be governed similarly, and present and prospective
applications to the U.S. Export-Import Bank were to be put on hold.[55]

Paragraph 9 of the report, running a full page (and still not declassified),
presumably incorporating recommendations for concrete actions to further
American objectives, was apparently especially controversial and the subject of "reservations and differences" among the members of the interdepartmental committee that submitted the report.[56]

Reaching any sort of consensus apparently did not come easily. After
"several formal meetings" the committee reported that the CIA had "not
yet determined its position as between two alternatives" and that "the
Committee agreed that a proposed appendix on covert operations should
be eliminated on the understanding that the Director of Central Intelligence
will brief the [National Security] Council on this point as necessary and
appropriate."[57] (Presumably the annex was to be eliminated because, as is
often the case, details of covert activities were regarded as too sensitive to
be put in writing.)

Preparatory to the National Security Council's consideration of this
special report, Assistant Secretary Robertson sought to clarify for Secretary Dulles the premises on which the recommendations were based.[58]
He noted:

1) That the Communists on Java have not only a relative but also an *absolute majority* [emphasis added—this was a grossly inaccurate and highly inflated estimate without foundation in fact and apparently based on CIA and certainly not U.S. Embassy reporting] and that the trend cannot be reversed by any action we might take; 2) that we wish to strengthen the dissident regional elements so that in their negotiations with the Central Government they will be negotiating from a position of strength and the government from one of weakness; 3) that failing successful negotiations, and should the regional elements break away, we will have laid the groundwork for strengthening the outer islands; 4) that in the event of a civil war the anti-Communist forces will have greater strength; 5) that time is running in favor of the Communists and against us.

Although highly inaccurate, this description of political conditions on Java fitted perfectly the prerequisite for American endorsement of a breakup of Indonesia posited by Eisenhower and Dulles in their oral instructions to Cumming when he was appointed ambassador.

Had Allison seen this hyperbolically apocalyptic memorandum, he would have been outraged and severely critical. But he was not made privy to it or to the full text of the Interdepartmental committee's report. Even so, in his cable to the State Department commenting on the milder condensed version of the report that was sent to him, he took strong issue with several of its assumptions and recommendations.[59] He noted that it provided for no attempt to influence Sukarno's ways, and that presumably he was being regarded as "beyond redemption." There was no "real consideration of the reasons for the great Communist gains or for Sukarno's increasing reliance on Communist support." Observing that he did not believe "valid recommendations can be made for a cure without considering the causes of the disease," he noted that "apparently Washington has not considered what the effect of United States policies present and past may have had on recent Indonesian developments." He had in mind primarily the role of the United States with respect to West Irian and its unwillingness to sell the Indonesian army equipment and spare parts for its largely American weaponry. His embassy's military attachés found "exactly an opposite trend" to the committee's conclusion that "the Army on Java is rapidly becoming less reliable politically" and that many of its anti-Communist officers had been removed from positions of influence. And at the most fundamental level he was critical of the assumption that American policy could lead to the establishment of an *anti*-Communist government in Indonesia in the near future. The "most we can reasonably expect is a truly independent non-Communist government." The United States "should recognize that premature or too vigorous insistence on an *anti*-Communist government may prevent the establishment of a *non*-Communist government. We should remember that there as in other cases the perfect is often the enemy of the good [emphasis added]."

Assistant Secretary Robertson, in conveying the interdepartmental committee's Special Report on Indonesia to Secretary Dulles, recommended that no action yet be taken on the report and that no final decision be reached on a course of action until the decisions made at the Munas conference in Jakarta and the prospect for their implementation by the Indonesian government had been clarified.[60] Cumming, however, with his views on Indonesia having moved close to those of Secretary Dulles, was impatient for action. He pointed out that the National Security Council's planning board had endorsed the report's recommendations and insisted that there was no evidence that Munas had produced solutions that would "stem the steady growth of Communist strength on the island of Java." He warned that if the current of anticommunism of the outlying islands were to lose its present momentum, it could lead either to "an inevitable creeping extension of Communism to the whole country or perhaps to a civil war."[61]

Three days later, on September 23 the National Security Council, with the president and both Dulles brothers present, met to discuss and decide on the recommendations in the Special Report on Indonesia.[62] Both of the brothers took positions in support of the report and reflected views that accorded with Cumming's September 20 memorandum. Allen Dulles referred to the Munas conference as having served as only "a sedative," reducing the pain but effecting no cure. A stalemate continued, he reported, with efforts to solve the military problem "a complete failure." His CIA estimated that the Jakarta government would be "unwilling or unable to meet the economic demands of the outlying provinces of Indonesia." He concluded by observing that the estimate of Sumatra's oil resources had been "upped a great deal recently, a 20-billion-barrel reserve is currently estimated, and this is only the beginning."

The secretary of state, urging flexibility in carrying out the committee's recommendations, focused on the pivotal issue of West Irian. While preserving for the present its stance of "neutrality," the United States should not be placed in a frozen position. Thus, if the Indonesians accepted Communist rule, "we will be obliged to oppose their efforts to secure control of Irian." "On the other hand," he said, "we might find ourselves in a position of desiring to support the claims of a strong anti-Communist government to Irian." As on other occasions, the secretary of state did not appear to appreciate that the American policy of "neutrality" stood for acquiescence in a status quo that meant nothing less than complicity in a continued Dutch occupation of the contested territory. Nor did he appear to heed his brother's warning that, "if the United States were to support the Dutch thesis as to New Guinea, we might find ourselves alienated from Indonesian Nationalists just as completely as from Indonesian Communists."[63]

There was, then, still no indication that the secretary was aware of the extent to which the West Irian issue transcended the clashing views of all political elements in Indonesia, the degree to which it had become the touchstone for Sukarno in assessing the attitudes of foreign states toward Indonesia, and the extent to which the PKI drew popular strength and the appreciation of Sukarno for its highly activist role in championing Indonesia's claim to the territory.[64] Yet this was just the assessment that his ambassador to Indonesia, John Allison, had for months been sending him. Ironically, Allison's predecessor, Hugh Cumming, who had earlier reported in the same vein, was now ignoring his own previous advice and had become one of the most ardent of those pressing for aggressive interventionism, though as yet apparently less so than Acting Secretary of Defense Brucker, who in the context of still-classified article 9 of the interdepartmental committee's recommendation urged a revision that he said was "very much along the lines of the original Defense-JCS proposal [still classified] which had been supplanted in the Planning Board" of the NSC. The proposal went too far for President Eisenhower and prompted him to interject that it "contained elements that could not appropriately be placed in an N.S.C. policy." The National Security Council's executive secretary, Robert Cutler, seconded the president's position, saying that its planning board had "rejected the Defense-JCS proposal for much the same reason."

The recommendations contained in the Interdepartmental committee's Special Report on Indonesia, then, were adopted subject to amendments, apparently all centering on the implementing features of the still-classified paragraph 9, which presumably bridged some of the language between the apparently more heavily military intervention advocated in the Defense-Joint Chief of Staffs version and that proposed by the National Security Council planning board. The broad directives of the special report were to serve as the fundamental charter of the Eisenhower administration's Indonesia policy over the next five months.

Shunted aside by both Cumming's interdepartmental committee and the CIA's Jakarta station, Ambassador Allison was initially unaware of their efforts. Gradually he began to suspect he was being bypassed by the Jakarta CIA—which had its own direct channel of communication to Washington—but he did not learn of Cumming's interdepartmental committee until after it had been launched, and he subsequently stated that, even then, he did not know the committee's membership and received only "a cabled summary" of its special report, with no clue as to the nature of the proposed American military actions (presumably contained in paragraph 9).[65] Allison saw that his own cables to Washington were having scant effect and became increasingly aware that the Jakarta CIA station and Cumming's group were both bypassing him and urging policies that largely contradicted his own recommendations.[66] It is understandable that on September 25 he cabled his old friend in the State Department, Walter Robertson, complaining that the department evidently preferred the CIA's reporting to his own and stating that, if the department no longer had confidence in his judgment, he was "prepared to resign as Ambassador and request retirement from the Foreign Service."[67] Not until two months later did he receive a reply. His offer to resign went unremarked, but just a month later he was shocked to learn that after serving less than eleven months in Indonesia he was being transferred—"sent into exile," he later termed it—to be ambassador to Czechoslovakia.[68]

5. Polarization

In the closing months of 1957, there was an increasing political polarization between the Indonesian government and its opponents, driven primarily by the growing assertiveness of the dissident military leaders in Sumatra and Sulawesi and by the conviction of Sukarno and other leaders in Jakarta that the Dutch had closed off the road to a negotiated settlement of the West Irian dispute. The polarization was intensified by the continuing unwillingness of the United States to moderate its tacitly pro-Dutch policy of neutrality on West Irian and its growing disposition to encourage and provide material support to the regionalist dissidents.

In many ways the series of meetings that took place before and after the Munas conference—those of the rebel colonels in Palembang and Padang and those of the interdepartmental committee and high members of the Eisenhower administration in Washington—were of much greater significance than the Munas conference itself. These meetings in Sumatra and the United States served to vitiate any chance that the conference in Jakarta would open up a road to compromise between the central government and its regional opponents.

After Munas: From Dissidents to Rebels

The three dissident colonels who participated in the Jakarta conference—Sumual, Barlian, and Husein—were anything but articulate spokesmen for their regions' grievances. They went along with the proposals put forward by the government and in the aftermath of the conference expressed optimism about its accomplishments, with Sumual publicly describing the results as satisfactory.[1] But this optimism was soon dashed by their colleagues who had remained behind in Sumatra—Simbolon, Zulkifli Lubis, Dahlan Djambek, and Sumitro. These four had adopted a position with respect to a compromise with Jakarta strikingly close to that expressed by John Foster Dulles in his cable to Ambassador Allison on August 24—namely, that the dissidents should "develop further strength before attempting direct negotiations with Sukarno."[2] After the Munas conference Sumual returned to Sulawesi while Husein and Barlian went to Padang to meet with their colleagues, who firmly quashed any euphoria they might have felt in the aftermath of the Jakarta conference. According to Sumitro, by the end of a meeting of the six dissident leaders held in Padang September 15-18, the consensus among them, again closely paralleling Dulles's view, was "that the outcome of the National Conference [Munas] had greatly enhanced Sukarno's scope for maneuvering and political manipulations."[3] A document that they drew up at the end of the Padang meeting stated that the substantive results of the Munas conference all constituted a victory for Sukarno, while Hatta's position had been further restricted.[4] The statement criticized the composition of the "Committee of Seven" established by the conference to negotiate the center-regional disputes, viewing only two of its members, Hatta and the Sultan of Yogyakarta, as sympathetic to regional aspirations. It particularly deplored the inclusion of Nasution among the seven, "notwithstanding the fact that one of the main issues to be dealt with by the Committee was the position of Nasution himself as Chief of Staff of the Army." This, the dissident colonels held, "should have ruled him out for membership."[5] They asked, "If it was felt necessary to include a military officer on the committee, why should it not have been Major General Simatupang," known for his close association with the PSI?"[6]

The evaluation of the Sukarno-Hatta duumvirate that appeared in the documents issuing from the Padang meetings differed strikingly from that in the original Palembang Charter drawn up before the Munas conference. The "guidelines" for the future struggle put forward in the later document rejected the "myth of the *dwitunggal*" and expressed their growing disillusionment with former vice president Hatta, a disillusionment that was now also beginning to take root in the United States. The guidelines prescribed holding a presidential election and added that their abandonment of "the idea that everything can be solved if only the *Dwitunggal* were re-established" should for the present "be kept secret, because the change in attitude toward Bung Hatta will have a great effect that could be used by our opponents."[7]

While the colonels were dissatisfied with Hatta's performance at the Munas conference, it is worth noting that the former vice president expressed similar discontent with the role played there by the dissidents' spokesmen. He too was cynical about the "*dwitunggal* myth," for he had experienced several years of acting as the junior partner in a duumvirate in which he had no defined powers while having to accept responsibility for government actions to which he had not been privy and over which he had no control. Already having taken the step of resigning from the position of vice president on December 1, 1956, he was unwilling to return to the government unless he had a defined role and responsibilities. According to his principal Indonesian biographer, Deliar Noer: "Apparently he was willing to become Prime Minister; or second man as before in a Presidential cabinet under Sukarno,"[8] but not simply a powerless vice president.

Thus, in response to the Padang dissidents' complaints about his role in the Munas conference, Hatta wrote to Dahlan Djambek: "If some of the regions now feel dissatisfied, this is a result of their having participated in the unanimous acceptance of the imprecise formula presented to them." The "joint oath" accepted at the conference, according to him, "was completely without content." A friend had apparently reassured him beforehand that the conference would reject the formula and would demand that Hatta's position be clarified and defined. "How surprised I was," he wrote, "when the formula was accepted by the conference without debate. Now don't turn this problem round by asserting that the declaration was accepted [by the regions] because I'd already agreed with it." Similarly, he argued that, if the colonels were opposed to Nasution's inclusion in the Committee of seven, their representatives at the conference should have rejected it: "Why was it just accepted without demanding and pressing for a different composition? This was also an error, to accept something that was basically disliked."[9]

In their meetings after the Munas conference, the colonels in Padang not only abandoned their faith in the *dwitunggal* formula; they also —probably reflecting Sumitro's and Simbolon's contact with the CIA— markedly strengthened their anti-Communist stance. While the earlier Palembang meetings had for the first time called for the banning of communism, this call now became more outspoken and strident. Communism was portrayed as "anti-God" and "antinationalism" and as such "in opposition to the State ideology [i.e., *Panca Sila*]." And in their mid-September meetings in Padang, the colonels' dissidence escalated toward rebellion as they for the first time threatened formation of a countergovernment, announcing:

> So long as the PKI still has a seat in the Center (the island of Java), this Center cannot be acknowledged as the Center of the State of the Republic of Indonesia, and to remedy these matters efforts have to begin now towards forming an Emergency Central Government for the Republic of Indonesia (Pemerintah Pusat Darurat Republik Indonesia) located outside the island of Java.[10]

They called for establishment of an all-Sumatran military command led by Colonel Simbolon that would then join with the East Indonesian Permesta movement under Colonel Sumual to form a joint military command. They also urged formation of an anti-Communist front, a call quickly answered by Dahlan Djambek, who established, initially in Bukittinggi, a joint movement against communism, Gerakan Bersama Anti-Komunis (Gebak), which soon had branches throughout West and South Sumatra.[11] These provisions constituted the main features of a document entitled "Guiding Principles and Joint Program of the Regional Struggle," which was officially regarded as an "annex" to the Palembang Charter and was then carried by Husein and Barlian to Sulawesi for Sumual's approval and there signed by all three colonels on October 5.[12]

The colonels were now moving along a very different path from the one they had initially pursued, with its emphasis on greater fiscal autonomy and decentralization of administrative power. Regional grievances were still being voiced, together with calls for formation of a senate to represent the interests of the regions; still present as well was the demand for a change in the leadership of the armed forces (in other words, the ouster of Nasution), coupled now with a proposal for a wide-ranging conference on problems within the armed forces, in which all the military leaders involved in the regional struggle could participate. But the agenda was changing and the demands becoming more confrontational. By repudiating Hatta, demanding elimination of the Communists, and threatening the establishment of a competing central government, the dissidents were drastically narrowing any remaining area for compromise with the Sukarno government. The three colonels who had participated in the Munas conference in Jakarta and had seen significant movement by the center toward some of their positions were now being impelled by their more extreme colleagues toward an open split. Thus, for the group as a whole, dissidence was escalating toward full-fledged rebellion.

Beginning of Direct American Contacts

Following the Munas meetings the rebels publicly argued for "using the results of this Conference to change the international atmosphere" so as "to activate help from abroad in the field of development, particularly regional development projects."[13] But, as some of their CIA contacts were well aware, their hopes for outside assistance went far beyond such projects, with many of the statements in their meetings, particularly the blanket condemnations of the Communist party and their proposal to establish a rival central government, made with an outside audience in mind.[14]

The CIA's first contact with the rebels, according to Joseph Burkholder Smith, had been with Colonel Simbolon in early April 1957, with Smith's Washington office getting involved soon afterward. The connection began with a field report that a CIA agent (presumably an Indonesian) had offered a Jakarta-based CIA case officer information from representatives of Husein, who, it will be recalled, had then been heading the largely autonomous West Sumatra government for some four months. The FE/5 desk officer promptly directed Jakarta to insist on "direct case officer contact with Hussein's representatives," and within a few days the case officer himself went to Padang to talk with Husein.[15] The American agent then learned the range of grievances of the "rebel colonels" and that they "had gone further than anyone in the CIA had yet realized in developing the nucleus of a genuine separatist movement." The colonels explained to the agent that they had already opened their own bank accounts in Singapore and that these accounts might be useful to anyone wishing to help them with any kind of assistance. They already had representatives at work in Singapore, including Sumitro.[16]

At this point, Smith states, "we hid the fact we were supporting their aspirations to form a separate state independent of Sukarno's government from higher authorities in Washington until we were certain we could win approval for this course of action" from the National Security Council's special group.[17] "Premature mention of any such idea [i.e., before special group approval] might get it shot down" by Ambassador Allison, the Department of State, or the Department of Defense. As in other instances, "we made the action program up ourselves after we had collected enough intelligence to make them appear required by the circumstances." In short, the objective was one of "making a situation appear to require that CIA step in to correct it."[18] It was, of course, the often tendentious and alarmist character of this reporting that—insofar as he learned of it—so upset Ambassador Allison. But given the existing prejudices of senior members of the Eisenhower administration, it is apparent that most of this reporting had a plausibility that was in tune with their own developing concern about Indonesia. Ambassador Allison was clearly correct in his belief that their worries about Indonesia were being heightened by the CIA's field reports.[19]

Former finance minister Sumitro was particularly active in seeing that the rebel decisions reached sympathizers in the United States and Britain. Almost immediately after the colonels' meetings in Padang ended on September 18, Sumitro used the decisions reached there to increase enthusiasm particularly in Washington for the rebel cause. On October 2, via CIA back (Roger) channel, the special assistant for intelligence at the U.S. embassy in London (presumably the CIA's office there) cabled that one of Sumitro's assistants, Roland Liem, had called at the embassy, apparently to ensure that certain information be conveyed to Washington. According to several reliable sources, Liem was an old friend of Sumitro and an official of the Nationalist (Kuomintang) government on Taiwan, serving until shortly before this time on its delegation to the United Nations.[20] He gave the American embassy official a report on the September 7 Palembang Charter, which he described as providing for a "National Front Against Communism" whose members were prepared to "join with any other block which wishes to crush communism." Liem explained that Sumitro had in mind a program for implementing the Palembang Charter, which called for the marketing of all Sumatran products through London to finance the movement. The British government, Liem stated, had granted Sumitro, then in Singapore, a visa under an alias for an early visit to London and advised that he also wished to visit the United States "to meet with friends there."[21]

Two days later Liem returned to the office of the special assistant for intelligence to convey additional information, including a personal letter he had received from Sumitro dated September 22 enclosing a copy of one dated September 20 sent by Sumitro to Colonel Sumual, the Permesta leader on Sulawesi.[22] Sumitro's letter to Liem included an analysis of the Munas conference, stating that the rebels would now seek to reverse its "relatively unfavorable outcome" so as to regain the initiative, consolidating their operations and preparing for a "long siege against Djakarta." In its struggle against the central government the rebel movement was to "accelerate all means to strengthen its armed forces"; it must "retrieve West Irian for Indonesia and take wind from Sukarno's sails by denying him this issue to exploit politically"; and it must obtain foreign aid for economic development "to help diminish communist influence." The movement "must accomplish changes in [the] high command of [the] Indonesian armed forces" and "in particular get rid of [the] present chief of staff, Nasution"; furthermore; it "must strengthen" the rebel armed forces "so that if civil war occurs [the] rebel movement will be ready to defeat its enemies." More generally, Sumitro instructed Liem to pass on to "friendly" powers the following seven points:

> Sukarno-Hatta dual unity must be restored but not at expense of those principles which Hatta stands for.
>
> Nasution must be dismissed.
>
> A senate should be set up for all Indonesia. Government should be decentralized from Djakarta. . . .
>
> There must be complete prohibition and crushing of all communist organizations (including SOBSI [the Communist party's labor federation]).
>
> Coordination in struggle should be achieved. . . . United military command must be established first in Sumatra. . . .
>
> Principles contained in the Palembang charter are binding force for the establishment of this new anti-communist front. . . . Movement has now taken on a national character. It has armed forces. It controls territory. It has an embryonic government with social and economic institutions. Most importantly it has popular support of the people it controls including some in Java (Lubis). Even Sundanese [major ethnic group in West Java] want autonomous state now. Rebel movement is acting from own volition and not at instigation of any foreign power.
>
> Rebel movement needs help now and anything which can be given to it will be appreciated and remembered in future. It will increase its military equipment . . . and prepare for civil war if necessary.[23]

Anti-Communist histrionics marked Liem's next discussion with Whitney on October 8—an apparent attempt to generate greater American interest in Sumitro.[24] Liem alleged that Sumitro was "becoming increasingly fearful of murder or kidnapping by Communist agents," that when Soviet president Voroshilov had visited Jakarta during the first half of May, the Soviets had "pressed Sukarno strongly on necessity [of] 'getting rid of Sumitro at all costs,'" and that Peking radio had been reporting his movements. In view of this, Liem stated, he had asked the British to provide protection for Sumitro during his forthcoming visit to London and planned subsequent visit to the United States.

The Liem-Sumitro information clearly received attention at high levels in the United States government, as is evidenced by the cable Hugh Cumming sent over Dulles's signature on October 25, via Roger Channel (thereby bypassing Allison), to the CIA station within the U.S. embassy in Jakarta.[25] This cable briefly encapsulated the information provided during Liem's visits to the London embassy and Sumitro's talks with Robert H. Scott, commissioner-general for Britain in Southeast Asia, in Singapore on October 10-11. In these meetings, Cumming observed, the British "were sympathetic with rebel aims but presently cool toward covert support." Cumming noted that Sumitro planned to hold a meeting, probably in Bangkok, between October 25 and 29, to discuss implementation of rebel strategy; the British were not interfering with Sumitro's movements or with his commercial activities in behalf of the rebels, and he was planning to visit London soon to "discuss marketing arrangements [for] rebel products."[26]

Sumitro was well positioned to serve as the rebels' principal outside fund-raiser and, along with Colonel Sumual, he had important contacts with American and other intelligence agents and commercial houses outside Indonesia. During the early years of the revolution he had been pivotal in the republic's rather modest success in obtaining outside funds — primarily from business interests in the United States and elsewhere anxious to compete in a field previously so heavily dominated by the Dutch. He had maintained some of these contacts after the revolution when he became the main fund-raiser in Sjahrir's Indonesian Socialist party (PSI). But now in the fall of 1957 Sumitro nursed legitimate grievances against both the PSI (in which he had been unfairly discriminated against in appointments to its governing "politbureau") and against Nasution, whom he, rightly or wrongly, believed to be behind the charges of corruption that in May had induced him to flee the country (see chap. 3). Although himself Javanese, the fact that his wife was Menadonese probably gave him greater sensitivity to the Outer Islands' grievances than would otherwise have been the case, and he was not, or at least no longer, an admirer of Sukarno. He was an ambitious man of considerable intelligence and great energy. It was not surprising, then, that, already being a fugitive from the Jakarta government, he early on elected to work with the rebel military leaders — none of whom, except perhaps Sumual, had he known well before. According to a broad spectrum of Indonesian sources — both friendly and unfriendly — during the fall of 1957 Sumitro was in frequent touch with a large number of overseas contacts, including the CIA's Singapore station, run by a friend whom he had previously known in Jakarta; at least one person from the CIA's Jakarta station (who operated out of a house in the salubrious climate just below the Puncak Pass); a retired United States rear admiral in Hong

Kong, widely believed to represent the CIA; and with government officials in Malaya, the Philippines, Thailand, and probably Taiwan, as well as British, Dutch, and overseas Chinese business houses.[27]

· · · · ·

It is difficult to assess the relative influence of Frank Wismer, Al Ulmer, Joseph Smith, and their CIA colleagues in the field compared with the more formal, if similarly covert, efforts of Hugh S. Cumming and his supporters in the State Department and Pentagon in shaping the aggressively interventionist administration policy that emerged during the fall of 1957. But their influences were evidently complementary and in a fundamental way mutually supportive. Furthermore, both the available documentary evidence and the consensus among State Department and CIA members interviewed indicate that, among the top leaders of the Eisenhower administration, John Foster Dulles was the most aggressive and consistent in forwarding this policy.[28]

While in the fall of 1957 no decision had yet been made as to major American intervention in behalf of the regional rebels, this was a period during which the United States sought to build up its "assets" in Indonesia and increase their strength so that, either through their acting alone or ultimately in conjunction with a more activist American policy, greater leverage would be available against Jakarta. In the meantime, the rebel leaders, now actively encouraged by CIA agents and receiving significant covert American financial support and weapons, were further expanding their ties abroad.

Jakarta's Growing Alienation from the West

During the closing months of 1957 the issue of West Irian increased the alienation of Sukarno's government from the West. Deeply rooted support for the national claims to West Irian existed throughout Indonesia, stretching all across the political spectrum.[29] It will be recalled that even the rebels in their post-Munas statements had argued that they needed to strengthen their struggle with regard to West Irian "in order 'to take the wind out of the sails' of the Communist groups that are influencing Sukarno."[30] The breadth of this support was appreciated in the Far Eastern Division of the U.S. Department of State, which in its recommendation of October 2, 1957, observed: "All elements in Indonesia, whatever their political, ethnic, or religious differences are agreed on Indonesia's 'right' to West Irian. It is a national claim and an irredentist issue of universal emotional appeal."[31] The recommendation noted that the Indonesian request to the United Nations General Assembly, similar to that of the previous year, was simply for "a resolution looking toward the resumption of negotiations under U.N. auspices between the disputants." Foreign Minister Subandrio, the memorandum observed, had told the U.S. Jakarta embassy that this was the most he hoped to obtain and that if these negotiations could go on for " one or two years or more," the government would be able "to keep the situation under control."

Events in Indonesia were not strengthening the hand of those in the State Department who hoped to moderate Dulles's inclination to continue giving tacit support to the Dutch on the West Irian question. Provincial elections during the fall of 1957 appeared to lend additional credibility to a U.S. National Intelligence Estimate of August 27 that "over the next 12 months the prospect is for a continued increase in Communist influence over the central government."[32] Especially important was the election of November 7 for the regional council in the Special Area (*Daerah Istimewa*) of Yogyakarta, which confirmed and reinforced the trend established in the Central, East, and West Java elections and correspondingly raised the level of American concern. Increasing its vote by more than 17 percent over the 1955 election for the Constituent Assembly, the Communist PKI displaced the nationalist PNI as the largest party in Yogyakarta. (The PKI total in the November 1957 election there was reported as 298,257, as against 164,568 for the PNI. The two major Islamic parties, the Masjumi and Nahdatul Ulama, roughly maintained their positions, together polling almost 213,000.) This meant that in Java as a whole (including the provinces of East, Central, and West Java, Greater Jakarta, and Yogyakarta) among the four largest parties the PKI garnered almost 30.5 percent of the vote (as against 19.8 percent in the 1955 parliamentary elections). If returns from the minor parties were added, this would probably have given the Communists around 25 percent of the total votes for these provincial elections on Java. The situation was, of course, different throughout almost all the rest of Indonesia, where the Islamic and Christian parties were strong and, except in a few areas, the PKI's support was inconsequential.[33]

That this manifestation of increasing PKI strength reinforced American worries over Java's leftward political drift was not lost on the dissident Outer Island colonels and their principal foreign liaison agent, Professor Sumitro. As the U.S. embassy reported on the eve of the Yogyakarta elections:

> From the point of view of obtaining foreign assistance they [the dissident regions] also consider their proclaimed anti-communist position, when contrasted with the pro-communist [sic] position of Sukarno, as an element that the United States cannot ignore. As a result, they are prepared to go ahead on the assumption that they will be able to obtain support from the United States government.[34]

Given the power realities within the Department of State, and Secretary Dulles's increasing criticism of Sukarno and his government, the Far Eastern Division was not inclined to follow Ambassador Allison's urgent recommendation that the United States move to support the General Assembly's discussion of the West Irian issue. Nor was it possible for Allison, although firmly backed by the embassy's military attachés, to overcome the secretary of state's unwillingness to permit the sale of arms and spare parts to the Indonesian military forces, despite the fact that they had equipped themselves almost exclusively with American arms.[35] During the second half of 1957 Nasution repeatedly and unsuccessfully requested such material from the United States. Under siege from the European and International Organization Divisions of the State Department who were arguing strongly to move from neutrality to clear support of Dutch retention of West Irian, Assistant Secretary of State Frank Robertson's Far East Division felt that the most it could achieve was just to hold the line. It therefore recommended that the United States keep to its existing "neutral" posture by abstaining in the General Assembly on consideration of all aspects of the issue.[36]

With his troops' effectiveness declining because of the deterioration of their equipment, Army Chief of Staff Nasution had concluded by the end of the year that, if the United States was going to continue to hold out, he would be obliged to accept long-standing Soviet bloc offers of arms. Having already advised the United States of this prospect, he finally on December 30, 1957, again called in Major George Benson, the American deputy military attaché, now requesting an immediate cable be sent to General Maxwell Taylor, the U.S. Army chief of staff, informing him that "if an affirmative response was not forthcoming by December 31 the army would have to look to Eastern Europe for its equipment." Taylor, who himself had met Nasution and was personally sympathetic to his request, cabled within twenty-four hours that "while military training of Indonesian officers in the U.S. could continue (arrangement for this being within his competence) he could still give no assurance with regard to arms, since that question was being considered at a high level on a political basis."[37]

In the face of continued United States intransigence, Nasution felt he had no other option but to go forward in the subsequent months with arrangements for the purchase of Eastern bloc arms, on the basis of the concessionary terms already available.[38] Such orders, even though actual delivery did not commence for another four to five months, gave some of the regional leaders an opening to buttress their charge that the central government and its armed forces were subject to Communist influence. Already during 1957 senior administration officials had repeatedly queried Major Benson as to the political complexion of the Indonesian army, which he consistently reported as non-Communist. (He notes that even by 1965 only four out of roughly 120 battalions were pro-Communist.[39]) Despite these assurances and despite corroborative reporting by the Jakarta embassy, those officials who were dominant in policy-making in Washington were inclined until April or May of 1958 to give more credence to the CIA's alarmist assessments as to the political orientation of Jakarta's armed forces.[40]

Ambassador Allison's West Irian Plan

Indonesian leaders (including those in opposition, such as Hatta and Natsir) were frustrated with their inability for a third straight year to muster the two-thirds majority in the United Nation's General Assembly necessary even to put the West Irian issue on the agenda for discussion. This was a source of growing anxiety for Ambassador Allison who knew that Indonesians would perceive another United States abstention on the issue in the upcoming United Nations' vote at the end of November 1957 as influencing many countries dependent on American aid or tied to it militarily to follow suit. He felt that some new formula had to be advanced to get American policy off what he termed "a dangerous dead center."[41] His sense of urgency was heightened when, in a speech before the General Assembly on October 3, Foreign Minister Subandrio—clearly reflecting Sukarno's view on West Irian—stated: "The only question is whether the United Nations is the place where its solution may be worked out, or whether we must embark upon another course, even at the risk of aggravating conditions in South-East Asia and perhaps invite 'cold war' tensions to muddy further the waters of peace in that region of the world."[42]

To break out of this impasse Allison now sought a new approach. After some informal testing of the waters with Djuanda's cabinet, he worked out "a suggested plan" that he believed could serve American, Australian, Dutch, and Indonesian interests. According to Allison the Indonesian ministers encouraged the plan and Sukarno implied he looked on it favorably.[43] Allison viewed the plan as a politically respectable basis for discussion of a compromise solution that would get Sukarno "off the hook of his commitment to take action with regard to West Irian" and keep him "from being pushed into a position whereby he needed to work more closely with the Communists." Allison did not regard his plan as flawless or fixed but felt it offered the basis for a fresh start that might be minimally acceptable to all parties and head off what, given the drift of events, might become a catastrophe.[44] The proposal that he outlined to the Department of State on November 4 called for "action by stages" along the following lines:

1. Indonesians publicly renounce use of force or threat of force with reference to West Irian problem.
2. Dutch announce willingness to negotiate providing negotiations include consideration of repudiated Indonesian debt, North Sumatra oil and position of Dutch commerce and industry in Indonesia. I make no attempt at this time to indicate what debt settlement should be but certainly Dutch aide-memoire given on September 27 [1957] to Assis-

tant Secretary Wilcox could be taken as basis for discussion. [The aide-mémoire given to Wilcox by Ambassador van Roijen on September 27 requested U.S. good offices in helping to initiate Netherlands-Indonesian discussions leading to a settlement of the debt issue.[45]]

3. At end of negotiations (which would probably take at least six months) it would be announced that at end of stated period, say five years, sovereignty over West Irian would be turned over to Indonesia and that:

a. During those five years Dutch would undertake training at accelerated rate of Indonesian and native administrators, et cetera [for service in West Irian]; Indonesians would provide, at their expense, such administrators as possible to work under Dutch for this period. Upon transfer of sovereignty Dutch would agree to allow certain administrators and officials to remain for a further stated period, under nominal Indonesian control and at Indonesian expense.

4. Indonesia would agree that ANZUS [Australia, New Zealand, United States] pact might be extended to cover any hostile attempt to attack West Irian and might even agree to be associated with ANZUS powers in limited area of West Irian.

5. Indonesian Government would undertake to control strictly all Communist activity within Indonesia and would accept American assistance and guidance in anti-subversive activities.

6. United States would undertake expanded aid program in Indonesia with understanding that large part of it would be designed to aid regions and assist in solution regional problems.

After his retirement from the Foreign Service, Allison wrote that point 4 relating to ANZUS, which was "designed to bring Australia into the picture was the only one which my Indonesian friends boggled at, but they admitted that if all other parts of the plan were agreed to there would not be much reason not to go along with this point." The provision in point 5 relating to the control of Communist activity was "designed to make Sukarno live up to his oft repeated statement that if America would only agree with his position on West Irian he could cut the Communists down to size."[46]

There were certainly grounds for criticizing elements of Allison's proposal, as he himself acknowledged, but whereas the Indonesian leaders with whom he discussed all or part of it thought that, despite flaws, it might serve as a basis for fruitful discussion, the State Department clearly did not. It gave him no response, although he was sure that Secretary Dulles read it.[47]

With Allison's proposal dead and Dulles making clear that the ambassador had no authority to mediate the West Irian dispute, American policy kept to the same sterile course that the secretary had set. To the keen disappointment of the whole gamut of Indonesian leaders, in the vote on West Irian in the General Assembly on November 29, 1957, the United States and ten other states voted to abstain, so that once again the proposal for negotiations on the issue fell short of the two-thirds majority necessary to put it on the United Nations agenda (forty voted in favor, twenty-five against, and eleven abstained).[48]

Rebuff in the United Nations and Seizure of Dutch Properties

Sukarno, together with the entire Indonesian leadership, had lost patience. Kenneth Young, then one of the senior U.S. representatives at the United Nation, recalls that, during the month of November, the Indonesian delegation in talking to Americans, Netherlanders, and others in the halls of the United Nations made clear that, if the vote in the United Nations once again would not permit discussion of the issue, the Indonesian reaction would be very strong and "would certainly involve a take-over of Dutch enterprises and the ejection of Netherlanders" from the country.[49]

The Indonesian government had not been bluffing, and the day after the vote an exasperated President Sukarno, refusing to accept the national and personal humiliation he felt inherent in the Dutch victory at the United Nations, encouraged Indonesian labor unions and the Indonesian army to take over Dutch properties and ordered the departure of most of the 46,000 Netherlanders living in Indonesia. The army quickly asserted its ascendancy in this operation, taking over supervision of the running of the Dutch properties, so that the labor unions were soon shunted aside. Army paramountcy was firmly and formally established on December 13, when General Nasution issued a decree of martial law authorizing army officers to take over enterprises that unions had seized. Few of the military officers now in charge of most of the properties had adequate qualifications either to supervise their management or to engage in it directly. Some key Dutch managers were induced to stay on, but the economy was badly jolted—the greatest strain on it arising from Indonesian efforts to take over the Koninklijk Paketvaart Maatschappij (KPM), the Dutch inter-island shipping company. Understandably the Dutch simply removed as much of this fleet as possible from Indonesian ports, thus leaving the country bereft of this vital commercial linkage. Efforts to secure replacements for the shipping from Japan and Eastern European countries were not completely successful and in any case required too much time to fill the most urgent needs.

Overall there had been no preparation for these takeovers and, in addition to the disruption of shipping, there was enough economic dislocation to strain severely an already-weak Indonesian economy. Indonesian reactions varied. The army leadership, with the sudden windfall of patronage for retired or redundant officers, welcomed them. Some Indonesians were too stunned by Sukarno's action to voice criticism, while others were reluctant to protest because in the supercharged nationalist atmosphere surrounding the West Irian issue they did not wish to be accused of a lack of patriotism.

It was soon evident, however, that within the progressive Islamic Masjumi party there was strong dissent—even though mostly muted. This dissent became overt at the meetings commencing November 25 of the National Economic Development Conference (Munap), the successor to the Munas conference, convened to address regionalist dissatisfaction in the economic field. Here, in Sukarno's presence, one of the Masjumi party's senior leaders, Sjafruddin Prawiranegara, governor of the Bank of Indonesia and one of the country's most respected economists, delivered a blistering critique of the ill-prepared takeovers, cogently arguing their disastrous impact on the economy. Although he was fully supportive of Indonesia's right to West Irian, as were other members of the Masjumi, he argued that the takeovers were not a sensible way to proceed if the national interests of the country were considered. Such opposition by one of the party's top leaders tended to highlight the criticism felt by most Masjumi leaders at Sukarno's initiative. Hatta, though less outspoken than Sjafruddin, was also opposed. And, predictably, American policymakers were antagonized, with those already critical of Sukarno seeing their doubts justified, though Djuanda's government gave firm assurances that American and British properties would not be touched.[50]

The moves against Dutch properties also worried other Indonesian pragmatists, but they could not reverse the operation Sukarno and the avid army leadership had set in motion. The adverse reaction from most Masjumi leaders reinforced the growing polarization within Indonesian politics that had been marked some six months earlier by the party's withdrawal from the second Ali Sastroamidjojo cabinet. And the likelihood of a Hatta-Sukarno rapprochement was also diminished.

Cikini: The Attempt to Assassinate Sukarno

But even more polarizing was a totally unexpected event that occurred less than thirty-six hours after Sukarno authorized the takeovers—a nearly successful assassination attempt against him. On the evening of November 30, as the president was walking out of a school in the Cikini area of Jakarta in the company of two of his children, hand grenades were thrown in an attempt to assassinate him. An aide saved Sukarno's life by pushing him flat to the ground as the first grenade exploded, but eleven people were killed and at least thirty seriously injured—most of the victims being schoolchildren. The Cikini affair, as this episode became known, had wide ramifications—reaching into internal army politics as well as the national political scene. The chief suspect behind the assassination attempt at that time and in general thereafter was Colonel Zulkifli Lubis, the former army intelligence chief and deputy chief of staff who had been among the contenders for the position of chief of staff in 1955 when Nasution was appointed to the post.[51] Despite the failures of Lubis's coup attempts in late 1956, he still had enough backing among elements of the army—both combat and intelligence—to constrain Nasution from arresting him. Smarting from his failures and still restively ambitious, Lubis had continued his quest for power.

Working with intensely Islamic youth leaders, mostly Bimanese from the strongly Islamic Dompo area of the east Indonesian island of Sumbawa, Lubis established an underground organization that, though unconnected with the Masjumi youth organization, Gerakan Pemuda Islam Indonesia (GPII), drew a number of members from it, some of whom had ties to the West Java Darul Islam.[52]

According to the government's official account of the Cikini affair, Lubis's organization reflected his effort to build a Jakarta-based anti-Communist paramilitary group, Gerakan Anti-Komunis (GAK), which was at the same time anti-Nasution, anti-Sukarno, and anti-Sukendro (the current head of army intelligence)—thus paralleling Lubis's own orientation.[53] An American assessment five months after the event corroborated this account and concluded that members of the GAK had already been involved before Cikini in grenading the headquarters of both the Communist party and SOBSI (the Communist-controlled labor federation) as well as in an attempt to assassinate Nasution.[54] A key aide of Lubis, Saleh Ibrahim, who headed the GAK and was a member of Masjumi, escaped after the assassination attempt, but three of the youths involved were tried and executed, with a fourth sentenced to life imprisonment.[55] When asked at the trial why they had attacked Sukarno, the four youths had answered: "Allah told us to."

That response is perhaps relevant to Lubis's own 1971 account. Acknowledging that "the leader and chairman of the Bima group," understood to be Saleh Ibrahim," came to him shortly before the action, Lubis stated that he told him he was opposed to an assassination and counseled him to urge the boys to "go to the mosque to pray." However, Lubis recalls, "the prayer, instead of diminishing their desire to assassinate Sukarno, simply reinforced their feeling that this was the right thing to do."[56] There is no way of knowing to what Lubis expected these prayers would lead. Whatever his actual intentions and role had been, he was widely suspected of being involved in the affair, and, in the view of a good many, of being the *dalang* (puppet master) behind the scene. A retired and generally circumspect CIA officer then serving in Indonesia has stated categorically that this was so.[57] There was no question that this time, if apprehended, Lubis would be brought to trial, so he promptly went underground, soon emerging in West Sumatra, where Colonel Husein immediately extended him protection.[58]

Since several of those in the GAK were members of the GPII, and Saleh Ibrahim was then using a car belonging to an official of the Masjumi's Jakarta office,[59] Sukarno's initial reaction was to believe that some influential Masjumi leaders were behind the assassination attempt. This conviction gave impetus to the already-considerable antagonism between him and this major Islamic party, contributing to the mounting political polarization in the country. Only later, after clear proof emerged of major CIA support to the dissident colonels in Sumatra and Sulawesi, was Sukarno convinced that the agency had played a decisive behind-the-scenes role in the Cikini affair.

Whether or not the CIA did in fact play any such part in the attempt to assassinate Sukarno remains unclear, although the release of still-classified United States documents for this period might shed some light on this. One of the more balanced histories of the CIA states: "There is scattered evidence . . . that the C.I.A. was at least in contact with groups who planned to kill Sukarno and Nasser."[60] In any case, eight years later within the U.S. Congress doubts arose as to whether the United States's record was clean.

Serious concern as to possible American involvement in an assassination attempt against Sukarno was evident in the investigations initiated in 1975 by Senator Frank Church, chairman of the U.S. Senate's Select Committee on Intelligence. This was reflected in the still-unreleased text of the testimony given before the committee by Richard M. Bissell, Jr., who had served in the Eisenhower administration, as CIA Director Allen Dulles' deputy director for plans, the office charged with covert operations. But the committee's published report, Alleged Assassination Plots against Foreign Leaders, while dealing with the Congo (Zaire), Cuba, the Dominican Republic, and South Vietnam, eschewed all mention of Indonesia, save for a single Spartan footnote that stated:[61]

> In addition to the plots discussed in the body of this report, the Committee received some evidence of CIA involvement in plans to assassinate President Sukarno of Indonesia and "Papa Doc" Duvalier of Haiti. Former Deputy Director for Plans Richard Bissell testified that the assassination of Sukarno had been "contemplated" by the CIA, but that planning had proceeded no farther than identifying an "asset" whom it was believed might be recruited to kill Sukarno. Arms were supplied to dissident groups in Indonesia, but according to Bissell, those arms were not intended for assassination. (Bissell, 6/11/75, p. 89) [This page reference presumably refers to a still-classified record of Bissell's testimony.]

Details from Bissell's testimony were not released, but the committee was sufficiently interested in the possibility of CIA involvement in assassination attempts against Sukarno that, after this official's appearance, the committee asked several Indonesia specialists to testify before it, including one of this book's authors, who held preliminary discussions with members of its staff. But when the committee—which had been under great pressure from the CIA and Secretary of State Kissinger to drop the hearings—agreed to put in charge of its investigation of events in Indonesia a CIA official who had recently served as the agency's station chief on Taiwan, a thorough investigation could hardly have been expected. It was not altogether surprising, therefore, that, not long after one of this book's authors met with the committee's staff, its operations coordinator phoned on December 23, 1975, to say that a return to Washington would no longer be necessary, since the committee now "chose not to pursue" the question of American involvement in assassination attempts against Sukarno. When pressed as to why, the operations coordinator explained that it was difficult to discriminate "between the actual efforts of carrying out an assassination attempt and those involved in the effort [on the one hand] and the actual authorization for the effort as it involved American authority." No further clarification was forthcoming.

Ambassador Hugh S. Cumming, who headed the Inter-Agency Task Force on Indonesia at the time of Cikini, had a somewhat similar experience. He stated he was "surprised the Church Committee did not ask" him about the affair. He had "fully expected they would—especially in view of their interest in CIA involvement in assassination attempts against Chiefs of State"—and had expected, and prepared himself, to respond to questioning about Cikini.[62]

Whatever the facts, President Sukarno soon came to regard Cikini "as having been masterminded by the CIA" and was sure that Lubis "acted for and was backed by" the agency. And when within a few months Sukarno had clear evidence that the CIA was working with Lubis and the other dissident colonels seeking to displace him, he became fully convinced that the agency had been and remained "out to get him." He apparently continued to hold that conviction until after he was ousted from power some eight years later.[63]

Compromise Efforts Break Down

The growing atmosphere of crisis during December 1957 brought Ambassador Allison to make a final and rather desperate effort to solve the West Irian problem—the issue that he believed lay at the root of Indonesia's disintegrating domestic political situation as well as the increasing strain in Indonesian-American relations. In this effort he recognized that his scope for action had been narrowed as a consequence of the Dulles brothers' strong antipathy toward Indonesia's president. The secretary of state, he recalled, had become "intensely and instinctively suspicious of Sukarno and quite prepared to listen to the Dutch and Australians concerning the proper view to take of Sukarno and Indonesia. . . . He had already written

Sukarno off, and with him Java, as being pro-Communist and eventually Communist controlled; he believed we should and could keep Sumatra free of Communism."[64]

Allison had already laid the basis for a new approach in a cable to Assistant Secretary Robertson on the eve of the expected United Nations rejection of Indonesia's request for negotiations on West Irian. In effect Allison told the Department of State that it had just two possible courses of action: either to continue to work with Sukarno's government—as he preferred—or else to "isolate or get rid of" Sukarno. In his opinion, the middle course he believed the Eisenhower administration to be following would fail. The anti-Sukarno policy, he reckoned, had about a fifty-fifty chance of succeeding "if well thought out and definitely decided upon."[65] Dulles soon made clear that the anti-Sukarno course was the appropriate one, his views being reflected in Assistant Secretary of State Robertson's December 7 cable to Allison:[66]

> Dept has considered Amb Allison's recommendations at high level and concurs that a policy along general lines of course two is desirable. Agree that a middle course is insufficient to halt the trend, and that course two is consistent with NSC's Special Paper on Indonesia. . . . The considered and firm U.S. . . . view is that we *have* reached the point of no return with Sukarno. If he should show signs of turning against Communists, this would probably be only because effective political action by his anti-Communist opponents forced him to do so in order to remain in office. He must at very least be relegated to less dominant position in political scene. Our best opportunities lie with the Masjumi leaders, the right-wing elements of Indo Nat Party, the opposition groups, and the anti-Communist elements in the military and minor parties.
>
> Our immediate objective is the formation of a government in Indonesia supported by the major political parties and the opposition group, which would be sufficiently strong to halt the present [sic] towards Communist domination and eventually reverse it. Our active support should be engaged in this endeavor.
>
> In view of the foregoing, we are not prepared to provide military equipment to the present government, nor are we prepared to consider greater economic aid. . . . If a new regime satisfactory to us is formed, we would promptly negotiate these points.

During the second and third weeks of December an unhappy Allison sought as best he could to follow these guidelines, working together with the head of the State Department's Division of Southeast Asian Affairs, Gordon Mein, who was sent to Jakarta on December 11, rather than have the ambassador return to Washington—as Allison had requested.[67] If he had been welcomed in Washington Allison could have gotten a fuller understanding of the covert-level approach to Indonesia being carried out by Cumming and his interagency committee on Indonesia. Undoubtedly Mein knew much more about this level of policy than did Allison, but he nevertheless had strongly supported the ambassador's plea that at least token amounts of U.S. military equipment and spare parts be provided the Indonesian armed forces, and there is reason to believe he supported Allison's fresh effort along the track of open diplomacy.[68] Indeed, the embattled ambassador continued to feel that, while Mein was privy to much more of covert policy than the Jakarta embassy, he probably was making an honest attempt to support him.[69] It should be noted that at this point Allison still had received no more than a brief résumé of the ad hoc committee's recommendations, did not know whether they had ever been approved, and did not know the identity of the members of the committee.[70]

Before it became clear to Sukarno that CIA agents were working with the dissident colonels and that he was personally an object of the Eisenhower administration's enmity, he had come to see the modernist Islamic Masjumi as his most formidable opposition. And in fact that party's leaders, aware of the Indonesian president's mounting antipathy against them and convinced he was wrecking the economy, began in December to maneuver, together with the right wing of the nationalist PNI, to displace the Djuanda cabinet with one less amenable to Sukarno's influence. The embassy strongly encouraged this move and did its best to procure the United States's active encouragement of it. Thus, Allison cabled on December 20:

> Gordon Mein and I believe we should be prepared immediately upon formation of new govt to offer economic and military assistance and most important be able to give new govt some assurance that we would use our influence to get talks with Netherlands opened.

Allison suggested—probably unrealistically—that the talks could initially be confined to economic matters: "We believe that a more conservative govt might be able to hold ground locally if talks were opened even if it was not specifically stated that they were dealing with New Guinea."[71] But in fact he expected that the Indonesians would be made to understand that the talks would ultimately deal with West Irian.[72]

Only a few days before this, Mein had met with Masjumi leader Sjafruddin Prawiranegara—the governor of the Bank of Indonesia who had openly opposed the takeovers of foreign properties—and with the right-wing PNI leader and economist Lukman Hakim about their plans to establish a new government. Mein cabled Assistant Secretary Robertson that Sjafruddin had told him that anti-Communist elements were negotiating for the formation of a strong government that would replace the existing cabinet "and would stand up to Sukarno." When Sjafruddin asked Mein if the United States would be prepared to assist such a government if it came to power, Mein indicated that this might be possible.[73] Mein told Sjafruddin and the right-wing PNI leader Hardi, Allison recalled, that Mein would soon return from Washington with "detailed recommendations."[74]

But, as the embassy had already reported, the Cikini affair had damaged the cause for those seeking a "middle of the road government which would be able to hold loyalty of the dissident elements in the regions and the non-Communist forces generally." Embassy officials expected that the government in Jakarta would now take a stiffer stand against opposition groups both in Java and the regions. They also predicted that repercussions from the affair would make it "more difficult, if not impossible, for Hatta to continue his strong stand against Sukarno's policies and actions. In the name of patriotism and as a good Indonesian, Hatta may very well find himself deprived of much of his former leverage."[75] This evaluation was fairly prescient. The Masjumi-right-wing PNI effort to establish a middle-of-the-road government never developed real momentum, and the United States appears never to have given it serious backing, while knowledge of the attempt further alienated Sukarno.

In the last part of December, a campaign of harassment was mounted, with Sukarno's acquiescence and probable encouragement, against Mohammad Natsir, chairman of the Masjumi, and Sjafruddin Prawiranegara. Newspapers close to Sukarno, the left wing of the PNI, and the PKI attacked their patriotism and accused them of being involved in the Cikini assassination attempt. Natsir's nephew, also charged with involvement, was arrested in the Masjumi chairman's house, while both leaders received a series of abusive phone calls and paramilitary elements jeered at them from the street. When Natsir and another prominent Masjumi leader, Mohamad Roem, protested to the attorney general, he indicated that only President Sukarno could restrain those mounting the campaign. In the face of these actions, Natsir and Sjafruddin finally concluded that, for the time being at least, they and their families would be safer in Sumatra than in Jakarta.[76] A third Masjumi leader, former prime minister Burhanuddin Harahap, hearing that he was slated for arrest in connection with the Cikini affair, had already departed for Sumatra in early December.[77] Sjafruddin left with his family for South Sumatra, in late December, moving from there to Palembang and later to Padang. Natsir arrived with his family in Medan on January 6 and then went to Padang, where he met with both Sjafruddin and Burhanuddin. Zulkifli Lubis, in the aftermath of the Cikini assassination attempt, had already fled to Sumatra, gaining asylum first in South Sumatra with his friend Major Nawawi, chief of staff in Barlian's South Sumatra Command, and then with Colonel Husein in Padang.

Prime Minister Djuanda reported on December 20 that Sukarno, still badly shaken by Cikini, was a "very sick man" on the verge of a nervous breakdown. The government had, therefore, agreed that the president should take a vacation abroad of "at least 3 or 4 weeks and perhaps longer, depending on his health."[78] Sartono, the widely respected speaker of parliament and a centrist PNI leader, was sworn in as acting president. His function was largely ceremonial, and the actual running of the government was left primarily in the hands of Djuanda and Nasution, with assistance from Subandrio, the foreign minister. After a delay in plans, Sukarno finally left the country on January 6, 1958, on a month-long rest cure—something these three officials felt he badly needed and strongly encouraged.[79]

$$\cdot \; \cdot \; \cdot \; \cdot \; \cdot$$

By the end of December, it being clear that Washington would not provide advance encouragement to elements of the Masjumi-PNI to replace the Djuanda cabinet, and in view of their inability to develop any real political momentum on their own, Ambassador Allison cabled the Department of State that he had lost hope in the capacity of these Indonesians or Hatta to succeed in such an effort.[80] The political middle ground had shrunk—having been heavily eroded by American policies that served to encourage and whet the ambitions of the rebellious colonels, raising their expectations of American support to a level that was incompatible with any viable compromise with Jakarta. Certainly by January 4, when Allison was stunned by news of his imminent transfer to Prague, it was clear that the United States had not only eschewed efforts at reconciliation between Jakarta and the dissidents on Sumatra and Sulawesi but was relying on a covert policy from which it had consciously excluded its ambassador.[81]

6. The Rebels Challenge Jakarta

Escalation of Covert United States Support

By THE FALL of 1957 the United States had decided to back the rebel colonels in their efforts to supplant or change the Jakarta government but had not yet determined the extent of the support it would offer and how open its backing would be. For their part, during the last three months of 1957 the rebels—with funds from the American government, monies raised by Sumitro from business and various governmental sources abroad, and income already being garnered by the dissident colonels from smuggling copra, rubber, and other products—had been purchasing a considerable quantity of weapons and jeeps abroad and had generally strengthened their military position vis-à-vis Jakarta.

Beginning in early October the CIA had started turning over funds to Colonel Simbolon—first in Bukittinggi (following his earlier contact with the agency) and soon thereafter in Singapore. At the meeting in Bukittinggi on October 3 or 4, Simbolon was given $50,000, which he said he needed to feed the 300-400 troops that had accompanied him there from Medan. Shortly afterward, he received instructions from the CIA to go to Singapore, as did the senior CIA officer stationed in Medan. There, according to this officer, Simbolon and the subordinate officers who accompanied him "played up the anti-Communist act because they knew we were interested in that." Simbolon told the CIA officials there that his Padang group was "intending to rebel against the Jakarta government and that they needed money and arms." The CIA station in Singapore then cabled this information to Washington and was quickly authorized to tell Simbolon that he would get both. Before he left Singapore he was given "more money and the promise of arms delivery to Padang." Arrangements were also made to have some of his entourage remain in Singapore for training in radio communications. "I remember," states the CIA officer who had accompanied Simbolon, that "he left happy." Thus began a process whereby "over the next five months the US provided the rebels in Sumatra with arms for 8,000 men"—in addition to much smaller amounts believed to have been supplied by the British and substantial additional arms the rebels purchased abroad on their own.[1]

Initially at least, the U.S. arms were supplied to the rebels with considerable discretion. For example, a U.S. Isthmian Line freighter bound from the United States to Thailand, with a large supply of modern U.S. arms aboard, was boarded by Colonel Husein's agents in late November or early December when the ship docked at Dumai, a port under his control on the east coast of Central Sumatra, ostensibly simply to unload pipes for oil operations. Their confiscation of this arms shipment officially destined for Thailand elicited no known protest from the Thai government, from United States officials, or from American shipping circles, and Indonesians privy to the episode do not question that it was the American government's intent that these arms go to Colonel Husein's forces.[2] The *New York Herald Tribune* correspondent Keyes Beech, on running into this account during a visit to Padang in late 1957, checked it out later with a CIA friend in Bangkok and was told: "This isn't the first time that sort of thing has happened in Sumatra."[3]

During November and December of 1957 there was a considerably greater influx of modern U.S. weapons, financed by the United States and delivered to rebel-held ports by commercial freighters and over the beach by U.S. submarines.[4] Especially effective in eluding Jakarta's intelligence were the U.S. Navy's nighttime deliveries of tons of arms and ammunition via submarine to the small port of Painan, some twenty miles south of Padang. The submarines were also useful in taking out some of Husein's soldiers (he recalls that these totaled about fifty) for special training in communications and weaponry at American military facilities on Okinawa, Saipan, and probably Guam. Later another twelve soldiers were taken out, equally removed from the sight of Jakarta's intelligence agents, by a U.S. Catalina flying boat that landed on Lake Singkarak, some thirty miles northwest of Padang.[5] Solution of the problem of discreetly bringing in large quantities of heavier arms was pioneered in December when a freighter from Taiwan left a barge (apparently acquired up the coast in Aceh) laden with weapons off the coast not far out from Padang, which was then picked up by Colonel Lubis's old aide Saleh Ibrahim and towed by his powerful speedboat into the coast near Padang.[6]

Apparently not until January of 1958 were arms less discreetly delivered by airdrops from airfields in the Philippines, Taiwan, Thailand, and Malaya—some of the planes flying directly and some via Singapore's Changi airport.[7] According to the veteran Southeast Asian correspondent Dennis Bloodworth, then stationed in Singapore, the pattern was for these planes to drop their arms in Sumatra and then repair to British fields at Singapore for refueling before returning to their home bases.[8]

All this pertained to the first, already agreed upon, phase of American intervention—the building up of the military strength of the dissident military leaders on Sumatra and Sulawesi. It took longer, however, to reach a clear decision as to whether the United States should embark on a more direct involvement and provide air cover to the rebels as well as pre-position U.S. naval elements for deployment as needed. As of November 29, the Eisenhower administration was still undecided regarding this level of intervention, as is clearly indicated in Secretary of State Dulles's phone call on that day to his brother, Allen, head of the CIA, pressing him to act while the United States still had strong "assets" in Indonesia. (The secretary had one of his office personnel listen in and take notes on many of his most important phone calls.) The record of this exchange recorded, among other things, the following:

> The Sec [John Foster Dulles] said what was happening was that one by one they were gradually being eliminated. Our assets were gradually shrinking. Today we have substantial assets with which to deal. We will, however, have only half of those assets six months from now. AWD [Allen W. Dulles] said we had been held up because of the duality of policy. We haven't reached a firm policy decision. He said they were working on this and would come in a day or two with specific recommendations. Sec. said how important it was to have some world developments that were definitely favorable. This thing might be it.[9]

Within a week, the impasse clearly had been overcome, probably because the Indonesian takeover of Dutch properties provided a stronger rationale for the United States to take further action. A new forward policy involving major direct American intervention was set in train, even though its implementation was initially aborted because of a lack of access to the necessary forward staging area at Singapore.

The United States's decision to adopt this more open policy of intervention was indicated in Secretary Dulles's telephone conversations with President Eisenhower and "a military man":

> *Telephone call with the President Dec. 7, 1957, 5.53 p.m.*
> Re the situation in Indonesia
>
> *Telephone call with a military man 5.57 p.m.*
> They discussed sending some ships out—but the Sec does not want to be conspicuous. The Sec said AWD will be in touch after talking with Herter, Murphy or Jones . . . they may want it on a smaller scale. The Pres. mentioned having some amphibious equipment.

That same day substantial U.S. naval units had been put on four hours' notice to move from the Philippines toward Indonesian waters. Assembled at Subic Bay and led by the cruiser *Princeton*, the task force then sailed south, carrying elements of the Third Marine Division and at least twenty helicopters.[10] The urgency felt was evident in Chief of Naval Operations Admiral Arleigh Burke's orders of December 7 (7:39 pm) to CINCPAC Admiral Stump:

> Indonesian situation may become critical. Sail under command of flag officer not COM7thFLT one cruiser one destroyer division all U.S. amphibious forces available Philippine area with embarked Marines plus necessary logistic forces.

Keep out of sight of land if at all practical. Forces to be prepared any contingency including evacuation U.S. personnel and landing Marines to protect U.S. lives and property in Indonesia especially Java and Sumatra.

Make movements as inconspicuous as possible. Do all possible to avoid comment by shore based personnel and news media. If queried force on training exercise in South China Sea.

Sail force and detachments cruiser and desdiv proceed at 20 kts others maximum sustained speed. Do not put in at any port.

Be prepared sail *Kearsarge* and one desdiv for additional support if ordered.[11]

Effective implementation of these orders for deployment of this large task force required use of Britain's naval base at Singapore and less restrictive use of the military airport there. Permission for such access took time—more than impatient American senior officials seem to have anticipated. In considerable measure this was because of the delicate political situation then facing the British in Singapore.[12]

In April 1957, when Malaya was given full independence, Britain had granted Singapore limited independence (excluding internal security, defense, and foreign policy). But Lim Yew Hock, the Singapore prime minister who, along with four other leaders (including People's Action party head Lee Kuan Yew), signed the agreement with the British, was under siege by his political opponents for aligning himself too closely with British policy. Indeed, Lee Kuan Yew had already taken advantage of these tactics in his attacks on Lim Yew Hock as "a colonial stooge." During the first weeks of December 1957 the election campaign for Singapore's City Council was especially volatile. Conditions became only moderately more stable after December 21, when Lee Kuan Yew's party won a decisive plurality of the votes, garnering almost twice as many as Lim Yew Hock's party. In this competition for power, few contestants felt any particular sympathy for Indonesia's rebellious colonels, and all felt the need to lean over backward vis-à-vis British foreign policy—covert or overt—to avoid attacks from their competitors that they were not sufficiently independent of Britain. In the words of a high-level British security officer, active during this period:

Singapore was internally in turmoil; domestic politics were heated and effervescent. Left wing students and labor strongly influenced politics and would have been sympathetic to the left in Indonesia. The PAP [People's Action party] would have been more partial to the left wing in Indonesian politics than to the rebels. . . . Thus the British would fear that any overt support to the rebels would give local parties in Singapore another stick to beat the British with.[13]

All this meant that the British, still responsible for Singapore's defense and foreign policy and worried about their ability to control internal security, had to be extremely cautious and quiet about extending air and naval base facilities to the United States—then regarded as a "nefarious imperialist power" by most politically active Singaporeans.

The U.S. naval task force reached "a point approximately 500 miles north of Sumatra,"[14] before it was realized that the British would not permit it to be based on Singapore—a condition essential for its effective operation. The whole exercise displayed a lack of foresight and political preparation, especially an absence of good intelligence regarding Singapore's internal politics and a remarkably complacent assumption that Britain would, without prior agreement, obligingly cooperate. London's unwillingness to do so was soon clear to an evidently much surprised Eisenhower administration. The flavor of this is reflected in the secretary of state's log of phone conversations during the operation with the CIA director and senior State Department officials:

> *Telephone call to Allen Dulles, Dec. 8, 10.10 a.m.*
> . . . Sec asked if we brought the pressure of the Dutch and Australians on the British. Sec asked what was the explanation of the British attitude. Sec said if this thing goes on the way it is we will have something across there which will be pretty bad.
>
> *Telephone Call to Governor Herter [Under Secretary of State] December 8, 10.16 a.m.*
> Re Indonesia situation. Sec asked if he had talked more to [Admiral] Burke last night. They are not moving down toward Singapore? You thought it was not wise to have them move down to Singapore? Sec asked what we were doing with the British. Sec said AWD [Allen W. Dulles] was very disturbed because the British at Singapore were taking a very negative attitude and blocking his efforts. . . . *Sec said what he would like to do is see things get to a point where we could plausibly withdraw our recognition of the Sukarno government and give it to the dissident elements on Sumatra and land forces to protect the life and property of Americans; use this as an excuse to bring about a major shift there.* Sec said we may never have a better opportunity. Sec said he would have thought it was wise to get something down there; it would take 2 or 3 days. Sec mentioned a transport with amphibious possibilities; that would be slower moving but would contain more useable elements than naval vessels. Sec said when he spoke to the President yesterday he spoke of having near there some amphibious possibilities so if need be they could move in to protect Americans. Sec asked if they were near there? Sec asked how long they could stay at sea. [emphasis added]
>
> *Telephone Call to Mr. Cumming. Dec. 12, 10.46 a.m.*
> C replied there is nothing the Sec needs to know before he goes [presumably to the NATO meeting in Paris]. Indonesia bubbles along the same. C hopes the Sec will get the British with us in Indonesia. MI6 wants to move and cooperate with CIA and Caccia is pushing this [Sir Harold Caccia was Britain's ambassador to the United States].

Jakarta Asserts a Twelve-Mile Limit

If there was a final precipitating development that brought Britain into alignment with the United States on policy toward Indonesia, it was undoubtedly the unexpected announcement by the Djuanda cabinet on December 13 that Indonesia was moving from a three- to a twelve-mile limit for its territorial waters and embracing the archepelagic geopolitical principle.

In anticipation of the upcoming Geneva Conference on the Law of the Sea (scheduled to begin February 24, 1958), this change would make it easier for Jakarta's tiny navy and air force to reduce the government's loss of revenue due to smuggling of export crops to Singapore by the regional military commanders in Sulawesi and Sumatra, as well as facilitate interdiction of arms shipments to them. Prime Minister Djuanda's announcement of his cabinet's decision was certainly a departure from the status quo. Referring to the "Indonesian archipelago" as "an entity" it affirmed that

> all waters around, between and connecting, the islands or parts of islands belonging to the Indonesian archipelago irrespective of their width or dimension are natural appurtances of its land territory and therefore an integral part of the inland or national waters subject to the absolute sovereignty of Indonesia. The peaceful passage of foreign vessels through these waters is guaranteed as long as and insofar as it is not contrary to the sovereignty of the Indonesian state or harmful to her security. The delineation of the territorial sea, with a width of 12 nautical miles, shall be measured from straight base lines connecting the outermost points of the islands of the Republic of Indonesia.[15]

This Indonesian move raised an important new strategic issue of immediate concern to Australia, Britain (and Malaya and Singapore), as well as to the United States. Their strong affinity of interest in this matter could not help but promote a closer alignment in their approach to Indonesia. Prodded by the U.S. Navy, the Department of State, now quickly joined by the British, on December 28 formally protested Djuanda's announcement.[16] It was clear that Jakarta's assertion of sovereignty over adjacent territorial waters could not only have threatened the viability of the Singapore and Malacca Straits but could also have led to Indonesia's interdiction of the important Lombok, Sunda, and Makassar Straits. Malaya and Singapore, being directly affected, joined in the protest. In spite of U.S. urging, the Philippines could not do so, for it had already itself, two years before, announced a similar twelve-mile limit. Indeed, the United States's prior tacit acquiescence to the Philippine claim made it awkward to protest subsequent parallel action by Indonesia. But Indonesia's much greater size and more strategic positioning—lying athwart all the main passages from the Pacific to the Indian Ocean north of Australia—presented a more serious problem for the U.S. Navy. The threat appeared all the greater because, while the Philippines was an American ally, linked by a mutual defense treaty and regarded as friendly to the United States, Indonesia was not an ally and its possible course of action could not be predicted.[17]

It now took only a little longer than a week to get the British aboard with respect to utilization of their naval and air facilities in Singapore. On December 16 at the NATO Heads of Government meeting in Paris, Dulles broached the question with Prime Minister Harold Macmillan, who promised a quick response. In the discussions that extended to December 19 the United States provided assurances that appear to have overcome British anxieties. The talks concluded with the establishment on December 23 of a "joint operational working group on Indonesia" with the rather Spartan mandate "to exchange information and consider courses of action." Records of those discussions have not been made available from State Department files, but Ambassador Howard Jones in preparing his book *Indonesia: The Possible Dream*, copied some of the most pertinent documents relating to them.[18] The still-unpublished retrospective account that Jones, while deputy assistant secretary of state, prepared for Secretary Dulles some seven weeks after the December 19-23 meetings, provides a fairly clear picture:[19]

> In talks last December with British and Australians, U.S. objective was to obtain from British the "maximum accommodation for our operational requirements". Meeting revealed British objective was to get firm statement of U.S. policy towards Indo as they seemed to fear U.S. policy was for a fragmentation of the country.
> In course of meeting we explained we envisaged two-pronged operation in Indo: first designed to bring about new government on Java by encouraging non- and anti-Communist elements to cooperate with each other in face of PKI threats; at same time, both to reinforce non- and anti-Communist elements on Java and assure a fall back position should Java be lost, and explained we were giving some support to dissident Colonels in outer islands. Explanation seemed reassuring to British, and we were promised the maximum use of Singapore for operations, keeping in mind no arms shipments to dissidents would come thru that port, that knowledge of British consent to our operations be tightly held, and neither it nor our operations become subject of pol. comment in Singapore.

In Jones's minutes of the organizational first meeting of this joint American-British operational working group on Indonesia on December 23, no reference was made to the U.S. Navy's frustrated move south some two weeks earlier. The groundwork for a more effective second attempt had, however, clearly been laid in the discussions held a few days before the December 23 meeting. There the U.S. representatives, of whom Jones was one, stated that the United States was "not writing off Java," but since the non-Communist forces were stronger in the Outer Islands, especially Sumatra, "we consider [the] most promising approach at this time lies in exploiting potential political and economic resources available in the Outer Islands," employing "all feasible covert means to strengthen will and cohesion" of anti-Communist forces there, "with two objectives: 1) to affect through their strength [the] situation in Java and 2) to provide a rallying point if the com[munists] should take over Java." But *if the "situation on Java continues to deteriorate"* then the United States would *"move to more forthright means"* (emphasis added).[20]

The way was now clear to base the U.S. Navy and Marines openly on Singapore and its anchorages and to make discreet use of its military airfield.

· · · · ·

From the beginning of January 1958 the actions of the dissident colonels on Sumatra were marked by a sense of great urgency. Sukarno had departed from the country on January 6, for a wide-ranging international tour aimed both at recouping his health and securing international support for Indonesia's claim to West Irian. In Washington, CIA chief Allen Dulles "speculated that Sukarno might be making this extensive trip in order to permit certain changes to be made in the Government of Indonesia without loss of face for Sukarno himself."[21] And the dissidents felt sure that during the president's absence the Djuanda government would be more likely to succumb to their pressure. Several of them argued that they should take preemptive actions before Sukarno returned and Jakarta had time to consolidate opposition to them.

The Rebels' Sungai Dareh Conference

South Sumatra commander Barlian had been hoping for some compromise between the dissident colonels and Chief of Staff Nasution, and he pinned his hopes on a possible meeting between the two sides on the island of Bangka, off Sumatra's east coast, in December or early January. Plans for this meeting foundered in part because of Nasution's insistence that only military leaders with actual commands should be present, which would have excluded Simbolon and Lubis.[22] In addition, both sides were presumably awaiting the outcome of a power struggle in South and Central Kalimantan (provinces of Indonesian Borneo), which had reached a critical stage at the end of December when some military and civilian leaders were intent on taking steps to join Sumatra and Sulawesi in demanding greater autonomy. (Not until the beginning of January did Nasution's local supporter, Colonel Hassan Basry, with the backing of locally stationed Javanese units, manage to end this threat to Jakarta's dominance.)[23]

When it was clear that a Bangka meeting with Nasution would not mate-
rialize, Barlian called for a gathering at Sungai Dareh in the southernmost
part of West Sumatra on January 9-10, a meeting that he originally planned
to be limited to Husein, Sumual, and himself.[24] By now, however, Simbolon
had asserted a dominant position among the Sumatra rebels, and he clearly
overruled Barlian, later claiming that it was he who "summoned the military leaders"—Husein, Sumual, Barlian, Dahlan Djambek, and Zulkifli
Lubis—to Sungai Dareh.[25] Also present was Major Alamsyah, formerly an
intelligence officer in South Sumatra who had participated in its Garuda
Council but who was now more closely tied to Nasution than the others
attending the conference knew at the time and who later reported the discussions to him.

At Sungai Dareh, these military leaders were joined by several prominent
civilians—not only the colonels' close associate, former finance minister
Professor Sumitro, but also the three newly arrived prominent Masjumi
leaders—former prime ministers Burhanuddin Harahap and Mohammad
Natsir and former governor of the Bank of Indonesia, Sjafruddin
Prawiranegara. A few days before the Sungai Dareh meeting Burhanuddin
and Sjafruddin had met in Palembang with Barlian, who invited them to
attend. In earlier discussions with the colonels, these two Masjumi politicians had opposed the extent of confrontation with Jakarta reflected in the
colonels' plans, and when Natsir arrived in Padang on January 8 his
Masjumi colleagues asked him to accompany them to Sungai Dareh to
strengthen their hand against the army officers.

Sungai Dareh was still regarded as primarily a military conference. The
army leaders had met in an initial session the night before to discuss what
they termed "purely military technical" problems, to which the Masjumi
leaders were not invited, and only on the following day were the civilians
allowed to participate.[26] Over the next few weeks the three Masjumi leaders
and Dr. Assaat, a respected nonparty civilian leader close to Hatta who had
now joined them, gradually learned the nature of these "military technical
matters" to which initially the colonels and Sumitro alone were privy.[27]
They discovered that the colonels already had well-developed contacts and
sources of funding and supply abroad, especially with the CIA, and had
been promised more, including air cover. The military leaders, Natsir
recalled, had "logistical cards and cards relating to their outside contacts
that they kept close to them." He found that "an outside power" had provided the colonels with sophisticated radio communications that gave them
"better contact with the world outside than they ever could have had in
Jakarta." Sjafruddin stated that they had not known of "Husein's previous
CIA contacts," and he observed, with visible annoyance, "We were left
completely in the dark with respect to his daily telegraphic contact with
Singapore," the CIA's major headquarters for covert U.S. operations in the
area."[28] Natsir realized the seriousness of American support to the colonels

when they arranged for a man they identified as the American consul in Medan to come down to Padang for a private lunch with him. At this lunch, Natsir states, the man told him to wait just one week and there would be an air drop of weapons. Precisely a week later the air drop occurred.[29] This demonstration undoubtedly helped convince the Masjumi leaders that the colonels were not exaggerating their claims of American backing.

In formulating the final decisions of the Sungai Dareh conference, at least some of the colonels felt the need for civilian backing, while the political leaders, fearful that the military would push for a separatist solution, welcomed an opportunity to dissuade them from this course. Although the military leaders still deny it, apparently some of them were prepared to contemplate a separate state of Sumatra that, temporarily at least, could secede from Indonesia, and the central government contended that this was their aim.[30] But the weight of the opinion of Natsir, Sjafruddin, and Burhanuddin tipped the scales decisively against the proponents of secession. The Masjumi leaders were not necessarily opposed to the formation of a countergovernment, but as *Time* correspondent James Bell accurately reported: "Unlike the military leaders, Sjafruddin and Natsir wish to move slowly. Forming an emergency government would not be easy since it must be broad enough to represent all of Indonesia and not just Sumatra since it must not appear to be a separate government." They felt that "civil war must be prevented and nothing rash should be done until all possible steps have been taken to replace Djuanda with Hatta."[31] They also stipulated that the rebels must be prepared to rejoin the central government, if it succumbed to rebel pressure and changed its nature and composition. Colonel Lubis argued forcefully for a government dominated by the military, "a military dictatorship," as the civilians in the conference interpreted it. To counter this, the three Masjumi leaders found it all the more difficult not to pledge their participation in an all-Indonesian countergovernment were it established.[32]

Possibly as a compromise between the two positions, shortly after the Sungai Dareh Conference both sides supported formation of a single all-embracing council—the Dewan Perjuangan (Struggle Council). This council, with Husein as its chairman and Padang as its headquarters, subsumed all the regional councils including Central Sumatra's Dewan Banteng, South Sumatra's Dewan Garuda, and the Sulawesi-based Permesta.[33] Even though their own positions at Sungai Dareh had been relatively restrained, the three Masjumi leaders realized that by participating in the conference they had crossed a Rubicon and that it would not be possible to return to Jakarta.

It was not only the discord between the aims of the military and those of the Masjumi leaders that made the Sungai Dareh meeting so inconclusive. In addition, the South Sumatra commander, Colonel Barlian, refused to commit himself to supporting establishment of a countergovernment,

wanting first to return to Palembang to consult with his military and civilian supporters there. His reluctance prevented any consensus among the
participants regarding concrete plans for action. This vacillation must have
been intensely frustrating to those rebel leaders—Sumitro and Simbolon
and possibly Sumual and Lubis—who apparently were attempting to coordinate their activities with those of the Americans. Actual agreement, with
Barlian's concurrence, was achieved only on three vague principles: "facing
Sukarno, anti-communism, and reconstruction of the daerah [regions]."[34]
Beyond that, the colonels had decided to continue to "exploit the weaknesses of the Central Government" and now make anticommunism "the
main issue." The only other steps proposed were at the regional level,
namely, to establish an all-Sumatra military command, improve interregional coordination, and increase regional economic and financial power in
anticipation of a severance of relations with the central government.

Evidently anxious to reassure their foreign backers, the military leaders
took advantage of the presence in Padang of *Time* correspondent Jim Bell,
who would soon visit the U.S. embassy in Jakarta, to convey their message.
Referring to the Sungai Dareh conference, Simbolon told him that "all military leaders at the meeting, except Barlian, are ready to move now and
want to take action before the end of January," because they had learned
that "the Djuanda cabinet has decided to get tough by the end of February"
when Jakarta would have received arms supplies from Italy and some Eastern bloc countries.[35] (It will be recalled that, after repeated but unsuccessful
efforts to purchase American equipment and spare parts, Nasution had
threatened to turn elsewhere.)

Colonel Barlian's Misgivings

Despite the discord at Sungai Dareh, within eight weeks the rebels issued
their challenge to Jakarta and proclaimed a countergovernment in Padang.
They took these actions despite clear indications of the probable defection
of South Sumatra commander Barlian from their cause. Support from his
region was absolutely pivotal to any realistic expectation that the rebels
could, at least on their own, exert sufficient pressure, either economically or
militarily, on Jakarta to ensure their success. Sjafruddin Prawiranegara had
forcefully argued that if South Sumatra's oil fields and refinery were in their
hands, the rebels would be in a position to cut off oil and gasoline supplies
to Jakarta, denying the government's air force its source of fuel and thus
significantly weakening both the central government's economic position
and its ability to respond militarily to the rebellion. If they controlled these
oil installations, the dissidents believed that the outside world, particularly
those Western countries whose nationals owned these properties, would be
sympathetic enough to their cause to prevent Jakarta from obtaining alternative sources of oil from outside Indonesia.

Barlian's allegiance to the rebel cause was therefore critical to its hopes of success, and soon after the meeting at Sungai Dareh he made it clear that, while he was willing to deny Nasution the use of South Sumatra as a base or staging area for an assault on Central Sumatra, under no circumstances would he go along with either a countergovernment or any open rebellion against Jakarta. On January 21, he stated publicly that he firmly opposed the use of force to achieve any such aim and rejected the idea of forming a separate state, saying that a state of Sumatra, Java, or anywhere else in Indonesia would be unconstitutional and should be condemned.[36] Although Barlian had seemed to go along with the statements of Husein and Sumual until Sungai Dareh, his aims had in fact always been relatively limited. He later affirmed he had been working for greater autonomy for South Sumatra, for its economic development, and for establishment of an Indonesia-wide Senate that would provide greater representation for the regions, but not for a break between Sumatra and Jakarta or any actions that could lead to a civil war in Indonesia.[37]

Barlian's own position was tenuous because of his region's proximity to Java and also because of the large number of Javanese laborers working there and the contingents of Javanese troops stationed in the province. Perhaps most critical, air force troops loyal to Jakarta ringed the only major airfield. It must also be remembered that Barlian had been appointed territorial commander in Palembang only in July 1956 and had narrowly escaped a coup attempt against him in April of the following year.[38] His predecessors as South Sumatra commander had both been Javanese, and many of his subordinate officers still owed loyalty to them. On several occasions Nasution sent these former commanders back to South Sumatra both to keep contacts open with Barlian and to rally as many waverers as possible to the side of the central government.[39] Funds supplied by Jakarta helped them expedite this process through generous bribes. Few of Barlian's officers did, in fact, favor the rebels, and the only senior officer who finally joined them was the battalion commander of Palembang, Major Nawawi.[40]

After the Sungai Dareh conference, Sjafruddin went to Palembang to try to persuade Barlian to go along with the rebels but became convinced that he could not be relied on.[41] In an interview with *Time* in Palembang on January 21, just after his talks with Barlian, Sjafruddin told correspondent Bell that he "had reconsidered the whole problem and had decided that Padang should not move as fast as planned. Sjafruddin agreed that Simbolon's goal was right but said there was a developing conflict between the civilian and military as to the correct means to the end."[42]

Without consulting his military colleagues, Sjafruddin had sent an open letter to Sukarno, dated January 15, and released a week later, that strongly criticized the president's economic and political policies. Here Sjafruddin called on Sukarno to abandon his "fascist concept of guided democracy" and return to a constitutional position within a government led by

"national leaders of proven integrity" such as Hatta and Hamengkubu-
wono (Sultan of Yogyakarta). Although Sjafruddin did not directly
threaten in his letter the formation of a countergovernment, he seemed to
be preparing the ground for a break with Jakarta unless Sukarno accepted
such changes. "We are squarely faced," he said, "with the choice of either
replacing the present government, with a truly national government . . . or
allowing Indonesia to be reduced to the position of Hungary under Janos
Kadar, dependent solely on assistance from Russia."[43] Although Sjafruddin's letter seemed hardly to evoke an atmosphere of compromise, he
reportedly hoped it would induce Sukarno to return to Indonesia and enter
into discussions with Hatta. Masjumi party leaders in Jakarta shared
Sjafruddin's optimism. Thus, Mohamad Roem told a British embassy official that they hoped the letter would cause some resignations from the government, while another Masjumi leader reportedly told a member of the
United States embassy that "Dr. Sjafruddin expected that this letter would
bring the president home from his foreign tour."[44]

On his return to Padang, Sjafruddin—still unaware of the extent of the
colonels' commitments to and the expectations of American agents—
urged these military leaders to halt plans for serving an ultimatum on
Jakarta. He argued that their position was weakened too greatly by Barlian's unwillingness to join them and that, before resorting to an ultimatum,
they should have time to bargain with Sukarno.[45]

American Pressure

As outlined above, since at least October 1957, the United States had been
providing the rebel leaders with tangible support—initially funds, then
weapons as well as equipment and personnel training in communications
and other fields at U.S. Pacific bases in the Philippines (where the Tawi-
Tawi airstrip had been reactivated), Okinawa, and the Marianas. In early
December, at the time the Eisenhower administration was marshaling
American forces for a possible military intervention in Sumatra, Secretary
of State Dulles had expressed his desire to "see things get to a point where
we could plausibly withdraw our recognition of the Sukarno government
and give it to the dissident elements on Sumatra."[46] At American urging, the
British Foreign Office was also looking into the legal aspects involved in
granting "*de facto* recognition of the dissident authorities in Indonesia in
the event that they were to declare themselves independent of the central
Government in Djakarta or as the legitimate government of all Indonesia."
A senior British official concluded at the end of December:

> The central Government in Djakarta, whom we should continue to
> recognise (for the time being, at least) as the *de jure* government of

Indonesia and the *de facto* government of the area which it controlled, would not, I think, have any valid legal grounds for complaint if we recognised the dissident authority as the *de facto* government of the area under its control—assuming, of course, that that authority control was effective and had a reasonable prospect of permanency.[47]

Dulles's desire to accord belligerent status and at least *de facto* recognition to the rebels remained salient in American policy through December and well into the spring of 1958. With the top levels of the American government having taken this position, it is understandable that by January 1958 or earlier American agents were suggesting to the rebel colonels that, once they precipitated a break with Jakarta, they could expect to be accorded belligerent status and at least *de facto* American recognition—a status that would permit open assistance by the United States, Taiwan, and the Philippines.

In an "eyes only" memorandum of January 31, 1958, to the president and secretary of state, Allen Dulles outlined what the CIA viewed as "probable developments in Indonesia."[48] The memorandum stated that "the Padang group probably will deliver its ultimatum to the central government on or about 5 February," though the CIA director thought that "the Padang leaders are still reluctant to take the final step of breaking with Java and possibly causing a civil war." Nevertheless, "if the central government should reject their demands . . . the chances are better than even that the Padang group would break with Java and establish a 'Provisional Government of Indonesia.'" Evidently unaware of—or else consciously ignoring—Barlian's probable defection, the assessment stated that "the group of provincial army leaders, Hussein, Barlian, and Sumual, plus Simbolon, Djambek, and Lubis, seem fully united on undertaking some action to force a change in the central government." The memorandum anticipated that the government would respond to the ultimatum by suggesting negotiations and that "the Padang group would probably agree to the government's offer to negotiate." It further stated that "we believe that the chances are better than even that Sukarno will accede to the appointment of a new government," though not one that would meet all the demands of the rebels. If, however, "a full break should occur," the CIA chief was sanguine about the military prospects of the rebels. In addition to being able to count on "the loyalty of the people and of the forces directly under its command on Sumatra and northern Celebes," the rebel government "would probably also have the support of the Atjehnese in northern Sumatra, the Darul Islam forces in South Celebes, the Amboinese and groups in the other Moluccas which support the East Indonesian Republic movement [a movement actually seven years dead], and some elements on Borneo." Even on Java, "at a minimum, the Padang group could probably launch fairly widespread guerrilla warfare," being able to "count on the Darul Islam, the Moslem Youth Group (GPII), possibly some units from the Siliwangi Division in West Java, and some volunteers from the

Masjumi and possibly from the PNI and NU." (Clearly, the CIA was now deep in Alice's Wonderland.)

Thus in foreseeing—and encouraging—proclamation of an ultimatum, the CIA was anticipating that the probable central government response would be toward negotiation and compromise. Even if this were not the case, the agency was confident that the military capacity of the rebels would prevail against the center's military power, at least outside Java.

Moreover, as the CIA well knew, Indonesia was surrounded by countries willing to provide aid and facilities to the rebels—and as noted in the next chapter, Taiwan, the Philippines, Thailand, and Malaya were already doing this. Although the semiautonomous Singapore government maintained a public façade of opposition to British use of facilities there for supporting the rebels, by February 1958 it no longer actually opposed such use.[49] As noted earlier, while the British themselves were initially reluctant to cooperate fully with the United States, after being assured that the goal of American policy was not a fragmentation of Indonesia, they had "promised the maximum use of Singapore for operations," provided no military supplies to the rebels came through there, that their consent be kept confidential, and that neither it nor American operations "become subject of political comments in Singapore"—criteria that in fact were soon largely ignored.[50] The Australian government apparently made Christmas Island available as a forward base for American submarines engaged in supplying and transporting the rebels, and its Defense Department deployed ships to stand off the Sumatran shore to provide logistic and medical support to them.[51] Moreover, Australia's minister of external affairs was soon engaged in an effort, ultimately abortive, to get SEATO to take some sort of action on the rebels behalf.[52]

Rebels Press Ahead

Throughout January and early February political leaders in Jakarta strove to induce the rebels to negotiate a peaceful compromise while simultaneously using the threat these dissidents posed to pressure the government into meeting some of the regional demands. Masjumi leaders in Jakarta were especially active in these efforts. They urged that a new government should be formed there, but neither Djuanda, Hatta, nor Nasution wanted to act while the president was out of the country. Mohamad Roem stressed to Prime Minister Djuanda that Jakarta would have to make concessions if rebellion were to be avoided. In response, the prime minister expressed his willingness to urge Sukarno, after his return, to form a new government, a message Roem carried to the civilian leaders in Padang on January 30.[53] Hatta and Socialist party leader Sjahrir also sent out emissaries to both military and civilian dissident leaders to draw them back from confrontation.[54]

There appeared to be a consensus among the rebels' sympathizers in the capital that many of their aims could be realized so long as they did not press too far—that is, did not serve an ultimatum on Jakarta, did not form a countergovernment, and left room for compromise. It was widely believed that if the situation remained short of an actual break, the central leadership would find it impossible to send Javanese troops against the rebels. According to Hatta, Nasution had twice previously tried to mobilize an expeditionary force against West Sumatra, but in each case the military commanders in Java had refused to cooperate.[55] And the Sultan of Yogyakarta now sent a message to the rebels in Padang that, on the basis of his discussions with the commanders of the East and Central Java divisions, he was convinced that none of their troops would be sent to Sumatra unless a countergovernment was proclaimed.[56]

Nevertheless, the military leaders and Sumitro had apparently already decided to pursue a confrontation with the central government, and were prepared to ignore the defection of Barlian, any moderating influence from the Masjumi leaders who had joined them, or any moves by Jakarta toward a partial compromise.

A number of factors, in addition to their foreign commitments, influenced the rebels in pressing forward with what appears in hindsight to have been a disastrous course, rather than move less precipitately toward obtaining many of their demands. With several of them, considerations of personal advantage clearly weighed heavily. For well over a year Lubis and Simbolon had been aware that their own positions could only deteriorate if a compromise were reached with the central government. Neither had a military command, and a major impulse behind their actions was the rivalry and antagonism between them and Nasution that made it inevitable that they would lose out under any compromise settlement. Lubis's position had become even more tenuous than that of Simbolon, for on January 22, 1958, an order went out to all commanders for his arrest because of his alleged role in connection with the Cikini affair.[57] Simbolon too, as the American consulate in Medan reported, was aware that his own "position [was] deteriorating with Sumatran followers necessitating imminent action," if it were not to be irreparably eroded.[58] Husein still held his military command, but he had achieved the most he could hope for within the context of a Jakarta-controlled Indonesia. He was strongly influenced by Simbolon and Lubis, and also by Djambek, all of whom had been his superior officers during the revolution.[59] Sumitro, having burned his bridges with the Jakarta government, had little to hope for from anything less than a rebel victory. He had now been in exile for nearly a year, and the corruption charges from which he had fled in May 1957 were still pending. He too had been the most outspoken of the rebels in persuading their foreign contacts that under Sukarno Indonesia would inevitably fall into the Communist camp.[60] Among the top rebel military leaders based in Central Sumatra, probably only the devoutly Muslim Colonel Dahlan Djambek was motivated primarily by religious and ideological concerns. The intensity of his religious beliefs and of his anticommunism made him perhaps the most intransigent of the colonels, and he had considerable influence over Husein.

Two other calculations were undoubtedly important in the apparently dogmatic insistence of these rebel leaders on proclaiming an ultimatum and forming a countergovernment. First, they feared the cleverness of their opponents, particularly Sukarno and Nasution, and they were convinced that Sukarno could outwit their sympathizers in Jakarta—Hatta, the Sultan, and Djuanda—and come out on top in any bargaining. If a new government were formed in his absence, they believed, Sukarno could more easily accept it; and his widely acknowledged skill in manipulating domestic politics was, of course, also curtailed while he was away from the scene. They also feared—with some justification—that Nasution, through threats, promises, and bribes, could draw many of the rebels' military supporters to his side. Second, their decisions were clearly affected by wishful thinking. They seem to have persuaded themselves that the government would not dare move against them militarily, and they hoped that, if they acted quickly enough, Barlian, despite his misgivings, would be swept along with them.

However much affected by wishful thinking, the rebels' assessment was no more off the mark than that of numerous reasonably well informed observers. Thus, the British ambassador reported on February 20: "The great majority of the Army in Java is tied down with internal security duties and attempting to control the Darul Islam forces. It is difficult to see how many troops could be spared from Java but, unless the Government is prepared to take the very real risk of large sections of the island, including large towns, falling into control of the Darul Islam, then very few troops indeed could be spared to attack either Sumatra or the Celebes [Sulawesi]."[61]

Finally, even if they were forced to confront Jakarta, the rebels apparently felt that foreign backing would ensure their success. These calculations help to explain the Sumatran dissidents' reluctance to pursue possibilities for a compromise settlement and their insistence on taking a series of rapid steps toward a confrontation with the central government that their civilian supporters regarded as unnecessarily precipitate and provocative.

The Rebel Ultimatum on Jakarta

Shortly after the Sungai Dareh conference the colonels had dispatched envoys from Sumatra to argue their case to foreign audiences. And it was these envoys abroad, notably Sumitro, Warouw, and Sumual, who, together with Simbolon, tried to accelerate the pace of the rebels' actions. In a press release from Geneva on February 2, 1958, Sumitro reported that three days earlier Simbolon had broadcast a belligerent and uncompromising statement over Radio Padang. According to the press release, Simbolon had outlined the rebels' demands and the steps they would take if these demands were not met. He had called on the Djuanda cabinet to resign and on Acting President Sartono to appoint a new cabinet "free from communist influence" led by Hatta and the Sultan of Yogyakarta. He threatened that, if the Djuanda cabinet refused to resign, the rebels "would set up an alternative government for the whole of Indonesia under the Prime Ministership of Sjafruddin Prawiranegara." This new countergovernment would again demand the Djuanda government's resignation, and if this were again refused it would request international recognition as the legal government of the Republic of Indonesia.[62]

It seems unlikely that Simbolon actually broadcast this statement, and Sumitro's press release may have constituted part of a propaganda campaign that the colonels had decided on at the Sungai Dareh conference to which the Masjumi leaders there were not privy.[63] Then four days after this press release, Sumitro announced from Switzerland that Sukarno's government would probably topple within ten days. Sumual, who had gone to Singapore immediately after the Sungai Dareh meetings to try to obtain weapons for the rebels, met in Hong Kong with Warouw, now military attaché in Peking. Together they went to Tokyo, where on February 3 Warouw informed Sukarno, then visiting Japan, of the rebels' intentions, while Sumual told the press that the rebel plan to "save the Indonesian Republic" would be announced from Padang "today or tomorrow."[64] Both colonels then made press statements anticipating a rebel ultimatum to Jakarta several days before it was actually proclaimed.

While they and the colonels in Padang pressed toward an ultimatum, political leaders in Jakarta intensified their efforts to find some formula for a solution short of civil war. In early February, Prime Minister Djuanda sent a message via Roem to the Masjumi leaders in Padang, "pleading with them not to take overt action that could block a compromise." He informed them "that within two weeks after return of Sukarno he would resign and pave way for Hatta-Sukarno government."[65] According to Roem, Djuanda further pledged to use his influence to induce Sukarno to change the membership of the National Advisory Council so that it would be more representative of the regions and function as a sort of "pre-Senate." Roem sensed that the Masjumi leaders in Padang reacted favorably to Djuanda's plea, but they said that they would have to discuss the proposal with their military colleagues. According to Roem, Burhanuddin observed that Djuanda's only actual leverage was his ability to resign and thereby bring about the cabinet's fall, but that this would not ensure that Sukarno would appoint Hatta as the new prime minister.[66]

Throughout early February Sjafruddin, too, continued to argue forcefully against issuing an ultimatum at this time, and he refused to sign it, delaying its proclamation for several days. He was joined in his opposition by several members of the Banteng Council itself, who feared that what had been essentially a move for regional autonomy and better conditions for soldiers and civilians in West Sumatra had assumed a life of its own, with outside forces pushing the movement and its local leaders toward catastrophe. Already some of the Jakarta-based Banteng Council members had shifted their allegiance.[67] Within West Sumatra itself Husein was facing strong opposition to any confrontation with the central government. This came in part from local Socialist party elements who were persuaded by arguments of prominent visiting national leaders of the party. But more threatening for Husein was the opposition from within the Banteng military forces. Three of his battalion commanders — Major Nurmathias, Major Johan, and Major Iskander Martawijaya all opposed any military confrontation with the central government, as did his police chief, Kaharuddin Datuk Rangkayo Basa.[68]

In the face of this pressure, Husein wavered, and none of his broadcasts in the early days of February met the expectations raised by the vociferous rebel spokesmen in Tokyo and Europe. A PSI courier reported from Padang as late as February 8 that "Husein is opposed to proclamation [of a] counter-government until every opportunity [is] exhausted to coerce Sukarno to change his attitude toward Outer Island interests and PKI," adding that Husein "favors allowing Sukarno until beginning March to work out new government in face-saving manner."[69] However, Simbolon, Djambek, and Lubis were exerting counterpressure, and Husein had already cast his lot with them at Sungai Dareh. It must have seemed to him at this time that there was no alternative to a public confrontation. So finally, in the face of Sjafruddin's continuing, adamant refusal to serve the ultimatum, Husein proclaimed it on February 10, 1958, over his own signature alone. He did this with the backing of Simbolon, Lubis, and Djambek, and in his capacity as chairman of the Dewan Perjuangan, which, as above noted, had superseded the Dewan Banteng and subsumed all the regional councils (including Permesta).[70]

The ultimatum formed part of a substantial document titled "Struggle Charter: To Save the State." Simbolon first read an introduction to the charter, giving the rebels' view of the national events that had precipitated their struggle against Sukarno and the central government.[71] President Sukarno and the Communists were there portrayed as the prime movers in leading the Indonesian nation toward disaster. Sukarno was charged with blocking parliamentary democracy, violating the constitution, and using his concept of guided democracy as a cloak for giving the Communists power in the central government. He was accused of having made no attempt to understand the real grievances underlying the regionalist movements and simply trying to suppress them by force. Simbolon asserted that Sukarno's refusal to grant Hatta any real power had undermined all attempts, through such means as the national political and economic conferences (Munas and Munap), to solve the regional and internal military problems on a national basis.

In addition, the charter's introduction attributed the decline of the Indonesian economy partly to the unwillingness of the Djuanda government to solve the problems between Jakarta and the regions and saw the decline as having been accelerated by the precipitate takeover of Dutch enterprises, which it alleged was undertaken at the initiative of the Communist party. Curiously—and very likely so as not to alienate foreign supporters—this statement disapproved of Sukarno's acceleration of the campaign over West Irian, which the military leaders had appeared to support in the Palembang Charter. While internally strengthening the power of the PKI, the charter aserted, the Sukarno regime was, at the international level, breaking off connections with the Western world and leading Indonesia into the Communist bloc. The Djuanda cabinet's de facto authority over the Indonesian archipelago was seen as progressively diminishing, with the number of regions that opposed its authority inevitably growing, raising the imminent danger that these territories would sever their ties with the Republic of Indonesia and pursue their own destinies. "It was not," this introductory statement concluded,

> to surrender our fate to one man who uses his position as President to break all valid laws and violate the basis of democracy, while taking steps that result in destroying the unity of the Republic of Indonesia, it was not for this that we struggled and sacrificed lives and wealth for our independence.

In the charter itself Husein issued a five-day ultimatum, demanding that Sukarno resume his constitutional position and rescind his unconstitutional actions of the past year, that the Djuanda administration return its mandate, and that Hatta and the Sultan of Yogyakarta be appointed to form a new cabinet to hold office until new general elections were held.[72] If these demands were not met, Husein warned, all consequences would be the "responsibility of those that do not comply, especially President Sukarno," and the Struggle Council would respond by taking "prudent steps" (which were not elaborated). He did not, however, yet threaten formation of a countergovernment. As Gordon Mein reported from Jakarta: "The 'or else' portion of the regionalists' demands is not clear," while Masjumi leader Mohamad Roem was reported as regarding the "significant feature" of the Husein broadcast as being the fact that "he stopped short of threatening proclamation [of a] counter-government."[73]

Nevertheless, the rebels' supporters in Jakarta were dismayed at Husein's ultimatum, and the British embassy reported that "even those who approve of most of the rebel objectives consider the ultimatum has been a bad move because it was too forthright and uncompromising."[74]

The government's response was immediate and clear. Neither Djuanda nor Nasution was disposed to postpone action until after Sukarno's return. The cabinet promptly rejected the ultimatum, and on February 12 Nasution dishonorably discharged Husein, Lubis, Djambek, and Simbolon from the armed forces, issuing warrants for their arrest the following day.[75] The government cut all sea, air, and land communications with Central Sumatra and at the same time froze its military command (placing it directly under General Nasution's Central Headquarters). The air force dropped leaflets over Sumatra on February 14 explaining the government's position.

The Rebels Proclaim a Separate Government

On February 15, after the expiration of the five days stipulated in the ultimatum, Husein made a speech over Radio Bukittinggi announcing formation of the Pemerintah Revolusioner Republik Indonesia (PRRI), the Revolutionary Government of the Republic of Indonesia, to serve until a cabinet headed by Hatta and the Sultan of Yogyakarta, Hamengku Buwono, was formed.[76] If "in a suitable period of time" it had become clear that Sukarno was not prepared to return to his constitutional position and to appoint Hatta and the Sultan to head a new cabinet, the PRRI leaders would consider themselves "free from obligatory obedience to Sukarno as Head of State." The declaration stated that the rebels would be ready to hand over power to Hatta and the Sultan whenever the two agreed either to assume leadership of the countergovernment or to form a new cabinet in Jakarta with guarantees that this cabinet would observe the ideals set out in the struggle charter. Husein listed the following as members of the PRRI cabinet: Sjafruddin Prawiranegara as prime minister and minister of finance; Colonel Maludin Simbolon as minister of foreign affairs; Colonel Dahlan Djambek as minister of internal affairs; Burhanuddin Harahap as minister of defense and justice; and Dr. Sumitro Djojohadikusumo as minister of trade and communications. In positions of lesser importance, the cabinet also included several of the Permesta leaders.[77]

Sjafruddin, as PRRI prime minister, then read his government's program.[78] Domestically, its main feature was a wide delegation of powers by this government to the regions, with the center's responsibilities limited to matters of external defense, finance, interisland traffic, justice, education, and the coordination of regional activities. It further called for a change in the leadership of the armed forces, improvement in the living standards of lower-ranking military personnel, and provisions to prevent members of the armed forces from participating in political party activities. Its economic program laid great stress on the development of regional economies and proposed industrialization of Java and other regions of high population density to help overcome the problems of overpopulation.[79]

In foreign affairs, the program called for adherence to an independent foreign policy, with stress on the United Nations as the means for the settlement of disputes, and on close cooperation with other Afro-Asian states. It stipulated that within this framework the struggle for West Irian must be continued "in an orderly and complete manner." It informed the Netherlands that normal relations could not be resumed between it and Indonesia until West Irian was returned and called on Holland to open the door again to a solution of the problem through diplomatic negotiation.

Sjafruddin concluded by guaranteeing the safety of foreign personnel and property in areas controlled by the PRRI so long as the laws and regulations of the revolutionary government were obeyed, and—ironically—he warned outside powers not to interfere in the dispute within Indonesia.

On February 17, Colonel Simbolon, in his capacity as minister of foreign affairs, called on all ambassadors domiciled in Jakarta to report home and for their governments to then send representatives to Padang. On the same day Sjafruddin, as prime minister, ordered the American oil companies in Sumatra to end the flow of oil and oil revenue to Jakarta and cabled the Federal Reserve Bank in New York and the Bank of England to freeze Jakarta's assets.

· · · · ·

After months of maneuvering, then, both the rebels and the Jakarta government had taken decisive actions that within five days had placed them in positions from which it would be difficult to retreat. The dissident leaders had in fact escalated to the level of revolution, by proclaiming a counter-government and by requesting for national and international recognition as the sovereign government for the whole of Indonesia. Sjafruddin and Simbolon sent out envoys to establish diplomatic relations in Western countries and to seek financial aid and credit, as well as to arrange for currency to be printed in London.[80] The directness of this confrontation with Sukarno excluded almost any possibility for compromise, for on his return to Indonesia on February 16 the president was faced either with concurring in his own removal from real power or with consolidating his supporters to defeat the challenge.

The Indonesian public became convinced that there was an American dimension to the now-explicit rebellion when the American secretary of state made a tactlessly partisan public statement on February 11, the day after the rebels' ultimatum. In this, Dulles denigrated the Sukarno government and implicitly approved the actions being taken by the rebels, declaring

We would like to see in Indonesia a government which is constitutional and which reflects the real interest and desires of the people of Indonesia. As you know, there is a kind of a "guided democracy" trend there now which is an evolution and which may not quite conform with the provisional constitution and apparently does not entirely satisfy large segments of the population.

We doubt very much that the people of Indonesia will ever want a Communist-type or a Communist-dominated government.[81]

In Indonesia as well as in the United States, it was generally understood that Dulles's statement was deliberately designed to indicate the Eisenhower administration's support of the rebels and its opposition to the Jakarta government.[82] Foreign Minister Subandrio made a public announcement on February 12 expressing his government's displeasure at Dulles's remarks, and before leaving Tokyo President Sukarno issued a statement that "Indonesia cannot possibly tolerate any interference in our domestic affairs from anyone or from any direction," a remark that "appeared aimed at Dulles' press conference statement."[83] The whole spectrum of the Jakarta press, including the official Masjumi newspaper, *Abadi*, registered outrage at what was uniformly regarded as American interference in Indonesian affairs.[84] The British ambassador, evidently noting this reaction, cabled London that "the Dulles intervention has given an unexpected and valuable weapon" to the Jakarta government.[85]

But Dulles did not alter his posture, reiterating the central points of his theme in hearings before the House Foreign Affairs Committee at the end of February.[86] There he stated that he feared Sukarno's "guided democracy" "would end up to be communist despotism" and that he would be "very happy" to see non-Communist elements "exert a greater influence." And from the Indonesian perspective the U.S. Navy appeared to be joining in on the same chorus, when the Seventh Fleet's Admiral Beakley was reported in the Indonesian press to have announced in Manila that Indonesia was the only chaotic country in Asia and that he would like to see a stable government there.[87]

7. Civil War

THE REBELS' PROCLAMATIONS of February 10 and 15, 1958, set the stage for civil war between the central government and the PRRI. The Eisenhower administration had anticipated this possibility and laid plans to support the insurgents, but, despite the uncompromising nature of their demands and statements, war was not what the Sumatran rebels themselves had expected.

Jakarta's Response

Sukarno returned to Indonesia on February 16, the day after the formation of the PRRI countergovernment. He initially refrained from responding publicly to the rebels' challenge. When he met with former vice president Hatta to discuss the situation on February 19, Hatta told Sukarno that he had two alternatives—either peaceful negotiations, the course that Hatta himself favored, or all-out military action that would probably destroy national unity and whose outcome no one could predict. Hatta proposed a formula under which (1) all parties would return to the constitution; (2) the National Council would be transformed into a sort of presenate by having its members nominated by and representative of the regions; (3) the rebels would withdraw their ultimatum, dissolve the PRRI, and return to the status quo ante of January 1, 1958, with the government declaring an amnesty; (4) Sukarno would form a presidential cabinet with Hatta as prime minister.[1]

As so often before, the two men clashed. Hatta refused to join Sukarno in issuing a public condemnation of the rebels, saying that "though he disapproved the rebels' position, he also disapproved Sukarno's policies which provoked them."[2] Despite their arguments, Hatta left with the impression that Sukarno agreed with his formula, so long as Hatta also resumed his position as vice president as well as that of prime minister (as had been the case in 1948-50). But two days later, on February 21, the president issued a statement praising his government's uncompromising stance against the rebels and asserting that "we must take drastic actions . . . with all the forces in our possession."[3] When, at Hatta's request, the two leaders met again on March 3, Hatta once more thought there had been "a meeting of minds" and that "Sukarno had agreed in broad principle to a compromise."[4]

Hatta and Sukarno were scheduled to meet once more on March 7 to work out the details of the program, but Sukarno postponed the meeting with the excuse that he was still sounding out party leaders. Some of Sukarno's advisers leaked the contents of the compromise proposal to the newspapers *Pemuda* and *Bintang Timur*, which denounced Hatta as a traitor. Feeling Sukarno had been consciously misleading him, Hatta wrote the president on March 9 saying there was no further need to talk.[5] By then the government had decided not to negotiate with the rebels until after military steps had been taken against them.

From this time on Hatta's actions became largely irrelevant to the major confrontation between the regional dissidents and the central government. Disappointed with his refusal to back them, the rebels abandoned any remaining hope that he would be their champion and perhaps future leader.

From the point of view of many of the PRRI leaders, the picture of Hatta that emerged during this period was one of a man unsure and indecisive in meeting the challenges presented by the regional councils and unable to summon the courage to back his belief in greater regional autonomy. From the record of his words and actions after December 1956 when he resigned the vice presidency, however, it seems clear that Hatta was in fact consistently maneuvering to use the leverage provided by the regional dissension so as to regain a position of real power within the Jakarta government—that of prime minister, through which he could deal with the economic and political problems besetting Indonesia, especially the underlying causes of regional discontent. During his years as vice president he had increasingly chafed at the impotence of the position that contrasted so markedly with the political power he had enjoyed during the anti-Dutch struggle. Each time he tried to influence the course of events in the early 1950s, he was reminded that his actions were inconsistent with the role of vice president under the constitution. It seems pretty certain that, when he resigned the vice presidency, it was with the hope, if not the firm expectation, that the parliament, faced with the crisis in the regions, would be compelled to turn to him to restore unity. And indeed, when the second Ali Sastroamidjojo cabinet resigned in March 1957, it looked as if Sukarno would then be forced to call on Hatta to form a new government. By this time, however, Sukarno already had his own vision of the future shape of the Indonesian state and had proclaimed his *konsepsi* of "guided democracy," an idea absolutely alien to Hatta's view of the fitting governmental order for Indonesia. Thus, it was Djuanda, not Hatta, whom Sukarno then appointed as the new prime minister.

Again at the time of the Munas conference in September 1957, Hatta was apparently planning to resume a pivotal role, but his hopes were dashed by the passivity of the regional representatives at the conference. He came to believe that he could then have taken the lead in forming a new political order more in tune with regional demands, had Husein, Sumual, Barlian, and their civilian sympathizers been willing to stand up to Sukarno at that conference.

Through February 1958 Hatta had continued trying to use the leverage provided by the developing rebellion, convinced that Sukarno would be forced to call on him to end the crisis by mediating with the colonels and achieving a compromise solution short of war. This hope, though it continued until Sukarno rebuffed his compromise proposal after these late February meetings, had, in fact, already been seriously undermined by the PRRI declaration of a countergovernment, a government which his legalistic mind would never approve and one that directly challenged Sukarno and Nasution, convincing them they had no alternative to confrontation.

Sukarno was under pressure from some of his closest advisers and from PKI leaders not to take any path of compromise. But they were not alone in urging a military response to the rebels. In the face of the open challenge presented to them by the proclamation of the PRRI government, both Prime Minister Djuanda and Army Chief of Staff Nasution had abandoned their earlier conciliatory posture and now insisted on military actions against the PRRI.[6] Djuanda told Ambassador Jones that "it was only with great reluctance" that Sukarno "yielded to pressure to take military action" and that "he [Djuanda] himself was as much responsible as anyone for military action after [the] ultimatum because, he said, he felt it necessary to establish for all time in Indonesia that open rebellion was not [the] way to accomplish objectives."[7]

Nasution's immediate response to the establishment of the PRRI had been to order the arrest of its military leaders, and he promptly followed this up by outlawing the regional councils—the Garuda Council of South Sumatra, as well as the Banteng and Permesta councils. During his tour around Sumatra in late January, he had come to the conclusion that the commanders in Medan (Gintings) and Palembang (Barlian) were not in the rebel camp and that there was an opportunity to isolate Husein's command in Central Sumatra.[8]

The next day, February 16, on Sukarno's return from abroad, the Djuanda government ordered the arrest of the leading civilian members of the PRRI cabinet (Sjafruddin, Burhanuddin, Sumitro) and demanded that the subordinate cabinet members (Mohammad Sjafei, Saladin Sarumpait, Abdul Gani Usman) and those from Permesta (Warouw, Saleh Lahade, Muchtar Lintang) make clear their loyalty to the Jakarta government. (Natsir was not then a cabinet member.) Permesta leaders responded by declaring their solidarity with the PRRI, and the following day Colonel Somba officially announced from Manado Permesta's full support of the revolutionary government and the severance of its relations with the Jakarta government.[9] In response, Nasution immediately dishonorably discharged Sumual, Somba, and his chief of staff Runturambi and ordered their arrest, together with that of other Permesta military leaders.

After over a year of negotiation and efforts to persuade the military dissidents to compromise, Nasution—backed by Djuanda—now became the driving force behind the forceful actions against them.[10] On February 21, the Indonesian air force destroyed a bridge in Painan on the southern coast of West Sumatra, and the following day bombed Padang and Bukittinggi, the two main towns of West Sumatra, as well as Manado, the capital of Northern Sulawesi, knocking out their radio communications.[11]

This was an initial show of force and intent. But in contrast to the reactions in Jakarta to earlier rebel statements, proclamation of the rebel government and the subsequent bombing produced no flurry of diplomatic activity by PRRI sympathizers there. It seems to have been generally accepted in Jakarta that the crisis had reached the point of no return. With the support of Prime Minister Djuanda, Nasution was mobilizing his forces and formulating his strategy against the rebels. He assigned two of his most loyal subordinates to head the campaign against them: Deputy Chief of Staff Brigadier General Gatot Subroto was appointed to take over command in East Indonesia and Brigadier General Djatikusumo was appointed deputy chief of staff to coordinate the commands in North and Central Sumatra.

Rebel Preparations in Padang

With Nasution's dishonorable discharge of Husein and the other rebel colonels, West Sumatran students and soldiers resident in Java began streaming back to rally to the cause of their home region. One informed estimate was that some 400 students from universities and colleges in Java made their way back to Padang over the next two to three months. There they joined high school and college students from West Sumatra, whom military leaders of the Banteng Council had begun recruiting during late 1957 and who had been given two to three months of military training by regular soldiers of the Banteng division.[12] Additionally some young Minangkabau soldiers, particularly those stationed in Bandung, began arriving in Padang during April to join the rebels.[13]

At the time of the proclamation of the rebel government, Husein and his colleagues arrested many who opposed its formation, together with others whose loyalty they suspected, imprisoning these dissidents in three main West Sumatra detention camps—at Muara Labuh, Situjuh, and Suliki. They had jailed some local Communist leaders beginning in early 1957 shortly after the Banteng Council was formed, and the number of Communist detainees had increased after Dahlan Djambek joined the rebels in August 1957 and established the Gebak (Joint Movement against Communism) in the wake of the Palembang conference. Djambek acknowledged to visiting journalists in February 1958 that he had locked up "two hundred leading leftists in a 'kind of concentration camp.'"[14] By March about 150 prisoners were held in the camp in Situjuh, an unknown number at Suliki, and nearly 400 at Muara Labuh. While most detainees in the first two of these camps were apparently members of the PKI, those in the last were mostly from the Nationalist Communist party (Murba), the Socialist party (PSI), and other non-Communist officials who disagreed with the formation of the rebel government.[15]

The anti-Communist theme had by this time assumed major importance in the rebels' propaganda, particularly to their overseas backers. Salient from the outset in the appeals Sumitro and his lieutenant Roland Liem made to their overseas sympathizers, by the time of the February ultimatum to Jakarta anticommunism dominated the interviews given by most rebel leaders to visiting Western journalists. Thus, Colonel Dahlan Djambek asserted to William S. Stevenson: "We must win American support by emphasizing the Communist danger" and assured James Mossman that "it was important to stress the anti-communist danger in the argument 'so as to interest the Americans'. Naturally our appeal must be made to fit our audience. For the Western powers we stress the very real danger of communism."[16]

Most of the sixty-nine battalions enrolled in the central government's three Javanese divisions (Siliwangi, West Java; Diponegoro, Central Java; and Brawijaya, East Java) were tied down in fighting Darul Islam forces in West Java and South Sulawesi. Nevertheless, by drawing directly on the Diponegoro division, remarshaling elements from the other two Javanese divisions, and adding to these its strategic reserve (especially its elite paratroop units, RPKAD), the central government enjoyed a significant superiority over the less than twenty battalions scattered throughout much of Sumatra and Sulawesi available to the PRRI and Permesta. No more than six of these rebel battalions were under Husein's command in Central Sumatra, and he could be sure of the loyalty of only three of these.[17] Nevertheless, even now neither the rebels nor their outside sympathizers seem to have worried seriously about the threat of military action by the central government. On March 9, *New York Times* correspondent Tilman Durdin reported that "Jakarta lacks the means for anything more than a small land attack or a light naval blockade and harassing air attacks."[18]

There were several reasons for outside observers to underestimate the capacity of Jakarta's armed forces: first was the belief that the central government would not dare to test the loyalty of many of its troops, particularly those in the West and East Java divisions, by asking them to move against the rebels, with many of whose demands they sympathized. And, indeed, during 1957 Nasution had been largely unsuccessful in his efforts to draw further on the three Java-based divisions for service in Sumatra.[19] Second was a perception that government airpower was too weak to be effectively employed;[20] and third was the recollection of the previous botched air actions Jakarta had mounted against Medan and Palembang.[21] In view of Nasution's perceived hesitation and indecisiveness over the previous year, both domestic and foreign observers also underestimated his will and capacity to move against the rebels. They believed, too, that the central government would fear transferring substantial forces from Java and leaving residual forces there vulnerable to attacks from the Darul Islam.[22] They clearly did not take seriously enough Nasution's speech of February 22, 1958, in which he declared that

> If a government allows several of its subordinate Commands to serve an ultimatum on it, and then fulfills their demands, we can appreciate that no future government will be able to stand. It could at any time be served an ultimatum by an army officer. And thus we would no longer have any military norms and state norms. So whatever happens a matter of this kind must be condemned. . . . So it is very clear that no government what-soever that calls itself a government, or Army Chief of Staff who calls himself an Army Chief of Staff, or CPM [Corps Polisi Militer, Military Police Corps] that calls itself a CPM, or soldier who calls himself an Indonesian army soldier could approve of a subordinate serving an ultimatum like this on the Chief of Staff, and could permit in that upheaval cooperation with bands of the DI [Darul Islam] that is no longer recognized by the Republic, and also cooperation with forces of foreign powers. . . . These are the bases for the government's decision and the steps that will be taken by the government and armed forces to resolve the problem.[23]

The rebels themselves were also clearly anticipating that support from the United States and other outside powers would greatly augment their military power not only through a continuing and increased flow of military supplies but especially by providing them with air cover. They were convinced that the air cover in particular would deter the central government leadership from moving against them. But Jakarta's recognition of the threat posed by foreign intervention on the side of the PRRI had just the opposite effect from that anticipated by the leaders in Padang. For it served to accelerate Nasution's schedule for action and encouraged him to move rapidly to organize his military campaign against the rebels before the United States had time to provide them such open support.

Seventh Fleet to Singapore

In contrast to the previous December, American and British policies toward Indonesia had now become closely aligned. Singapore was politically much more settled, and British facilities there were now open and welcoming to the U.S. Navy. As early as February 21, 1958, the two Dulles brothers, Undersecretary of State Christian Herter, and Chief of Naval Operation, Admiral Arleigh Burke were discussing the possibility of again sending a naval force toward Indonesia, with John Foster Dulles and Herter agreeing that "it would be well to repeat our previous maneuvers" (presumably the abortive move to Singapore of December).[24]

Two days later the commander of the U.S. Seventh Fleet established Task Force 75, which he ordered to proceed to Singapore. Drawn from several points in the Western Pacific the force initially comprised the heavy cruiser *Bremerton*, the destroyers *Shelton* and *Eversole*, and the attack aircraft carrier *Ticonderoga*, itself carrying two battalions of marines. It is not clear on what date the destroyers left base, but by March 2 they were steaming south through the South China Sea and early in the morning of March 7 anchored in Singapore's Man O'War naval harbor. The *Bremerton* entered Singapore roads late on the night of March 10 and dropped anchor just after midnight close to where the destroyers were positioned. The *Shelton* and *Eversole* departed Singapore on the early morning of March 11, with orders to rendezvous with the *Ticonderoga*, which had been ordered south by the commander of the Seventh Fleet on March 9, departing Subic Bay at 6.18 a.m. the next day.

As the Seventh Fleet's task force was now well on its way to Singapore, the Eisenhower administration was still groping for the most plausible excuse for using it on behalf of the Sumatran rebels. On March 4 Dulles had privately suggested to the CIA chief that a threat by Jakarta "to bomb US property and people" might provide "a case for usefully doing something" and asked him whether he did not think it desirable "to send forces in to protect American lives and property." (Clearly he was referring to the Caltex oilfields in Husein's bailiwick in Central Sumatra.) Allen Dulles felt it would be better to wait, for if Jakarta did in fact bomb the oil fields "then we have a good basis for yelling and screaming and also get a better reception."[25] Jakarta, however, was unwilling to oblige with such a pretext, and, apparently to pave the way for justifying such an intervention, Secretary of State Dulles had the State Department spokesman, Lincoln White, announce publicly on March 5 that the department had asked its embassy in Indonesia to investigate a report that Jakarta's air force planned to bomb Caltex.

Soon after the two American destroyers took up station at Singapore on March 7, and before the arrival of the *Bremerton*, Prime Minister Djuanda was already worrying that Seventh Fleet units in the area "would land Marines and go to the Pekanbaru area [the principal Caltex oil center] with the announced objective of protecting American lives and properties at the Caltex operation."[26] His fears had been aroused even before the destroyers had actually appeared, when the American embassy began applying heavy diplomatic pressure to secure Jakarta's acquiescence for such an intervention. After repeated visits by Cumming's appointee, U.S. Chargé d'Affaires Sterling Cottrell, to Prime Minister Djuanda and Foreign Minister Subandrio demanding in the strongest terms that the Jakarta government give public agreement for such a "protective" move by American forces, these two officials and General Nasution became acutely alarmed and concluded that they had little time to forestall a move for which the United States was well prepared and needed only a pretext to execute.[27] As the then U.S. military attaché to Jakarta later recalled, "The US was anxious to have a pretext to send in marines," and two battalions of them, "fully equipped and ready for battle were prepared to be helicoptered within twelve hours notice to the Sumatran oil fields."[28] The Indonesian ministers' alarm was undoubtedly heightened by the arrival of the *Bremerton* and by decoding messages between the rebels and the Seventh Fleet. It was during this tense period that Colonel Husein recalls he received a coded message from the Seventh Fleet that they would intervene if he would have the Caltex installations burned.[29]

To forestall any action by the United States, the Jakarta government now insisted that a number of the foreign personnel from the Caltex area be evacuated and that others be concentrated in camps:

> On March 8 the American Chargé d'Affaires was informed by the Foreign Minister that the Indonesian Government wished the dependents and a certain number of employees of Caltex and Stanvac to be evacuated from Central Sumatra. . . . The remainder would have been concentrated in a camp. . . . With considerable misgivings the Caltex representative, on the advice of the American Ambassador [Howard Jones, who had just arrived in Jakarta to take over from Cottrell] accepted the Indonesian proposals.[30]

Under these proposals, foreign personnel at Pakning and Dumai (about 150 Americans) were to proceed to Singapore by tanker or merchant ship ("*but not* by American naval craft"). The foreign personnel from Duri, Menas, and Pekanbaru would be concentrated in a camp at Rumbai.[31]

But the problem remained. The possibility of U.S. military intervention seemed all the more imminent, with U.S. naval officers in Singapore now publicly announcing plans to use the American force assembled in the area "for evacuating American nationals from Sumatra—in case their assistance is called for," and reports circulating that ships from the British navy based at Singapore had plans to evacuate British nationals and protect British property.[32] Colonel Zulkifli Lubis, the PRRI's senior military strategist, recalled that the rebels believed that the very presence of this formidable American armada would intimidate the Jakarta government, especially since any doubts as to the United States partiality for the rebel cause were concurrently being dispelled by Secretary Dulles's well-publicized statement of March 9 before the American House Foreign Affairs Committee.[33] There Dulles spoke of "a fear that the trend of the Sukarno Government may be to put the Communists in control there," and stated: "We would be happy to see non-Communist elements who are really in a majority there, the Moslem elements, the non-Communist parties, exert a greater influence in the affairs of Indonesia than has been the case in the past, where Sukarno has moved toward this so-called 'guided democracy' theory which is a nice sounding name for what I fear would end up to be Communist despotism."[34] This statement was understandably regarded as the United States's call for the displacement of Sukarno's government.

As Nasution's deputy, General Djatikusumo recalled, "regardless of which party threatened" the oil fields—the PRRI or Jakarta—the marines remained "prepared to disembark in Sumatra to secure the oilfields if they should be threatened by fighting."[35] This view was independently seconded by Lubis, who recalls, "It was figured that a scorched-earth policy in the oil fields by Husein's troops would bring in the 7th Fleet. From our standpoint it didn't really matter on whose side it would appear to be; but by intervening with its [the Seventh Fleet's] forces it could stop the fighting and this would oblige the parties to have peace talks." Lubis's close associate, E. S. Pohan, who had served as the PRRI's chief resident representative in Singapore during this period, added, with Lubis's evident approval: "As far as those in charge of the 7th Fleet themselves were concerned, given their attitude towards Jakarta, they would say [to us] 'go ahead and blast the oilfields.'"[36] Thus, however restrained Jakarta's forces were, the rebels still had the option of launching a scorched-earth policy against Caltex properties that would give the United States the pretext for sending in the Marines.

Without a forcible preemptive occupation there was no way the Jakarta government could prevent the rebels from embarking on such measures. Indeed, as Husein recalled, he had already "given orders to our troops to destroy the Caltex operations as a scorched-earth policy [with at least the ostensible purpose] to deny the oil to the central government if they attacked."[37] Thus, Prime Minister Djuanda sent Nasution an emphatic message to move his forces to Pekanbaru and the Caltex installations three days ahead of schedule to preempt an American move having "the announced objective of protecting American lives and properties."[38] Nasution secretly advanced his assault timetable accordingly and moved in some of his best troops with a speed and decisiveness that surprised and bewildered both the PRRI military commanders and the United States.

Several convergent factors speeded Jakarta's actions, in addition to the presence of the U.S. Seventh Fleet in Singapore. The most important of these was the SEATO foreign ministers meeting in Manila March 11-12. Almost immediately leaked from the conference's "secret" sessions was the fact that the situation in Indonesia was high on its agenda, and it was widely known that a PRRI representative had flown to Manila to be present at the meeting. Moreover, in Indonesia as well as in the United States, Dulles's March 9 statement was generally regarded as designed to encourage the rebels. All this, together with indications from Cottrell and the British Foreign Office that the United States and Britain were looking into the possibility that they might accord "belligerent status" to the PRRI presented a menacing backdrop to the activities of American and British naval units in the area.[39] Such status could have opened the way for foreign powers to provide open and direct support to the PRRI.

Any remaining disposition on the part of Djuanda and Nasution to defer preemptive action was undoubtedly dissipated by the report that a DC4 aircraft (believed to be of ultimate U.S. provenance and presumed to have flown from Taipei, Bangkok, Manila, or Saigon with a refueling stop at Singapore) had on the night of March 11 repeated an operation carried out February 26 and dropped a substantial amount of arms on the Pekanbaru airfield.[40]

The Government Attacks

By now Nasution had established his headquarters at Tanjung Pinang on Bintan Island—Indonesian territory close enough to Singapore to monitor Pacific and Indian Ocean shipping into and out of its harbor—and had finalized preparations for mounting his operation against the Riau area of Central Sumatra. The Army Command planned a three-pronged move: (1) paratroops were to be dropped at Pekanbaru airfield (near the Caltex oil operations) to secure it and permit airborne troops to land; (2) a contingent of marines was to move up the Siak River toward Pekanbaru; and (3) Brawijaya Division troops were to land at the Caltex port of Dumai, regroup there, and then fight their way to the same town.[41] These plans, however, had to be streamlined and rearranged to preempt further American actions.

On Sumatra's other coast, Indonesian government ships had been patrolling the seas between Padang and Painan to give the impression that any initial government offensive would be launched against Sumatra's west coast. Then on March 12 in a lightning preemptive stroke that clearly caught both Husein and the U.S. Seventh Fleet by surprise, a full five battalions of government marines and paratroops were airlifted to eastern Central Sumatra, where a staging area had been quietly secured on Bengkalis Island—opposite the Siak river approach to Pekanbaru. Two companies (about 250 men) of paratroops (RPKAD), under Lieutenant Colonel Kaharuddin Nasution, parachuted directly onto the Pekanbaru airfield.[42] Shortly before landing they received reports of four-engined planes cruising the area, and, after they parachuted in, the Jakarta troops found cases of modern American-made weapons on the landing strip, including heavy machine guns, antiaircraft guns, and ammunition that had been dropped only a few hours before.[43]

The rebels had only one company of troops at Pekanbaru when government forces landed, as they anticipated the initial assault would be against Padang. Despite their orders to destroy the Caltex operations as part of a scorched-earth policy if the government attacked, these PRRI soldiers,

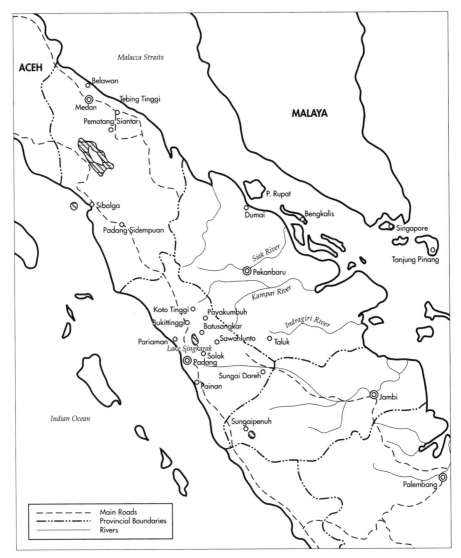

Map 5: Jakarta's Operations against the PRRI in Sumatra

taken by surprise, made no attempt to carry out these orders before they fled.[44] By evening, Chief of Staff Nasution had landed with his staff and established their headquarters in the town of Pekanbaru.

Meanwhile, some Indonesian marines proceeded up the Siak River while others landed at Dumai on March 12 and also made for Pekanbaru, reaching it just a day after the paratroopers. These forces were able to "rescue" the Caltex oil installations situated between Dumai and Pekanbaru, freeing their foreign personnel from the camps in which they had been held. By March 22, Caltex was able to resume its regular operations in Pekanbaru and restore its tanker voyages down the Siak River the same day.[45]

With Jakarta's forces having occupied Pekanbaru and the nearby Caltex oil fields and "rescued" its American personnel before Husein's troops could carry out their scorched-earth orders, there was no longer any plausible role for the Seventh Fleet's marines and helicopters in Indonesia. On the afternoon of March 13 (approximately a day and a half after the fall of Pekanbaru) the carrier *Ticonderoga*, after nearly reaching Singapore, abruptly reversed course and returned to Subic, with the destroyers *Eversole* and *Shelton* doing the same. In the words of the head of the U.S. Navy's Ships Histories Branch: "One might speculate that some form of air operation had been contemplated, but then canceled, which could have explained the destroyers' diversion from the planned rendezvous." (Air operations would have required the presence of the destroyers close to the carrier for "plane guard duty.")

But a substantial task force remained based on Singapore, two other American destroyers, the *Nicholas* and *Phillips*, joining the cruiser *Bremerton* in Singapore's Man O'War Anchorage on March 15. These three ships then went to sea for two days, after which they returned to Singapore. The destroyers then departed, but the *Bremerton* (now designated flagship of Task Force 75) remained at Singapore until at least the beginning of May.[46] American options as to its use remained open, its commander having earlier (March 11) advised Secretary of State Dulles he would make recommendations after March 20 "as situation develops."[47]

Thus, on March 13, Admiral Roy Benson, commander of Task Force 75, somewhat gratuitously announced in Singapore that his forces would not act in Sumatra without permission from the Jakarta government.[48] That same day Jakarta announced that henceforth all foreign warships would be excluded from Indonesian waters.[49] But with the U.S. destroyers remaining on for another week and the task force's flagship, the cruiser *Bremerton*, for at least six more weeks, an interventionist American naval option had apparently not been abandoned.

Prime Minister Djuanda's prescient assessment of the joint PRRI-Seventh Fleet's plan and his order to Nasution to preempt it by suddenly moving forward the army's schedule of operations by three full days had caught the United States and the PRRI flatfooted. And Nasution's logistical and tactical skill and speed in executing this advanced timetable effectively closed the door on a strategy by which the Dulles brothers and Eisenhower had set great store. No longer available to the United States was that apparently easy shortcut to providing not only a measure of protection to the rebels but a belligerent status, one that could open up avenues of overt foreign support to them.

Over the next few weeks, the rebel forces in eastern Central Sumatra withdrew rapidly in the face of attacks from government marines and commandos. There was, however, a brief rebel upsurge in Medan, where Major

W. F. (Boyke) Nainggolan, a Toba Batak, who was widely regarded as one of the army's ablest combat officers, launched a coup against the pro-Jakarta Medan command, took over the city, and forced Nasution's deputy chief of staff, Colonel Djatikusumo, to flee to the east coast port of Belawan.[50] But again government reaction was swift. Nasution feared that, if Nainggolan's forces were successful for even only a few days, not only military units in Tapanuli but possibly also the Aceh command might join forces with the PRRI. The following day the Indonesian air force (AURI) bombed the rebel-controlled radio station in Medan while government reinforcements landed at Belawan, where they joined with those of Djatikusumo to advance on Medan. After a three-hour fight, Nainggolan's forces withdrew before government troops reached the city. Over the next month Nasution's forces gradually succeeded in advancing east into Tapanuli and reasserting government control over most of that province. Already cut off from potential supporters in Barlian's South Sumatra command, the rebel government was now sealed off from access to the north by Djatikusumo's forces.[51]

Western Reactions

The Eisenhower administration was clearly shocked and disappointed by the opening salvos of the insurrection. From the time of the PRRI proclamation officials in Washington had been discussing how best to strengthen the rebels in Sumatra and Sulawesi, whom they now referred to as "the patriots," against a government attack.

At this stage John Foster Dulles seems to have been the senior American official most eager for U.S. forces to become directly involved in the confrontation on the side of the rebels. By the end of February, over the cautions of his brother Allen, he was urging greater American activity in their support, stating that "if it is going to work we should take some risk of showing our hand." Allen Dulles reassured his brother that "we are ready to give them a bird [presumably an airplane] as soon as they can eat it. We are pushing ahead as daringly as we can. It is a vigorous program and they are very happy with it and cooperate very well." But the secretary of state was still impatient, reiterating his belief that "we can't play too safely here and we have to take some risk because it looks . . . it is the best chance we have."[52]

SEATO

At the Manila SEATO conference Dulles found his impatience and willingness to take risks matched by Britain and Australia. Recently declassified Australian documents disclose that on March 11 Australian foreign minister Casey informed Prime Minister Menzies that Britain's foreign secretary, Selwyn Lloyd, had told him that Lloyd and Prime Minister Harold Macmillan, agreed "that it is essential in the interests of the UK Government and the West that the dissidents in Sumatra should at the worst be able to make a draw of it" and that "this means considerable support for the dissidents from the West." The British foreign secretary, Casey reported, had advised Macmillan that "as to the implementation you and I discussed on Saturday night of covert action and what we called the 'overt but disavowable' aspect, I feel we have got to take considerable risks to see our policy succeed."

The debacle of the early morning of March 12 at Pekanbaru appears to have increased the feeling among these three allies at Manila that risks had to be taken. Later that day in Manila, Dulles met with Lloyd and Casey, and Casey cabled Menzies: "It is agreed between the UK and the US that all help that is possible to provide should be given to the dissidents although every possible care should be given to conceal the origins." Casey advised Menzies that same day that the rebels in "central Sumatra had already received from friendly sources all supplies then needed (including [from] Australia) except aircraft," but that "Dulles said we might have to take some further risks provided the central Sumatran forces are able and willing to continue to resist." Particularly singling out assistance in the air, Dulles mentioned "two possibilities: (a) to give the dissidents aircraft, but as [Casey] pointed out, the dissidents now lack adequate airfields, fuel and facilities for operations. Dulles said they also lack pilots so we would have to find pilots as well as aircraft; (b) to carry out bombing operations ourselves." There appeared to be agreement between the three representatives that even "scattered raids" from places such as Singapore and East Borneo (presumably Jesselton or Sandakan) "could not be concealed if continued." Nevertheless Dulles, clearly aware of the loss of Pekanbaru to Jakarta's forces earlier that morning, suggested that if its airfield could be knocked out "it would be a great thing." Sir Robert Scott, Britain's Singapore-based commissioner for Southeast Asia, suggested that as a "longer-term proposition" the three countries "should look into the possibility of encouraging rebellion on Amboina and the Moluccas [in eastern Indonesia], to widen the basis of any international attitude that the Indonesian Government was not in control of the country." The possibility of covertly "alerting and possibly helping" a now-dormant movement for independence in these parts of eastern Indonesia (overcome by Jakarta seven years before) was discussed. There was, however, "general assent that the immediate need was to prevent central Sumatran resistance from collapsing."[53]

Casey was hardly the moderate among the three Western representatives at SEATO. His diaries, released in 1989, made him appear, according to two Australians who drew on them, at times "more gung-ho than the Americans."[54] Casey's discussions at the SEATO meeting concerning the possible use of Australian aircraft on bombing missions in Indonesia were serious enough to alarm Australia's minister of defense, who cabled him to that effect. In his answer, Casey sought to soothe the minister but made clear that it might be necessary to take the risk:

> Under the present conditions, any bombing of Indonesia would have to be covert and under conditions that would be most difficult to shoot home. There would be a risk, of course, but Dulles recognises this. If this risk were taken it would be lest much worse befall. I may say that no decision was taken as to action, although I believed the situation had a considerable degree of urgency and reason for taking the risk.[55]

Just after the SEATO meeting, Casey broached another idea as well, advocating to Canberra

> not only a secret plan to undermine Indonesia's economy, but a covert action operation to justify it.
>
> It occurs to me as a possible move in the game that the Americans (and others with oil interests in Sumatra) might stop their oil activities in Sumatra on the plea that conditions are too disturbed to enable them to carry on. This might follow some minor *alleged* [emphasis added] sabotage of their installations and/or threats to their employees. Stoppage of oil activity would substantially add to the Djakarta Government's financial difficulties. Danger of such action would be nationalisation by the Djakarta Government and substitution of America and other friendly operators by Russians and others. The above suggestion might equally apply to any other commercial activities conducted by European interests in Sumatra.[56]

While there is no evidence that either Casey's bombing or economic sabotage scenarios were actually adopted, such thinking makes more plausible other clandestine activity in which Australia did engage.

It was just after the final SEATO meeting of March 13 that Dulles, in what he described as a "highly confidential talk" with Lloyd and Casey, "threw out [the] suggestion that if the rebel movement did not immediately collapse and if sustained fighting seemed likely US might say to Sukarno that since early military solution seemed unlikely US must inquire as to likelihood of a political solution, and that in the absence of this likelihood, US would have to consider according belligerent rights to rebels."[57] Dulles argued that "if accurately timed" such a move "might strengthen the hands of those seeking a political solution." The British foreign minister, he reported, "at least appeared unsure as to whether it would have a 'productive or counter productive result.'"[58]

On the secretary's return to Washington, he found President Eisenhower eager to know whether at the SEATO conference "there was much concern about Indonesia and desire that we should take a stronger course." Secretary Dulles replied that there was such a concern "particularly on the part of the Philippines and Australia."[59]

Even before this meeting the secretary had picked up on the belligerent-status scenario that he had broached to Lloyd and Casey, instructing the newly arrived American ambassador to Jakarta, Howard Jones, to discuss this matter with Sukarno. Accordingly, on March 18 the hapless ambassador called on Sukarno to inform him that Secretary Dulles wished to "alert him to the possibility that if hostilities continued," the United States government "might have to give consideration to recognizing the belligerent status of the rebels" and that "an early settlement of the internal conflict would avoid the necessity of facing the question of recognition of the rebels." Sukarno, Jones recalled, bridled: "This is the way to hell," and "threatened that such a move would bring a violent reaction not only throughout Indonesia but elsewhere."[60] "We will reach a settlement as soon as the rebellion is quelled," Sukarno said, pointing out that the "Central Government was not using great force or violence and did not wish to but that it must reestablish its position and authority on Sumatra."[61]

By now the Indonesian army was exhibiting to foreign journalists evidence of outside arms shipments to the rebels, though thus far the only foreign country named as supplying them was Taiwan (Nationalist China). On March 21, Chief of Army Intelligence Lieutenant Colonel Sukendro referred publicly to the arms dropped to rebel forces by a DC4 aircraft on February 26 and March 12, and some of these were put on display at the Ministry of Information three days later. He also charged—correctly—that the rebels had purchased a DC4 aircraft themselves—though unbeknown to him it was the CIA's wholly owned subsidiary CAT headquartered on Taiwan that had "sold" the plane at a concessional rate in a deal probably arranged by Sumitro.[62] It was by now no secret—at least in Indonesia—that American CIA agents were working with the rebels in Central Sumatra, not only providing them with very modern American arms, including recoilless rifles and bazookas, but also with training. American correspondents in Sumatra saw—but refrained from reporting—both the newly arrived weaponry and U.S. agents. Even though they observed them, for instance, directing the Sumatrans in the use of weapons, in putting up pointed stakes around the airfield in Padang to hinder a parachute attack, and placing oil drums on the airstrip to keep planes from landing, "we did not write about it. Maybe it was kind of a patriotism that kept us from doing so."[63]

View from Washington

Administration leaders were expecting that the PRRI's forces would perform more satisfactorily in their main base area of western Central Sumatra than they had done heretofore. They were particularly hopeful that Colonel A. E. Kawilarang, who had been Indonesia's military attaché to the United States since being relieved of his command of the Siliwangi division in September 1956, would make a difference. Kawilarang, a Manadonese, had commanded republican forces in Tapanuli during and after the Dutch Second Military Action in 1948-1949, and because of his superior performance there he had been made North Sumatra commander at the end of 1949, just after the transfer of sovereignty.

The CIA's Joseph Smith claims that by February 15, 1958 (with the expiration of the rebels' ultimatum and the establishment of the PRRI), it looked as though the agency's efforts to get Kawilarang to defect were proving successful.[64] Whether or not the agency had been able to influence him, Kawilarang states that Colonel Sumual's agents approached him in Washington on March 10, 1958, and because he agreed with their aims he resigned his post as military attaché and flew to Manila.[65] Shortly before he left he had cabled Nasution offering to help mediate between the PRRI and Jakarta by going to Padang and Manado to talk to rebel leaders, but he had been ordered by Nasution to stay in Washington.[66] Until his arrival in Manado on April 13, the record of Kawilarang's activities is murky.[67] On April 3, at a meeting of the National Security Council, General Cabell reported that Kawilarang "would assume control of all dissident forces. His [Kawilarang's] estimate of the prospects for the rebels was said to be one of guarded optimism."[68] Jakarta's military spokesman Rudy Pirngadie reported that Kawilarang had been scheduled to enter Medan on March 18 to take over "Operation Sabang-Merauke" from Major Nainggolan.[69] Kawilarang, according to his close friend, ex-colonel Daan Jahja, was in Singapore in late March and scheduled to go to Central Sumatra to look over the situation before deciding whether he would fight there or in northern Sulawesi.[70] But either because the plane promised by the British could not then take off or because of Kawilarang's own misgivings regarding the quality of the PRRI forces on Sumatra after the Pekanbaru landings and Nainggolan's defeat, he instead went on to Manado, traveling there, according to Kawilarang himself, on a CIA plane from Manila.[71]

· · · · ·

After the unexpected efficiency and success of the government's operations at Pekanbaru and other parts of Sumatra, the Secretary Dulles was beginning to realize by the end of March that the Jakarta forces "must be better than we thought."[72] He acknowledged to his brother that "sharp differences of opinion" were emerging in the administration, and they would soon have to "take serious decisions re the archipelago."[73]

The reports Washington was receiving from CIA operatives in the field were by early March being balanced by a Jakarta embassy now led by a man with greater influence in the Department of State than his two predecessors. Howard Jones, appointed as the new ambassador, had arrived to take up his post on March 6, five weeks after John Allison had been sent to

Prague, during which period Sterling Cottrell had been brought in as chargé d'affaires.[74] Having served during the previous three years as deputy assistant secretary for Far Eastern economic affairs and been a member of the working group of Cumming's Inter-Agency Committee on Indonesia, Jones was au courant with the Indonesian situation and with both the covert and overt levels of U.S. policy there.

His initial move after a meeting with former vice president Mohammad Hatta was to alert the State Department to two misapprehensions he felt they were laboring under. First he informed them that, despite his differences with the government, Hatta did not support the rebels and had stated that, while the Communists referred to Hatta himself as enemy number one, they viewed "Nasution as enemy number two."[75] "Thus," Jones later observed, "while Washington was acting upon information to the effect that a pro-Communist Djakarta government with a heavily Communist infiltrated army was fighting the anti-Communist forces of Indonesia in Sumatra and Celebes—it was clear that an anti-Communist Indonesian army led by one of the country's top anti-Communists was locked in combat with the other principal anti-Communist force of the nation."[76]

The new ambassador also bluntly dismissed any hopes of a rebel military success. As early as April 6, he cabled his estimate of the military situation:

> Rebels are losing ground fast militarily. Pakanbaru was serious blow and expectations they would take advantage mountainous terrain resist central forces advances across Sumatra have not (repeat not) been realized. It now appears they may not (repeat not) defend Padang, and from reports of progress made by GOI [Government of Indonesia] troops overland toward Bukittinggi, it begins to look as though rebels will not (repeat not) even attempt defend that city (their capital). This leaves guerrilla warfare as their only resort.

Jones felt that Sukarno had left the door open for a compromise settlement, as the president was "deeply worried about [the] difficulty [of] rebuilding national unity," and that the PKI, lacking any capacity to seize power, was prevented from making any violent move "by fear of offering opportunity which anti-Communist army officers have been vainly seeking for years to suppress PKI by force." All these factors led him to conclude that the "army is emerging as most reliable machinery available for anti-Communist action at present and heightened prestige over Sumatran successes may be expected [to] increase its confidence in [its] ability to handle Communist action of any kind, whether violent or subversive."[77]

In contrast to the ambassador's portrayal of the situation, the chairman of the U.S. Joint Chiefs of Staff, Air Force General N. F. Twining, presented the next day an apocalyptic vision of events should the Jakarta forces be successful, and he called for overt U.S. action in support of the rebels:

Present restrictions do not permit sufficient timely aid to the dissidents to insure victory. Defeat of the dissidents would almost certainly lead to Communist domination of Indonesia. Such a turn of events would cause serious reaction in Malaya and Thailand, probable trouble in Laos and possible trouble in Cambodia. It could result in the disappearance of SEATO as a viable pact, and an extension of Communist influence in the Moslem Middle East. Consequently, if Communist domination of Indonesia is to be prevented, action must be taken, including overt measures as required, to insure either the success of the dissidents or the suppression of the pro-Communist elements of the Sukarno government.

The Joint Chiefs of Staff recommend that you support a relaxation of restrictions on United States policy toward Indonesia and accelerated efforts to prevent the fall of the nation to Communism.[78]

The concerns of the Joint Chiefs of Staffs had been heightened, as their preface to this memorandum had indicated, by Jakarta's announcement on April 6 of an extensive program for the purchase of arms from the Soviet bloc that had begun after the United States had made absolutely clear at the end of December that it would not permit Jakarta to buy either new U.S. military equipment or spare parts for those previously purchased from the United States.[79] As late as May 1, John Foster Dulles himself reported that only "small quantities of Soviet-bloc military equipment [primarily Soviet jeeps] have arrived in Indonesia to date and none has been used by Government forces against dissidents."[80] But heavier equipment was known to be in the pipeline. With the possible exception of a few troop transports (for the most part, if not exclusively, purchased from Japan or Italy), none of this equipment reached Indonesia in time or in a condition to affect the outcome of the civil war (planes, for instance, had to be assembled there and then pilots and mechanics trained). Nevertheless the Joint Chiefs of Staff remained worried over the possible impact these arms might have.

The contradictory assessments from Ambassador Jones and the Joint Chiefs of Staff pressed in on the top levels of the Washington administration in the middle of April as concern mounted that Jakarta forces might soon launch an amphibious invasion against the west coast of Sumatra, the main center of rebel power. On April 12, representatives of the JCS met with Allen Dulles and the secretary of state, and the group concluded that action needed to be taken, but preferably if it could be kept covert. There were three possibilities to be explored:

1. Recognition of a state of belligerency (dependent upon the Indonesian government's failure to drive the rebels into the mountains);
2. Secession of Sumatra from the Indonesian Republic, with the U.S. recognizing Sumatra and guaranteeing its independence (similar to Panama [its detachment from Colombia] and T[eddy] R[oosevelt's] recognition). Perhaps, too, [the] regional concept in the United Nations that Indonesia be a loose confederation of independent [sic!] states should be explored;

3. Possibility there would be so much damage to U.S. property that U.S. troops will have to be sent in. (No real precedent—one with good cover would have to be established.)[81]

In marshalling his forces for an amphibious assault on Padang Nasution advanced his timetable to preempt what he feared might be a U.S. effort to block it. His fear appears justified, for at a meeting of the National Security Council on April 14 President Eisenhower suggested that "what the dissidents most badly needed was a submarine or two to deal with the Djakarta Government's amphibious attack," and that one such "considerable disaster to the Djakarta forces might change the whole direction of the struggle."[82]

Whether or not Eisenhower held to this position, only three days elapsed before the assault on Padang began, probably not enough time for the American submarines that had earlier been active in the area to be deployed to sink the invasion transports. In a phone conversation with his brother a couple of hours before the critical meeting of senior U.S. policy makers the next day, John Foster Dulles made clear that he now felt the rebels had to give some demonstration of their military ability before the United States could make overt moves in their support. He asked if there was "any way of indicating if they repel this [expected invasion] they have a brighter prospect" and "thought they might fight with a great deal more heart if they saw a prospect ahead."[83]

When the Dulles brothers spoke again an hour later, the CIA chief observed that "we are reaching the hour of decision and little time will be left to do that so as to have the impact on what is happening." Recognizing President Eisenhower's interest in offering some direct support to the rebels without exposing American military personnel, Secretary Dulles thought the important thing was to "find a political basis to do it overt rather than get caught covert." If the president "thinks it worth pursuing then get word to these people we are giving consideration to it and if they survive the first assault then they could look forward to something."[84]

This line of thinking came out later that day in the 3.30 meeting between President Eisenhower and his advisers, when Secretary Dulles stated that "it did not seem likely that the patriots [i.e., the rebels] could gain a victory or in the long run sustain themselves at least without overt outside support. On the other hand it seemed as though their willingness to fight needed to be better demonstrated." The secretary went on to suggest that the "*CIA might convey communication to rebel leadership of 'patriots' on highly confidential basis our feeling . . . if they put up a stubborn resistance to the imminent attack by the Central Government threatened on the West Coast off Padang, the United States would be disposed to consider some form of recognition which might permit of overt support from the U.S. or Asian countries which might join in that recognition. But if they did not show real will to fight and dedication to their cause, they could expect no aid or such support.*"[85]

Dulles's minutes of the meeting continued:

> We discussed various alternatives which recognition might take. One was the recognition of belligerency against the Central Government. Another was recognition of the government of the Sumatran State on the assumption, however, that that state would be part of an Indonesian federation as soon as an appropriate constitution was adopted. A third step was merely to recognize them as the *de facto* government of the area they controlled. A fourth measure that might be considered was for the United States to land forces for the protection of American life and property on Sumatra, notably at the oil fields. [The U.S. navy still had ships at Singapore, where at least the cruiser *Bremerton* remained until mid-May or later.][86]

Dulles recommended against the last option because of the adverse international reaction it would incur. President Eisenhower concluded that consideration of the question of recognition should be left open in the event that the rebels did some active fighting that would justify such a move.[87]

Jakarta's Military Successes

The Fall of Padang

The reluctance of the senior officers of the three Java-based divisions to release troops for Nasution's use against the rebels had been greatly diminished with the establishment of the PRRI on February 15 and the break with the central government that this entailed. By late March, as it became clear to them that the United States and its allies were supporting the rebels, their patriotic outrage at this foreign intervention removed any residual constraints and they were ready to provide Nasution with what troops they could spare.[88] Natsir himself later acknowledged: "There is no doubt that in terms of marshalling support in Java the fact that we were getting outside support played into the hands of Sukarno, and his information ministry kept hammering on this theme with good effect."[89] While the West Java division was still heavily engaged against the Darul Islam in its area and could spare few soldiers, the Central Java and East Java divisions were now prepared to release substantial forces for Nasution's use in the campaign he wished to mount against the rebels in Sumatra and Sulawesi.

After ejecting Nainggolan from Medan, Nasution turned his attention to preparing an attack against the center of PRRI strength in West Sumatra, drawing primarily on troops from the East and Central Java divisions. He appointed Colonel Achmad Yani, recently returned from a training course in the United States at Fort Leavenworth, to head this major campaign, "the 17th August Operation."[90]

As it had become clear that Jakarta's response to the formation of the revolutionary government was to be one of force rather than negotiation,[91] until at least the capture of Padang, the strategy being worked out by the PRRI's West Sumatra command bore little resemblance to the expectations of their foreign supporters. Husein had decided to resort immediately to guerrilla tactics rather than organize frontal resistance to the invading forces, in part because he knew that several of his battalion commanders were still opposed to a military clash with Jakarta,[92] and also presumably because the airplanes requested from the CIA to carry out tactical bombing had not arrived.[93] (Probably this was in part because the British were still too worried over the fragility of the political balance within Singapore to risk direct and open use of its airfields for this purpose and the fact that airfields to which the United States had access for covert operations in South Vietnam, Taiwan, the Philippines, and Thailand were too distant to permit round-trip flights and any significant time for tactical operations over Sumatra.) Husein states that he had readied the Padang airfield to accommodate the basing there of two B-26 bombers being sent him from the airfield controlled by Colonel Sumual at Manado that were due to arrive on April 16, but that following their attack en route against shipping at the oil port of Balikpapan, the two planes exploded in midair and never reached Padang.[94] Moreover, apparently by the time the rebels had purchased their own DC4 and found a crew for it, they had lost the airfield at Padang where it could have been based, and their negotiations for two amphibious planes (presumably to have been based on Lake Singkarak) had not yet been completed.[95]

Ships from the Indonesian navy had been patrolling off the coast of West Sumatra even before the landings at Pekanbaru, so the dissident forces had plenty of opportunity to prepare their defenses. They chose instead to withdraw their major strength to what they termed "more defensible positions." Confronted with what they perceived as overwhelmingly superior government forces, Husein and his colleagues decided to move from the coastal towns into the interior and from there to launch sporadic counterattacks and, if necessary, long-term guerrilla warfare, against the invading forces. Reflecting this strategy, even before Jakarta's troops began to land, the PRRI leadership had ordered government officials and teachers to withdraw from the major towns or their salaries would not be paid.[96]

At 4.30 in the morning of April 17, government warships began a systematic bombardment of Padang and the coastal areas north of the town, followed immediately by an hourlong airraid.[97] At 6.40 a.m., a company of government paratroopers landed near the runway of Tabing airfield, while forces from the Central Java division, under command of General Yani, made an amphibious landing north of Padang. The attacking soldiers met virtually no opposition. The rebel forces—mostly high school students—who had remained to defend the coastal town were reported by the U.S. military attaché in Jakarta to have "offered no resistance and surrendered to army troops."[98] Had the rebels chosen to contest the landings the government troops would have been exposed to their fire as they waded ashore, but that would, of course, have been at the cost of the rebels' exposing themselves to strafing and bombing by the government's airplanes—modest though these were in number.[99] Shortly after midday Yani's seaborne troops were able to land and advance on Padang, with his forces securing the town before the end of the day.[100]

Defections in South Sumatra

Meanwhile Nasution had handed over responsibility for operations in South Sumatra to his second deputy, Colonel Ibnu Sutowo, a former commander of the area who still enjoyed some influence there. The South Sumatra commander, Colonel Barlian, had remained in an openly neutral position since the declaration of the PRRI in mid-February. There was still a very strong "pro-Padang" group within his territory, with Major Nawawi, deputy chief of staff and commander of the Palembang area, the leading PRRI adherent. But in the wake of the string of government military successes further north, the pro-Jakarta forces in South Sumatra had been gaining strength, resulting in "a definite swing of the center of political gravity . . . from the pro-Padang to the pro-Pusat [i.e., Jakarta] tendency."[101]

On April 26 Nasution fired Barlian's deputy chief of staff, Nawawi, and ordered Barlian to send him to Jakarta. Barlian, however, ignored the order: "I did not want Nawawi to be caught, so I remained inactive and he was able to escape."[102] Similar to Husein's actions in the Caltex area, Nawawi had been requisitioning weapons and transportation and radio equipment in Stanvac's Sungei Gerong oilfield and was reportedly planning to set up a rebel headquarters within the Stanvac refinery there.[103] Before he was able to put any of these plans into effect, however, Colonel Ibnu Sutowo disarmed his troops.[104] Nawawi himself managed to escape, "with one jeep and one truck . . . considerable arms, ammunition and money." He eventually moved up to the border of Bengkulu to join with the forces retreating from the Padang front. Barlian was induced to return to his home "to rest for two or three months," and on June 26, Nasution dismissed him from his command and replaced him by his chief of staff.[105]

· · · · ·

In West Sumatra, the speed of the government advance slowed in the aftermath of the Padang invasion. A rebel battalion led by Major Johan stayed the advance of Jakarta's forces in the steep Anai Valley on the way to the upland town of Padang Panjang, until AURI planes were brought in to strafe his troops and he was outflanked by a second battalion of Jakarta's forces.[106] And not until May 4 did the government battalions finally occupy the rebel capital of Bukittinggi. American observers commented that its takeover which Jakarta had "long anticipated[,] was also long delayed."[107] With this defeat, the PRRI government on May 5 transferred its capital to the Permesta stronghold of Manado in northern Sulawesi, where Colonel Warouw was appointed to head the government as deputy prime minister.

The United States quickly adjusted to these changes in the rebels' fortunes. On April 17, even before news of their retreat from Padang reached him, Secretary of State Dulles was telling his brother that the government attack "has happened with far greater efficiency, speed and precision than he had expected from what he heard" just four days before. But CIA chief Allen Dulles had clearly anticipated the Sumatran rebels' retreat. He had sent a message to his agents the night before stating that "if fighting resulted in the boys moving to the mountains don't deliver [possibly an airplane?]." The secretary noted that the CIA chief thought that government forces "can take Padang but does not think it is the end. He thinks we should reinforce the north [Sulawesi?] which we can do—better than [setting up] a govt in exile. But we have to be careful not to get too far out on a limb."[108] In fact, in the Sulawesi area the United States now did get out on a fairly long limb—in military terms longer than the one it had been on in Sumatra.

The rebels on Sumatra were now obliged to confine their operations to the level of protracted guerrilla warfare, a struggle that they were to sustain—with diminishing success—over the next three years. But in the northeastern theater, centered on Sulawesi, the United States organized the introduction of supportive air power that significantly altered the military equation and ushered in a very different kind of warfare. The action also served to quash Jakarta's expectation that the fall of Bukittinggi would permit it to move toward a negotiated settlement with the rebels.

8. Climax and Turning Point

Negotiations Rejected

WITH ITS FORCES on Sumatra achieving such a striking success, it is understandable that Jakarta believed the time was ripe for making a major effort to reach a settlement with the rebels on Sulawesi. Accordingly, Nasution authorized Lieutenant Colonel Andi Jusuf, a prominent aristocrat from the South Sulawesi realm of Bone, to travel to the headquarters of Colonels Sumual and Warouw in Manado to try to reach an accord that would end the fighting. Jusuf, who had been commander of the central government's Hasanuddin regiment in South Sulawesi since 1956, had been one of the signers of the original Permesta charter in March 1957, but he had never taken up the position as head of the Security Section of the Permesta military government to which the rebels appointed him. And he had maintained close ties with army headquarters in Jakarta.[1]

Jusuf left Jakarta for Manado on May 2, 1958, with a message from Nasution promising that he and the Sultan of Yogyakarta would direct formation of a new government, in which Nasution himself, Hatta, the Sultan, and the deputy chief of staff, Colonel Gatot Subroto, would hold dominant positions. This "cabinet will not (repeat will not) contain any leftist type members," assured Nasution, apparently also adding that he had a "definite plan for the elimination of the Communists."[2] Jusuf's mission failed, for Sumual and his colleagues "wanted no part of peace talks and in fact tried to convince Jusuf that the smart thing for him and the people of South Sulawesi to do would be to join the rebel cause."[3]

During his days in Manado, Jusuf became convinced of the wholehearted support the United States was providing the rebels. As the U.S. army attaché in Jakarta reported:

> While in Menado Jusuf saw four F-51s and four B-26 bombers at the airfield. Pilots were American and Chinese and very young. Jusuf stated "If these are adventurers they are the youngest group of adventurers I have ever seen. They looked like a group of young kids, like I saw when I visited West Point". Col. Sumual . . . told Jusuf that the rebels only had to ask and they would get any piece of equipment they wanted. Since they now had an airfield that can handle jets (presumed to be Morotai) they expect to have jets flying for them real soon. Jusuf said "The rebels were not worried about Govt air attacks because the field is now protected by US 90 mm AA guns. I saw them with my own eyes". Some Chinese colonels [from Taiwan] are training the 90mm gun crews.[4]

When the American army attaché asked Jusuf, "Do you think that Secretary Dulles can stop the air attacks?" Jusuf answered, "Many people here believe so, but I know so. After seeing the operations in Menado, [I] am sure that the Americans are running the show."[5] This was clearly the message he conveyed to Nasution and his colleagues, and it undoubtedly removed any remaining doubts they had as to whether the United States itself was *directly* backing the rebels. It was now evident that not merely were U.S. arms being channeled to the rebels via Taiwan and the Philippines but that military *personnel* from both the United States and the government of Chiang Kai-shek were directly supporting the rebels and that Philippine government personnel were also giving them significant assistance.[6] As early as April 30, Prime Minister Djuanda publicly gave official credence to reports that had been circulating for over a month that Taiwan and the United States were helping the rebels in Sulawesi, with American and Chinese pilots flying missions out of Taiwan bases in their support. A few days later a Jakarta military spokesman for the first time publicly accused the Philippines of supporting the rebels and offered proof.[7]

The now-overwhelming evidence of foreign military intervention on behalf of the rebels in eastern Indonesia, especially the clear air superiority this gave them and their lack of restraint in using it, severely altered the political as well as the military equation. Contrary to their earlier inclinations, Nasution and the army commanders—together with Prime Minister Djuanda and the centrist politicians heading the government in Jakarta—now abandoned their plan to initiate negotiations with the rebels once Jakarta's forces captured the PRRI capital of Bukittinggi. On May 6, Djuanda informed Ambassador Jones that "he had originally hoped that capture of Padang and Bukittinggi would make it possible to bring about political settlement in conflict with rebels. Foreign bombings however had introduced new element which had so aroused Indonesians that government was determined to push on with military campaign." Jones added that Djuanda "implied he knew we were involved and could not understand our motives. It now looked to GOI [government of Indonesia] as if purpose of US was to split Indonesia in two in order to insure that one part of Indonesia at least would remain non-Communist." The prime minister's entreaty to Jones on May 15 that the United States "do everything in its power to discourage further support to [the] rebels from [the] Philippines and Taiwan"[8] was followed by Dulles's instructions to the ambassador to tell Sukarno that "he cannot move his country to the Communist camp without expecting reaction from the free world and that some of the free peoples are bound to help the rebels . . . that if he takes actions to stop this [Communist] trend we are willing to discuss the allegations with the Philippines, Chinats [Chinese Nationalists], etc. . . . They [the Indonesians] cannot turn over their country to Communism without something being done about it by the free world." Jones was at the same time to offer a carrot: if a trend to stop communism showed "real significance" the United States would be prepared to give Jakarta economic and military assistance.

Air Power: Pivotal

Both Americans and Indonesians had long recognized that a critical element in the course of the struggle in Sumatra and Sulawesi would be control of the air. Nasution stated baldly: "Air cover was critical. If Sumatra had gotten air cover we would have been finished."[9] Just before the proclamation of the PRRI, Sumual had stated that "our only concern is the Air Force of the Djakarta Government." The day after government forces landed in Sumatra, CIA chief Allen Dulles expressed the fear that the "Djakarta Government's control of the air above Sumatra might prove to be crucial." But when a week later he emphasized that "the great need of the dissidents was for aircraft," he was rebuffed by Eisenhower who argued on the basis of what appeared to be a very limited understanding of the terrain in the key strategic areas of Sumatra.[10]

The Jakarta government found itself severely disadvantaged by having relied so exclusively on the United States for its military planes, most of which were now no longer operational because the United States was not willing to permit spare parts to be sold to Indonesia. But soon after Jakarta's last appeal (December 31, 1957) was turned down, it sent missions abroad to make purchases that would help compensate for the continuing rapid diminishment of its own air combat power. The United States's allies in Western Europe were not forthcoming, but Communist bloc countries were. Thus, at the end of April 1958, U.S. military intelligence reported that Jakarta had ordered twenty IL14 Soviet transports to arrive over the next few months, though none had yet reached Indonesia, and they would still have to be assembled there once they had.[11] Soviet MIGs and Ilyushin bombers were also ordered, but it would be longer before their Indonesian crews training abroad would be qualified to fly them. None of this augmentation of Jakarta's air power arrived in time to affect the outcome of the civil war, even in the Permesta-controlled areas of Sulawesi and the islands to its east.

In its assistance to the rebels, the Eisenhower administration was unwilling to commit U.S.-marked Navy planes beyond reconnaisance missions in both the Sumatran and eastern Indonesian theaters, an exercise in which they were joined by British and probably Australian planes.[12] Even such limited activity, however, involved the top reaches of the American government and exposed them to acute embarrassment should it come to light. One dangerous incident occurred on March 27, when Indonesian government forces fired on and damaged a U.S. navy photo reconnaissance plane flying on a mission in eastern Indonesia. Reports that the plane had been downed caused brief panic among senior members of the administration. On being alerted to the news by his brother, Secretary Dulles tried to get information from Admiral Burke on where it had been shot down, fearful that the Indonesians would now have incontrovertible proof of American involvement in support of the rebels.[13] As "the Indonesians knew they shot this one," he feared that "if we deny it they will know we have a guilty conscience." He and Burke frantically tried to concoct a plausible story, with the admiral suggesting:

> We may want to claim that this was on a normal flight to Australia and raise a rumpus with them for shooting it down. The Sec[retary] said it seemed to him that we would not want to deny this until we know how to handle the matter. Burke said what we could do was to have the plane commander say it was an engine explosion and then when he looked at it further discover that someone had shot at it.[14]

It eventuated that the reconnaissance plane had been able to limp out of Indonesian airspace and make an emergency landing at Davao in the southern Philippines, with a gaping hole in one wing.[15] By late that afternoon, Allen Dulles was able to reassure his brother about the downed aircraft, saying "we can relax re the plane. There was a friendly reception [in the Philippines]. Our Boys."[16] The secretary of state responded that this was "a great relief" and apparently felt secure in continuing to deny that the United States was providing any physical support to the rebels.

With Jakarta's minuscule air force tied up over Sumatra, however, the United States soon felt there was an opportunity to introduce camouflaged American air power in support of the Sulawesi-based rebels. Nasution noted that during the first half of April rebel forces on Sulawesi began to receive American B-25s and B-26s and expressed fears that, if a B-26 were also provided to their forces in Padang, this would enable them to bomb Jakarta as well as Medan, Pekanbaru, and Palembang. At that time, he received reports that the United States was also planning to provide the rebels with B-29s that would be based at Padang and later at Morotai. It was, he said, "in order to secure" Padang "before the rebels got air cover" that he advanced his schedule for invading the west coast of Sumatra.[17] But because of the Sumatran rebels' rapid retreat, with their successive loss of the crucial Pekanbaru and Padang airfields, the Eisenhower administration concluded that rebel forces had to demonstrate a willingness to fight before the United States could risk providing them with aircover by basing planes for operations in Sumatra on foreign airfields.

During its March-April 1958 military campaign against the PRRI forces, the Indonesian government had felt obliged to concentrate its limited air fleet over Sumatra, leaving air defenses on Java vulnerable to rebel

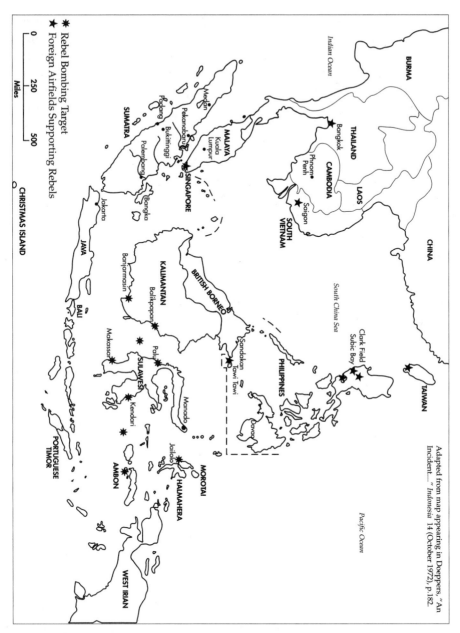

Map 6: The Air War

air power in eastern Indonesia. The Indonesian air force, AURI, was dangerously weak: Nasution recalled that "all we had were B-25s inherited from the Dutch—planes they had actually used against us in the revolution, and a few old Mustangs."[18] To defend the Indonesian capital against possible attack by rebel forces, the Indonesian air force tried to convert its Vampire jet trainers to operational use, but because of the lack of spare parts only three could be put on alert, together with one F-51 Mustang to protect Jakarta.[19]

Certainly by mid-April the rebels in Sulawesi had been strengthened by planes and pilots from abroad. They were thereby able to establish an air force, Angkatan Udara Revolusioner (AUREV), headed by Air Vice Commodore Muharto, previously the Jakarta government's base commander at Manado.[20] In addition to that city's airport and to fields on the eastern Indonesian islands of Halmahera and Morotai, AUREV was also able to use airfields in the southern Philippines, including the now-resurrected field at Sanga Sanga in the Sulu archipelago. The Indonesian government verified that the rebels in Sulawesi had bombers and Mustangs and "had established [the] fact that [the] planes were from Taiwan and they were being piloted by Americans and [Taiwan] Chinese."[21] In fact, by mid-April, according to Harvey, "the AUREV had eight to nine planes, with American, Filipino, and Taiwanese Chinese pilots, available for its use from fields in the Philippines and in Minahasa."[22] The rebels' air campaign began on April 13, when a single plane, reportedly "a B-26 with Taiwan markings," bombed Makassar airport.[23] Three days later a raid on Balikpapan destroyed an Indonesian air force Catalina and a Dakota owned by BPM Shell.[24]

The threat posed by the Permesta rebels to the Jakarta government increased on April 21, when their planes attacked Ternate, Jailolo (on Halmahera), and Morotai, and their ships were able to land occupation forces at both Jailolo and Morotai. Once Padang fell, Morotai airfield (constructed for American use during World War II) was the only one in rebel hands with a runway long enough to accommodate the four-engined B-29s.[25] With a B-29 based there the rebels could bomb Surabaya, Bandung, and Jakarta. And, according to Nasution and Sumual as well as the U.S. military attaché, this was what the Permesta strategy envisaged.[26] Ambassador Jones reported that Jakarta was anticipating such attacks before the end of May.[27]

Indeed, the plans of the rebels on Sulawesi went considerably further. Their senior military leader, Colonel Ventje Sumual, was convinced that, with the amount of air cover the United States had provided him by mid-April of 1958, he could do much more, and the capture of Jakarta itself now became his objective. Air cover of this magnitude meant control of the sea as well as the air, and he laid plans to move his troops by stages down from north Sulawesi to Java. The first step, he states, would be to move them across the Straits of Makassar to Balikpapan on the eastern coast of Borneo. From there his forces planned a move down around the southeast corner of Borneo to capture Banjarmasin that would provide the final staging area for an assault on Java's northwestern coast near Jakarta. Evidently the Jakarta government misread his preparations, states Sumual, for it "made the mistake of reinforcing the Lesser Sundas, particularly Bali and Lombok—the wrong area in view of our plans. . . . We planned to use coastal ships such as we used against Morotai and Halmahera and were confident that with the continuance of air cover our landings would be easy to execute. . . . It was technically possible to land our forces in the Jakarta area on the basis of continuing air cover . . . our plan was to land in the Jakarta area three months after the Banjarmasin landing." Sumual was confident his plan would have succeeded had the United States not abruptly ended its covert supply of planes and pilots toward the end of May.[28]

A May 6 report, "Unidentified B-29 makes long reconnaissance flights over East Indonesia from Manila to Singapore," increased fears among Jakarta's leaders regarding Sumual's plans.[29] Several rebel aircraft had attacked Ambon Harbor on April 27, heavily damaging a Greek freighter, and on April 28 they destroyed a British tanker off Balikpapan. They sank the Indonesian frigate Hang Tuah, flagship of the fleet, killing all on board, and many of Jakarta's troop transports, five at Dongala alone.[30] They bombed and strafed government air force headquarters for eastern Indonesia at Kendari in southeastern Sulawesi, and on May 1 and 2 they sank a Panamanian and an Italian vessel off Ambon.[31]

Until well into May, the Permesta forces remained on the attack. According to an American intelligence report they were initially planning to gain control over the whole of eastern Indonesia by advancing from three directions: first, securing East Kalimantan by taking Tarakan and Balikpapan; second, securing the rest of Sulawesi by attacking directly south to take Poso, Pare-Pare, and Makassar; and third, securing the Moluccas by occupying Morotai, Jailolo, Ambon, and Kupang. These attacks would all have air protection from the rebel air force "aided by American and SEATO pilots."[32] By early May they were well on the way to achieving many of these objectives. On May 8 rebel forces occupied Parigi in Central Sulawesi, arriving by ship with strong air cover.[33] They continued their bombing campaign against Ambon, attacking the government airfield, destroying planes on the ground, and also shooting down a government fighter aircraft.[34] By this time military sources in Jakarta were expecting that the "rebels will air attack Djakarta within two weeks using radar equipped long range aircraft operating from Morotai."[35] But although "from mid-April to mid-May the rebel air force controlled the skies over East Indonesia,"[36] their ability to use this superiority to affect the course of events on Java was critically dependent on decisions made the United States as well as in Indonesia.

Jakarta's military successes on Sumatra meant that by May the government was in a position to withdraw planes from the Sumatra theater for use in Sulawesi, and since Nasution "no longer had difficulty in getting forces from the three large Java divisions," he now could considerably augment his forces on the ground in eastern Indonesia.[37]

By the middle of that month government forces had begun to focus on crushing the Permesta wing of the PRRI. On May 10, AURI planes began an all-out offensive against the rebels' air power in eastern Indonesia. After a surprise attack that destroyed at least five rebel planes parked at Manado's airbase, they targeted the airfields of Morotai and Jailolo (Halmahera) in the northern Moluccas. In the wake of this assault, Jakarta mounted ground attacks, recapturing the island of Morotai on May 20.[38] It also launched ground assaults against rebel strongholds on Halmahera, and then began attacks on northern Sulawesi itself.[39] By mid-June, the backbone of the rebel air power had been largely broken, with only five planes still based in northern Sulawesi, and the government was preparing to open its offensive against the rebel headquarters in Manado.[40]

Pressures for Change in American Policy

The rebels' ignominious withdrawal from Padang had immediately strengthened the hands of those arguing for a change in American policy. Since April 8 Ambassador Jones had been recommending that the United States reassess its attitude toward Indonesia's armed forces. He had then cabled that he was "inclined [to] feel our best hope in Indonesia lies with army," on the basis of his assessment that it was the "only powerful non-Communist political element on Java" and that it "has become influential in all fields [of] administration and is last word in some of them." This had "greatly increased its political power." On April 15, he cabled that the "time may have arrived to make some positive gesture of support toward Indonesian military if we are to preserve pro-American anti-Communist loyalties among top officer group here."[41]

The fall of Padang had also clearly affected the thinking of the Joint Chiefs of Staff, who on April 8 had recommended that "if Communist domination of Indonesia is to be prevented, action must be taken, including overt measures as required, to insure either the success of the dissidents or the suppression of the pro-Communist elements of the Sukarno government."[42] Ten days later, immediately after the fall of Padang, the Joint Chiefs of Staff reversed themselves and now backed up the ambassador's assessments. General Maxwell Taylor sent a message to the secretary of defense informing him that, as only "overt US military assistance" to the rebels could prevent their "defeat and ultimate liquidation," the Joint Chiefs urged that the United States should now "ally with Nasution, rather than send U.S. troops." They recommended that "the matter of an approach to Nasution be re-examined on an urgent basis, taking as a point of departure the recommendations of Ambassador Jones in his Message . . . of 15 April 1958." Taylor suggested that "U.S. support of Nasution or other influential Indonesian Army leaders . . . might influence him [Nasution] to take positive action to prevent a communist take-over by political or other means."[43] Thus, American military leaders had now adopted a position significantly less hawkish than that of the Dulles brothers.

As the extent of the military debacle in West Sumatra became clearer, even Allen Dulles acknowledged that as far as rebel forces were concerned "there is no fight in them." By late April Secretary of State Dulles too was finally becoming somewhat aware of the disastrous miscalculations that had been guiding American policy and was considering the possibility of "our switching around and backing the government."[44] American support of rebel forces, however, had been too long in the making for it to be reversed easily, even if senior officials wished to do so, and neither of the Dulles brothers seems at this point to have beem willing to cut their ties with the dissidents.

By early May, although both Dulles brothers had become disillusioned with the fighting capacity of the rebels on Sumatra, they still had not lost hope in the Permesta group in Sulawesi. In this they were backed by the British foreign minister, Selwyn Lloyd, and after talking with him on May 6 in Copenhagen, Secretary of State Dulles cabled Washington the next day:

> In private conversation with me evening May 6, Lloyd said he thought most recent news from Indonesia encouraging and we should not rpt not give up hope of keeping on the pressure through the rebellious forces now rpt now principally in the Celebes. He expressed view that it not rpt not impossible that activity in Sumatra might revive if there were success in the Celebes. He said his Ambassador Djakarta strongly favored trying for a political solution and abandoning any assistance to the rebels, but that Rob Scott [commissioner-general for the United Kingdom in Southeast Asia], whose judgment Lloyd valued more highly, did not rpt not share this view.[45]

Against the advice of their ambassadors in Jakarta, then, the foreign-policy heads on both sides of the Atlantic still saw the rebels as providing leverage through which Jakarta could be pressured into adopting leaders and policies more in keeping with the priorities of the United States and Britain.

Both Eisenhower and Dulles, when queried at news conferences, steadfastly denied any U.S. government support of the rebels and held that any Americans who might have been involved were simply "soldiers of fortune," whom the U.S. government had no legal obligation to restrain. While the Indonesian press carried extensive accounts of American, Philippine, and Taiwanese personnel participating on the side of the rebels — especially in eastern Indonesia,[46] reporting in American newspapers was in most cases nominal. This was true of the *New York Times*, which remained generally partisan, in favor of the rebels and uncritically supportive of Dulles's and Eisenhower's positions on Indonesia.[47] Thus, as Roger Hilsman has noted, the *New York Times*, as late as May 9, 1958, responded to

Jakarta's charge that the rebels had received aid from the United States with "a long and indignant editorial denouncing the Indonesian Government for circulating a 'false report'" and then asserting: "Our Secretary of State was emphatic in his declaration that this country would not deviate from a correct neutrality. The President, himself, at a news conference reiterated this position. [Jakarta's] cause is not promoted by charges that are manifestly false."[48]

By this time, Ambassador Jones was arguing that further aid to the rebels would be counterproductive, reiterating that the "rebels newly found air strength has been given privately as reason for breakdown of earlier plans to attempt solution of rebellion by negotiation once rebel capital in Sumatra had fallen." Jones's opinion that American policy should rapidly shift away from the rebels had been reinforced by his first meeting with General Nasution, in which the ambassador was most favorably impressed by the army chief of staff, describing him as "a highly intelligent, determined man of character with definite philosophy and most attractive personality." Further, Jones was convinced by Nasution that the "army would never permit Communists to take over government," and he understood Nasution's message to be "that Indonesian Army would in effect be policeman of constitution and guardian of Indonesian liberties and that he was determined to weld it into effective instrument for this purpose."[49] Nasution's reassurances were being backed up by the American military attaché's conversations with other central government commanders, who emphasized the fact that American-trained officers headed Jakarta's operations against the rebels. As Jusuf told the American assistant military attaché: "In Army Headquarters, they refer to the operational commanders as 'the sons of Eisenhower,' Jani (CO in Sumatra), Rukmito, Huhnholz [who led the operation against Morotai] and myself, all US trained."[50]

Admiral Felix Stump, commander of U.S. forces in the Pacific, had begun on May 8 to pressure the administration to change its policy. Reacting to Jones's May 6 conversation with Djuanda in which the Indonesian prime minister deplored foreign support of the rebels and expressed his fear that "relations between U.S. and Indonesia were at cross roads," Stump cabled:

> Djuanda's presentation of views to Jones . . . reveal that the situation is grave indeed and that there is an imminent possibility of a break of relations between Indonesia and us. If this should transpire, the fat is really in the fire and we will have forced beyond the point of no return anti-Communist elements which may still exist within the framework of the Djakarta government.

Remarking that "it is obvious that Djuanda knows of our active assistance to the rebels," the admiral went on to contend that "further bombings, etc, can only be counter-productive during the period when we are trying to develop a response and sense of gravity to the communist danger among the the anti-communist elements left in Djakarta."[51]

There was a further closing of ranks between the American military and the Jakarta embassy when Admiral Laurence H. Frost, chief of U.S. Naval Intelligence, met the next day with General Nasution and other government leaders in talks arranged by Jones and emerged from these discussions as close to the ambassador's views as the latter could have hoped. As Jones later wrote:

> Frost's conclusion was the same as my own: the Indonesian military leadership was the key to remedying the internal political situation. He found no indication that anyone was thinking of trying to unseat Sukarno; indeed, the President was still a potent symbol of Indonesian independence, and it was time for the United States government to accept this as a fact of life. Frost also supported my feeling that our government must now show the Indonesian military leadership tangible evidence of its willingness to support them.[52]

In responding to this pressure from his ambassador in Jakarta and from the military, Secretary of State Dulles on May 13 suggested the possibility of a "cessation of military activities in order to permit the anti-Communist elements in Djakarta to take the contemplated steps in attainment their objectives which in essence are the same as those of the dissidents." He saw this in the context of a cease-fire by all forces, during which "there would be no build-up by either side," and expressed the hope that "during the cease fire period Nasution would take such action as he contemplates to bring about a change in the Cabinet and against the Communists." In return for this, "he can be assured of receiving U.S. military and economic support." In accompanying instructions to Jones, sent the same day, however, Dulles expressed skepticism, writing that it was "not clear what specific action government or Nasution intends to take against Communists or whether what they say is more than talk." In instructing Jones to reiterate American concern regarding the "growing influence and ambitions of the Communist Party in Indonesia," he again urged him to make clear: "It is not possible for us to control the activities of all Americans, some of whom are 'soldiers of fortune' and interested in freedom, and there is no international obligation on our part to do so." Nevertheless, he offered what probably seemed to him a major concession, stating that, if the Indonesian government "takes definite measures for the elimination of the Communist threat . . . we would use full extent of our influence . . . to try to compose the situation," as well as extend economic aid "and such military aid as would seem appropriate to maintain internal order as against any Communist subversive threat."[53]

This halfhearted olive branch held out by Dulles in the form of a possible cease-fire between the rebels and the government forces was "seed sown on stony ground" in Jakarta. When the American ambassador presented the cease-fire proposal to Djuanda, the "Prime Minister interrupted and inquired what I meant by 'cease-fire.' When I explained, he shook his head incredulously and said, 'but this would mean negotiating with the rebels. This we could never accept.'" When Jones expressed the United States's willingness to take the initiative by publicly suggesting the cease-fire itself, if the Indonesian government would agree to this,

> Djuanda rejected this flatly, commenting that there was one thing upon which he, President Sukarno, Suwirjo, head of PNI, and Army were in complete agreement—that was that there would be no negotiations with Indonesian Army officers who had sought foreign assistance in fighting other Indonesians. They were adamant on this point, he said.[54]

As a result of his talks with Djuanda and parallel talks by the U.S. army attaché with Sukendro, Jones cabled Washington on May 15 that

> Sukarno, Djuanda, Subandrio and Nasution are united in conviction GOI [government of Indonesia] can work with US only on following basis:
> 1. US to exercise its influence to bring about cessation of foreign support to rebels, especially air support.
> 2. GOI to reorganize Cabinet.
> 3. GOI to proceed to win military victory over rebels in Menado area.
> 4. GOI to move against Commies with US military aid supporting GOI forces.
> 5. GOI economic rehabilitation and development with US support.

Recognizing that several of these points would be anathema to some policy-makers in Washington, Jones hoped to overcome their objections by asserting that the Indonesian government was in fact preparing to move "in parallel line toward objectives originally set forth by rebels." Arguing for a "reassessment of current rebel objectives," he stated that "it would appear time has arrived to put brakes on rebel military effort" that "has served constructive purpose but I believe this is as far as it can go without pushing GOI to breaking point and alignment with Soviet bloc." In view of all the above he recommended the following series of actions:

> 1. Statement by Secretary at next press conference deploring bombings, expressing hope conflict will soon be concluded and peace and stability restored to area and assuring GOI that US will do what it can to discourage foreign adventurers.
> 2. Take any steps available to us to slow down further material support for rebels.
> 3. Arrange if possible approach to rebels to:
> (A) Ascertain present objectives, pointing out probable early fulfillment of their primary political objectives.
> (B) Convey view of US that point has been reached at which further military action will play into hands of Communists.
> (C) Urge rebels to move toward peaceful settlement of dispute.

Having reached the conclusion that the Indonesian government "will not take first overt move and covert move on their part was flatly rejected," he proposed "that next step should be to induce rebels to make covert overtures toward settlement."[55]

The secretary of state, however, was not ready for such a prescription, and his more militant posture still precluded the moves toward a possible compromise that Jones and General Taylor sought. It took an altogether shattering and unexpected event to shake Dulles's dogged determination to sustain the Sulawesi rebels' air superiority.

Capture of an American Pilot

The Eisenhower administration's first tentative steps toward changing its policy were accelerated by an event that turned out to be disastrous for the rebels. In the same telegram of May 18 in which Assistant Secretary Robertson notified Jones that Secretary Dulles was planning to hold a press conference during which he would make a statement in line with Jones's first recommendation, Robertson also stated:

> Have just heard of bombings today at Amboina. Regret they occurred at time when you exploring situation further, but trust their effect may be offset to a certain extent by steps we are taking and assurance we exploring matter with neighboring countries.[56]

But this particular incident was a decisive one. On May 18 a rebel B-26 bomber carried out apparently indiscriminate raids against the city of Ambon, a port on the eastern Indonesian island of Amboina. After sinking an Indonesian naval vessel at its pier the plane bombed a church and the central market, resulting in heavy civilian casualties. Before the plane left, however, antiaircraft fire brought it down, and its American pilot, Allen L. Pope, and his Indonesian radio operator were captured.

Pope's capture provided Jakarta with incontrovertible evidence of direct American involvement in support of the rebels. The administration persisted in its contention that he was an independent "soldier of fortune" for whom the United States was not responsible. But the fact that he carried not merely a diary containing detailed accounts of recent bombing missions but also U.S. military identification papers, a copy of recently dated orders from a U.S. army base, and a current post exchange card for Clark Air Force Base in the Philippines made it difficult for this argument to be given much credence.[57]

Sukarno and other Indonesian government leaders, however, used the leverage provided by this new card with remarkable restraint and skill, and no public announcement was even made of Pope's capture until May 27, nine days after he was shot down.[58] On that day, however, before he could be briefed by his superiors in Jakarta, Lieutenant Colonel Herman Pieters, the government's eastern Indonesia commander who brought Pope to Jakarta, gave some details of his capture and service with the rebels in an airport interview. Outraged at the heavy loss of civilian lives in this and previous bombings of Ambon, Pieters quoted Pope as saying there were three other American pilots at the rebel forward airbase at Manado, as well as Philippine and Taiwanese pilots, with the Americans having previously been stationed at Clark Field, the major American base in the Philippines.[59] Before he could go into further detail Pieters was ordered by Nasution and Djuanda to stop talking, but what he had divulged was carried in all the major Indonesian newspapers. The Communist press now had positive proof to substantiate its earlier charges. The U.S. army attaché in Jakarta was very worried and cabled Washington: "If rebel aircraft again start bombing effect on U.S.-Indon relations could be disastrous."[60]

Ambassador Jones credited the Jakarta government with "great maturity" in its efforts to avoid "making use of the bombings of the church and market place for purposes of propaganda—domestic or international." When discussing this matter with one of the authors only seven months after the bombing, this normally calm and composed ambassador was still seething with anger over what his sources had indicated to have been "several hundred civilians killed." (In the book he wrote twelve years after the bombing, he stated that the civilian casualties were reported to be "in the vicinity of 700," but while pursuing his official duties he abided by the Jakarta government's "official" casualty figure of six civilians and seventeen members of the armed forces.)

Having sensed from Jones some movement by the United States toward a more friendly position in the week before this incident, the Indonesian government did its best to downplay Pope and the implications of his actions. Prime Minister Djuanda, in a conversation with a British embassy official, voiced his government's concern "lest the remaining Americans should not get out of Minahasa in time—he didn't want any more to be captured!" and expressed his relief that the incident was not worse, for "just before Pope's aircraft was shot down it had 'near-missed' a transport with no fewer than 1,000 troops on board." "Casualties on this scale," Djuanda said, "would have provoked violent reactions. He would have preferred to keep the capture and casualties a secret but that had proved impossible."[61]

To help dampen public outrage at what information had gotten out, casualties at Ambon remained officially calculated at only six civilians and seventeen armed-forces personnel. Pope was hidden away from the press at the pleasant mountain resort of Kaliurang where, according to Jones, he was "treated well and given excellent medical attention" for the hip he had broken after bailing out of his plane. Most important in defusing the public outrage, his trial was delayed for nineteen months. Jones correctly observed:

Indonesians maintained that the delay was to let Indonesian tempers cool down, and privately admitted that the PKI would have a field day if Pope were tried while the whole matter was fresh in the minds of the public. Certainly from the standpoint of the American government, an early public trial of Pope would not have helped matters.[62]

In Pope's diary, log, and other papers found on his plane and person, there was much information that was disclosed at his trial but never made it into the press—either in Indonesia or in the United States. Any reading of the trial transcript discloses how gently Pope was treated and how many obvious questions were not pursued. The trial record of the military court that sat in judgment on Pope provides a sketchy account of his twelve bombing and strafing missions against government naval and merchant shipping, airfields, and port cities—with accounts of ships sunk and airplanes destroyed at airports. This record shows that the attack on Ambon in which he was shot down was the fifth he had made on this city and its environs. But potentially most embarrassing to the United States was not only that Pope's immediate employer was the CIA—through its wholly owned subsidiary CAT (Civil Air Transport, based on Taiwan)—but also that he had been released to CAT on April 21 on 120 days temporary duty while assigned to the headquarters of the U.S. Army command at Camp Bruckner in the Ryukyu Islands.[63] (In fact, Pope was one of eight names listed in this order from Camp Bruckner, but only that part of the order pertaining to him—where his name stood third—was excerpted and actually incorporated into the trial record, no reference being made to the other seven individuals.[64])

It was with respect to Pope's action that CIA Chief Allen Dulles in April 1961, in a highly classified report in response to a request from President Kennedy, formally acknowledged in rather Spartan terms that in November 1957 the Eisenhower administration had approved "a special political action program in Indonesia calling for the maintenance as a force in being of the anti-Communist, pro-West dissident movement established by anti-Sukarno military commanders in Sumatra and the Celebes [Sulawesi]," and that this

> later authorized the provision of arms and other military aid to the dissidents including air support. Several C.A.T. pilots volunteered for this work, *ostensibly* took leave from their C.A.T. jobs and and as "Soldiers of Fortune" employed by the dissidents, undertook combat missions. On 18 May 1958 one of these pilots, Mr. Allen Lawrence Pope, was shot down. [emphasis added][65]

Dulles further observed that "preservation of Pope's cover story has required considerable circumspection on the part of U.S. officials."

Pope was convicted and sentenced to death on April 29, 1960—nearly two years after his capture and well after public interest in his actions had died down and United States-Indonesian relations had been considerably repaired. The sentence was never carried out, and he continued to live in comfort under house arrest until quietly freed shortly after U.S. Attorney General Robert Kennedy spoke with Sukarno in Jakarta during a "good-will visit" to Indonesia in February 1962 concerned with trying to settle the West Irian dispute. It is possible that Pope's release helped induce the Kennedy administration to play a more active role in helping resolve the issue.

It is not entirely clear whether it was Robert Kennedy or Pope's wife, mother, and sister who exerted the most influence in getting Sukarno to grant Pope a pardon. Women's tears were known to make Sukarno extremely uncomfortable, and all three women cried profusely when being received by him. Whatever the case, not long after these visits Sukarno sent word to Pope that he was pardoning and releasing him. The president admonished: "I want no propaganda about it. Now go. Lose yourself in the U.S.A. secretly. Don't show yourself publicly. Don't give out news stories. Don't issue statements. Just go home, hide yourself, get lost, and we'll forget the whole thing."[66]

Shortly after that, on the night of July 2, 1962, an Indonesian army lieutenant colonel quietly drove Pope to the airport where an American plane was awaiting him, his evident fear subdued by a note from Ambassador Jones, saying that everything was all right.[67]

Washington Reverses Course

The Pope incident and Jakarta's handling of it were probably significant in accelerating a shift in Washington's official policy toward Indonesia. On May 20, apparently complying with Ambassador Jones's recommendations, Dulles made a press statement as the first in a series of steps aimed at indicating Washington's change of heart toward Jakarta. During his press conference, when asked to comment on the situation in Indonesia, the secretary made the marvelous statement:

> I would say this that the United States believes that the situation in Indonesia can be and should be dealt with as an Indonesian problem. The U.S. itself is a nation which has suffered civil war, and we have sympathy and regret when another country undergoes the losses in life and economic dislocations that are incidental to civil war. But we do believe that the situation can be and should be dealt with as an Indonesian matter by the Indonesians without intrusion from without, and we hope that there will be quickly restored peace and stability in the Indonesian Republic.[68]

That same day, in a meeting with Australian ambassador Howard Beale, Assistant Secretary for Far Eastern Affairs Walter Robertson spelled out the change in United States policy, stating that "in view of the collapse of the Sumatra dissidents due to their unwillingness to fight and of the small leverage provided by the Celebes group, we had come to the conclusion that a solution would have to be found through development of assets on Java."[69]

The Eisenhower administration now clearly regarded its "assets on Java" as consisting of the army leadership, Prime Minister Djuanda, and other moderate political elements in the Jakarta government. Within a few days thereafter, American policy toward the Indonesian government and the rebels underwent a reversal, with further support for the rebels being officially discouraged—even if actually not completely ended. Ambassador Cumming and Graham Irwin, assistant secretary of defense for international affairs, were sent to Singapore to "stand down" the by now well known center of American operations in Sumatra.[70] Although American military supplies from Taiwan (mostly via the Philippines) continued to reach the rebels on Sulawesi, most of the air power supplied to them through the CIA appears to have been abruptly withdrawn. And a small amount of American aid now, after a long lapse, began slowly to go once again to the central government and its armed forces.

Coupled with Dulles's May 20 press statement, the administration took a number of further steps: on May 22 it arranged for the sale of $5.5 million of rice to Jakarta under an earlier PL-480 agreement signed in March 1956; it issued export licenses for approximately $2 million worth of spare parts for aircraft belonging to the Indonesian airline, Garuda, and the Indonesian air force, in addition to 250 revolvers for the navy and ammunition for the police; it undertook to provide sixty-one diesel generating plants, most of which were to be located in the outer islands; and it initiated measures to implement an economic development loan of $15 million agreed to in 1957 for work on the Sumatra north-south highway.[71]

Dulles, however, was still dragging his heels on committing the United States to inaugurate any really substantial or binding change in American policy, and in his instructions to Jones of May 23 he made it clear that he intended to reverse the policy shift if there were no quid pro quo from Jakarta. His instructions for Jones's "background guidance and for discreet use at times and with persons of his choosing" contained an implicit threat:

> It is utterly unrealistic for anyone to believe that Indonesia can in tranquillity wend its way into the Communist camp. Once it becomes clear that that was the course, the now dying embers of revolution would burst out in flames and it would not be possible for the United States, even should it so desire, to restrain the impulses of governments and individuals who are dedicated to freedom and some of whom would feel they were imperiled by the course Indonesia was taking.[72]

He concluded that "we are hoping to see concretely, the start of a new trend and some action responsive to our own" from the non-Communist forces in Jakarta.

These hopes were to a large extent undercut by the popular reaction in Indonesia to the Pope affair. Although the Jakarta government did its best to restrain Indonesian outrage in both the military and civilian arenas, Jones concluded that Pope's downing and the "ensuing emotional reaction" to it in Indonesia "were serious setbacks to new favorable trend in US-Indonesian relations" and that Pope's capture had stimulated the campaign by "Communist and leftist elements who identify US as power behind rebellion."[73] The pro-American deputy chief of staff, Ibnu Sutowo, expressed the feelings among the military, stating

> that Pope case will have serious reactions throughout Indonesia, especially in army. Before there was a large group of officers who were on fence, but appearance of Pope has changed that. GOI . . . troops in Sumatra are mostly anti-American now because of large amount of American made equipment supplied to rebels. Troops in East Indonesia blame U.S. for permitting air attacks and capture of Pope removes any doubt these people may have had as to who actually behind support to rebels.[74]

Jakarta's Victory in Northern Sulawesi

By early June, in eastern Indonesia, after the withdrawal of American and other foreign personnel from Manado, the central government had gained air superiority and captured the principal airfields at Gorontalo, Jailolo, and Morotai. Its forces were then in a position to press their campaign from all sides against the major rebel strongholds in northeastern Sulawesi. Reports came in that the chief of staff of the Permesta armed forces, Colonel Sumual, apparently at American urging, was seeking to open negotiations with Jakarta, but the Jakarta military leadership now dismissed any such overtures until after an unconditional surrender by his troops.[75]

On June 8 Indonesian naval ships began shelling the city of Manado. Jakarta followed this with air attacks on Manado and other rebel strongholds and with ground assaults along the coast. The battle for Manado was one of the fiercest of the rebellion, and not until June 24 did Warouw, deputy prime minister of the PRRI/Permesta government, finally order evacuation of the city, with the government forces occupying it two days later.[76] After a further six weeks of fierce fighting, the Permesta government under Warouw retired to the border area of Bolaang-Mongondow, while the military district commanders established their headquarters in mountainous areas of southeastern Minahasa that could serve as bases for guerrilla warfare.[77]

The United States and Its Allies: Keeping Options Open

When the United States began its policy shift in late May 1958, it needed at least to inform the Asian allies whose assistance it had enlisted in support of the rebels. Even if the United States had been wholehearted in wanting to reverse this policy, it would have been difficult and certainly awkward to enforce its allies' compliance. But, the Eisenhower administration was in fact ambivalent in approaching its allies, for its own change of tack was initially uncertain and tentative, dependent in part on Jakarta's response as well as on shifts of influence among American policymakers. One apparently influential school of thought argued that it was important to keep the rebel movement alive in order to leave open the option—and a base on which to build—for a reintroduction of major military support to those opposed to Jakarta.

The Roles of Taiwan and Korea

The two major external adjuncts of the Eisenhower administration's Indonesian intervention had been the Chinese government of Chiang Kai-shek on Taiwan and the government of the Philippines. Of the two, Taiwan had been by far the most important: providing the major channel for American war materiel going to both groups of rebels and itself selling them additional arms, as well as providing pilots and artillery instructors to the Permesta forces on Sulawesi. Taiwan was not only host to the CIA's CAT airlines, whose planes were so heavily involved in behalf of the rebels, but some of its own air force delivered weapons to them in Sumatra and probably Sulawesi as well.

Moreover, many soldiers from both rebel areas were sent for special training in the use of weapons and communications equipment to Taiwan, as well as to Okinawa, Saipan, and probably Guam and Thailand. And apparently in late December 1957, a Chinese Nationalist team from Taiwan arrived at Manado in northern Sulawesi, traveling either by air or by submarine. According to Colonel Alex Kawilarang, who was especially knowledgeable of developments in the Sulawesi theater, they were not instructors, as sometimes alleged, but "five or six pilots and a ground crew."[78]

While Taiwan acted as the United States's major foreign agent in furthering its intervention in Indonesia, the actions of the Taiwanese government also stemmed from its own political convictions and agenda. Until at least the watershed event of Pope's capture these appeared to be roughly parallel with those of the United States.

A further complication for U.S. officials, which affected Taiwan's approach to the civil war, was the sudden introduction of a wild card in the person of South Korea's unpredictable president, Syngman Rhee. As early as March 29 he had stressed that Korea was ready to offer the rebels in Indonesia army, naval, and air support. President Rhee's generally well controlled press then began to float a trial balloon calling for the dispatch of Korean troops to fight on the side of the rebels, in view of what was claimed to be "every probability" that mainland China would "openly intervene by sending [a] People's Volunteer Army to Indonesia."[79] While in fact the People's Republic of China had as yet given no indication of any such intention, Rhee's initiative was politically unsettling and proved useful to those elements in Taiwan's leadership who favored continuing support to the Indonesian rebels. Their clamor became progessively louder and, together with Dulles's public announcement that the United States had "no legal obligation to control" American adventurers, precipitated a warning by the Chinese Communist government that, if requested, it would send its own "volunteers" to Indonesia to support the Jakarta government in the civil war.[80]

It was against this background that, in a speech on May 2, Sukarno alluded to the Chinese offer and warned the United States: "Don't play with fire" (giving additional point to his warning by rendering this part of his speech in English). Sukarno never gave any indication that he would accept China's offer, and, of course, it would have been logistically impossible for it to have gotten any significant number of soldiers past the barrier of the Seventh Fleet and air power based on Taiwan. But there is no doubt that the offer stimulated further threats from Rhee.

On May 19, the American embassy in Seoul reported that South Korean volunteers were in fact being recruited to assist the Indonesian rebels as part of a government-supported effort in their behalf that "included several Presidential statements; editorials [in the] pro-Government press; and [a] reported deal [to] sell 'surplus' ROK [Republic of Korea] arms to Indonesian rebels." Within a week Dulles sought to put a damper on this activity—at least for the time being—and signaled the change in the United States's official policy toward Jakarta in a telegram to the American ambassador in Seoul. In this he urged that the South Korean foreign minister "and in your discretion Rhee" be discouraged from any further support for the rebels. But Dulles did not want to close the door on possible Korean military involvement should this at a later date conform with American interests. Thus, in concluding this cable to his ambassador to Seoul, he wrote: "We will of course advise you should there be any change in our thinking at a later date to encourage such action as Korean group apparently contemplating at this time as means increasing pressure for action [on] Djakarta." In accordance with these instructions, the American ambassador told South Korea's foreign minister, "I was not rpt not asking ROK government to discontinue consideration which it might be giving to desirability of assistance to rebels at some future time . . . but rather that public statements and demonstrations be stopped."[81]

President Rhee remained outspoken in his conviction that Jakarta would be receiving "volunteers" from outside and that the "anti-Communist forces must get there first." He informed the American envoy that he therefore had a "plan to communicate with govts. of China [Taiwan], Philippines, Australia, Thailand and perhaps Vietnam [Saigon] to ascertain if there was a basis for common action." The American ambassador, nevertheless, was confident that South Korea "will remain responsive to US views and will avoid rash action."[82]

Rhee's prophecy seems to have been based on press reports in Jakarta, attributed to a high government source, that asserted that China had offered "thousands of volunteers" to the Indonesian government. A more realistic concern for the United States was Jakarta's clear threat, first suggested on May 3 but then repeated, of following Burma's course and taking the case of Taiwan's military intervention to the United Nations. Such a move—even if yielding no more results than it did in Burma's effort—would certainly have exposed American complicity in Taiwan's support to the rebels in Indonesia. It was a prospect that clearly worried Ambassador Jones.[83]

Rhee's fears that the mainland Chinese "volunteers" would be sent to assist the Jakarta government soon appeared to be shared by Taipei, and American diplomacy was presented with a neat dilemma regarding how to keep the threat of military action by Taiwan alive as a deterrent to Jakarta while at the same time improving relations with the Indonesian government. Thus Dulles warned his ambassador in Taipei, "In view of delicate situation in Indonesia [we] believe it desirable that public statements be avoided and that if unavoidable they be couched in terms which not likely embarrass us or local governments."[84] The State Department also made clear that it was paying only lip service to the Indonesian request that the United States restrain Taiwan, cabling its embassies there and in Jakarta in early May:

> Since [Taiwanese] Chinese participation, if any, is according to Subandrio and Djuanda's statements by "adventurers", we do not feel we can do any more than inform GRC [Government of the Republic of China—Taiwan] of Subandrio's request. As pointed out by Secretary in his press conference May 1, U.S. has no legal obligation to control the activities of this character by Americans. We are not, therefore, in position ask GRC to take any different action.[85]

Taipei followed this hint and issued a public statement on May 10 asserting that it "could not exercise control over actions [of] its citizens residing abroad but [that] no GRC Air Force pilots [were] taking part in foreign military operation." Nevertheless, as late as July 9 bombers believed to be based in Taiwan were still making sorties against government forces in northern Sulawesi.[86]

Taiwan also continued to provide military aid to the rebels, in mid-June having sent them an "unspecified quantity of old Japanese-type light artillery" and despatching a number of Chinese military officers to Sulawesi "to train the Indonesian dissidents in modern means of warfare." Although most of these military advisers had returned to Taiwan before the end of June, as "the Indonesians had been adept at learning how to use the artillery," two or three remained, with "the necessary means to escape if that became necessary."[87]

As usual, it was the local Chinese in Indonesia who suffered for Taiwan's support to the rebels, and between May 5 and July 11, nineteen pro-Kuomintang leaders of the Chinese community in Jakarta, including publishers, editors, school officials, businessmen, and party functionaries, were arrested for "subversive activity." A few months later, Nasution placed all Kuomintang Chinese business firms under government control.[88]

Input of the Philippines

The Philippines cooperated with the United States in setting up training camps for the rebels and by making its airfields as well as those at the U.S. Clark Field available to the rebels and the mostly foreign (Taiwanese, Filipino, and American) pilots who by the spring of 1958 under CIA contract were flying for the Permesta rebels in eastern Indonesia. Numerous Filipinos worked with the CIA in logistical aspects of these operations, probably the most important being Benigno (Ninoy) Aquino. At President Carlos Garcia's request, he opened up his family's Hacienda Luisita in Tarlac as a training camp for the rebels and, as he recalled, "We even set up an elaborate radio network so the rebels could contact their people."[89] According to Colonel Ahmad Husein, "Ninoy Aquino was instrumental in getting arms to Sumual's group in Sulawesi, making several trips there in the process with arms brought from Taiwan."[90] Aquino himself stated that in early February Garcia sent him and two Philippine army radio technicians to Manado to establish a secret radio transmitter through which he kept the Philippine president regularly informed of the situation in Sulawesi. He added that this assignment went well beyond gathering information. Referring to divisions among the Permesta rebels, he said, "My main mission was to fuse these two groups together and get them organized. Otherwise the supplies we were flying in would be useless." He recalled that when Pope was captured, "He must have sung like a canary, because they were identifying everybody in the Menado operation. The Americans backed out, packed up, flew off. 'This isn't so long, this is goodbye,' they said." Aquino then filed his last report to Garcia, and told him he also was pulling out.[91] But apparently Aquino's most important function during the nearly four months that he was based in Manado was as a channel of American funds to the rebels. According to his close friend, Senator Jose Diokno, he had been appointed by President Carlos Garcia as one of the principal paymasters for funds channeled through the Philippine president's office by the CIA for support of Permesta's military operations.[92]

Jose Fuentabella, the Philippine ambassador to Jakarta, emerged as an eloquent critic of Philippine support of the rebels and publicly differed with President Garcia and Defense Minister Vargas. As early as May 5 the *Manila Times* reported that in congressional circles there was "mounting support for Fuentabella's stand in his controversy with [Foreign Minister] Serrano." Even before news broke of Pope's capture and Clark Field's involvement, the Philippine press was accusing Serrano of being "an American tool" and attacking him for publicly acknowledging his reliance on the American embassy in Manila for information regarding Indonesia's civil war. And with the publication of the circumstance and background of Pope's capture, Garcia's and Serrano's dogged claim of strict neutrality in the civil war was seriously discredited. Defense Minister Jesus Vargas, who had been outspoken in his criticism of Sukarno's government and wild in his charges against it, was left in an even more awkward position.[93] His blatantly false charge, clearly mirroring the most extreme rebel propaganda, that "Soviet technicians and military experts" were aiding Jakarta's forces finally so crystalized the Djuanda cabinet's anger against Philippine aid to the rebels as to remove its previous restraint in publicly criticizing Philippine intervention.

The United States clearly did not keep the Philippines up to date with its policy shift in mid-May 1958, and not until the end of July did the American embassy in Manila report Foreign Minister Serrano's resentment that the United States had not informed it of the change, "particularly," the embassy noted, "since the Phils had been so heavily involved in the previous phase."[94]

· · · · ·

Events seemed to reinforce the conclusion that the United States was of two minds as to whether it wanted its Asian supporters to go along with its official change in policy. For despite American moves to provide token military aid to the Jakarta government, military support from outside Indonesia was clearly still also reaching the rebels. Through June and until at least July 19, one or more B-26s based outside the country continued to attack government forces in eastern Indonesia.[95] In reporting one of these attacks in mid-June, Foreign Minister Subandrio complained that, "since all useable airfields in Menado and vicinity are now under GOI control, including Morotai, only airport from which plane could have come . . . was Sanga Sanga in the Philippines." Ambassador Jones himself expressed the opinion that the plane had been based in Taiwan (presumably refueling at Sanga Sanga) and warned the administration that the Indonesians knew that its government "could not exist without US support and consequently will continue to believe US lending tacit support" to the attacks. The B-26 attacks continued, with the Indonesian government and army becoming ever more outraged, as they were sure the Americans could stop these if they wished. On July 21 Sukarno expressed the view to Ambassador Jones that "the psychological situation between Indonesia and the U.S. was not good and was beginning to deteriorate" and that the "improvement [in United States-Indonesian relations] that had occurred few weeks ago had been pretty well wiped out by continuation of bombings by B-26s."[96]

End of the Dulles Policy

The wholesale military defeats of the rebels left the United States in an unenviable position. All the factors in Indonesia that had worried American government leaders and their allies when they decided to promote and support the rebellion were still in place, and in fact Sukarno had been further strengthened by facing down the threat posed by the uprising. Foreign support to the rebellion had also given greater legitimacy to anti-American elements in Indonesia, notably the PKI, and undercut the generally pro-American Masjumi and PSI parties that were seen as tied both to the rebellion and to its foreign backers. The vast majority of the leaders in Jakarta whom the United States had regarded as its allies and "assets" had either been weakened, discredited, or alienated.

Dulles could not escape these facts as he confronted the deteriorating situation that had resulted from his policies. Reluctantly, he began to recognize that, if the United States were not to lose all its influence in Indonesia, it would have to make gestures of reconciliation beyond its mostly symbolic steps of late May (see above), by now providing the Jakarta government with a significant amount of the military and economic support it so badly needed. He continued, however, to contend that, if the United States were now to start furnishing some of these supplies, Sukarno and other leaders in Jakarta should be so grateful that they must switch from a neutral international stance to a pro-American one and begin to crack down firmly on the PKI. He seemed to believe that Sukarno should adopt the American view that the PKI and the Soviet bloc posed the greatest threat to Indonesia's "security and independence,"[97] despite the fact that the Indonesian president was still in the throes of suppressing a major internal rebellion mounted by local anti-Communist elements critically dependent on support from the United States and its allies.

Nevertheless, Sukarno and Djuanda were pragmatic enough to recognize that it was in Indonesia's interests to ease the tensions in relations with the United States, and in the government reshuffle that was being negotiated throughout June they tried to bring the Sultan of Yogyakarta into the cabinet, both to achieve this purpose and to strengthen national unity. But the president was unwilling to give him an important position such as either the minister of defense or deputy prime minister, offering him instead only the position of minister of trade. His refusal of this lesser ministry disappointed Sukarno, Djuanda, moderate political leaders in Jakarta, rebel forces, and the United States.[98] Even after it became clear that the Sultan would not enter the cabinet, U.S. officials continued to hope that the government reshuffle would remove leftist leaders—none of them members of the PKI but nevertheless radical in their socioeconomic orientation.[99] But in the new cabinet, finally announced on June 25, all these ministers retained minor posts (with or without portfolio).[100] Such cabinet changes fell far short of American expectations, leading to Dulles's "general disappointment that [the] reshuffle did not produce [a] decided shift to right" and his conclusion that it represented a "failure to live up [to the] many assurances given us" by friends in the Jakarta government, in connection with the initial grant of American aid.[101]

For its part, the Jakarta government was equally exasperated with the Eisenhower administration's refusal to stop American and Taiwanese assistance to the rebels. Toward the end of June Assistant Secretary of State Robertson repeated to Dulles Jones's earlier warning that "anti-Americanism is reported increasing among the [government's] troops because of what they consider to be evidence of U.S. assistance to the rebels while refusing to sell military equipment to the Government."[102] That feeling increased as air attacks against government forces continued after the last rebel airfield in Indonesia had been captured. The bombers involved were clearly based in either Taiwan or the Philippines, so it was plausible for Jakarta's officer corps to conclude that the United States was keeping open the option of renewed rebel air attacks—a prospect that the British embassy appeared to take seriously.[103]

These officers and the Jakarta government also remained deeply anxious about the continuing presence of U.S. Marines in Singapore. When Sukarno raised this concern with Jones, the unhappy ambassador tried rather lamely to reassure him by stating that they were there for recreation. The president, who was widely acknowledged to be something of an expert on the "recreational" facilities at Far Eastern ports of call, responded: "Hong Kong and Manila are much better for recreation; what has Singapore to attract Marines?" Jones concluded his dispatch to Washington: "I believe he did not accept my statement that the Marines presence in Singapore had nothing to do with Indonesia."[104]

But the rapidly eroding position of the rebel forces meant that the United States had few options except to begin to move slowly toward an accommodation with the government led by Djuanda and Sukarno. Thus, at the end of June Jones cabled Dulles "(1) That rapid anti-Communist movement by Indonesians cannot be expected, but steady, step-by-step progress is in the cards and (2) that U.S. cannot afford to sit and wait for Indonesian moves before extending help."[105] It was not until a month later, however, that Washington began to follow this prescription. Then, in the hope of strengthening anti-Communist elements in Jakarta, "particularly Nasution and pro-U.S. officers in Army," it resumed—albeit somewhat haltingly—its modest assistance to the Jakarta government. During the first week of August the aid was still little more than token, but by the middle of the month a corner seemed to have been turned and its level became significant.[106]

In this process the secretary of state appeared increasingly to disengage from active involvement, delegating policy both to Under Secretary of State Herter (who in Indonesian matters appeared to hold views generally similar to Dulles but who was far less forceful in advancing them) and especially to Assistant Secretary of State Robertson, who was much more knowledgeable and apparently more certain of himself than Herter with respect to Indonesia and more closely aligned with Ambassador Jones.[107] Whether this bespoke Dulles's own frustrations over the failure of his Indonesian intervention or the draining of his energy because of the onset of what would prove to be a fatal illness or both, it is difficult to say. Moreover, crises in Lebanon and especially in Iraq during mid-1958, the mounting tension with the Soviet Union over Berlin, and in particular the sharp escalation of Chinese pressure on Quemoy during August undoubtedly commanded a higher priority than Indonesia in Dulles's allocation of his waning stamina. In any case, by early August the previously strong stamp of John Foster Dulles on policy toward Indonesia had become far less evident. With his withdrawal from an active role, a more pluralistic input ensued, with the National Security Council as well as Robertson, General Taylor, and Ambassador Jones exerting greater influence and Herter unwilling or unable to maintain the degree of rigidity in policy toward Indonesia that Dulles had. And with Allen Dulles's brother no longer active on the Indonesian front, the CIA was clearly less influential than before.

The increased loss of coherence in administration policy toward Indonesia was clearly evident in Herter's August 20 cable to Ambassador Jones that, in an apparent reference to a new National Security Ccouncil (NSC) Special Intelligence Estimate, observed that not only was there "divided counsel" over the new approach but that "debates over it were not only "within the Executive Branch but within the Department [of State] which have occupied us right down to present. There has been no unanimity of conviction on our present policy at any time."[108]

The next day Herter cabled an undoubtedly relieved and elated Jones the "summary conclusions" of this benchmark NSC assessment that underlay the new approach. Sober and cautious and quite devoid of the wishful thinking and dogmatic views that had characterized Dulles's analyses and prescriptions, it demonstrated that the Eisenhower administration's appraisal of the situation in Indonesia had finally begun to come to grips with reality. It acknowledged that, while the rebels could "continue guerrilla actions for [a] prolonged period of time and place considerable military and financial burden on [the] gov't," they "could not however develop widespread political support nor create sufficient pressure [to] cause gov't [to] seek negotiated settlement."

The NSC concluded that the PKI had been "greatly strengthened by events of [the] past year," so that if elections were held in 1959 it would "probably emerge as largest party," and predicted it would "continue present policy seeking [to] retain power by legal means." The leaders of the armed forces were seen to have "gained prestige in rebel operations," and although they had "considered measures [to] move against PKI," they would not "take any decisive action without at least tacit approval Sukarno." According to the report, Sukarno was "concerned by growing power [of] PKI," but "reluctant however [to] use force or abandon [his own] position above party struggles." He would "first seek [to] consolidate [and] strengthen non-commie parties to achieve balance between them and PKI. If convinced Commies seriously threaten his position, he will probably yield to Army pressure [and] postpone elections."

It predicted that

> Continuing and substantial US military and economic aid would increase ability and determination non-commie leaders, especially army, persuade Sukarno take stand against PKI and deal with threat Commie violence. US aid by itself, however, will not persuade Indo gov't take vigorous action against PKI, much less suppress it. Most that can be hoped for would be that non-commie forces would be so strengthened PKI could not come to power, although it would remain major political force with overall power, however reduced.[109]

On August 13, the day after this new National Intelligence Estimate, the United States signed an agreement with the Jakarta government wherein it undertook to

a. Furnish token military aid [totalling $7 million] particularly to the Army ... on a phased basis and at military level so far as practicable ...
b. Provide additional slots for Indonesian officers in US military schools.
c. Agree [to] use of counterpart funds for construction barracks Indonesian Army.

General Vittrup, whom the Pentagon had put in charge of arms deliveries and who appeared to have had little sympathy with Dulles's support of the rebels, agreed to supply four H-19 Helicopters to the Indonesian air force and a submarine chaser to the Indonesian navy, apparently without State Department approval.[110]

Nasution had become the linchpin of the new policy, and American officials put their faith in his assurances that his major aim was to restrict the power of the Communist party. They were even willing to acquiesce in his actions when on September 5 throughout the areas in rebellion he outlawed the Masjumi, PSI, and Parkindo (the major party of non-Catholic Christians), precisely the political parties the United States had hitherto been supporting.[111] Much more gratifying to American officials was a new and more permissive foreign-investment law and the almost-concurrent government decision announced by Djuanda on September 22, 1958, that the national elections scheduled for 1959 would be postponed—a move about which the four major non-Communist political parties (PNI, Nahdatul Ulama, PSI, and the Masjumi) on Java were in either tacit agreement or unwilling to contest, for they were convinced that if elections were held then the Communist PKI would easily emerge the strongest party, with an increased plurality and stronger credentials for insisting on participating in a coalition government.[112]

For much of this improvement in its fortunes the PKI had reason to thank the Eisenhower administration. Most important in the party's rise in popularity was the windfall it had garnered by having correctly charged the United States with military support of the rebels well before the other parties had been convinced this was the case. Indeed, PKI leaders could legitimately assert that they had pioneered and sustained this protest, with others subsequently climbing aboard the bandwagon it had launched. In this process it had both increased its credibility and been the principal beneficiary of the explosion of widespread patriotic outrage against the destructive intrusion of the United States and its Asian client states into Indonesia's domestic affairs.

But the decision of Sukarno to back Djuanda and Nasution in postponing the national election long scheduled for mid-1959 meant that the patriotic momentum that was currently buoying the PKI so strongly would probably gradually dissipate—assuming, of course, that no further indications of American support to the rebels were discovered. For the Communists the parliamentary road was the only feasible route to power, and, as Daniel Lev concluded in his classic study of Indonesian politics during this period: "By far the strongest and most vital party, the P.K.I. lost most from the postponement of elections, for with deferral the bed began to wash away from underneath the parliamentary road."[113] It was a rather ironic commentary on publicly professed global American foreign policy that U.S. officials now pointed with satisfaction, as evidence of their growing influence and success in Indonesia, to this postponement of free elections, a postponement that would in fact prove permanent.[114]

Sizing up the changes in Jakarta's policies, Ambassador Jones on September 29, 1958, cabled the secretary of state:

There is little need for further proof of the position of Djuanda and cabinet than the two major actions of passage of the foreign investment bill and postponement of the elections, both bitterly opposed by PKI.

With the postponement of elections formerly scheduled for 1959, Indonesian Government has arrived at a kind of plateau in which there is a chance of political stability for a minimum of two years. . . . General Nasution has stated he intends maintain status quo for five years.

This situation provides US and free world with excellent opportunity [for] removing Indonesia for good from danger Communist take-over if we promptly exploit available possibilities.[115]

However belatedly, the Eisenhower administration now, with a somewhat clearer view of Indonesian realities, sought to exploit those possibilities.

9. End of the Rebellion

HAVING BEEN ENCOURAGED and sustained for so long by the United States, the rebels only belatedly grasped the full extent of the shift in American policy that gradually began during the second half of 1958 and the full implications of this change for their own prospects. Their lack of awareness was attributable not simply to the wavering of American policymakers and the initially tentative and conditional nature of the American shift toward supporting Jakarta. It was also a consequence of rebel hopes being kept alive because elements within the Eisenhower administration continued to feel that the prudent pursuit of American interests necessitated keeping the dissidents' residual military forces sufficiently viable as to constitute an option that could be resorted to and built up should Jakarta change its course and depart widely from the newly consummated but fragile and uneasy détente between it and the United States. Maintenance of that option required that the United States and its Taiwanese ally, with continuing logistical support from the Philippines, maintain a significant, even if drastically reduced, flow of arms to the rebels, mostly in Sulawesi, where these were now almost all dropped by air or delivered by small boats. Despite the diminished volume of this flow of arms, it was understandable that rebel commanders, at least in Sulawesi, interpreted it as a commitment to continued American backing of their cause.

Moreover, despite the well-publicized mid-August "token package" of American arms to the Jakarta government, the rebels had assumed, along with many senior United States officials, that there would be no more such support to Jakarta unless there were major changes in the character of its government along the lines for which they and the United States had pressed; and they could clearly see this was not the case. They had no way of comprehending the increasing divisions within the Eisenhower administration as to what course it would follow in Indonesia, and in view of the public rhetoric of American foreign policy, it was logical for the rebels' leaders to assume that American knowledge of Jakarta's receipt of Soviet bloc arms, well under way during the fall of 1958 (see below), would strengthen their own appeal to the Eisenhower administration—making more credible their allegations that Sukarno and the Jakarta government were pursuing a pro-Communist policy and prepared to align Indonesia with the Soviet Union. They could hardly be expected to have foreseen that the Pentagon's anxiety over these purchases would result in its pressuring the administration to react with a massive program of U.S. arms deliveries to Nasution and provide an increased incentive for the United States to reach an accommodation with the Jakarta government.

Protracted Guerrilla Warfare

Beginning in the second half of 1958, the military contest between the government and the rebels became increasingly one of guerrilla warfare, even though large PRRI/Permesta units—sometimes more than a battalion—were frequently employed. The early months of this guerrilla phase found the rebels widely dispersed as well as considerably weakened. Within Sumatra, communications between the different pockets of rebel forces had broken down as their defenses against the advancing government troops crumbled. But even after three months of devastating defeats, it was reported on June 12, 1958, that none of the rebel leaders had been captured on Sumatra,[1] and most of them were in fact to continue in rebellion for more than another three years.

From the middle of 1958, the two major segments of the rebellion—the PRRI on Sumatra and its Permesta branch on Sulawesi—carried on virtually autonomous struggles, although some radio contact was maintained.[2] After the fall of Bukittinggi, Sjafruddin had approved the formation of a working cabinet in Manado, with Colonel Warouw as acting prime minister and Sumitro as acting foreign minister.[3] This reflected the geopolitical reality that Sumatra had become relatively more isolated from the outside world. With Singapore increasingly difficult for rebel agents to work from, the Minahasa area of Sulawesi was geographically much better placed for rebel contact with external channels of American arms, especially Taiwan and the Philippines.

Minahasa, the eastern third of the long northern arm of Sulawesi, now constituted the Permesta heartland. For more than a year after the fall of Manado on June 26, the rebels maintained open Permesta control over substantial parts of the central and southern part of Minahasa. Outside this area, government forces dominated the towns and rebel forces the countryside of most of the peninsula.[4] Large-scale fighting continued and in fact increased in the closing months of 1958 and the first half of 1959.

On Sumatra, the last major town in rebel hands, Payakumbuh, had fallen on May 20. After government forces occupied the towns, the PRRI forces withdrew to bases in the surrounding hills. And throughout the next three years the rebels continued to exercise control over a major—though gradually diminishing—part of the rural areas of Central and North Sumatra while the government controlled the towns. The PRRI government established its headquarters in the small upland town of Koto Tinggi, which had been the capital of the military government of West Sumatra during the final year of the Indonesian republic's struggle against the Dutch. Its leaders—both civilian and military—were indeed still trying to repeat the strategy they had followed during that earlier struggle, when, after the Dutch had captured most of the republican leaders on Java, Sjafruddin headed the republic's emergency government and spent 1949 leading a guerrilla movement in the jungles of West Sumatra. But the strategy that had been successful in 1949 was not suitable for the very different character of the struggle now being waged.

In the months after the defeat of the PRRI's main forces, the fighting in the interior of Sumatra was much fiercer than during the initial government assault. At the end of June the British military attaché reported to his government that "hostility to the occupying Javanese army in Sumatra is growing" and that visitors to the interior felt that "the Central Government control little more than the major towns and throughout vast areas of the country are holding down the population, which is at best sullen and in many cases openly hostile."[5]

Hatred had grown between the contending forces during the initial government advance into the highlands, when on May 27, before they retreated into the hills, the PRRI forces burned down a schoolhouse at Situjuh Padang Kuning, not far from Payakumbuh, where PKI prisoners were being held, killing nearly 150 of them.[6] This massacre heightened tensions between the Communists and anti-Communists as government forces advanced into the interior. Evidence of American and Taiwanese involvement with the rebels further embittered the advancing government forces. Moreover, most of the units brought into West Sumatra to occupy the area were from the Diponegoro Division of Central Java, many of whom were considered to be pro-Communist.[7] As they occupied the highland areas, they brought with them anti-PRRI administrative officials from Padang who had been jailed by the Banteng Council.[8] These former prisoners, often affiliated with local branches of the PKI, had been the Banteng Council's strongest opponents and were even more opposed to the revolutionary government; consequently, Jakarta's forces now put a number of administrative positions into their hands. Numerous officials from outside the area were also appointed to take up administrative positions in the local bureaucracy, for "in central Sumatra the majority of the civil administrative staff departed into the jungle with the rebels."[9] The British embassy reported: "Local officials, many of them very junior rank, village policemen, postmen and telegraph operators, are being dismissed for assisting the rebels, and their places are being taken by Indonesians from outside Sumatra."[10]

The rebellion developed into a protracted guerrilla war. The PRRI forces themselves, certainly in Sumatra, long remained confident of their ultimate victory. In fact during the later months of 1958, as on Sulawesi, the rebels did experience marked successes in the field, with their forces demonstrating their strength by frequent forays into the government-controlled towns, which, in much of Central and West Sumatra, as well as Tapanuli and Aceh, remained isolated pockets within the rebel-controlled countryside.

By the end of the year it had become clear that there was a virtual stalemate between the government and rebel forces and that Jakarta's stated expectation that it would be able to quash the rebellion within two to three months had been wildly optimistic. Two or three more years of guerrilla warfare seemed to be the best that the Jakarta government could hope for. A "tentative Departmental appreciation," drawn up by the British embassy in Jakarta in December 1958 "on the basis of recent intelligence reports," summed up the situation:

> In East Sumatra the Government . . . hold[s] the main towns and [is] strong enough to send armed convoys along the principal highways in the daytime. Large tracts of the countryside are dominated by rebel forces and at night their control extends to the outskirts of the towns. . . . In Central Sumatra and Tapanuli the picture appears much the same. . . . It seems probable that the various pockets of rebel strength are still in communication with each other. . . . In North Celebes the Government forces have captured the major towns though not until after some heavy fighting and much later than they originally anticipated. . . . [I]t is thought that Kawilarang still has substantial numbers of troops in the jungle. . . . From the dissident angle at least a situation approaching a military stalemate appears to have been reached in Sumatra and the Celebes.[11]

New Attempts at Negotiation

Given this situation it clearly made sense for both sides to try to reach some sort of agreement to end the fighting, and in the closing months of 1958 there were indications of movement in this direction. American officials too were reportedly pushing compromise efforts. Sutan Mohammad Rasjid, a member of the Indonesian Socialist Party and former Indonesian ambassador to Italy, who after his resignation had become PRRI representative in Europe, wrote to Sjafruddin on November 20, 1958: "A few days ago I got news from an agency in Western Europe that the US is trying very hard to achieve peace between Jakarta and the PRRI."[12] Rasjid himself was clearly hoping that some compromise could be effected, for PRRI supporters abroad had found it increasingly difficult to arrange for further outside help to the rebels, particularly those on Sumatra, after the debacle of their military operations the previous April and May. Rasjid, however, well aware of the rebels' bitterness toward Jakarta's armed forces, realized that it was not possible at that time for either side to seek a reconciliation openly. He therefore urged on Sjafruddin a proposal that they seek a third party either from within Indonesia (such as Hatta) or from outside (such as the United States) to act as intermediary.[13]

At the same time Nasution was apparently also seeking to end the confrontation with the rebels. In early December two of the most senior members of his staff, Colonel Hidajat and Colonel Sukendro, visited PRRI representatives in Paris to probe the possible grounds for compromise. In these meetings, Hidajat assured the rebel representative that "all levels in Jakarta saw that the sole way out was through compromise but no one was courageous enough to take the first step, fearing that anyone doing so would be arrested." Hidajat gave the impression in his discussions that the army was sympathetic to the possibility of compromise but that the navy and air force opposed moves in that direction, as did a "majority of Djuanda's government."[14]

Sukarno's stance at the time was unclear, but he does not appear to have been adamantly opposed to eventual negotiation with the rebels. In his letters to foreign diplomats Rasjid argued that "we know that from the very bottom of his heart Sukarno wants peace; Sukarno is neither so confident nor so uncompromising as his public pronouncements suggest." Prime Minister Djuanda apparently concurred, American Ambassador Jones reporting that the prime minister stated that he himself wanted compromise with the rebels and "Sukarno agreed with him and would like to get this over as soon as possible."[15]

But the rebels still fighting within the country were thinking along different lines. The tactics of the Jakarta forces sent in to subdue opposition in West Sumatra had convinced the PRRI dissidents there that compromise was out of the question. This conviction, particularly among the civilian leadership in Koto Tinggi, stemmed in large part from the formation and activities of the army's paramilitary defense force, the People's Youth Organization, Organisasi Pemuda Rakjat (OPR) numbering approximately 6,000 mainly young Communist party members. These local youths were generally charged with identifying and arresting suspected PRRI followers.[16] They operated initially in the towns, but eventually spread throughout the countryside. Natsir later described the difficulties they came to pose for the PRRI:

> As long as we were fighting just Javanese troops there was no problem about maintaining our guerrilla bases and controlling areas just outside towns such as Padang and Bukittinggi. While I was in the jungle we got food every day from the market in Bukittinggi. . . . But the situation was drastically altered when the Javanese troops developed a technique for using members of the local PKI's pemuda Rakjat [Communist youth] as scouts to track down the guerrillas in the jungle. Being local lads they knew every creek and path just as our people did and could guide the Javanese forces.[17]

At the same time additional numbers of PKI and national Communist Murba party members were appointed to fill administrative positions, down to the level of village head, throughout government-held areas of West Sumatra.[18] The growing pressure these local political opponents exerted against the PRRI led its prime minister, Sjafruddin, to proclaim in mid-February 1959 that the "Sukarno regime is moving toward a communist regime, particularly in Central Sumatra."[19]

The Rebels Shift to a Federal Order (RPI)

Thus, despite the efforts at negotiation by their representatives abroad, from the end of 1958 Sjafruddin and Natsir began to guide the PRRI-Permesta movement away from any compromise with Sukarno. They both now reversed the earlier PRRI moves aimed at pushing the central government to return to the Indonesian republic's 1945 constitution. It had become clear that, under existing circumstances, returning to the original constitution would legitimize increased power for Sukarno and the army, further eclipsing that of the elected political parties. Thus, Sjafruddin announced that the "regions and people alienated by the cruelty of the Sukarno regime's reaction [to the PRRI] feel freed from any obligation . . . to the centralized Republic."[20]

Natsir and Sjafruddin began to urge formation of a federal form of government that would incorporate all the regions under rebel control in both Sumatra and Sulawesi. They also commenced discussions with the major Darul Islam leaders, particularly Daud Beureuh in Aceh and Kahar Muzzakar in South Sulawesi. Their aim was to create a federal system of government, made up of autonomous regions, in which the center's role was limited largely to foreign relations, defense, and communications. A strongly Islamic minority of the PRRI argued for splitting completely from Java, eventually setting up a Sumatran state, and even exploring the possibility of allying such a state with the newly independent state of Malaya, but their view clearly did not prevail.[21]

During the second half of 1959, the PRRI leadership held meetings in isolated regions of Central Sumatra to formulate ideas for constructing a new constitution that would eventually embrace the whole of Indonesia. These discussions led to an agreement to change the state structure in favor of a federal system, the Republik Persatuan Indonesia (RPI), United Republic of Indonesia, with the ten component states choosing their individual governments in accordance with the culture and wishes of their peoples.[22] But it took nearly a year to work out the extensive details for the RPI constitution, it being finally proclaimed at a meeting held near Koto Tinggi in March 1960.[23]

Cleavages in Rebel Ranks

The moves toward forming the RPI and particularly the rebel leadership's approaches to the Muslim rebels in the Darul Islam increased tensions within rebel ranks. The issue of religion had always been a sensitive one, for two of the major PRRI regions, North Sumatra and North Sulawesi, were predominantly Christian and, as Simbolon later expressed it, "We feared the right extremists (DI faction) as much as the left (communist)."[24] This split also exacerbated the civilian-military tensions, for most top military leaders, particularly such non-Muslims as Simbolon, Kawilarang, and Sumual, opposed any cooperation with the Darul Islam in establishing a new government. One of the major civilian leaders, Sumitro (a Javanese without any strong religious attachment) also opposed the idea of a RPI "ostensibly at least on the grounds that it should be a unitary state." Even Zulkifli Lubis, among the most ardently Islamic of the Muslim officers, recognized the potential tensions inherent in cooperating with the Darul Islam. He stressed that proposals for joint action with them were "a tactical move." "We had the same enemy; it was not a strategic move because our ideas were different. . . . It was not feasible to have Islam as a state ideology."[25]

At the same time, the central government had some successes in provoking rifts even within Darul Islam ranks. In Aceh on March 15, 1959, one of Daud Beureueh's lieutenants carried out a "bloodless coup" against this leader and established a "revolutionary council" prepared to discuss peace terms with the Jakarta government.[26] As a result of these negotiations, in response to the council's "return to the fold of the Republic," Jakarta agreed to create a "special region"of Aceh (Daerah Istimewa Aceh), promising the region "the widest possible autonomy, in particular in the fields of religion, education and customary law."[27]

This coup within the Darul Islam in Aceh weakened Daud Beureueh, although he retained the loyalty of a substantial minority of its army there and apparently continued to receive shipments of American arms at least as late as February 1960.[28] In shoring up his power, he intensified his cooperation with individual commanders of the PRRI and aligned himself with the newly formed RPI. The parts of Aceh he controlled now became the Islamic Republic of Aceh, one of the ten component states of the RPI.

Jakarta apparently also instigated a dissident movement within the ranks of the Darul Islam in South Sulawesi, and in September 1959 arranged the defection of some 5,000 of Kahar Muzakkar's followers. Sukarno encouraged further defections by promising amnesty to all those in South Sulawesi who surrendered by the end of November. It was estimated that Kahar Muzakkar lost altogether 70 percent of his following.[29]

• • • • •

Intensifying the tensions raised within the PRRI by the approaches to the Darul Islam were the moves by Nasution and Sukarno, ultimately supported by Hatta as well as Djuanda, to strengthen the executive branch of government at the expense of the parliament and the political parties. Although these moves further incensed the Masjumi members of the PRRI leadership, they seemed to its military leaders to open for them the possibility of a face-saving accommodation with Jakarta. After several months of preparation and under strong pressure from Nasution and other army leaders to move somewhat more rapidly than he had planned, Sukarno proclaimed on July 5, 1959, a return to the revolutionary period's constitution of 1945 and nullified the 1950 constitution currently in effect. Rather than provide for a parliamentary system in which major power lodged with the political parties, the older constitution posited a political order that at the national level was more akin to that in the United States: the center of authority was lodged in a president and a cabinet appointed by and responsible to him, which shared legislative power with an elected congress.[30]

Natsir and other civilian PRRI leaders, together with the residual Masjumi leadership in Jakarta and the country's second largest Islamic party, the Nahdatul Ulama, had opposed a return to the 1945 constitution, unless it also incorporated the 1945 Jakarta Charter. Dating from June 22, 1945—and therefore slightly predating the 1945 constitution, the Jakarta Charter prescribed guarantees that those who embraced Islam should "be able to fulfill their religious duties." Although mild enough, this statement had worried Indonesian Christians as well as Sukarno and Hatta, who saw it as setting one religion (Islam) above all others and feared that it might constitute the first step toward an Islamic state. The Jakarta Charter had never been incorporated into the 1945 constitution during its period of operation from 1945 through 1949. But in 1959 all Islamic parties represented in the national Constituent Assembly that had been elected in 1956 united in an effort to have it incorporated as a preamble to a revised 1945 constitution. The vote in this still-sitting Constituent Assembly, however, was far short of the two-thirds majority needed to pass the amendment.[31] Three days later the assembly addressed the more fundamental question as to whether the 1945 constitution, with the greater power it gave to the executive branch and tacit marginalization of the political parties, should supersede the 1950 constitution. The majority who voted in favor (263 to the 203 opposed) again fell well short of two thirds, and the effort failed.

During June 1959 Nasution and his senior officers mounted an intensive effort to create a situation whereby Sukarno, then abroad, would be able to dissolve the Constituent Assembly and put the 1945 constitution into effect by decree. To achieve the right atmosphere Nasution temporarily banned all political meetings, prohibited all ideological propaganda, and forbade any public discussion for or against a return to the 1945 constitution. Although Sukarno did want to return to this constitution he was worried by the extent to which Nasution had taken over, and he resented being pushed faster than he wished. Faced, however, by a solid phalanx of senior officers when he returned to Jakarta on June 29, he moved rapidly ahead on a timetable closer to Nasution's than his own. On July 5 he decreed a return to the 1945 constitution and abolishment of the Constituent Assembly. As a bow to Islamic forces he said that the Jakarta Charter had inspired the constitution of 1945 and that the two together should be regarded as constituting one whole, but this gesture was without substance and did not affect the readoption of the 1945 constitution.[32]

Although for the PRRI's Islamic leaders this development was a keen disappointment, the move was welcomed by its military leadership (except for Dahlan Djambek), for it seemed to open up for them the possibility of an advantageous accommodation with Jakarta. A rebel source in Singapore appeared to reflect this assessment, reportedly stating: "Our demands have been complied with"; the 1945 constitution "is compatible with our goal of forming a stable Government in Indonesia which . . . would not provide maneuvering room for communism because it would be controlled by a single executive body."[33] After Sukarno's speech announcing the return to the 1945 constitution, the PRRI military leaders, according to Natsir, "began to have second thoughts" about continuing the fight. With this speech "there began something of a rift, a sort of undercurrent whereby the military began to think in terms of how to make the best of things," that is, accommodation with Jakarta.[34]

The moves by the civilians in the rebel leadership toward closer ties with the Darul Islam and Sukarno's return to the 1945 constitution were the two main issues on which lines began to be drawn between the civilian and military leadership of the PRRI. Another important cleavage that developed in PRRI ranks, not necessarily following the same fault lines, was over the supply of arms. In these transactions there were large amounts of money involved, and much was embezzled by some of the rebels' overseas agents.[35] By late March 1959, there were three competing channels for "transporting arms/ammunition and finances from Taiwan," involving "independent discussions with foreign governments." One axis, and probably the largest, was that directed by Sumitro and his ally Pohan (based in Singapore), a second by Taher Karim Lubis, and a third by Nukum Sanany (also apparently based in Singapore) and Hasanuddin.[36]

Sumitro, now largely unsympathetic toward PRRI leaders on Sumatra, had always felt closer to Sumual, and he and his protegé Des Alwi (Sjahrir's adopted son) focused their major efforts on obtaining supplies for the Sulawesi rebels.[37] They were relatively successful in this task, for it had always been much easier to smuggle arms into Sulawesi than Sumatra. Overall, during 1959 and 1960 the Sulawesi branch of the movement continued to be much the better armed and supplied.[38] But Mohammad Natsir noted ironically that the day after he surrendered at the end of September

1961 "there arrived for us via Singapore a large shipment of ammunition and uniforms."[39]

In fact, relatively few arms reached central PRRI headquarters on Sumatra after the major American supply effort ended in mid-1958. In 1957 and early 1958 the rebels had been able to make Singapore into a major base for their overseas operations, and through their agents there they had been able to export Sumatran rubber and copra to other parts of the world, import arms to Sumatra, and coordinate their Sumatran military and political activities with those in Sulawesi. These activities had to be curtailed after it had become evident to the British that Jakarta had gained the upper hand against the regional rebellions. Protests by the Indonesian government against continuing rebel activities in Singapore took on greater weight after the posting in November 1958 there of Colonel Djatikusumo as consul general. When the British refused to restrain rebel activities further, Djatikusumo applied pressures that, he states, induced them to be more cooperative: first, he arranged with Jakarta to have all copra exports from Indonesia to Singapore suspended for one month, and second, he had anti-aircraft guns placed on an island in the Riau archipelago close to Singapore to shoot near, but not directly at, planes using Changi airport when they flew over Indonesian airspace.[40] And after Lee Kuan Yew's People's Action party (PAP) won the first elections in the newly independent Singapore in 1959, the PAP government moved to improve relations with Jakarta. As prime minister, Lee Kuan Yew declared his government's "intent to assist Indonesia in every possible way, including the denial of facilities in Singapore to enemies of the Djakarta regime."[41] The rebel community in Singapore soon declined in numbers as PRRI agents shifted their major activity to more hospitable Asian territory—Manila, Hongkong, Macao, and Taipei—which were also much more accessible to the rebels on Sulawesi than those on Sumatra.

The Catalyst of Soviet Arms

Helping bridge the continuing divided counsels within the American government during the latter part of 1958 and reinforcing the position of those arguing in favor of greater support to Jakarta had been a new external factor—the United States government's mounting anxiety over the rapidly growing size and pace of arms delivery to Jakarta from the Soviet bloc. It soon dwarfed the token U.S. arms shipments of August, and the disparity continued to grow. Exacerbating this concern was the Jakarta government's long-delayed agreement to accept the $100 million in economic assistance that the Soviets had offered three years before.[42]

It will be recalled that when, at the end of December 1957, Washington had turned down Nasution's last urgent appeal for purchase of at least replacements and spare parts for the decaying inventory of American-manufactured infantry weapons and airplanes with which his forces were largely equipped, he had then in January turned decisively to other sources of supply. The United States's allies in Europe and Asia almost without exception refused to sell military equipment or spare parts to the Jakarta government.[43] (Not until after the United States had reversed its arms policy with its token $7 million package of military support in mid-August 1958 did Britain, West Germany, and Italy begin to open their gates to Indonesian purchasers.) Thus, the purchasing missions led by Colonel Yani in the first months of 1958 turned primarily to the Soviet bloc, especially Poland and Czechoslovakia, and to Yugoslavia. Orders were promptly accepted on easy credit terms. The magnitude of Jakarta's orders for equipment from all non-U.S. sources, preponderantly from Soviet bloc countries, was enormous. For 1958 alone, its value was calculated by U.S. intelligence at $229,395,600, with an additional $100,456,500 for the period January through August 1959. Of the total for these two periods $132,412,500 went to the army and included, in addition to small arms, mortars, artillery, and ammunition, 275 tanks and armored cars, and 560 other vehicles. The $126,201,700 for navy purchases included four destroyers; twenty-four torpedo boats, submarine chasers, and patrol boats; two submarines; eighteen airplanes; as well as guns, ammunition, and spare parts. The $69,916,200 total for the air force covered fifty jet interceptors, forty jet and piston trainers, twenty bombers, twenty transports, eight helicopters, as well as antiaircraft artillery, electronic equipment, and ammunition.[44]

· · · · ·

Mounting anxiety over this heavy Soviet bloc supply to Indonesia brought the United States in November 1958 and especially in January 1959 to augment enormously its flow of arms to Indonesia, in a major effort to offset and outstrip the Soviet bloc war materiel that Yani had contracted for in the spring of 1958.[45] During this period the United States's European allies swung into line, albeit on a much smaller scale.[46] As the Eisenhower administration had hoped, this cornucopia of Western arms induced Jakarta to place no further significant orders with the Soviet bloc. But it also, of course, spelled a heavy American commitment to Jakarta—at the expense of the insurgents on Sumatra and Sulawesi, with the most serious adverse implications for their expectations of continued political backing from the United States. But arrangements for this greatly augmented supply of U.S. arms were made so secretly that the rebels—and for that matter most U.S. congressmen—were unaware of the arrangement until well after the pipeline for delivery had been established and the new second-phase deliveries begun.

The publicly acknowledged "second military aid package" of $14,900,000 to Jakarta approved by President Eisenhower on December 3, 1958, reflected actual purchases—on highly concessionary terms—in *Indonesian currency* rather than U.S. dollars.[47] That modest sum was miraculously made to encompass "materiel to equip 20 infantry battalions" including trucks and radio equipment, "small ships" for the navy, equipment for a company of marines, including a 60-mm mortar section, and pilot training for the air force.[48]

For the period immediately after fiscal year 1959-60 (i.e., mid-1959 through mid-1960) Jakarta was not really expected to make repayment— even in Indonesian currency. As the National Security Council reported, this next round of military assistance (officially calculated to value $27,900,000) was an even cheaper gift, it being "nominally on a reimbursable basis but for all practical purposes [to] be treated as grant aid insofar as the MAP [Military Assistance Program] is concerned. Repayment when it is made is expected in rupiahs and at only a fraction of the original cost to the MAP."[49]

But all this was not the major component of American largesse as it did "not include the value of excess stocks." The category of "excess stocks" constituted a largely hidden package, apparently many times larger, that did not show up on ledgers available to most U.S. congressmen, for it masqueraded under the rubric of military equipment the Pentagon conveniently classified as "surplus." Declaring war materiel "surplus" meant making it a virtual gift. Thus, for twenty F-51 "surplus aircraft and 50,000 lbs. spare parts," the Indonesian government was charged a total of just $22,055, probably no more than 2 percent of the world market price for these secondhand planes. Fifteen "surplus" B-25 aircraft were offered soon afterward on apparently similar "government to government" terms.[50]

This enormous inventory of U.S. military equipment made available at these virtually cost-free levels to Jakarta during the year after the well-publicized token package in mid-August 1958 was sufficient that, together with arms made available by Western allies of the United States, it had by mid-1959 exceeded the accumulated orders from the Soviet bloc. Indeed, as a "consequence of this encouragement from Washington and these allies," during the second half of 1958 and in 1959 "Indonesia placed its orders almost exclusively in Free World countries."[51]

All this decisively tipped the scales away from the Communist bloc so far as Indonesia's army was concerned, but not for its air force or especially its navy. The memory of the deaths and wounds inflicted by the CIA's planes and American and Taiwanese pilots was too fresh for them to reverse their procurement policies in favor of the United States. This was especially the case for the navy, which had lost much of its elite corps when its flagship and several other vessels had been so recently sunk by what was clearly understood as American air power. As earlier noted, neither of these two services would for many years be willing to become heavily dependent on U.S. equipment. Moreover, the air force had invested heavily in Soviet-manufactured airplanes during the first half of 1958 and was preoccupied with the training of pilots and ground crews, and only the virtually free gift of U.S. planes induced it to augment these earlier purchases with American planes and training. And while the navy bought some ships from Western Europe it balked at close ties with the United States. Thus, an internal U.S. memorandum of September 8, 1959, noted: "Much of the navy's and air-force's modern equipment is of Bloc manufacture, and to maintain a sustained operating level these two services must rely on spare parts and replacements from the Bloc."[52]

If the rebels had had any idea of the magnitude of military equipment being injected after the August 1958 "token package" into the pipeline to Jakarta from the United States and its European allies their senior military leaders would probably have given up much earlier than they did—despite the continuing trickle of American arms still coming to them via Taiwan and the Philippines, deliveries which reportedly continued to Sulawesi until at least early 1961, going to Kahar Muzakkar's Darul Islam there as well as to Permesta.[53] Moreover, as noted above, the sustained and massive delivery of Soviet arms during the fall of 1958 and early 1959 had a different effect on American foreign policy than the rebels had expected. The United States became less, not more, insistent on major changes in the Jakarta government and was now prepared to settle for only the deferral of elections, a more welcoming foreign-investment law, limitations on PKI public rallies, and a constitution that, while significantly reducing the power of all political parties, including the Communist party, lodged greater power with Sukarno, as well as Nasution—the two men the rebels regarded as their major adversaries.

Nor could the rebels have been expected to know of the fortuitous change in the balance of power among those Americans charged with responsibility for U.S. policy in Indonesia that occurred in late 1958 and early 1959. For, as noted above, that balance was considerably affected by the complete withdrawal during this period of the rebels' most powerful and persistent champion, Secretary of State Dulles, from his previously highly influential role in the shaping of that policy. And while Eisenhower had been staunchly supportive of Dulles on Indonesia as on most issues, he too was now heavily preoccupied in dealing with Khruschev over the German crisis and with China's apparently continuing minatory stance toward Taiwan. The under secretary of state, Christian Herter, now more frequently signed cables as "acting secretary" until on April 18, 1959, just five weeks before Dulles's death, he officially replaced him as secretary. Usually never more than marginally involved in policy toward Indonesia and apparently poorly informed concerning it,[54] Herter was now absorbed by European matters and certainly had had insufficient interaction with the rebels to be much interested in trying to sustain them. Allen Dulles, as head of the CIA, had, of course, been a close supporter of the rebel cause, and it was only his agency apparently that now maintained what slender ties there were with them and saw to it that they continued to be nourished by at least a trickle of small arms and ammunition. But to whatever extent he may have felt his organization owed a loyalty and responsibility to its "assets" on Sumatra and Sulawesi, in the absence of his brother, he had presumably lost considerable clout with respect to the administration's policy toward Indonesia. And after John Foster Dulles's withdrawal from policy-making on Indonesia the influence of Ambassador Jones and his allies in the Pentagon continued to grow, and by the end of 1958 it had become dominant.

Washington's Final Reassessment

Taken as a whole, Jakarta's massive program of arms acquisition from the United States and its European allies during the fall of 1958 through 1959 reflected a major shift in American policy. This process culminated in late January of 1959 with the preparation by the National Security Council of a statement of policy on Indonesia drawn up to supersede previous directives (including the recommendations of the "Special Report on Indonesia" of September 25, 1957), which was approved by President Eisenhower on February 3, 1958.[55]

This new directive coincided with the United States's decision to massively augment its supply of arms to the Jakarta government and U.S. efforts to press both Jakarta and the rebels toward rapprochement. It clearly reflected a reinforcement of administration concern over Communist prospects in Indonesia arising from the infusion of a substantial amount of military equipment and economic assistance to Jakarta from Communist regimes abroad. Its very first sentence read:

> The chief danger confronting U.S. policy with respect to Indonesia is that a combination of domestic instability, Sino-Soviet Bloc economic and military aid, and growing Communist strength may lead to a Communist takeover or to a policy increasingly friendly toward the Sino-Soviet Bloc on the part of whatever regime is in power.

The nineteen-page policy statement effectively downgraded and seemed virtually to write off the Sumatran and Sulawesi rebels as significant factors in American policy. It assigned them no immediate constructive role or any future, devoting just three sentences to them. They were credited with "some local support" and the capacity to "continue guerrilla warfare for a prolonged period, creating serious economic and political problems for the central government." Though guerrilla fighters were capable of "seriously harassing the government forces and hampering the reestablishment of civil authority in North and Central Sumatra and North Celebes," they were "no match for the government forces in regular military operations" and "lack the military capability and the political following to reestablish their control of major populated areas." There was no longer any mention at all of their providing leverage on the central government or even a fulcrum for the United States to do so. But when the statment was discussed in the NSC, Allen Dulles urged that the new policy "not prevent the U.S. from providing small arms to the rebels later if this appeared to be a desirable action," with Eisenhower then observing the CIA chief was advocating "that we play both sides."[56]

Most striking in the new directive was the change shown in the Eisenhower administration's attitude toward Sukarno. No longer was he regarded as an obstacle to be gotten rid of or at least needing to have his wings clipped. He was now portrayed as pivotal in Indonesian politics — and someone the United States had to work with — not against. He was "Indonesia's paramount political figure" not only "because of his personal magnetism and hold on the masses, but because he represents to the Indonesian people the symbol of their revolution and mystical incarnation of their state. . . . Sukarno the symbol is still indispensable; he is a living national monument, a political fact of life which must be lived with."

There was evident, moreover, a more accurate picture of Sukarno's attitude toward the Indonesian Communist party. "He appears concerned by the growing power of the PKI but is reluctant to use force or to abandon his position above party struggles. He will probably seek to manipulate non-Communist elements to counter-balance PKI strength." Although not joining Sukarno in advocating the PKI's nominal representation in the cabinet, the policy statement took over some of his principal arguments for urging this course, pointing out that the PKI "is free of any responsibility for government failures and inadequacies since it has not been formally represented in any cabinet" and that "open measures of repression against the PKI would be difficult to justify on internal political grounds, and would expose any government undertaking them to charges of truckling to Western pressure." Moreover, Sukarno was no longer attacked for his non-aligned foreign policy, and it was acknowledged that "basically any non-Communist Indonesian regime likely to come to power will desire to follow a 'neutralist' policy, seeking aid on its own terms from both the West and the Bloc and balancing each off against the other."

The army was seen to "represent the principal obstacle to the continued growth of Communist strength" and as having "assumed an increasingly powerful position in the political arena including a growing policy-making role," which, "barring an open break between Sukarno and Nasution" was likely to continue. Its increased power was attributed to "the considerable authority it is permitted under the present 'state of war,' and the prestige accruing from its success in suppressing the regional revolt."

The NSC policy statement noted that non-Communist political parties had "won approximately 75% of the total vote in the 1957 election," and while they were "faction-ridden and sharply divided among themselves," they did "represent nevertheless a significant element of Indonesian society seeking to steer a course between military dictatorship on the one hand and Communist dictatorship on the other," and were "presently exercising some stabilizing influence, and to the extent that they are able to reconcile and subordinate their inter-party differences, they could, with the backing of the Army, turn the tide against the Communist party in the political field."

The NSC now gave a more sober and realistic estimate of Communist strength and prospects than had accompanied the recommendation of September 25, 1957. It acknowledged the possibilities for the PKI's further growth and that, if the election scheduled originally for 1959 had not been cancelled, it "would probably have emerged as the largest party in Indonesia and would have been in a strong position to demand cabinet representation." But the panic and apocalyptic projections that marked earlier assessments were no longer evident. The party's political future was now seen in fuller political context and as subject to constraints from both Sukarno and the army. "Direct Government action to suppress the Communist Party would not bring lasting results unless non-Communist forces in Indonesia at the same time demonstate to the masses some progress in solving Indonesia's social and economic problems."

In this situation, the NSC concluded, the United States should "maintain and strengthen . . . ties with the Indonesian police and military establishment; and increase their capability to maintain internal security and combat Communist activity in Indonesia by providing appropriate arms, equipment and training, on a limited but continuing basis." And it should "give priority treatment to requests for assistance in programs and projects which offer opportunities to isolate the PKI, drive it into positions of open opposition to the Indonesian Government, thereby creating grounds for repressive measures politically justifiable in terms of Indonesian self-interest."[57] This last prescription in fact was to remain the hallmark of American policy toward Indonesia for the next six years.

• • • • •

Developments within the Indonesian government during 1959 continued to increase the United States's disposition to rely on Jakarta rather than gamble further on support to the rebels. As American analysts could readily see, with the government operating under the 1945 constitution the prospects for the PKI—and all the elected political parties—would sink along with those of parliamentary government, for, as noted above, the parliamentary system provided the only feasible road to power open to the PKI. Nasution and his senior officers, their political position much strengthened by their successes against the rebels, the continuing state of martial law, and the introduction of the 1945 constitution, moved assertively to carry out their long-nourished desire for a much larger role in government for the army and the further emasculation, if not the full elimination, of political parties and the parliametnary system. As earlier noted, Sukarno in general shared this objective and saw a return to the constitution of 1945 as an appropriate step toward achieving it, although he sought to curtail Nasution's efforts to reserve for the army "representation in the cabinet as well as in all advisory and policy making bodies of government."[58]

The State Department regarded with satisfaction the new Jakarta government that took office on July 9, 1959, under the aegis of the 1945 constitution, with Sukarno as premier as well as president, Djuanda as first minister, Nasution as minister of defense, and with almost one quarter of cabinet members from the armed forces. It noted that Sukarno's appointments to the cabinet left it "more conservative in political orientation than the previous cabinet." Sukarno now very consciously prepared to assume greater direct responsibility.[59] The United States saw this as a "willingness to be an active, day-to-day leader" and as "the key to the effectiveness of this government," noting that "it is evident that he has not delegated sufficient responsibility to any other person to enable the government successfully to pursue a decisive course without his active participation."[60] The Eisenhower administration thus now acknowledged that, after two years of its active intervention in Indonesia's affairs, Sukarno had emerged not weaker but significantly stronger.

A State Department assessment at the very end of December 1959 was essentially consistent with the above-cited National Security Council policy statement made at the beginning of the year and reflected overall a general acceptance of the course of events in Indonesia:

> The major political forces in Indonesia at the present time are President Sukarno, the Army and the Communist Party (PKI). Sukarno retains his pre-eminence and appears to try to balance the Army and the PKI against each other, though he has gone along in recent months with efforts (enjoying some success) of the anti-Communist Army leadership to circumscribe Communist propaganda and activity. The political role and influence of the Army are great and continue to grow. Heavily represented in the present government, the Army enjoys added power as the principal implementing arm of martial law (indefinitely extended as of December 16, 1959) measures.[61]

That extension, the embassy noted, "is a blow to both the Communists and to parliamentary government."[62] The present Indonesian government's "composition and general orientation," it concluded, is "as favorable to free world interests as could be expected at this time."

Disintegration and Surrender of the Rebel Forces

After the rebels' proclamation of a federal government (RPI) in March 1960, the rebellion began to fall apart. Dissensions and cleavages within the rebel ranks on both Sumatra and Sulawesi were exacerbated by more forceful military action by the Jakarta forces aimed at crushing rebel strength. Concurrently the central government intensified its attempts, principally initiated by Nasution and other army commanders, to detach less fervid rebel leaders and attract them back to the central government's side.

Two incidents after the mid-1960 marked the beginning of the end of the rebellion. First was the culmination of the Jakarta forces' more aggressive military activity on Sumatra, when they occupied the rebel stronghold in Koto Tinggi in July 1960. Until then this mountain redoubt had provided a real headquarters for the rebel leadership, particularly its civilian politicians, who had been able to build up an administration and maintain relatively sophisticated communications with their main pockets of support on Sumatra. After Sjafruddin, Natsir, Burhannudin, and Assaat were set to flight by the government attack on Koto Tinggi, they lost their earlier security and were forced to abandon most of their radio equipment. Rather than be able to act effectively as government leaders they were now reduced to the status of refugees dependent on the strength and goodwill of their military commanders.

Civilian politicians had never played a major role in the Sulawesi branch of the rebellion, and any real coordination that may earlier have existed between the various military units constituting its major strength had disintegrated by 1960. As Kawilarang later described the situation: "By 1960 the forces of the rebels were very badly disunited. They had incorporated many robber gangs and these groups asserted much independence. The country was ruined by the fighting. Almost every battalion was on its own, many of them fighting each other. When a battalion commander moved from one place to another he would need an escort of at least 60 men to protect him, Sumual generally had a whole company."[63]

By this time the strongest and most independent of these bands was one led by Jan Timbuleng, who increasingly ignored any direction from the official Permesta leadership. The crisis reached a head in 1960. According to one account it was set in motion when in April Timbuleng's men arrested the deputy prime minister, Warouw, when he was crossing their territory, shooting him in the knees to prevent his escaping.[64] Permesta headquarters responded in October by arresting Timbuleng himself when he accepted an invitation to negotiate. A few days later, on October 5, he was killed in an escape attempt. Reportedly in retaliation, his followers shot Warouw to death on October 15.[65] Details of the incidents surrounding these deaths are widely disputed and many of the PRRI leaders both on Sumatra and Sulawesi believed in fact that Sumual was responsible for Warouw's death.

But whatever the precise course of events, the bloodletting within their ranks clearly sickened many of the rebel leaders and speeded their impulse toward negotiation with the central government. Kawilarang, in particular, long a reluctant rebel, was soon to go along with a compromise between Permesta and the army central command.

• • • • •

On March 3, 1961, Nasution renewed appeals for the rebels to return to the "arms of the motherland," and by the end of the month Kawilarang authorized the agreement for all Permesta forces to surrender. There were two ceremonies in April in which all the major Permesta leaders, with the exception of Sumual, officially surrendered to the republic. Within a week a cease-fire was in place, and more than 36,000 troops on Sulawesi had laid down their arms.[66]

The Permesta surrenders came as a shock to the rebels on Sumatra. Even before this news had come in, however, the leadership there had fractured. In early 1961 at the final meeting of the RPI, according to Sjafruddin, they were already contemplating abandoning the struggle, and Simbolon was appointed to represent the group as a whole in negotiations with the central government. "Then afterwards he betrayed us and set up with Husein a military government wherein they disavowed the Republic Persatuan Indonesia and its civilian leaders." (Natsir's account is similar.)[67] Simbolon's version, given to the British consul in Medan two months after his surrender, is largely consistent with this. He stated that in March or April 1961 he and Husein "dissociated themselves from the DI [Darul Islam] . . . dropped the RPI name and called themselves the Emergency Military Government" (Pemerintah Darurat Militer).[68]

Simbolon had evidently concluded that he and his military colleagues stood a better chance of receiving good terms from Jakarta if they negotiated merely on their own behalf with their army counterparts on the government side rather than act for the whole rebel group on Sumatra. According to Sjafruddin, the military government that Simbolon and Husein proclaimed as superseding the civilian-led RPI "was a largely paper operation, but it put them in a position to work out their own formal deal with Nasution providing for the unconditional surrender of themselves and their military regime." He understood that "one of the quid pro quos was that at least many of the regular officers involved could be given not only amnesty but reinstatement in the Jakarta army at ranks two slots below that which they then held."[69]

At the end of June 1961, shortly after pockets of rebel troops had surrendered in Aceh and in North, Central, and South Sumatra, Husein, following lengthy negotiations with the local government commander, surrendered with about 600 men.[70] He ordered all troops in West Sumatra to follow suit, according to some informants stating that "if they did not come down he would have them hunted down." Whether in accordance with his orders or on their own volition, between July 12 and 28 four other units in West Sumatra, totaling approximately 2,800 men, surrendered. Also during July, Simbolon negotiated his own terms and late that month he and Nainggolan surrendered with some 4,000 followers.[71]

Later in that month, Sjafruddin sent a representative to Nasution to begin to discuss surrender terms. After an exchange of letters with him, on August 17, 1961, Sjafruddin made a public radio announcement, calling on all RPI forces "to cease hostilities" (he refused to use the term "surrender").[72] That same day President Sukarno announced a general amnesty for all rebels who submitted by October 5, an amnesty that applied not only to the RPI (PRRI and Permesta) but also to the rebellions of the Darul Islam in Aceh and Java, Ibnu Hadjar in South Kalimantan, and the minor surviving remnant of the Republik Maluku Selatan (South Moluccas Republic) rebellion.[73] (There is no indication, however, that Darul Islam in either Aceh or West Java, then took advantage of the amnesty, and both retained considerable strength.) On August 18, Zulkifli Lubis surrendered, and a week later later, Sjafruddin and Burhanuddin Harahap, along with several other civilian leaders, reported to government military authorities near Padang Sidempuan in the southeastern corner of Tapanuli in North Sumatra.[74] On that same day Sjafruddin sent a further letter to Nasution, announcing the cessation of hostilities by the forces of the RPI and, on behalf of the RPI, acknowledging the 1945 constitution and stating his willingness to swear an oath to support it.[75] He later surrendered the PRRI's remaining liquid assets, twenty-nine kilograms of gold bullion, to Nasution for delivery to Djuanda and subsequently over the next four years was imprisoned in a series of military jails in Java.[76]

By the time of Sjafruddin's surrender few of the rebels remained in the field. On Sulawesi, Sumual was the last standout, not surrendering until October 15, 1961, after the amnesty deadline had passed, although his surrender was back dated to accord with it.[77] On Sumatra by the end of August, only a small group of civilian leaders, including Natsir, remained in the hills, with the one colonel who had not surrendered, Dahlan Djambek. Djambek and Natsir, both noted and outspoken Muslim leaders, were very conscious of the animosity felt against them by the Communist youth militia (OPR) and of the dangers inherent in surrender. In a letter written just over a month later to a friend abroad, Natsir recalled: "From the end of August there remained in all of West Sumatra only the late Colonel M. Dahlan Djambek, myself, together with a few friends (plus or minus 10 people). . . . We were surrounded by the 3rd force (PKI activists), uniformed and armed who were carrying out their activities around us."[78] Djambek had sent his wife and children back to Bukittinggi and had been in touch with the government commander to arrange his own arrest, demanding only that he should be brought to trial to clear his name of the charges of corruption made against him after his defection to the rebels in August 1957.[79] The place of arrest was agreed on, but the information was leaked to some members of the Communist OPR militia, and when Djambek, accompanied by a couple of followers, reached the assigned surrender place, on September 19, he was ambushed and killed.[80]

Bereft of any military protection, Natsir and his remaining six followers finally surrendered on September 25, 1961, and were taken to Padang Sidempuan. With the other defeated leaders they were eventually moved to Java and in 1962 were transferred to jail or house arrest in Jakarta where they were held until after the fall of Sukarno in 1966.[81]

• • • • •

Thus, well before the surrender of the PRRI's principal leaders in the spring and summer of 1961, senior American officials had radically shifted course, finding it expedient to do business with the same Jakarta government they had so assiduously encouraged the regionalist leaders to topple. For the mere handful of people in Washington who knew the facts,[82] Eisenhower and the Dulles brothers had been discredited by their dogged pursuit of disastrous policies—policies informed by their own stubborn a priori prejudices nourished by the CIA's egregiously flawed intelligence and tendentious interpretation of it. But knowledge of this fiasco was kept under tight wraps in Washington, and the little information concerning it that eventually did leak out was insufficient to embarrass them or sully their reputations after their deaths. Concealment of what had happened was, of course, made easier since apparently not a single American died in this intervention. But many thousands of Indonesian civilians and soldiers lost their lives.[83] Many others faced a warped and dismal future in a country where the political landscape and the political forces operating within it had been directly or indirectly severely altered. Nor was the impact of American power transitory, for even today its imprint on Indonesia's political character is distinctly visible.

CONCLUSION AND EPILOGUE

THE EISENHOWER ADMINISTRATION'S attempt to manipulate the politics of Indonesia had been glaringly counterproductive. Aimed at changing the character of that country's government to conform to what were perceived to be American interests, it actually strengthened those elements the administration had sought to eliminate or weaken and destroyed those whom it wished to reinforce.

The most immediate and at the same time most long term of the effects of the civil war were the strengthening of both the army and the presidency and the destruction of parliamentary government. Since then Indonesia has never again enjoyed a representative government, and the army and the president have continued to dominate its political and economic life.

At the same time the civil war struck a devastating blow against any future prospects for a devolution of power from the central government in Jakarta to the regions or any significant measure of decentralization and local autonomy. Indonesia became an authoritarian centralized polity, both in the closing years of Sukarno's rule and under the Suharto regime which succeeded it. Worse, for the region most heavily involved in the rebellion, West Sumatra, the war ushered in a decade of repression and authoritarian rule, from which the province only began to emerge in the early 1970s. After necessarily accommodating to Communist-dominated military units from the Central Javanese Diponegoro division that administered the region in the late 1950s and early 1960s, the people of West Sumatra were particularly hard hit by the swing to the right in 1965/66. Nor were their political leaders, who had been in the forefront of the Indonesian Nationalist movement and the early postindependence governments, ever again to play a significant role in the national government of Indonesia. Although Hatta never supported the rebels, their defeat removed any possibility that his vision of a decentralized Indonesia with a large degree of local autonomy would ever be accepted, and the discrediting of the leaders of the Masjumi and PSI and the abolition of their parties, removed the major political voices at the center representing the regions outside Java.

In the immediate aftermath of the rebellion the two leaders who emerged with their power significantly increased were Army Chief of Staff Nasution and President Sukarno. The defeat and elimination of the insubordinate officers in the Outer Islands left Nasution in unchallenged control of an army that was both more united and more capable of promoting its political interests than ever before. By crushing the rebellions, the top leadership of the Indonesian army on Java, whom the Eisenhower administration had mistrusted and sought to weaken through supporting countervailing regional military elements on Sumatra and Sulawesi, had become much stronger—politically as well as militarily. The army's overall cohesiveness and discipline had been increased and its public image brightened by virtue of the perception that it had faced down the might of the United States. Seen at home and abroad as the major actor in crushing the rebellion, with his chief challengers within the military hierarchy discredited and defeated, Nasution was finally in a position to put into effect his centralization and rationalization policies within the army while, through his concept of the "middle way," he asserted military control over economic and administrative matters previously left mostly in civilian hands.[1] At the time he was appointed minister of defense in July 1959, Nasution was strong enough to refuse to relinquish his post as army chief of staff so that for the first time in independent Indonesia's short history the army was not even nominally under civilian control.

President Sukarno emerged after the rebels' defeat significantly stronger as well, and the administration in Washington was now obliged to make a cynical about-face and work with him. His stature as the country's major political leader had grown as he, more than anyone else, was seen as symbolizing an enhanced national self-respect deriving from successful resistance to a superpower and its allies; indeed, so vivid in the minds of many Indonesians was the recent winning of independence from the Netherlands that resistance to American power less than a decade later seemed something like an extension of the old anticolonial struggle. And in the then-vigorous nonaligned group in the United Nations, where there was widespread satisfaction with Indonesia's ability to stand up to one of the great powers, Sukarno took on enhanced stature. Indeed, in view of the Eisenhower administration's hostility to neutralism, one of the salient ironies of its Indonesian intervention was that it left that country even more steadfast than before in its dedication to an independent foreign policy aligned with neither the Soviet Union nor the United States.

The reconformation of the Indonesian political landscape in the aftermath of the rebellions was heavily reinforced by the state of war and siege (martial law) imposed in reaction to them. It was also buttressed by the reintroduction in 1959 of the 1945 constitution under which both the army and the president could build up their power. In his efforts to move Indonesia toward his concept of "guided democracy" at the expense of the party system and parliamentary government Sukarno welcomed and supported Nasution's initiative in terminating the nearly concluded deliberations of the elected Constituent Assembly where a compromise agreement on a new constitution finally appeared possible.[2] With Nasution again taking the lead, the two were now able to reinstate the 1945 constitution, an instrument operative during the revolution, wherein the presidency was much more powerful than in the provisional constitution that had replaced it between 1950 and 1959.

In the process of fighting the rebels, army headquarters had found a legitimate basis—which after the rebellions it refused to surrender—for the imposition of martial law, which, in conjunction with its management of seized Dutch properties, permitted it to emerge as the strongest political force in Indonesia, paving the way for its later complete dominance of government.[3]

With the enhanced powers granted it under martial law, the army leadership moved to undermine and emasculate those political parties not already proscribed because of their involvement in the regional rebellions. In pursuit of this objective, as Daniel Lev has noted, "Army leaders often succeeded in weakening only the non-Communist parties, thus making their other—and increasingly important—objective of destroying the PKI in particular more difficult to prosecute."[4] In fact, the only party strengthened by the rebellion was the Communist party, which had become more powerful and respectable, with its nationalist credentials increased by its capitalization on the widespread patriotic outrage at the U.S. intrusion into the country's affairs.

Critics who had initially accused the Communist leaders of crying "wolf" and through sheer ideological animus opportunistically castigating the United States for covert trespass were humbled and the party leadership vindicated. Its early and continuing advocacy of firm military measures against the rebels put the PKI conspicuously in the winning camp of Nasution and Sukarno. Although the postponement of the scheduled elections meant that the Communists' parliamentary road to greater power was blocked, they did gain a greater measure of protection from Sukarno. For with so many of the other political parties proscribed or suspended, the president had greater need for the Communist party in his efforts to offset and contain the growing power of the army.

The major void in the old party lineup was, of course, created by the absence of the Masjumi, the whole party having been discredited because of the involvement of some of its leaders in the rebellion. That meant the elimination from the political spectrum of what was the country's largest and most progressive Islamic party and the major political organization in the islands outside Java. Indeed, if one seeks to understand why today in the world's most populous Muslim country Islam has not become a greater political force, it is essential to take into account the demise of the Masjumi. Its elimination was clearly one of the major factors in bringing about the post-civil war tripolarization of political forces in Indonesia. But this process was further advanced by the suspension or banning of several of the smaller parties tarred by the apparent ambiguity of their position during the civil war (of which the Indonesian Socialist and Christian parties were the most important).

Sukarno undoubtedly had few regrets over the elimination of his old parliamentary adversary, the Masjumi, but, facing a stronger, more unified military, he did have some pragmatic second thoughts about his opposition to a multiparty system as a whole. Thus, now shelving his plans for eliminating all remaining parties, he resisted the army's efforts to abolish them and used the more amenable of them as a base for political maneuver and organized support on issues on which he differed from the army. But among those parties only the Communists had sufficient organizational strength and mass backing to provide him significant help in his continuous effort to counterbalance the power of the army.

Thus, probably the most dangerous consequence of the American disruption of the Indonesian political scene was the fragile political polarization that it induced. Not only had that struggle badly scarred Indonesia's political face, but it had left the entire balance of domestic political forces severely skewed. With a much less pluralistic political spectrum than before, the country was left with a tense and brittle tripolarization of just three major political forces, each now stronger than before—the army, the Communist party, and Sukarno. That was a formula for neither effective government nor political stability. Indeed, it incorporated the necessary ingredients for a major political explosion.

· · · · ·

An early test of strength came in September 1959, a few months after Sukarno had appointed a new attorney general charged with eradicating corruption in government. One of this official's first targets was a group of high-ranking officers in Nasution's headquarters. The economic spoils of military office, especially after the windfall of the properties seized from the Dutch at the end of 1957, had provided army headquarters with a source of patronage of great importance in maintaining military cohesion. To make effective use of it Nasution was obliged to countenance numerous corrupt activities among the administering officers, although it appears he was never personally tainted by corruption. In the face of Sukarno's persistent attempts to weaken the armed forces by exploiting any divisions among them, Nasution was rarely inclined to abandon loyal officers who might also be vulnerable to corruption charges.[5] Consequently, he now stood by those under investigation by the attorney general and countered by arresting the prosecutor. Although Sukarno was able to obtain the official's release, he was unable to have him reinstated, and the corruption investigations were dropped.

In mid-1962 Sukarno recaptured some of the ground he had lost to Nasution over the previous few years when he "promoted" him from chief of staff of the army to the seemingly more exalted but actually much less powerful position of armed forces chief of staff. From Sukarno's point of view the new army chief of staff, General Achmad Yani (who had led Jakarta's attack on Padang) was considerably more flexible and amenable than Nasution, and this maneuver had the effect of removing Nasution from direct command and undermining his position as the major focus of army loyalties. But it should be emphasized that this move did not significantly weaken the political power of the army as a whole.

Periodically the now almost institutionalized competition between the army and Sukarno was damped down by their generally common front on the major issues of foreign policy: the final effort to gain control over West Irian and at least the first stages of Indonesia's subsequent confrontation with Britain and Malaya over their establishment of the new state of Malaysia.

The struggle for West Irian intensified between August 1960, when Indonesia broke relations with the Netherlands, and August 1962, when the region was finally brought under a temporary United Nations trusteeship that then passed control over to Indonesia in May 1963. During these years, as it became clear that the Kennedy administration supported Indonesia's claim to West Irian, relations with the United States considerably improved. Sukarno again visited Washington in April of 1961, and when Attorney General Robert Kennedy went to Indonesia, he was able finally to arrange for Allen Pope's release, an action that, as noted earlier, presumably increased the American government's disposition to support Indonesia on the West Irian issue. Nevertheless, Sukarno remained suspicious of the United States because of American activities during the regional rebellions and his continuing conviction that the CIA had been behind the Cikini assassination attempt. He continued to believe that, however friendly and trustworthy Ambassador Jones might be, what he regarded as an autonomous CIA remained out to get him.

As in the case of West Irian, the British plan to expand the state of Malaya, by incorporating Singapore and the British Borneo territories of Sarawak and North Borneo (Sabah) into a single entity to be known as Malaysia, united Sukarno and the Indonesian army in opposition. And initially Ambassador Jones, who was outraged at what he regarded as the British government's cavalier and provocative tactics in securing this goal, tried to prevail on the American government to remain neutral in the face of Indonesian and Philippine opposition. The trigger that transformed these two countries' grudging acceptance of the proposal into active opposition was when, even before a United Nations mission to ascertain whether the people of Sarawak and North Borneo wished to join a Malaysian Federation had finished its consultations with the local inhabitants and rendered its opinion, the British government and the Malayan prime minister announced that, regardless of the outcome of the UN mission, they would set up the new Malaysian state on September 16, 1963. This announcement violated the informal agreement that Indonesia,

Malaysia, and the Philippines had reached only a month earlier in Manila, which had been regarded as a face-saving way for Jakarta and Manila to acquiesce to Malaysia's formation.

These tactics angered the Indonesian army as well as Sukarno and brought them together again for well over a year in a common front ("Confrontation"), one that the PKI strongly supported, thereby again, as with the campaign for West Irian, gaining for itself popular favor by its association with a patriotic cause. Indonesia's militarization of the conflict was enormously expensive for the British, obliging them to withdraw large numbers of troops from Germany to marshal a force sufficient to deal effectively with the threat of an Indonesian invasion of Malaysia. The alarm in the United States at this drawdown of British strength in Europe undoubtedly contributed to its overruling Ambassador Jones's advocacy of an accommodationist policy toward Indonesia and reinforced American diplomatic support of Malaysia. Even Jones lost his sympathy for the Indonesian position when small Indonesian military units began cross-border probes into Sarawak, and especially when Jakarta began efforts to land paratroopers on the Malay peninsula on August 17, 1964—ill planned and undermanned operations that were generally regarded as fiascos.

Like Sukarno, Indonesian military leaders initially regarded the establishment of a Malaysian federation as a product of British neocolonialism, and, much more than he, they worried that inclusion of Singapore in Malaysia would lead to dominance of the whole federation by its resident Chinese and open it to Peking's penetration—not a very real prospect, but one they took seriously and regarded with alarm. Probably more important, the army was still resentful of British and Malayan leaders for providing the rebels with the use of military facilities in Malaya and Singapore during the PRRI and Permesta rebellions. Confrontation also provided army leaders with powerful arguments for deferring proposed cuts in Indonesia's military budget and for restoring as much as possible their partially lapsed access to martial law.

But as Britain began to assemble a heavy superiority in both air and naval power in the area and steadily augment its ground forces in Malaysia, more and more Indonesian military leaders drew back from any support of full-scale Confrontation, which they could soon see was likely to prove disastrous. Thus, increasingly during 1964 and early 1965, they simply went though the motions of mounting a campaign, doing substantively little to implement it. Nothing more clearly reflected the army's general unwillingness to escalate its own involvement than the fact that army paratroopers did not participate in the airdrops in Malaya that Sukarno approved, an operation which therefore had to rely on the much smaller number of airforce troops qualified for such missions. Thus, though senior Indonesian military leaders maintained a façade of unity with Sukarno in the anti-

Malaysia campaign, they held back from making a major commitment of their forces, husbanding most of them on Java and Sumatra, an action that some argued was necessary to ensure that the Indonesian Communist party did not take advantage of the Malaysian situation. Although it appears that Sukarno did not want Confrontation to escalate to an all-out war, he could not have been pleased at the army's footdragging, for it left him without the leverage for even a negotiated compromise.

Toward the end of the period, probably with the approval of General Yani, General Suharto, who had previously headed the West Irian command and was now deputy commander of the Malaysia campaign as well as commander of the Army Strategic Reserve Command (Kostrad), took steps to reassure the British and Malaysians that Indonesia would not escalate its confrontation. A few of Suharto's top aides made secret contact in Malaya with British, Malaysian, and possibly American intelligence with the object first of allaying fears of increased Indonesian military operations, and then of exploring possibilities for ending Confrontation.

During the late stages of the anti-Malaysia campaign, from mid-1964 through the first half of 1965, tensions grew between the army and Sukarno, as well as within the armed forces, where the air force and navy suffered casualties disproportionate to those sustained by the army. As Sukarno grew increasingly reliant on the PKI to offset army power, the Communists became more assured of his protection against the army, and consequently politically more assertive. The PKI was sometimes so aggressive in its efforts to enforce compliance with agararian reform legislation that bloodshed resulted; it mounted a propaganda campaign against "bureaucratic capitalists" that was clearly directed against the economic enterprises managed by active and retired army officers; it frightened conservative civil servants by demanding their political "retooling," and it worried the army by pressing Sukarno to support its proposal for a "fifth force." Envisaged as a sort of militia made up of workers and peasants willing to volunteer for the anti-Malaysia campaign, who were to be trained by one of the existing armed services, this plan ran into so much army opposition that it never really took hold (only the air force appears to have begun the training of a small number of candidates). Although "Sukarno himself was to remain uncommitted on this issue," the prospect of a "fifth force" was a source of serious anxiety for the army's leadership, which saw it as potentially an entering wedge to endow the PKI with a military capacity.[6]

The PKI did have a large following, most of its adherents knowing little of communism but often grateful for the party's efforts through its labor and peasant organizations to improve their lot. Many of the country's grossly underpaid teachers as well as many in the urban and peasant labor force had benefited from the efforts of the PKI-controlled SOBSI, Indonesia's only really effective labor organization. Although the party had intelligent leaders and could mobilize large demonstrations (a capacity often helpful to Sukarno), organize successful strikes (though often the army could limit these), and field able speakers, it had no guns and was consequently able to muster little physical power. Nor had it been able to carve out a significant position within the civil power structure. Despite Sukarno's efforts to secure some Communist representation in the cabinet, even by the end of April 1965 the PKI held only three of seventy-nine cabinet positions, one being the Ministry of Sports and the other two without portfolio; whereas the army held twenty-three cabinet posts, including Defense and Security (incorporating police as well as the military arms of government), Internal Affairs, Information, and the Attorney General. And of the twenty-four provincial governorships the army held twelve and the PKI none.

Not only within Indonesia were tensions rising during 1964–5; they were also intensifying between Indonesia and the United States. Sukarno had expected that the United States would back him in his demand for self-determination for the peoples of British Borneo through a plebiscite or referendum as to whether they would join Britain's Malaysia plan. When the United States would not support this approach he, along with General Nasution, began to suspect that it was in collusion with Britain.[7] Nasution expected even more than Sukarno, arguing that "the peoples of the Borneo states should first be given independence and then be allowed to choose whether or not they wish to join Malaya, the Philippines, Indonesia," or remain on their own.[8]

As during 1964, substantial economic support by the United States to the new federation was followed by a successful campaign to get Malaysia elected to the United Nations Security Council, Sukarno's antagonism toward the United States intensified. On March 25 he renounced American economic assistance to Indonesia. And he began criticizing American actions in Vietnam even more strongly than before, as did Nasution. They saluted the struggle of Vietnam's National Liberation Front, and at the beginning of August 1964 Sukarno arranged for Jakarta's full diplomatic recognition of the Hanoi government. Then on the last day of 1964, reflecting his outrage at the U.S. engineering a seat for Malaysia on the Security Council, he withdrew Indonesia from the United Nations. Charging that it was dominated by reactionary forces, he proposed the establishment of an "antiimperialist axis" of "New Emerging Forces" stretching from Peking via Pyongyang and Phnom Penh to Jakarta. Although this project never materialized, the envisaged closer relationship with China (bête noire of the Indonesian armed forces as well as the United States) was as upsetting to many senior army officers as it was welcomed by the PKI.

During the early months of 1965 relations between the United States and President Sukarno continued to deteriorate. As Howard Jones later wrote of this period:

Pressures mounted against the American community. There were demonstrations in Djakarta; "takeover committees" made threatening gestures against American-owned rubber plantations in Sumatra; apparently on the initiative of the Communist-dominated unions, a mail boycott was instituted against our embassy, the AID mission, and our consulate at Surabaja; electricity and gas service to U.S. installations in Djakarta were suspended and telecommunications personnel refused to handle copy for U.S. newsmen.[9]

American concern increased when offices of U.S. oil companies in Indonesia were seized, and although American managers were permitted to remain on there was fear that their oil operations might be nationalized without compensation.

Nearly a year earlier Ambassador Jones had tried to persuade Nasution that the army should take matters into its own hands against the PKI.[10] In March 1965, expressing fears of "some accommodation between the Army and the PKI," Jones went so far as to tell senior American officials: "From our viewpoint, of course, an unsuccessful coup attempt by the PKI might be the most effective development to start a reversal of political trends in Indonesia" (wherein the army would be free to crack down on the Communists). But, he acknowledged, "the PKI is doing too well through its present tactics of cooperation with Sukarno," and that "unless the PKI leadership is rasher than I think they are they will not give the army the clear-cut kind of challenge which could galvanize effective reaction."[11] Exasperated though he was with Sukarno, Jones had not completely abandoned hope of working more productively with him. But this was not the case with Jones's successors. His own deputy chief of mission, Francis Galbraith, had, together with the CIA station, long been waging a secret campaign to discredit Jones in Washington for his patience with Sukarno, and when Marshall Green succeeded Jones as ambassador at the end of June 1965, Galbraith had a more sympathetic superior. Indicative of the embassy's harder line was Galbraith's memorandum sent to Washington "For the Amabassador" on September 21: "It is our conclusion that Sukarno is pushing this country towards communist control . . . and that the longer he stays around the closer Indonesia is likely to move towards that goal . . . therefore anything that makes Sukarno feel more comfortable and prolongs his life span is not in the U.S. interest."[12]

In the descending spiral of mutual mistrust Sukarno concluded that he himself was the target of a new CIA assassination attempt. In a mid-February 1965 meeting with White House aide Michael Forrestal, he charged that the CIA was "out of control" in Indonesia and that Ambassador Jones did not know what it was doing.[13] According to Jones there had in fact been no less than seven "narrowly failed" assassination attempts against Sukarno, at least three of these having been made subsequent to that at Cikini.[14] When the ambassador paid his farewell visit at the beginning of

June he was obliged to deny Sukarno's allegation that the CIA was plotting to assassinate him, General Yani, and Foreign Minister Subandrio.[15]

From January 1965 there had been constant rumors of the possibility of a coup to be mounted against Sukarno by a "Council of Generals." Sukarno questioned General Yani in May about the existence of such a council and Yani told him that it existed but was merely a body to consider promotions and appointments in the army, not a political body.[16] According to a CIA study however, the council did in fact have a broader concern: "In January, General Yani and a group of his most trusted advisers in the Army began to meet together informally to discuss the deteriorating political situation and what the Army should do about it."[17] Presumably, the senior Communist party leaders were similarly preoccupied, and spasmodic signs that Sukarno might be critically ill provided both them and the army an urgent incentive to develop contingency plans in case of his sudden death. Sukarno himself, largely because of his earlier experience with the covert activities directed against him, clearly suspected not only that the council was much more minatory than Yani had admitted, but also that it was probably tied to his Western enemies. As the CIA's retrospective study of 1965 acknowledges:

> No doubt, at that point in time, Sukarno was predisposed to think the worst of both the U.S. and the British. He may really have believed that Britain and the United States were in collusion with the Indonesian military in plotting his overthrow. Ever since the PRRI-Permesta rebellion in the outer islands in 1956-61, in which the U.S. and Britain had been involved, he had been deeply suspicious of the U.S.; and of the C.I.A., in particular. By the summer of 1965, when the West Irian issue had been settled in his favor, Sukarno had transferred the full fury of his anti-Dutch complex to the U.S. and Britain. In the situation of growing tension between him and the Army, he might easily have been persuaded of the danger of a coup by a Generals' council, probably in foreign pay.[18]

Whatever the case, the period of rumor and uncertainty ended on September 30, 1965, when Lieutenant Colonel Untung, commander of one of the battalions of Sukarno's palace guard, ordered an action in which six top generals were kidnapped and (with or without Untung's orders) brutally murdered, including General Yani and several of the small group of high-ranking officers surrounding and supporting him. Nasution was also targeted but escaped, although his young daughter and one of his aides were killed. Untung announced that this was a preemptive action to forestall what he claimed was a CIA-backed coup by a "Council of Generals" (presumably made up of the six who had been kidnapped and Nasution).

If Untung's "preemptive" coup had been meant to succeed, it could hardly have been more gauchely handled. The troops it could deploy in Jakarta were vastly outnumbered by those available to Jakarta garrison commander General Umar Wirahadikusumah and General Suharto's Strategic Reserve. Although from their base of operations in the center of Jakarta Untung's troops occupied the offices of Radio Indonesia, they completely ignored the nearby headquarters of Suharto's Kostrad, with its vital communication links to military units throughout Indonesia. Untung stated that his move was to protect Sukarno, yet in the new government lineup he broadcast Sukarno's name was conspicuously missing and he gave no indication that the president supported his actions or this new government.[19] (In view of Sukarno's popularity this omission was striking to many of those who heard Untung's broadcasts.) And finally he made an announcement of what would be his new government's policies that could hardly have been better calculated to ensure it would draw no support from any army officer of the rank of colonel or above. While all privates and noncommissioned officers were to be promoted one rank (two if they had supported Untung's movement), all rankings above lieutenant colonel would be abolished.

General Suharto, who stood just behind General Yani in the chain of command, had nevertheless not been a target of Untung's men. He had no difficulty in promptly mustering his Strategic Reserve and in less than twenty-four hours overcoming the meager force of just three battalions upon which Untung's movement had relied in the capital. Suharto then took over leadership of the army. Alleging PKI responsibility for Untung's putsch, he unleashed army units in a massive pogrom aimed at eliminating all Communists, their trade unions, peasant and other mass organizations, and many individuals believed to have been sympathetic to them. Apparently in most cases soldiers carried out the massacres, but in the countryside of Central and East Java, North Sumatra, and Bali (where the incidence of killings was probably the highest), the army also turned over weapons to members of local non-Communist youth organizations, especially members of Ansor, the youth component of the Muslim Nahdatul Ulama party, and exhorted them to carry out the executions. Most of the killings took place outside the cities and larger towns, primarily in rural areas, where the deaths among school teachers were reported to be especially high. Sukarno's efforts to halt the massacres were largely unavailing. Charges of involvement in the coup attempt were leveled against him, and the army leadership publicly forced him to yield power to Suharto in April 1966 at a time when in some parts of Indonesia the massacres were still going on.

Preoccupied with their country's escalation of military intervention in Vietnam, the American public largely ignored developments in Indonesia, as did most of the rest of the outside world. But the 1965–66 massacres constituted one of the bloodiest purges in modern history: in the words of the CIA study, "In terms of the numbers killed the anti-PKI massacres in Indonesia rank as one of the worst mass murders of the 20th century, along with the Soviet purges of the 1930's, the Nazi mass murders during the

Second World War, and the Maoist bloodbath of the early 1950's."[20] Details concerning the killings have not been easy to come by, for as Robert Cribb observes in what thus far is probably the most comprehensive account: "With the regime which oversaw and approved the killings still in power, those who have stories to tell against it are understandably reticent about what took place in 1965–66 lest they themselves become victims." Reasonably dispassionate estimates, however, have fixed the number killed as at least half a million—450,000-500,000 being acknowledged by Admiral Sudomo, head of Suharto's Kopkamtib (Komando Pemulihan Keamanan dan Ketertiban—Command for the Restoration of Security and Public Order), who estimated that 750,000 others were jailed or sent to concentration camps[21] (where many spent the rest of their lives).

The genesis of Untung's putsch, the actions of the PKI and General Suharto, and the possibility of involvement of the CIA and Britain's MI-6 are still unclear and matters of ongoing dispute—at least outside Indonesia, where it is safe to differ with the incumbent government on this issue. Although it is quite possible for Untung's effort to have taken place without any outside assistance or even encouragement, serious scholars have certainly not ruled this out. As Frederick Bunnell has recently (1990) averred in what is by far the most comprehensive and careful analysis of American policy toward Indonesia during the first nine months of 1965 leading up to what he refers to as Untung's abortive "coup," it is

> premature for any analyst to render a final judgement on the CIA's role in the October coup plot, or in other clandestine activities both before and after the coup, including the tragic massacre of about half a million alleged Communists in the fall of 1965. Few documents relevant to CIA activities have yet been declassifed and censors have been skillful in "sanitizing" ostensibly declassified NSC staff memoranda. Conclusive judgement must therefore await the US government release of relevant classified documents, such as the complete file of the CIA's Jakarta station, and also the Indonesian government's granting of access to participants, such as Colonel Latief [still alleged to have been one of the key conspirators and known to have conferred with General Suharto on the night of the coup attempt], who are still imprisoned.[22]

While in the case of American intervention in Indonesia in 1957-58 the lack of released CIA documents is compensated for by Ambassador Jones's private notes and the record of the Dulles brothers' relevant phone calls, no comparable data are available to offset the CIA's withholding of pertinent documents relating to 1965. Britain, too, has yet to release government documents with respect to relations with Indonesia during this period. Yet of the external powers with motivation for bringing about major political change in Indonesia in 1965 Britain undoubtedly ranked first. Only through such change would it be possible to stem the heavy hemorrhaging of the British treasury brought about by the need to maintain a large expeditionary force to defend Malaysia against Indonesia's confrontation policy.

President Suharto's government has also done much to obscure what took place in 1965. So keen has it been to get across its version that the Communist party was in Harold Crouch's words "the sole *dalang* [puppetmaster] that had initiated the planning and organization of the coup attempt" with "the military participants" "mere puppets in its hands,"[23] and so insistent in asserting that there was no basis for regarding Untung's movement as fundamentally an "internal army affair" that its attempts to explain what happened soon lost credibility. The government's efforts to establish its case culminated in 1968 with its sponsorship of a study printed in English by two army officers, Colonel Nugroho Notosusanto and Lieutenant Colonel Ismail Saleh, which until this day remains the closest thing to an official version of the 1965 coup attempt.[24] As Crouch has noted, this version held that "the army and airforce officers involved in the coup attempt were conscious agents of the PKI without independent motivation of their own," that in the words of these two colonels, their action was "staged to look like an internal army affair." For their evidence the two authors relied largely on army-conducted trials the aim of which, as Crouch observes, was "to demonstrate that the PKI initiated the coup attempt."[25] Although it is not difficult to accept that there was some measure of Communist involvement, this officially approved account resorted to so much overkill in trying to exculpate the army and lodge responsibility with the Communists that it had the result of further undermining the credibility of the Suharto government's version. Its heavy reliance on a series of interrogations and trials of Communists and others alleged to have played roles in the coup attempt was less than convincing even for the CIA, which clearly tried to be supportive of the government's view. Thus in discussing the use of army interrogations at the trials, the CIA in its December 1968 study of the attempted coup acknowledged:

> If we accept the fact that the interrogation reports are verbatim transcripts of the actual interrogation of the various people in connection with the 30 September Movement, there is still the question of the validity of such evidence. It is certainly true that the evidence obtained from men under duress, either physical or mental, as these men certainly were, must be accepted with some reservation. It is always possible that the person under interrogation will sometimes say whatever he thinks the interrogators want him to say in order to end the ordeal of interrogation.[26]

Although no evidence has appeared that shows the United States to have been involved in Untung's failed coup, it is clear that the State Department and senior American embassy officers in Jakarta enthusiastically supported the Indonesian army's actions in its aftermath.[27] The U.S. embassy's attitude was clearly expressed when, almost a month after the mass killings had begun, Francis Galbraith, the deputy chief of mission (later to succeed Marshall Green as ambassador), reporting to Washington on his conversation with a high-ranking Indonesian army officer, said that he had "made clear" to him "that the embassy and the U.S.G[overnment] were generally sympathetic with and admiring of what the army was doing."[28] Careful study of all declassified U.S. government documents that bear on the physical liquidation of the PKI disclose no instance of any American official objecting to or in any way criticizing the 1965-66 killings. When later asked to comment on this finding, William Colby, who at that time served as head of the Far Eastern division of the CIA's Directorate of Plans (and later as the agency's director), concurred, stating that he had never been aware of any such objection or criticism.[29]

American input went beyond mere approbation and encouragement. As Bunnell has established from U.S. government documents and corroborative interviews with General Sukendro (in 1965 the ranking army intelligence chief), the United States quickly fulfilled the army's request, relayed by Sukendro on November 6, 1965, for weapons "to arm Moslem and nationalist youth in Central Java for use against the PKI" in the context of overall army policy "to eliminate the PKI."[30]

The PKI was indeed eliminated—root and branch—and even before the process of its liquidation was completed Sukarno had been obliged to yield power to Suharto and spend most of his few remaining years under house arrest.

For the United States the political landscape of Indonesia had become vastly simpler. Eight years before, it had been obliged to deal with a variegated, pluralistic polity. Its intervention in behalf of the rebels and its role in the ensuing civil war had left Indonesia with just three significant centers of power—competitive and unstable in their relationship and poised for an inevitable and very destructive explosion. After that took place in 1965-66 the United States had an even less complex situation with which to deal. For there now remained just one significant power factor—the Indonesian army under General Suharto.

Biographies of Key Figures

Indonesian government*

Djuanda, Kartawidjaja

b. Tasikmalaya, West Java, July 10, 1911, a Sundanese Muslim. Graduated with engineering degree from Bandung Technical School in 1933. No party affiliation. Deputy Minister and then Minister of Communications, 1946-48; Minister of Prosperity, 1950; Minister of Communications, 1950-52; Director General National Planning Bureau, 1952-56; Minister of Planning, 1956-57; Prime Minister, 1957-58; First Minister (Sukarno cabinet), 1959-62.

Hamengku Buwono IX (Sultan of Yogyakarta)

b. Yogyakarta, 1912. A Javanese aristocrat, son of previous sultan of Yogyakarta; studied law in Leiden University until illness of father, whom he succeeded as Sultan in 1940, obliged him to return to Indonesia. No political affiliation, but close to Sjahrir's Indonesian Socialist party. Governor of Military District of Yogyakarta, 1946-49; Minister of State, 1946-48; Minister of Defense, 1949-50; Deputy Prime Minister, 1950-51; Minister of Defense, 1952-53.

Hatta, Mohammad

b. Bukittinggi, West Sumatra, August 12, 1902. Master's degree from Rotterdam School of Commerce in 1932. An active nationalist leader, he led a political party on his return to Indonesia and was imprisoned and exiled by the Dutch from 1934 to 1942. He cooperated with the Japanese administration and became vice president under Sukarno after independence, a position he held until 1956. A devout Muslim, he believed, as did the religious socialists in the Masjumi, that Islam and Socialism were fully compatible. Like Sukarno after the revolution he was a member of no political party. Strongly favored a decentralized federal political order for Indonesia.

Jusuf, Andi

Aristocrat from southern Bone in South Sulawesi, he fought against and was imprisoned by the Dutch. In 1953 he attended the SSKAD and from

---

* Many Indonesians, especially from Java, have only one name.

1955-56 the Staff School at Fort Benning, Georgia, emerging as a Lieutenant Colonel in the Indonesian army.

Nasution, A. H.

b. Kotanopan, North Sumatra, 1918, Muslim Mandailing Batak. Received military training at the Bandung Military Academy under the Dutch, and at the time of the Japanese invasion was a second lieutenant in the Dutch Indies Army (KNIL). Inactive during the occupation, he joined the republican army in 1945 and in May 1946 was appointed commander of its West Java division, later known as the Siliwangi division. In 1948 he became deputy to Army Commander Sudirman and, as Chief of Operations Staff, was prime mover in the republic's plans for rationalizing the armed forces, working closely with Vice President Hatta. He was named Chief of Staff of the Army in December 1949, replacing the dying General Sudirman.

Roem, Mohamad

b. Parakan, East Java, May 16, 1908, of peasant parents. Earned degree from Jakarta Law School in 1939. Member of progressive wing of Masjumi. Minister of Internal Affairs, 1946-47; 1947-48; Without Portfolio, 1949-50. Appointed High Commissioner to The Hague, 1950; Minister of Foreign Affairs, 1950-51; Minister of Internal Affairs, 1952-53; First Deputy Prime Minister, 1956-57.

Sastroamidjojo, Ali

b. Magelang, May 21, 1903. Graduated from Leiden University 1927. Joined PNI of Sukarno and member of its central board in 1928. Cofounder of Partindo, Member of Executive Council of PNI 1945-66. Minister of Education and Culture, 1947-49; first Indonesian Ambassador to the United States, 1950-53; Prime Minister of the Republic of Indonesia, August 1, 1953-August 12, 1955, March 26, 1956-April 9, 1957. Indonesian Representative to United Nations, 1957-60; General Chairman of PNI, 1960-66.

Subandrio

b. Malang, September 15, 1915. Graduated from Medical College in Jakarta, 1942. Nonparty until 1958 when joined PNI. Representative of Republic of Indonesia in London, 1947-49; Ambassador to United Kingdom, 1950. Secretary General of the Indonesian Foreign Ministry, 1956-April 1957; Minister of Foreign Affairs, 1957-65; First Deputy Prime Minister, 1964-65. Imprisoned by the Suharto regime and still in detention.

Sukarno

b. Surabaya, June 6, 1901, the son of a Javanese school principal and a Balinese mother. Graduated from Dutch high school in Surabaya, then the technical faculty in Bandung, with a degree in engineering. He led the National-ist Party of Indonesia, until imprisoned by the Dutch from 1929-31 and then from February 1934 to 1935 when he was again arrested by the Dutch and kept under arrest in exile in Flores and Benkulen until released by the Japanese in 1942. Because of his leadership qualities and great gifts as an orator he was accepted as leader of the nationalist movement by all Indone-sian groups, and after cooperating with the Japanese during the occupa-tion, became first President of the Republic in August 1945, a position he held until succeeded by Suharto in 1967.

Rebels

Assaat

b. Bukittinggi, West Sumatra, September 18, 1904. Graduated from law school in Leiden, 1939. Nonparty. Head of the Working Committee of the KNIP (National Committee of the Republic of Indonesia), 1946-49; exiled by Dutch to Bangka with Sukarno, 1948. After transfer of sovereignty was Minister of Home Affairs in the Natsir cabinet.

Barlian

b. Palembang, July 23, 1922; graduated from Dutch Middle School in Malang, Java, in 1941. Received military training from the Japanese and during the revolution fought in South Sumatra, eventually becoming com-mander of the Sriwijaya division. After the transfer of sovereignty he was assigned to army headquarters on Java, then attended the SSKAD in Ban-dung 1951-52. He stood as a candidate for Nasution's IPKI party in the 1955 elections. Was appointed Chief of Staff of the South Sumatra military command in March 1956, and Commander in July 1956.

Djambek, Dahlan

b. Bukittinggi, 1917, the son of a famous West Sumatran Islamic leader. He first attended Islamic schools, then a Christian high school in Jakarta, but remained a devout Muslim. He was one of the first group of candidate offi-cers to be trained by the Japanese in West Sumatra. Was the first Comman-der of the Banteng division in West Sumatra after independence, and over-saw its dissolution in 1949-50. Was military attaché in London from 1952 to 1956. Before joining the rebellion he served as the Jakarta government's liaison with the West Sumatran dissidents.

Harahap, Burhanuddin

b. Medan, February 12, 1917. Received law degree from Gadja Mada Uni-versity, Yogyakarta. Member of progressive wing of the Masjumi. Prime Minister and Minister of Defense, August 12, 1955-March 26, 1956.

Accused, without proof, of involvement in the Cikini assassination attempt against Sukarno, he fled to West Sumatra at the end of 1957.

Husein, Ahmad

b. Padang, April 1, 1925, the son of a pharmacy assistant in the Dutch military hospital who was also a prominent Muslim leader. Husein attended the nationalist Taman Siswa schools. He received military training from the Japanese and was a regimental commander of the Banteng division during the revolution. As regimental commander in December 1956, he played a key role in establishing the Banteng Council and emerged as its leader.

Kawilarang, A. E.

b. Jatinegara, West Java, February 23, 1920, a Christian, with a Minahasan father and mother both of whom had served in the Dutch civil service. He was educated in Dutch high school and was a member of the 1940 class of the KNIL (Dutch Indonesian forces). During the revolution he was an officer in the republican army in West Java and in Tapanuli, and then in April 1950 he was appointed Commander in East Indonesia until being transferred to head the Siliwangi division in West Java at the end of 1951.

Lubis, Zulkifli

A Mandailing Batak born in Aceh in 1923, Lubis was a cousin but no friend of Nasution. Trained in intelligence by the Japanese during their occupation, he was responsible for setting up the republic's intelligence services in 1945, which he headed throughout the revolution. He became Deputy Chief of Staff of the Army in December 1953 until August 1956. He opposed Nasution in the October 17, 1952, affair and attempted a coup against him in 1956 that was unsuccessful. He was accused of responsibility for the November 1957 assassination attempt against Sukarno.

Nainggolan, W. F. (Boyke)

A Christian Toba Batak, whose mother and sisters had been murdered in the social revolution of 1946, allegedly by members of the Gintings clan. He was widely reputed to be one of the ablest oficers in the Indonesian army. Mounted the action in Medan in support of the rebels in March 1958.

Natsir, Mohammad

b. Alahan Panjang, West Sumatra, July 17, 1908, the son of a government clerk, he received both religious and Dutch education, graduating from Dutch high school in Bandung. Was active in modernist Islamic politics and education throughout the 1930s. A member of the Masjumi both during the Japanese occupation and after independence, he became a leader of its progressive wing, and served as the republic's Minister of Information during the revolution. He was Prime Minister of the Republic from September 1950 to April 1951. A strong believer in a federal political order, he remained Chairman of the Masjumi until he became involved in the PRRI rebellion.

Saleh Lahade

A Buginese-Makassarese, he graduated from the agricultural school in Bogor and was married to a daughter of the venerated Javanese nationalist leader Ki Hadjar Dewantoro. He had joined the armed Sulawesi unit (KRIS) which fought on Java during the revolution.

Simbolon, Maludin

b. Tarutung, North Sumatra, September 13, 1916, a Protestant Toba Batak, educated in a Christian school in Surakarta. Taught in several Dutch elementary schools, 1938-42, then received military training from Japanese in South Sumatra. During revolution in charge of South Sumatra command (1946-50), then in 1950, with rank of full colonel, succeeded Kawilarang as North Sumatra Commander in Medan, a position he held until 1956.

Sjafruddin Prawiranegara

b. Banten, West Java, Feburary 28, 1911, the son of a Bantenese father, a district head, and a Bantenese-Minangkabau mother. He graduated from Dutch high school in Bandung in 1931 and from law school in Jakarta in 1939. After independence became a leader of the progressive wing of the Masjumi party. He served as Minister of Finance in several republican cabinets during the revolution, then headed the emergency government on Sumatra after the Dutch captured Sukarno and his cabinet on Java. After full independence he again served as Finance Minister from 1950-51, then as Governor of the Bank of Indonesia until the end of 1957.

Sumitro Djojohadikusumo

b. Central Java, May 29, 1917, he earned his doctorate in economics at the Rotterdam School of Commerce, and remained in Holland during the World War II. Returned to Indonesia, 1946. Deputy Chief Indonesian delegation to United Nations, 1948-49, Minister of Trade, 1950-51; Professor and Dean, Faculty of Economics at University of Indonesia, 1951-57; Minister of Finance, 1952-53 and 1955-56. He was widely regarded as the country's leading economist and enjoyed considerable backing within the Indonesian Socialist party, ultimately challenging Sjahrir (unsuccessfully) for its chairmanship.

Sumual, H. N. Ventje

b. Minahasa, June 11, 1923, a Christian and son of a sergeant in the KNIL.

Attended merchant marine school in Makassar during Japanese occupation. Member of an armed Sulawesi unit (KRIS) on Java during the
revolution, and afterward served in North Sulawesi. Graduated from
SSKAD in 1953. In charge of training and education at the infantry in
spectorate in Bandung before being appointed Chief of Staff of the East
Indonesia Command.

United States Officials

Allison, John M.
Assistant Secretary for Far Eastern Affairs, February 1952- March 1953;
Ambassador to Japan, April 1953 to February 1957; Ambassador to
Indonesia, February 21, 1957 (Presented his credentials March 13.) -Janu-
ary 28, 1958.

Bell, James D.
Director of Office of Southwest Pacific Affairs, March 1956-April 1957;
Counselor of Embassy Indonesia, April-December 1957. Then Ambas-
sador to Malaya.

Benson, George
United States Army attaché in Jakarta Embassy, 1957-58.

Burke, Arleigh A.
United States Navy, Chief of Naval Operations from August 1955.

Cottrell, Sterling
Chargé d'Affaires, U.S. Embassy, Jakarta, January 29-March 5, 1958;
appointed at request of Hugh S. Cumming, Jr., after serving as Consul in
Singapore since July 1956.

Cumming, Hugh S., Jr.
Ambassador to Indonesia, September 3, 1953-March 3, 1957; Special
Assistant for Intelligence, Department of State, May-October 1957; then
Director of the Bureau of Intelligence and Research, Department of State
and Department Liaison with CIA. Chairman, Inter-Departmental Task
Force on Indonesia, 1957-58.

Dulles, Allen W.
Director of the Central Intelligence Agency, 1953-1961.

Dulles, John Foster
Secretary of State, January 1953-April 1959. Died May 1959.

Eisenhower, Dwight D.
President of the United States, 1953-1961.

Felt, Harry D.
United States Navy, Commander in Chief, Pacific Command (CINCPAC), from July 1958.

Herter, Christian A.
Consultant to the Secretary of State, January-February 1957; then Under Secretary of State until April 1959, thereafter Secretary of State.

Jones, Howard P.
Chief of the Foreign Operations Administration in Indonesia and Counselor of Embassy, July 1954-July 1955; Deputy Assistant Secretary of State for Far Eastern Economic Affairs, February 1956-April 1957; Deputy Assistant Secretary of State for Far Eastern Affairs, May 1957-February 1958; Ambassador to Indonesia, March 6, 1958-April 1965.

Mein, John Gordon
First Secretary of the Embassy in Indonesia to May 1955; Counselor of Embassy, May 1955-July 1956; Deputy Director of the Office of Southwest Pacific Affairs, Department of State, July 1956-May 1957; Director of Office of Southwest Pacific Affairs, May 1957-May 1960.

Radford, Arthur W.
United States Navy, Chairman of the Joint Chiefs of Staff to August 1957.

Robertson, Walter S.
Assistant Secretary of State for Far Eastern Affairs, April 1953-June 1959.

Stump, Felix B.
United States Navy, Commander in Chief, Pacific Command (CINCPAC), 1957-July 1958.

Taylor, Maxwell
United States Army, Chief of Staff, 1957-58.

Twining, Nathan F.
United States Air Force, Chief of Staff. Chairman of the Joint Chiefs of Staff, August 1957-September 1960.

Young, Kenneth T.
Director of the Office of Philippine and Southeast Asian Affairs to March 1956; thereafter Director of the Office of Southeast Asian Affairs to May 1957.

A Note on Sources

Our study draws on a broad range of written and oral data gathered over the course of some three and a half decades in Indonesia, the United Kingdom, and the United States. Some of our most important sources are unique and privileged, and our efforts would not have been successful without access to them. Thus, although investigation of the American dimension of this story has long been discouraged by the unwillingness of the CIA to declassify and release relevant documents, we have acquired other data that permit us to outflank and compensate for this bureaucratic stone wall. Among these are the abstracts of some of the most important of the still-classified relevant American government documents made by the late Howard P. Jones during and after the periods when he served on the secret interagency planning group on Indonesia and then through most of 1958 as U.S. ambassador to Jakarta. Supplementing these is his personal fifty-five-page annotated chronology of developments in Indonesia and American policy-making on Indonesia relating to the PRRI rebellion.

We, of course, make extensive use of the several thousand State Department documents bearing on our study that have been declassified (many through our efforts under the Freedom of Information Act) as well as a large body of British Foreign Office records and the deck logs of ships of the U.S. Seventh Fleet involved in Indonesian operations during the period we cover.

Also helpful to our study are the pertinent transcripts of Secretary Dulles's telephone conversations commencing in September 1957 and running into June 1958. Most extensive are the records of calls to and from his brother, Allen Dulles, director of the CIA, but also enlightening are the records of his discussions with Under Secretary of State Christian Herter, Assistant Secretary of State for Far Eastern Affairs Walter Robertson, and Chief of Naval Operations Arleigh Burke. There are records of only a few conversations directly with President Eisenhower, but references are made in several of Dulles's talks with others to discussions he has just had with the president and to the views he had then expressed. (These records exist because Secretary Dulles had his private secretary listen in and take notes on important telephone conversations, and they are now available to the public at the Eisenhower Library in Abilene, Kansas.) Although these records may often appear all too cryptic, much can be gleaned from them when one knows the context of the situation in which the calls were made and appreciates the meaning of some thinly disguised terms—e.g., that "the archipelago" stands for Indonesia and "eating a bird" refers to utilization of an American-supplied aircraft.) The absurdity of the U.S. government's reluctance to declassify official documents relating to the developments about which we write is starkly highlighted by the open access to the record of these phone calls—for presidentially authorized covert operations are unlikely to be enshrined in a document and more likely to be conveyed orally.

Our study also draws heavily on interviews between 1958 and 1993 with numerous active or retired U.S. State Department, CIA, and Defense Department officials. Especially valuable to our understanding of American policy were the discussions over many years made possible by our friendship with two of the three American ambassadors stationed in Jakarta during this period—John M. Allison and Howard P. Jones—both of whom wrote part of their memoirs while fellows in Cornell University's Modern Indonesia Project and Southeast Asia Program. (Also very helpful was a nearly daylong interview with the third of these ambassadors, Hugh S. Cumming, Jr., held when he felt too weak to write his memoirs but nevertheless wanted to "set the record straight.") All interviews cited, unless otherwise noted, are by the authors.

With respect to Indonesian sources, we have utilized published and unpublished documentation—both that of the central government in Jakarta and internal, largely typewritten records of the rebels. But most important has been the probably unique access we have had to all of the major Indonesian actors in interviews extending intermittently from 1958 to 1994. One of the authors, George McT. Kahin, as the only American in Indonesia's revolutionary capital in 1948-49, came to know well most of the men who played major roles on both the central government and rebel sides of the civil war of the mid-1950s. The other author, Audrey R. Kahin, has over many years carried out extensive research in West Sumatra, the original crucible of the rebellion. Without our discussions with participants at the national and local levels our study could not have succeeded, and we wish to record our gratitude to all those we have interviewed.

We would like to acknowledge our indebtedness to the works of those few scholars who have contributed major studies of the Indonesian political terrain that existed during the years our study covers—especially Herbert Feith's *The Decline of Constitutional Democracy in Indonesia*, Barbara S. Harvey's *Permesta: Half a Rebellion*, and Daniel S. Lev's *The Transition to Guided Democracy: Indonesian Politics, 1957-1959*.

And finally we wish to thank the helpful archivists and librarians at the Dwight D. Eisenhower Library in Abilene, Kansas; the John F. Kennedy Library in Boston; the U.S. National Archives, U.S. Naval Historical Center, and the National Security Archive in Washington, D.C.; the Seeley Mudd Library in Princeton, N.J.; the British Public Records Office in Kew, Surrey; the library of the Institute of Southeast Asian Studies in Singapore; and the John M. Echols Collection on Southeast Asia at Cornell University's Kroch Library.

Addendum

In November 1994, while our study was already at galley proof stage with the publisher, we obtained a copy of the just published *Indonesia*, Vol. XVII in the *Foreign Relations of the United States* series for 1958-1960. Although it was too late for us to make use of this, we found that we already had obtained the most significant of its documents (or Ambassador Howard Jones's abstracts of them) while the others of most interest were largely redundant with those we previously had acquired.

In view of the publicity attending publication of this volume we were astonished by the paucity of relevant information the CIA actually permitted to be released, and how much of the story that agency still insists be kept hidden. And thus we note that, despite the persistent efforts over many years of Robert McMahon, the volume's able editor (who actually completed work on this volume in 1981), the CIA still refused to permit publication of important information that, as the State Department's Bureau of Public Affairs acknowledges, relates to "the details of U.S. covert support of the Indonesian rebellion in Sumatra and Sulawesi (Celebes) and to liaison with other countries interested and involved in the operation." Even assuming the CIA should decide to be more forthcoming in the future, the State Department historians who personally have recently been "provided expanded access" to some of the most important data, but forbidden by the agency to publish them, realize that in view of the CIA's attitude the process of "submitting such documents for declassification review would have necessitated considerable [additional] delay in the publication of the volume." Consequently they "chose not to postpone publication" any longer.

The continued stonewalling by the CIA will, we believe, be regarded as all the more absurd by those who read our study, for it should be abundantly clear that through our access to other sources, as noted above, we have considerably more than made up for the documents that agency still insists on withholding.

Glossary & Abbreviations

ANZUS
Australia, New Zealand, United States—mutual security treaty

AURI
Angkatan Udara Republik Indonesia, Indonesian Airforce

CIA
Central Intelligence Agency

CINCPAC
Commander in chief of U.S. Pacific Forces

dalang
puppet master

Darul Islam (DI)
House of Islam—insurgents in West Java, Aceh, and South Sulawesi, dedicated to establishment of an Islamic state

dwitunggal
duumvirate—of Sukarno/Hatta

GAK
Gerakan Anti-Komunis
(anticommunist movement)

Gebak
Gerakan Bersama Anti-Komunis
(Joint movement against communism)

GOI
Government of Indonesia

GPII
Gerakan Pemuda Islam Indonesia—Masjumi youth organization

IPKI
Army Veterans' Party

KNIL
Koninklijk Nederlands Indisch Leger (Royal Netherlands Indies Army)

Kopkamtib
Komando Pemulihan Keamanan dan Ketertiban (Command for the Restoration of Security and Public Order)—under the Suharto regime

KPM
Koninklijk Paketvaart Maatschappij—Dutch Interisland shipping company

MAP
Military Assistance Program

Masjumi
Madjelis Sjuro Muslimin Indonesia (Indonesian Muslim Consultative Council), major Islamic political party

Munas
Musyawarah National (National Conference)

NASAKOM
Sukarno's acronym for the union of national, religious and Communist forces

NATO
North Atlantic Treaty Organization

NIE
National Intelligence Estimate

NIT
Negara Indonesia Timor (State of East Indonesia)—during revolution—Dutch sponsored

NSC
National Security Council

OPC
Office of Policy Coordination—CIA's covert political activities division

OPR
Organisasi Pemuda Rakjat (People's Youth Organization)—PKI controlled

Panca Sila
Five Principles; basis of the state propounded by Sukarno in 1945

PAP
People's Action Party (Singapore)

Permesta
Piagam Perdjuangan Semesta Alam (Charter of Inclusive Struggle)—
Sulawesi based insurgent organization allied to PRRI

Peta
Pembela Tanah Air (Defender of the Fatherland) Japanese-sponsored militia

PKI
Partai Komunis Indonesia (Indonesian Communist Party)

PNI
Partai Nasionalis Indonesia (Indonesian National Party)

PRRI
Pemerintah Revolusioner Republik Indonesia (Revolutionary Government
of the Republic of Indonesia), insurgent movement proclaimed in Padang,
February 15, 1958, and allied to Permesta

PSI
Partai Sosialis Indonesia (Indonesian Socialist Party)

RPI
Republik Persatuan Indonesia (United Republic of Indonesia)—formed by
rebels in 1960

RPKAD
Resimen Pertempuran Komando Angkatan Darat—Indonesian Army
Paratroopers

RUSI
Republic of the United States of Indonesia (1950)

SEATO
Southeast Asia Treaty Organization

SOBSI
Sentral Organisasi Buruh Seluruh Indonesia—All-Indonesia Federation of
Labor Organizations—PKI controlled

SSKAD
Sekolah Staf dan Komando Angkatan Darat (Army Staff and Command School)

TNI
Tentara National Indonesia (Indonesian National Army)

TT
Army Territorial Command

NOTES

Introduction

1. Oral history interview of Robert Lovett deposited in the J. F. Kennedy Library, Columbia Point (Boston), Mass., pp. 40-41.

2. For an informed account of Dulles's hiring of McLeod, see John Emmet Hughes, *The Ordeal of Power* (New York: Atheneum, 1963), pp. 84-86. See also Townsend Hoopes, *The Devil and John Foster Dulles* (Boston: Little Brown, 1973), pp. 152-55.

3. Stephen Ambrose, *Eisenhower*, vol. 2, *The President* (New York: Simon & Schuster, 1984), p. 442.

4. Piers Brendon, *Ike: His Life and Times* (New York: Harper & Row, 1986), p. 355.

5. Richard H. Immerman, ed., *John Foster Dulles and the Diplomacy of the Cold War* (Princeton, N.J.: Princeton University Press, 1990), p. 9.

6. Ambrose, *Eisenhower*, vol. 2, pp. 110-11.

7. Stephen Ambrose with Richard Immerman, *Ike's Spies: Eisenhower and the Espionage Establishment* (New York: Doubleday, 1981), Introduction.

8. Loch K. Johnson, *A Season of Inquiry: The Senate Intelligence Investigation* (Lexington, K.Y.: The University Press of Kentucky, 1985), pp. 58-59.

9. Papers of John Foster Dulles, Harvey Mudd Library, Princeton University, Princeton, N.J.

10. Ibid. Also discussion with Ambassador Cumming, Washington, D.C., 25 Dec. 1975. On that day, I had a wide-ranging, unusually candid five-hour discussion with Cumming, who, having decided not to write his memoirs, nevertheless wanted to set the record straight on his relationship with Indonesia(GMcTK).

11. For Truman's decision to open up a second front from bases in Burma using Chiang Kai-shek's forces and bypassing the U.S. ambassador see Thomas Powers, *The Man Who Kept the Secrets: Richard Helms and the C.I.A.* (New York, Alfred Knopf, 1979), pp. 81, 323, n.11. The fullest account of the intervention by Chiang Kai-shek's forces is in Robert H. Taylor's *Foreign and Domestic Consequences of the KMT Intervention in Burma* (Ithaca, N.Y.: Cornell Southeast Asia Program, 1973).

12. It was this situation that so incensed Alexander Smith, then chairman of the Senate Foreign Relations Committee's Subcommittee on the Far East, who

though apparently still quite oblivious of any American role in Burma, had discovered the actions of Chiang Kai-shek's forces there. To his committee he reported on 25 Jan. 1954: "Certainly the Burmese government, which is busily engaged in fighting Communist uprisings within its borders should not have to dissipate its resources and its energy chasing troops and trouble makers who claim to be on the side of the free world." For Senator Smith's report see the *Congressional Record* (9 Feb. 1954), 100: 1548. More than a year later when I visited Burma I found that a majority of the Burmese army's nongarrison forces were still tied down in trying to contain Chiang Kai-shek's marauding forces (GMcTK).

13. For the *New York Times* and this quote, see its special report on the CIA, 26 Apr. 1966. This view of the Burmese leadership was widely known in diplomatic circles and was forcefully expressed to me in May 1955 in my interviews with U Ba Swe, acting prime minister and minister of defense, and several other cabinet members (GMcTK).

14. I first learned of the extent of these Khmer Serei activities in 1967 when I was in Cambodia and was investigating cross-border intrusions of the South Vietnamese Army. In discussions in Phnom Penh with Western and Asian embassies and with the staff there of the International Control Commision (a legacy of the 1954 Geneva Agreements) I was struck by their astonishment that the United States was still continuing with its support of the Khmer Serei—a policy that they regarded as incredibly blundering and counterproductive (GMcTK). (At this time there was no U.S. embassy in Cambodia, Sihanouk having severed diplomatic relations in 1965, partly in protest against the continuation of Khmer Serei activities.)

15. In 1971 in Phnom Penh I had a discussion with Son Ngoc Thanh in which he vouchsafed that more than 10,000 of his Khmer Serei had been sent into Cambodia before or just after the coup against Sihanouk. He told me that if the funds could be made available he could raise an additional 10,000 (GMcTK).

16. The most comprehensive scholarly account of the Eisenhower administration's involvement in Laos and of Laotian politics during this period is Charles A. Stevenson's *The End of Nowhere: American Policy toward Laos since 1954* (Boston: Beacon Press, 1972).

17. Further information and relevant references concerning the Eisenhower administration's policies and actions in Vietnam can be found in George McT. Kahin *Intervention; How America Became Involved in Vietnam* (New York: Knopf, 1986; New York: Anchor, 1987), chaps. 2-4.

18. NSC 5492/2, "Review of U.S. Policy in the Far East," 20 Aug. 1954.

Chapter 1

1. For these statistics see *Indisch Verslag* [Indies Report, official statistical yearbook of the Netherlands Indies government] 2:343 (1941). In 1940, when the guilder was worth approximately 50 U.S. cents, imports into the Netherlands

East Indies totaled 430,160,000 guilders while exports were 940,256,000. Further data as well as greater detail on income tax and education can be found in George McTurnan Kahin, *Nationalism and Revolution in Indonesia* (Ithaca, N.Y.: Cornell University Press, 1952), ch. I.

2. The last official Dutch census of the Netherlands East Indies published was for 1930, but these population figures for the Indonesians are official estimates published in *Indisch Verslag* vol. 2 (1941), as are all the income statistics here cited. (See especially Tables 110 and 110A, pp. 181 and 184-85.) The population figures for the other ethnic groups are drawn from the authors' rough interpolations from the 1930 census.

3. Kahin, *Nationalism and Revolution*, chap. I. Most Dutch children from the colony were sent to the Netherlands for tertiary education, and a small handful of Indonesians were able to go, but the vast majority of those who received such an education were dependent on the few colleges available in the colony, where as late as 1940 only 637 Indonesian were enrolled, with just thirty-seven graduating in that year. See I. J. Brugmans and Soenario, "Enkele Gegevens van Socialen Aard," *Verslag van de Commissie tot Bestudeering van Staatsrechtelijke Hervormingen*, vol. 1 (Batavia, 1941); and Indisch Verslag, vol. 2 (1941), esp. p. 343.

4. *Hollandsch-Inlandsch Ondwerwijs Commissie*, 6a, pp. 73-78.

5. See Air Marshal Sir Paul Maltby, "Report on Air Operations during the Campaigns in Malaya and Netherlands East Indies from the 8th December, 1941 to the 12th March, 1942," *London Gazette*, 3d. suppl., 20 Feb. 1948, pp. 1401-1402.

6. H.J. van Mook, *Indonesia, Nederland en de Wereld* (Batavia and Amsterdam, 1949), pp. 104-105.

7. Sjahrir acknowledged on several occasions to one of the authors that without this shared calculation neither he nor Sjarifuddin would have occupied the office of prime minister.

8. For the classic account of this period see Benedict R. O'Gorman Anderson, *Java in a Time of Revolution: Occupation and Resistance, 1944-1946* (Ithaca, N.Y.: Cornell University Press, 1972). With respect to the British dilemma see also Vice-Admiral the Earl of Mountbatten of Burma, *Post-Surrender Tasks: Section E of the Report to the Combined Chiefs of Staff by the Supreme Allied Commander, Southeast Asia, 1943-1945* (London, 1969). An excellent account of British-Dutch relations, providing important recently released documentary data on logistics and training, can be found in J.A. Scholte's "Koloniale bondgenoten?" *Marineblad* 102 (Feb. 1992): 50-69.

9. Though the list of committee members was probably vetted by the Japanese authorities, nearly all of those selected represented bona fide nationalists of considerable stature. Japanese acquiescence to this conference reflected the expectation of an Allied victory and the desire to secure Indonesian goodwill in the postwar era.

10. See Robert J. McMahon, *Colonialism and Cold War: The United States and the Struggle for Indonesian Independence* (Ithaca, N.Y.: Cornell University Press, 1981), pp. 227-29, 311.

11. One of the writers witnessed the continued use of U.S. insignia on some planes, armored personnel carriers, and trucks in the Dutch attack on Yogyakarta, 19 Dec. 1948. A Dutch major, when queried, explained that he was wearing battle fatigues marked "U.S. Marines" because he was proud of having been trained at the U.S. Marines camp at Quantico, Va.

12. C.I.A., "Review of the World Situation As It Relates to the United States," 14 Nov. 1947, para 15, Southeast Asia.

13. For the most comprehensive account of the Madiun rebellion and its background, see Ann Swift, *The Road to Madiun* (Ithaca, N.Y.: Cornell Modern Indonesia Project, 1989).

14. I witnessed this operation as I was quartered in the same small guest house in which this agent was later given a room. (Since I was the only American resident in Yogyakarta, he felt I should help him, and when I refused he denounced me as pro-Communist.) The Indonesian interpreter the republic assigned the agent later informed me that he witnessed him offer Prime Minister Hatta an extensive financial subvention, which was refused (GMcTK).

15. The fullest account of U.S. policy toward the Indonesian Dutch dispute is McMahon, *Colonialism and Cold War*.

16. The attack and its aftermath, as witnessed by one of the authors, is described in Kahin, *Nationalism and Revolution*, pp. 336-50 (GMcTK).

17. The fullest account of the United Nations' role in the Indonesia-Dutch dispute is Alastair M. Taylor's *Indonesian Independence and the United Nations* (Ithaca, N.Y.: Cornell University Press, 1960). A perceptive evaluation of the importance of the United Nations factor can be found in Evelyn Colbert, "The Road Not Taken: Decolonization and Independence in Indonesia and Indochina," *Foreign Affairs*, April 1973, pp. 608-28.

18. This perception was evident in talks with middle-level U.S. officials in Jakarta and Washington in March-June 1949. Among the most concerned with this prospect was the U.S. Office of Naval Intelligence, which as early as the end of January warned: "The 'police action' and pursuance of repressive measures by the Dutch to quell the guerrilla activities of the Republican Indonesians will have the effect of weakening seriously the influence of the moderate Indonesian leaders, and strengthening the position of the extremists and Communists. The moderate Indonesian leaders, at present under custody of the Dutch, are the most capable of the native leaders and are oriented toward the U.S. A continuation of the present economic and social disorders will play into the hands of the Communists by providing a fertile field for the growth and spread of communism in an already chaotic area. Since the moderate Indonesians were unable to reach a solution of their problems with the Dutch by peaceful means, the more militant policy of the extremists and communists probably would appeal more

to those natives who are now convinced of the futility of further negotiation with the Dutch." Central Intelligency Agency, *Consequences of Dutch "Police Action" in Indonesia*, 27 Jan. 1949, ORE 40-49, p.5. (Document declassified and released by CIA, 21 July 1992.) Although Tan Malaka was actually killed by republican forces in the spring of 1949, news of his death was slow to spread and rumors continued for months that he was still actively leading the anti-Dutch struggle.

19. For more detail see McMahon, *Colonialism and Cold War*, pp. 300-301; and Kahin, *Nationalism and Revolution*, pp. 442-44, and Taylor, *Indonesian Independence and the United Nations*, pp. 239-49, 438.

20. This was the judgment of Indonesian specialists in the State Department with whom one of the authors talked at the time.

21. McMahon, *Colonialism and Cold War*, p. 321.

22. United States partiality to the Dutch position was bitterly remarked to me by Vice President Hatta, leaders of the Masjumi, PNI, and Socialist parties, as well as President Sukarno in discussions with them during 1954-1956. (GMcTK)

Chapter 2

1. The official population estimate for Indonesia as a whole in 1950 was 77.2 million, of whom 50.5 million lived in Java; Widjojo Nitisasastro, *Population of Indonesia* (Ithaca, N.Y.: Cornell University Press, 1970), pp. 116-17, 125.

2. This section draws heavily on numerous interviews and discussions that George McT. Kahin had with both these leaders between 1948 and 1963, but parts are also based on assessments in the following books: J. D. Legge, *Sukarno: A Political Biography* (New York: Praeger, 1972); Bernhard Dahm, *Sukarno and the Struggle for Indonesian Independence*, trans. Mary Somers Heidhues (Ithaca, N.Y.: Cornell University Press, 1969); Sukarno, *Nationalism, Islam, and Marxism*, trans. with an introduction by Ruth McVey (Ithaca, N.Y.: Cornell Modern Indonesia Project, 1970); Mavis Rose, *Indonesia Free: A Biography of Mohammad Hatta* (Ithaca, N.Y.: Cornell Modern Indonesia Project, 1987); Deliar Noer, *Mohammad Hatta: Biografi Politik* (Jakarta: LP3ES, 1990).

3. Cable: Ambassador Cumming to Secretary of State 2148, 27 Feb. 1957 (756D. 0012-2757 U.S. National Archives, Washington, D.C.).

4. First published in Claire Holt et al., eds., *Culture and Politics in Indonesia* (Ithaca, N.Y.: Cornell University Press, 1972), pp. 1-69; and more recently as the lead section in Benedict Anderson, *Language and Power: Exploring Political Cultures in Indonesia* (Ithaca, N.Y.: Cornell University Press, 1990), pp. 17-77.

5. The fullest coverage of the 1951 arrests is in Herbert Feith, *The Decline of Constitutional Democracy in Indonesia*, (Ithaca, N.Y.: Cornell University Press, 1962), pp. 187-92.

6. Interviews with Mohammad Natsir in 1955 and 1971.

7. In 1948, units of the republic's Islamic militias, together with several minor Masjumi politicians in West Java, had defied official Masjumi party policy and broken with the Republic of Indonesia because they held that the government was betraying the revolution when it withdrew its troops, in accordance with the United Nations-sponsored Renville agreement of Jan. 1948, from areas of West Java penetrated by Dutch forces. In the absence of the republic's power, Kartosuwirjo set up a rudimentary government structure in the region, and its guerrilla units were transformed into "the Islamic Army of Indonesia" (Tentara Islam Indonesia). See C. van Dijk, *Rebellion under the Banner of Islam: The Darul Islam in Indonesia* (The Hague: Nijhoff, 1981), p. 10; Deliar Noer, *Partai Islam di Pentas National* (Jakarta: Grafiti Pers, 1987), pp. 179-83.

8. Ulf Sundhaussen, *The Road to Power: Indonesian Military Politics, 1945-1967* (Kuala Lumpur: Oxford University Press, 1982), p. 53.

9. Benedict Anderson, *Imagined Communities*, rev. ed. (London: Verso, 1991), pp. 176-77.

10. See John Gordon Mein to Mr. Robertson [Assistant Secretary of State], "Historical Summary of Dutch Control and of the Indonesian-Dutch Dispute over the Area," 20 Sept. 1957. (U.S. National Archives, Washington, D.C.)

11. Gerald S. Maryanov, *Decentralization as a Political Problem* (Ithaca, N.Y.: Cornell Modern Indonesia Project, 1958), p. 41 (quoting the Sumatran leader Mohammad Sjafei).

12. Notable among them were Colonel T. B. Simatupang, who became chief of staff of the armed forces; Colonel A. H. Nasution, army chief of staff, Commodore Suryadarma, chief of staff of the air force; Admiral Subijakto, navy chief of staff; and Colonel Hidajat, who occupied a high post within the Ministry of Defense. These originally Dutch-trained officers, then, held nearly all the top armed-forces positions. See Sundhaussen, *Road to Power*, p. 52.

13. See Harold Crouch, *The Army and Politics in Indonesia* (Ithaca, N.Y.: Cornell University Press, 1978), pp. 28-29.

14. Sundhaussen, *Road to Power*, p. 61. See also Zulkifli Lubis, "Komandan Intelijen Pertama Indonesia," *Tempo* [Jakarta], 29 July 1989, p. 60. In a speech on 1 Oct. 1952, Minister of Defense Hamengku Buwono gave the total strength of the army as 307,500 and stated only half that number were needed. See A. H. Nasution, *Memenuhi Panggilan Tugas*, vol. 3; *Masa Pancaroba I* (Jakarta: Gunung Agung, 1983), p. 355. The whole text of the speech is in ibid., Appendix 8, pp. 345-68.

15. They were headed by Colonel Bambang Supeno, who was a distant relative of Sukarno and had been the formulator of the official army code of principles, the Sapta Marga. He had headed the recently dissolved Chandradimuka Military Academy in Bandung that had "mainly served to foster the ideological indoctri-

nation of the officer corps." See Sundhaussen, *Road to Power*, pp. 63, 65, Ruth McVey, "The Post-Revolutionary Transformation of the Indonesia Army," *Indonesia* 11 (April 1971): 145. The group charged Nasution and his colleagues with being supporters of Western imperialism and too strongly influenced by the Dutch advisory military mission (MMB) still operating in Indonesia. See also Manai Sophiaan, *Apa Yang Masih Teringat* (Jakarta: Yayasan "Mencerdaskan Kehidupan Bangsa," 1991), p. 317; Sundhausen, *Road to Power*, p. 68.

16. See Nasution, *Memenuhi Panggilan Tugas* 3: 165-66. The pamphlet is referred to as Laporan Atrap no. 40, "Sekitar demonstrasi parlemen dibubarkan." For Nasution's own account of the confrontation, see ibid., pp. 198-200. See also Sophiaan, *Apa Yang Masih Teringat*, pp. 340-41, for Lubis's version, see "Komandan Intelijen Pertama Indonesia," pp. 61-62.

17. While still under investigation for his role in the October 17 Affair, Nasution turned away from military affairs to writing and then to organizing an Army Veterans' party (IPKI) that competed in the 1955 general election.

18. At the invitation of Vice President Hatta one of the authors attended this conference and had the opportunity to talk with several of the officers, including Nasution's successor, Bambang Sugeng, who made very clear that he did not wish to stay on as army chief of staff.

19. Interview with Zulkifli Lubis, Jakarta, 27 Feb. 1971. See also "Komandan Intelijen Pertama Indonesia," pp. 59-60.

20. See Herbert Feith, *The Indonesian Elections of 1955* (Ithaca, N.Y.: Cornell Modern Indonesia Project, 1957), p. 58.

21. Interview with A. H. Nasution, Jakarta, 27 May 1971.

22. According to Nasution, Sukarno's change in attitude toward him had occurred because the president had been impressed by his political speeches in behalf of his IPKI party, particularly his advocacy of a return to the 1945 constitution and his defense of the rights of veterans. Nasution, *Memenuhi Panggilan Tugas* 3: 302-304. In the 1955 elections IPKI ranked ninth with 539,824 votes, thereby gaining four seats in parliament.

23. One of the first signals of further trouble in the officer corps had come in August 1956 when Kawilarang was only narrowly thwarted in his attempt to arrest Foreign Minister Ruslan Abdulgani on charges of corruption just as he was about to leave for the London Conference on the Suez crisis. Kawilarang's action apparently reflected both his dissatisfaction with the civilian politicians and open defiance of Nasution's rotation policies.

24. Interview with Zulkifli Lubis, Jakarta, 10 May 1991.

25. Sundhaussen, *Road to Power*, p. 101. See also A.H. Nasution, *Memenuhi Panggilan Tugas*, vol. 4; *Masa Pancaroba Kedua* (Jakarta: Gunung Agung, 1984), pp. 38-39.

26. The army leaders seem to have been perfectly aware of his location but did not arrest him, presumably because he still retained considerable support within the army.

27. On November 8, Lubis threatened Nasution's deputy that, if his subordinate in the coup attempt, Colonel Sapari, was not released, he would see to it that the First and Sixth Military Territories (North Sumatra and Kalimantan) would dissociate themselves from Nasution. Simbolon, of course, was still in command of the First Territory, and in Kalimantan (TTVI), Colonel Abimanyu, a Lubis supporter, had recently taken over. See Feith, *Decline*, p. 506. On Nov. 15 Abimanyu declared his opposition to Nasution's policies and ordered "that all central government officials, whether military or civilian who came to Kalimantan had to be arrested." See Nasution, *Memenuhi Panggilan Tugas* 4: 34, McVey, "Post Revolutionary Transformation," 1:163.

28. The results for the election to the Constituent Assembly (held in Dec. 1955) were close to those of the earlier parliamentary elections, with most of the smaller parties losing votes and the PNI garnering 635,565 votes more than in the earlier parliamentary election for a total of 9,070,218. The Masjumi lost 114,267, thereby bringing its total down to 7,789,619. The Masjumi's major loss was in West Java, but even so it remained the largest party there. The Nahdatul Ulama added 34,192 for a total of 6,989,333 and the PKI advanced by 34,192 votes for a total of 6,232,512. For further details, see Feith, *The Indonesian Elections of 1955*.

Chapter 3

1. It should be noted, however, that destruction in the struggle against the Dutch had been especially heavy on Java. One expert estimate was that in 1956, 71 percent of Indonesia's exports came from Sumatra (21 percent from North Sumatra, 15 percent from Central Sumatra, and 35 percent from South Sumatra). See S. Takdir Alisjahbana, *Perdjuangan Autonomi dan Kedudukan Adat Didalamnja* (speech before the all-Sumatra Adat Congress, Bukittinggi, 12-20 March 1957) (Jakarta: Pustaka Rakjat, n.d.), p. 16. See also J. D. Legge, *Central Authority and Regional Autonomy in Indonesia: A Study in Local Administration, 1950-1960* (Ithaca, N.Y.: Cornell University Press, 1961), p. 237.

2. In East and Central Java, the PNI received 65.5 percent of its total vote, the Nahdatul Ulama 73.9 percent, and the PKI 74.9 percent. See Herbert Feith, *The Indonesian Elections of 1955* (Ithaca, N.Y.: Cornell Modern Indonesia Project, 1957), p. 62. In Java overall the PNI received 86 percent of its total vote, the Nahdatul Ulama 85.6 percent, and the PKI 88.6 percent. While weak in Central and East Java (see chap. 1 above), the Masjumi was the strongest party (26.4 percent of the vote) in West Java and throughout Sumatra (50.7 percent in Central Sumatra; 43.1 percent in South Sumatra; 36.4 percent in North Sumatra). With 32 percent in South Kalimantan and 40 percent in South and Southeast Sulawesi, it was by far the largest party in those areas as well. Collectively, the several Muslim parties gained 80 percent of the vote in Central Sumatra, 63.4 percent in South Sumatra, 45.4 percent in North Sumatra, 81.3 percent in South Kalimantan, and 64.3 percent in South Sulawesi.

3. Ruth McVey, "The Post-Revolutionary Transformation of the Indonesian Army," *Indonesia* 11:152.

4. "Monthly Summary—December 1956," Enclosure to Mr. Consul Fish's Despatch No. 4 to Djakarta, dated Medan, 16 Jan. 1957, FO 371/129511 PRO, Foreign Office Files for 1957. Despite Simbolon's protestations, the consul reported suspicions that the colonel probably had a number of camouflaged financial interests in and around Medan.

5. Military Territory I covered Aceh, North Sumatra, West Sumatra, and Riau; Military Territory II embraced the southern half of the island and the smaller adjacent islands of Bangka and Billiton. The North Sumatra Command was made up of four territorial regiments, Regiment 1 (Aceh), Regiment 2 (East Sumatra), Regiment 3 (Tapanuli), and Regiment 4 (West Sumatra and Riau). It also incorporated a fifth major unit, the City Military Command of Medan, Komando Militer Kota Besar Medan (KKMP). See John R. W. Smail, "The Military Politics of North Sumatra: December 1956-October 1957," *Indonesia* 6 (Oct. 1968): 134. See also "Monthly Summary," January 1957, FO371/129511 p.2.

6. On his weakening position among his subordinate officers during 1956, see Smail, "Military Politics of North Sumatra," pp. 137-38.

7. C. Van Dijk, *Rebellion under the Banner of Islam: The Darul Islam in Indonesia* (The Hague: Nijhoff, 1981), p. 332.

8. "Monthly Summary," Jan. 1957, FO 371/129511.

9. Smail, "Military Politics," p. 138.

10. "Monthly Summary," Jan. 1957, FO 371/129511, p. 2.

11. R. Z. Leirissa, *PRRI Permesta* (Jakarta: Grafiti, 1991), p. 30; Nasution, *Memenuhi Panggilan Tugas* 4: 63; and Smail, "Military Politics," pp. 138-39. Quote is from Smail, "Military Politics," p. 140. See also *Haluan*, 14 Jan. 1957; Leirissa, *PRRI Permesta*, p. 66.

12. Including former prime ministers Mohammad Natsir (Masjumi) and Sutan Sjahrir (PSI); Mohammed Yamin (minister of education), Haji Agus Salim (former foreign minister), and Assaat (who had been head of the Working Committee in parliament during the revolution).

13. On all of these moves, see Kementerian Penerangan, *Republik Indonesia: Propinsi Sumatera Tengah* (n.p., n.d. [circa 1953]), pp. 597-98, *Sumatera Tengah*, 113/114 (17 Aug. 1953): 29, Legge, *Central Authority*, pp. 38-39; "Otonomi Daerah: Kesan2 Kab/Kota se Sumatera Tengah," *Sumatera Tengah* 123/124 (25 Jan. 1954): 8-14, 19.

14. Husein succeeded Lt. Col. Thalib, who had held the position since 2 Dec. 1950, when Colonel Dahlan Djambek, the original commander of the division was assigned to the army's central staff after, on Jakarta's orders, dissolving

the division. Djambek was soon thereafter appointed Indonesia's military attaché in London.

15. For the full text of the charter, see Departemen Penerangan R.I., *Kronik Dokumentasi. Djilid I Peristiwa Sumatera Barat* (Jakarta: Direktorat Publisiet-Penerangan, 1960), pp. 2-4. For a full account of the seizure see *Sumatera Tengah* 159 (15 Feb. 1957). See also Graham R. Alliband, "Upheaval in Sumatra: From Dewan Banteng to the P.R.R.I. Rebellion" (Master's thesis, Cornell University, Ithaca, N.Y., 1970), pp. 25-26.

16. Prime Minister Ali Sastroamidjojo bitterly complained to U.S. Ambassador Hugh S. Cumming, Jr., that Simbolon had agreed to the transfer "but had asked for postponement from December 23 to December 28 so he could carry on through Christmas and [the] government had acceded to this knowing Simbolon to be [a] devout Christian." Cable Jakarta (Cumming) to Sec. of State, December 24, 1956 (756D.00/12-2456 Nat. Archives).

17. Nasution, *Memenuhi Panggilan Tugas* 4: 64.

18. Since Lubis had removed himself from consideration for the position, Gintings had been Simbolon's scheduled successor. Despite this government order, on 26 Dec. Gintings initially reaffirmed his loyalty to Simbolon, but on hearing that Macmoer "had answered the President's call" and himself assumed the position, Gintings too proclaimed himself Simbolon's successor as commander of Military Region I.

19. See British Medan consulate's "Monthly Summary—January 1957," p. 4. Enclosure to Mr. Consul Fish's Despatch No. 5 to Jakarta (Medan, 11 Feb. 1957), FO371/129512 Ref. 150442 (PRO).

20. "Monthly Summary—January 1957," p. 4.

21. Smail, "Military Politics," p. 152.

22. Reports in *PIA*, 27 Dec. 1956, and *Pedoman*, 2 Jan. 1957, in *Kronik Dokumentasi*, vol. 3, *Peristiwa Sumatera Selatan* (Jakarta: Departemen Penerangan Daerah, 1960), pp. 2, 6-7. See also Alliband, "Upheaval in Sumatra," pp. 101-6, 108-10; and Nasution, *Memenuhi Panggilan Tugas* 4: 65.

23. Nasution, *Memenuhi Panggilan Tugas* 4: 18. Nasution notes that, while he was out of power, Barlian helped him in setting up his Veterans' Political party and that they campaigned together for the party in Lampung and Palembang during the 1955 elections.

24. "Notes on a visit to Palembang, Padang, and Medan by Mr. M. E. Heath, 2nd Secretary, H. M. Embassy, Djakarta, in Company with Mr. A. Y. Fish, H. M. Consul at Medan, February 15-23, 1956." (FO371/122373). BPM was controlled by the British and Dutch, with a minority American interest, while Standard Oil was American. The other major American oil company, Caltex, had greater production than Stanvac, mostly in the Pekanbaru area, but no refinery. The BPM refinery depended for about a quarter of its output

on imported Middle East crude oil, while Stanvac relied mostly on locally produced oil.

25. Harry H. Bell, "Political and Economic Pressures on Lt. Col.-Barlian," Foreign Service Desp. No. 522, 16 Apr. 1958, p. 7.

26. Feith, *Decline*, p. 535. *Antara*, 17 Feb. 1957, in *Kronik Dokumentasi* 3: 14. The reaction in Central Sumatra to these subventions from Jakarta was, however, one of outrage. The Padang daily newspaper *Haluan* (21 Jan. 1957) criticized the government for treating the people of the region as children, who if they were given a few hundred thousand rupiah for pocket money would come around.

27. See Legge, *Central Authority and Regional Autonomy*, pp. 68, 236; Feith, *Decline*, pp. 534, 552.

28. For a list of these groups, see *Sumatera Tengah* 159: 32. Such public statements cannot, of course, be taken at face value, and they did vary in the degree of support they expressed, but they seem to reflect a general sense that the Banteng Council was representative of and responding to general dissatisfaction in the region.

29. In the 1955 parliamentary elections the PKI had received 90,513 votes in Central Sumatra (5.75 percent) and increased this number to 98,583 in the Constituent Assembly elections of 15 Dec. 1955. See Feith, *Elections*, pp. 68, 78. Colonel Ismael Lengah, former commander of the Banteng division, who acted as the Banteng Council's liaison to Jakarta, had met there with the head of the Communist party's Politbureau, D. N. Aidit, in an unsuccessful attempt to moderate the PKI's stated view that the affair in Central Sumatra was instigated by the Islamic (Masjumi) and Socialist (PSI) parties and did not have the support of the people. According to Lengah, Aidit promised to withdraw this statement after their meeting, but in fact the Politbureau reiterated its charges on 27 Dec. *Sumatera Tengah* 159: 13.

30. See *Haluan*, 16 Jan., 22 Jan. 1957.

31. van Dijk, *Rebellion under the Banner of Islam*, pp. 267-68. For Hassan Basry's account of his exploits during the early part of the revolution against the Dutch, see H. Hassan Basry, *Kisah Gerila Kalimantan (Dalam Revolusi Indonesia) 1945-1949*, vol. 1 (Banjarmasin: Lambung Mangkurat, 1961). See also McVey, "Post-Revolutionary Transformation of the Indonesian Army," pp. 163, n. 48, 173; Nasution, Memenuhi Panggilan Tugas 4: 34-35; interview with Nasution, Jakarta, 27 May 1971.

32. The most cogent and comprehensive account of the Permesta rebellion, events leading up to it, and its consequences for East Indonesia can be found in Barbara Harvey's study, *Permesta: Half a Rebellion* (Ithaca, N.Y.: Cornell Modern Indonesia Project, 1977). The following section, and those in other chapters dealing with Permesta, draw heavily on her analysis.

33. On the efforts to incorporate South Sulawesi units into the TNI and the early

stages of Kahar Muzakkar's rebellion, see Burhan Magenda, "The Surviving Aristocracy in Indonesia: Politics in Three Provinces of the Outer Islands" (Ph.D. dissertation, Cornell University, Ithaca, N.Y., 1989), pp. 616-25; see also Leirissa, *PRRI Permesta*, p. 78.

34. See Nasution, *Memenuhi Panggilan Tugas* 4: 39.

35. For an account of the internal dissensions and demands within Sulawesi during the succeeding weeks, see Leirissa, *PRRI Permesta*, pp. 86-91.

36. These were Andi Pangerang Petta Rani (South and Southeast Sulawesi); Major D. J. Somba (North Sulawesi); Lieutenant Colonel Herman Pieters (Maluku and West Irian); and Lieutenant Colonel Minggu (Nusa Tenggara). Harvey, *Permesta*, p. 49. West Irian was, of course, still under Dutch control.

37. Jakarta (Spinks) to Sec. of State, #2264, 7 Mar. 1957, citing a source close to the PNI (756D.001 3-757 Nat. Archives); Magenda, "Survival of the Aristocracy," pp. 639 ff., where he shows that, despite central government policies in the economic and military sphere, the aristocratic and military elements in Sulawesi were more bitterly divided among themselves than opposed to the Indonesian state.

38. *Antara*, 10 March 1957, in *Kronik Dokumentasi* 3: 31-32.

39. Emb.Tel. 2529, 12 Apr. 1957 (756D.001 4-1257 Nat. Archives). Nasution, in his autobiography, confirmed that Djuhartono was a strong admirer of Sukarno. See also FO 371/129540, Military Attaché Djakarta's report for May 1957 (PRO).

40. NASAKOM was Sukarno's acronym for the union of the forces of nationalism (*NAS*ionalism), religion (*Agama*), and communism (*KOM*unism).

41. See Lev, *Transition to Guided Democracy*, pp. 15-16, 59-63.

42. British Embassy to Southeast Asia Department, 1 May 1957, Foreign Office, FO 371/129513.

43. Department of State 2707, 4 May 1957 (756D.00 [W]/5-457 Nat. Archives). For Col. Husein's speech, see *Haluan*, 4 May 1957.

44. *Haluan*, 15 May 1957; DOS 2793, 15 May 1957 (756D.001 5-1557 Nat. Archives). See also Noer, *Mohammad Hatta*, pp. 530-31, for an account of Hatta's visit and his assessment of the regional movement in Sumatra.

45. Amembassy Jakarta to Department of State, 2804, 16 May 1957.

46. All these quotations are from "Simbolon Emerges as a Strong Figure in Sumatra" Despatch #594 from Amembassy Jakarta to DOS, 27 Apr. 1957, with attachments (756D.001 4-2757 Nat. Archives). The foreign employees at Caltex had similar experiences. R. H. Hopper recalls: "We were summoned to Padang to meet Achmad Husein and Col. Simbolon, and given treatment

(orally) similar to Richardson's. I remember well how the PRRI military in Pekanbaru approached us in 1957 and indicated that they would like some quiet help. We told them (as our Jakarta office had instructed us) that for obvious reasons we as a foreign company had to maintain an *absolutely neutral* position. They understood." He notes however that the situation changed in early 1958 "when things heated up." Letter from R. H. Hopper, 16 May 1990.

47. Amembassy Jakarta to Department of State, 2804, 16 May 1957.

48. Referred to in Dulles to Amemb, 14 May 1957 (756D. 0014-157 Nat. Archives). It will be recalled that the "Madiun affair" in September 1948 was a Communist rebellion against the Hatta-Sukarno government.

49. "Increasing Communist influence in Indonesia," Amembassy despatch, 10 July 1957 (756D.00/7-1057).

50. See chap. 4 for detailed results. In Greater Jakarta and West Java, the Masjumi came in first, and in East Java the Nahatul Ulama was first. The great loser in these electons was the PNI. See Lev, *Transition to Guided Democracy*, pp. 84-95.

51. Simbolon, for example, was insisting that their aims were national, not local. "We are the channel of the people's desires, our struggle is not sukuism [ethnic group orientation], not regionalism, not separatism, not for the Minangkabau and Tapanuli regions, but for the welfare and totality of the Unitary Republic of Indonesia that we love." Speech in Solok, West Sumatra, reported in *Haluan*, 11 July 1957.

52. *Haluan*, 11 June 1957. A new South and Southeast Sulawesi Military Command (KDM-SST), with its headquarters in Makassar, was formed under Lieutenant Colonel Andi Mattalatta. The other regional commands were Nusantenggara (comprising Bali, Flores, Lombok, Sumba, Sumbawa, and West Timor), under Colonel Minggu; Maluku (including Ambon), under Colonel Pieters; and North and Central Sulawesi, under Major Somba, with its headquarters in Manado. See Harvey, *Permesta*, pp. 59-63; see also British Embassy in Jakarta to Foreign Office, 16 Jan. 1958 (FO 371/135847/ C150550).

53. Leirissa, *PRRI Permesta*, pp. 114-15, 119. Nasution's account of the incident, where he states that the proposal only concerned a temporary "planning staff," to oversee the change, appears in his *Memenuhi Panggilan Tugas*, 4: 106.

54. Harvey, *Permesta*, pp. 62, 66, 160. *Haluan*, 26 June and 28 June 1957.

55. "Dr. Sumitro Flees to Central Sumatra rather than Face Interrogation of Alleged Corruption," Foreign Service Despatch, Amembassy, Jakarta, 14 June 1957. (756D.00-1457). For Sumitro's explanation of his flight, see *Haluan*, 23 May 1957.

56. Joseph Burkholder Smith, *Portrait of a Cold Warrior* (New York: Putnam, 1976), p. 235, and interviews with several knowledgeable Indonesians.

57. "If the party system is buried," Natsir declared, "democracy will be dislocated, in which case the Masjumi will go to war and is willing to sacrifice itself for the democratic cause." "The Masjumi Maintains Party Unity Despite Internal Differences Over Policy," Foreign Service Despatch 80, 12 Aug. 1957 (756D.00/8-1257).

58. He had requested to be relieved of his post on 11 Aug. See *Haluan*, 19 Aug. and 20 Aug. 1957. He was subsequently accused of depositing army funds in his personal account. See ibid., 1 Sept. and 5 Sept. 1957. See also Jakarta to Sec. of State 488, 23 Aug. 1957 (756D.001 8-2357), where Allison noted that Djambek had been briefly arrested on 11 July "in company Banteng Council representative" and that a hand grenade had exploded in the yard of his residence on 15 Aug. Allison further commented: "Djambek has made no secret of his sympathy for Banteng Council and anti-Nasution feelings. Despite support for regional cause he is also reported on friendly terms with Sukarno and opposed to extremism in provinces."

59. See Jakarta to Secretary of State 771, 20 Sept. 1957 (756D.00 (W)/9-2057).

60. Cable Jakarta to Secretary of State 649, 7 Sept. 1957. (756D.00 (W)/9-757). Although it was rumored beforehand that the delegation from Sumatra might include Simbolon and perhaps Lubis, in the event Husein took with him Abu Bakar Djaar and educator Mohammad Sjafei.

61. In addition to Nasution were Col. Gintings from Military Territory TTI, Kosasih from TTIII, Suhartomo from TTIV, Sarbini from TTV, and Kusno Utomo from TTVI. Cable, Jakarta to Secretary of State, 575, 31 Aug. 1957 (756D.00(W)/8-3157); *Haluan*, 30 Aug. 1957.

62. See Penerangan Angkatan Darat, *Kini Tabir dapat Dibuka* ([Jakarta?]: Kementerian Penerangan RI, 1958), p. 30; Lev, *Transition to Guided Democracy*, pp. 36-37.

63. For the full text of the Palembang Charter see Nasution, *Memenuhi Panggilan Tugas* 4: 446-49; Sumitro, "Searchlight on Indonesia," p. 6.

64. Harvey, *Permesta: Half a Rebellion*, p. 90. See also Sumitro, "Searchlight on Indonesia," p. 6.

65. Cable: Jakarta to Secretary of State 761, 19 Sept. 1957 (7567D.00/9-1957).

66. Ambassador Allison commented that the "meeting of dissident leaders [in] Palembang probably contributed [to the] unanimity [of] their position at national conference Djakarta which is said to have impressed Sukarno." Jakarta to Sec. of State 761, 19 Sept. 1957 (FW-756D.00/9-1957).

67. Jakarta to Sec. of State 771, 21 Sept. 1957 (756D.00 [W]9-2057).

68. The committee was headed by President Sukarno and the other members were former vice president Hatta, Prime Minister Djuanda, Third Deputy Prime Minister Dr. Leimena, former minister of defense Sultan Hamengku Buwono IX, Minister of Health Dr. Azis Saleh, and Chief of Staff Nasution.

69. Interview with Hamengku Buwono IX, Jakarta, 25 Feb. 1959. He explained that the face-saving compromise called for dropping all political charges against the dissident colonels and then going through the motions of an investigation of criminal charges that would be found to be without basis and dismissed.

70. Cable Department of State to Amembassy Jakarta 13690, 24 Aug. 1957 (756D.00/8-2357).

71. Discussions with Ambassador Allison, New York (29 June 1960); Ithaca, N.Y. (spring 1969); Honolulu, 9 Dec. 1975.

Chapter 4

1. Papers of John Foster Dulles, Harvey Mudd Library, Princeton University, Princeton, N.J.

2. Ibid.

3. Discussion with Hugh S. Cumming, Jr., Washington D.C., 27 Dec. 1975.

4. Ibid.

5. From the outset Dulles had little faith in the capacity of Indonesians or other ex-colonials who achieved power through force to govern themselves. Expressing this to me in mid-1950, he stated that, where an ex-colonial power could not effectively assist in a former colony's governance after independence, the United States had an obligation to assume that responsibility (GMcTK).

6. Meeting of the National Security Council (NSC), 5 Apr. 1956, as reported in *Foreign Relations of the United States, 1955-1957*, vol. 22, *Southeast Asia* (Washington, D.C.: GPO, 1989) [hereafter *FRUS*, vol. 22], p. 254.

7. One of the authors was in Bandung during the conference and talked with a number of the sponsoring delegations then and afterward. Nehru's strong support for it, he explained, was in large part to provide China with a clearer and more realistic view and understanding of the world outside her borders; in this he felt that the conference had been very successful (interview, New Delhi, 1955). For a fuller account see George McT. Kahin, *The Asian African Conference: Bandung, Indonesia, April 1955* (Ithaca, N.Y.: Cornell University Press, 1956).

8. Telegram from the Embassy in Indonesia to the Department of State, 2084, in "For Allison," February 1957, printed in *FRUS*, vol. 22, pp. 351-53.

9. Telegraph no. 2214, 2 March 1957, in Ibid., pp. 359-61. This assessment of Sukarno's views was similar to the impression I received in talking with him and some of his close associates (GMcTK).

10. Discussions (GMcTK) with Sukarno, 8 Oct. and 12 Oct. 1954, 15 Feb.

1955, and with his chef de cabinet (and confidante) A. K. Pringgodigdo, Jan. 1959.

11. Discussion with Ambassador Cumming, Washington, D.C., 27 Dec. 1975. As late as Jan. 1955 when I drove the road between Ceribon and Bandung, more than two thirds of the route was empty of the republic's soldiers and apparently either contested or under Darul Islam control (GMcTK).

12. Joseph Smith, a CIA official who worked on Indonesia, has written that $1 million was made available to the Masjumi party. See his *Portrait of a Cold Warrior* (New York: Putnam, 1976), pp. 210-11, 215. Gordon Mein noted in his memorandum of 22 Apr. 1957, "U.S. Policy Towards the Djuanda Government," addressed to Assistant Secretary Robertson and his then deputy, Howard P. Jones, that "U.S. contacts, particularly in the covert field, have in the past been principally with the Masjumi." (National Archives)

13. Thus, Cumming cabled Dulles that Sukarno had observed to him that Darul Islam "was in his opinion as much a foreign controlled movement as I had said was the Communists'." Cumming to Secretary of State, 2214, 2 March 1957 (756D.00/3-257).

14. Discussion with Ambassador Cumming, Washington, D.C., 27 Dec. 1975.

15. Interviews by one of the authors with him and other U.S. embassy personnel, Jakarta, 1955-56.

16. Letter from the Ambassador in Indonesia (Cumming) to the Director of the Office of Philippine and Southeast Asian Affairs (Young), 20 May 1955, *FRUS*, vol. 22, pp. 162-67.

17. Prime Minister Menzies, Discussions in Washington, Memorandum of Conversation, Department of State, 15 March 1955, in ibid., pp. 143-44.

18. This included the Indonesian undertaking to consult with the Netherlands before any change in the Indonesian currency's exchange rate with the Dutch guilder. See Telegram from Herbert Hoover Jr. (March 9, 1956) to the U.S. Ibid., pp. 237-38.

19. National Security Council meeting of 26 Jan. 1956, as reported in ibid., p. 229; Telegram to the Embassy in Indonesia, 25 Feb. 1956, ibid., pp. 234-35; Memorandum of Conversation (including Dulles and the Netherlands Foreign Minister), London, 20 Aug. 1956, in ibid., pp. 296-97; and Telegram, Department of State (Dulles signature) to U.S. Embassy in the Netherlands, 14 Aug. 1956, ibid., p. 293.

20. Telegram from the Secretary of State to the Department of State (from Bangkok), 13 March 1956, ibid., pp. 239-40.

21. Finally consummated on Aug. 4, 1956. N.I.E. 65-66, 7 Aug. 1956. Ibid., pp. 290-91.

22. For a perceptive—though overly critical—commentary on Cumming's "over-personalized diplomacy," see John Osborne's "The Importance of Ambassadors," *Fortune*, April 1957.

23. This was clear as early as 1948 in discussions of one of the writers with Sukarno.

24. Telegram 289 from Djakarta, 30 July 1956, as printed in *FRUS*, vol. 22, p. 288, n. 3.

25. Discussion with one of the authors, Washington, D.C., 27 Dec. 1975.

26. Discussions with John Allison, Ithaca, N.Y., 1969, and Honolulu, 9 Dec. 1975. See also John M. Allison, *Ambassador from the Prairie* (Boston: Houghton Mifflin, 1973), pp. 312-13.

27. *FRUS*, vol. 22, p. 496.

28. This was the view of midlevel officials who then worked on Indonesia in the State Department and in the U.S. embassy in Jakarta in discussions with one of the authors in 1957 and 1958.

29. Allison, *Ambassador from the Prairie*, p. 301. Allison had served as ambassador to Japan since May 1953.

30. Discussions with Allison in Ithaca, N.Y., 1969, and Honolulu, 1975.

31. Interview with Joseph Burkholder Smith (28 July and 2 Aug. 1992), and his *Portrait of a Cold Warrior*, p. 205. Regarding Wisner, see also Fletcher Prouty, *The Secret Team* (New York: Ballantine, 1973), pp. 366-67, and Thomas Powers, who in his *The Man Who Kept the Secrets: Richard Helms and the C.I.A.* (New York: Knopf, 1979), p. 89, uncritically accepts this account of Smith regarding Wisner and Ulmer.

32. Smith, *Portrait of a Cold Warrior*, pp. 216-17.

33. Ibid., p. 205.

34. Interviews with Allison, Honolulu, 1960 and Ithaca, N.Y., 1979, and Allison, *Ambassador from the Prairie*, p. 307.

35. Telephone interview with Joseph Burkholder Smith, 28 July 1992.

36. For a detailed account see Smith, *Portrait of a Cold Warrior*, pp. 238-41. The quotation is from p. 239. See also William Blum, *The C.I.A.: A Forgotten History* (London: Zed, 1986), pp. 110-11.

37. Interview, 22 Jul. 1992.

38. Memorandum of discussion at the 316th Meeting of the National Security Council, Washington, D.C., 14 Mar. 1957, *FRUS*, vol. 22, pp. 370-71.

39. In later discussing this situation with Admiral Stump, one of the writers found his views on Indonesia strikingly simplistic: "Sukarno," he said, "was playing footsie with the Communists" and therefore the United States had the right to intervene. The admiral said he did not become convinced that Jakarta's government was actually anti-Communist until he had talks with Indonesia's deputy chief-of-staff, General Gatot Subroto, apparently in mid-1958. He paid particular attention to Gatot Subroto, he said, because he knew the general had played a major role in suppressing the 1948 Madiun rebellion. Interview, New York, 5 Jan. 1960.

40. Office memorandum from John Gordon Mein to Mr. Robertson, "The possible break-up of the Republic of Indonesia," dated May 17, 1957 (756D.00/5-1757 Nat. Archives). A slightly different version of the memorandum appears in FRUS, vol. 22, pp. 381-85; interview with Ambassador Allison.

41. See letter from Allison to Robertson, 8 Apr. 1957, FRUS, vol. 22, p. 372.

42. See letter from Allison, 1 June 1957, in ibid., p. 392.

43. See ibid., pp. 400-402.

44. N.S.C. Action No. 1758, 1 Aug. 1957.

45. Letter to the authors from Francis Underhill, who then served as Indonesia desk officer, 3 Dec. 1993 and telephone discussion 18 Sept. 1994.

46. See FRUS, vol. 22, pp. 402-3. The National Council, established by Sukarno on 6 May 1957, was an advisory body broadly representative of political, ethnic, religious, and occupational groups, as well as including key members of the cabinet and the chiefs of the armed services. Although regarded by critics as a potential rival of the cabinet, it never became so, nor did it more than marginally increase Sukarno's power.

47. Interviews with Allison.

48. Message from Allison to Robertson, 12 Aug. 1957, FRUS, vol. 22, pp. 409-11.

49. Memorandum for the Chairman, JCS, Subject: U.S. Policy on Indonesia, 12 Aug. 1957. Records of the JCS: General Nathan Twining (1957-1968), File 091, Box 9, Nat. Archives, Washington, D.C.

50. Message from Robertson to Allison, 16 Aug. 1957, FRUS, vol. 22, pp. 411-12.

51. Memorandum from the Secretary of State to the Deputy Assistant Secretaries of State for Far Eastern Affairs (Jones) and International Organization Affairs (Walmsley), 21 Aug. 1957, ibid., p. 418.

52. Telegram from Allison to the Secretary of State 505, 26 Aug. 1957 (756D.00/8-2657 Nat. Archives).

53. Telegram signed Dulles to Amembassy Jakarta, 31 Aug. 1957, ibid. Two days

earlier Dulles had sent out a telegram to the American embassies in Tokyo and Taipei, instructing them that "further information this subject [which is described in a handwritten notation as "Indonesian and Sumatra coup against central government"] should be communicated [by] your CAS [CIA station] and reported to Department through Roger Channel," presumably thereby bypassing the American embassy in Jakarta (ibid.).

54. Report prepared by the Ad Hoc Interdepartment Committee on Indonesia for the National Security Council, *FRUS*, vol. 22, pp. 436-40. It should be noted that parts of this report as declassified for *FRUS* are still sanitized.

55. These details are from Annex A of the Special Report (not included in the *FRUS* coverage).

56. In our own copy of the sanitized document the size of the deletion is clear. Memorandum for the National Security Council, 6 Sept. 1957, from James S. Lay, Executive Secretary [covering memo in the transmission of the Special Report on Indonesia].

57. Memo to James S. Lay, Jr., executive secretary, National Security Council from Hugh S. Cumming, Jr., special assistant to the secretary of state and chairman of the Ad Hoc Interdepartmental Committee on Indonesia, 3 Sept. 1957.

58. Memorandum from Robertson to Dulles, 19 Sept. 1957, in *FRUS*, vol. 22, pp. 445-48.

59. Telegram of 13 Sept. 1957, in ibid., pp. 442-44.

60. Memorandum: Robertson to Dulles, 19 Sept. 1957, ibid., p. 447.

61. Memorandum from Cumming to the Secretary of State, 20 Sept. 1957, ibid., p. 448.

62. Memorandum of Discussion at the 337th Meeting of the National Security Council, 23 Sept. 1957, ibid., pp. 450-53.

63. Ibid., p. 452.

64. Only six days before this NSC meeting of September 23, Assistant Secretary Robertson in a telephone call to Secretary Dulles had tried, with no apparent success, to convince him that it was not "just a question of Sukarno" but "a question of every Indonesian" feeling the same way about West Irian and that "the best way to alienate them" would be to abandon the position of neutrality and "join the Dutch." Dulles responded that the administration's position of neutrality over West Irian "has been that we wanted to keep Indonesia from going to the Left and they are going there." Robertson responded: "They have not gone yet. The people we have to work through to save them feel as strongly as Sukarno does." Telephone call to Mr. Robertson, 12 Sept. 1957, 3.56 p.m. Dulles Phone Calls, Eisenhower Library, Abilene, Kans.

65. Interviews with John Allison, spring 1969 and 9 Dec. 1975.

66. Cumming sent some of his own agents, Foreign Service officers Tom Conlon, Culver Gleysteen, and William Kelly to Indonesia to report independently to him—a move naturally resented by the embassy.

67. Allison, *Ambassador from the Prairie*, pp. 314-15.

68. Interview with John Allison, Honolulu, 9 Dec. 1975.

Chapter 5

1. Barbara S. Harvey, *Permesta: Half a Rebellion* (Ithaca, N.Y.: Cornell Modern Indonesia Project, 1977), p. 78. Husein agreed, stating: "When Munas was finished . . . we were satisfied with the decision." Interview with Ahmad Husein, Jakarta, 9 May 1991.

2. See chap. 3.

3. Sumitro, "Searchlight on Indonesia" (typescript, c. Feb. 1959), Section 2, p. 8.

4. This is included as "Memorandum C" in PAD, *Kini Tabir Dapat Dibuka* (Jakarta: Kementerian Penerangan, n.d.), pp. 45-47. Although the documents regarding the rebel decisions are contained in an official publication of the central government, Lubis has acknowledged that the government pamphlet was a compilation of genuine documents seized from his house. Interview, Zulkifli Lubis, Jakarta, 10 May 1991. The contents of the documents also accord with other reports of the September meetings among the rebel leaders, most notably those put out by Sumitro.

5. Sumitro, "Searchlight on Indonesia," p. 9.

6. PAD, *Kini Tabir Dapat Dibuka*, p. 47.

7. Ibid., pp. 55, 60-63. Hatta's departure immediately after the Munas conference on an extended trip to China and his speeches there probably further undermined regionalist (and American) confidence in him. Secretary of State Dulles reassured President Eisenhower about Hatta's planned trip, stating that "most Asiatic leaders visit Communist China at one time or another," and that he was not particularly worried "because Hatta was a strong anti-Communist." Memorandum of Discussions at Meeting of the NSC, 23 Sept. 1957. *FRUS*, vol. 22, p. 451. An embassy despatch from Jakarta the following day raised further misgivings, when it reported that "Hatta's speeches have had three themes: Socialism [is] Indonesia's goal, coexistence [is] essential for peace, Chinese and Indonesian histories [are] similar in respective struggle[s] for independence. In addition he advocated CPR admission [to the] UN." Jakarta to Sec. of State 821, 28 Sept. 1957 (756D.00 (W)/9-2857), Nat. Archives.

8. Deliar Noer, *Mohammad Hatta: Biografi Politik* (Jakarta: LP3ES, 1990), p. 528. Hatta had played such a role in 1948 and in 1949-50. On Hatta's attitude toward the "*dwitunggal* myth," see ibid., pp. 526-29.

9. Extract from a letter from Hatta to Colonel Dahlan Djambek, 2 Nov. 1957, in ibid., pp. 523-24. Noer notes that Hatta's younger sister was married to Djambek's elder brother, M. Zein Djambek. Ibid., p. 522, n. 58.

10. This is in a document dated 5 Oct. 1957, "Dasar, Pedoman dan Program Bersama dari Perdjuangan Daerah-Daerah jang Bergolak," signed by Barlian, Husein, and Sumual, in PAD, *Kini Tabir Dapat Dibuka*, pp. 56-57.

11. Ibid., p. 57. Interviews in Padang, Feb. 1991. Interviews with Ahmad Husein, June 1985 and May 1991. According to Husein, Djambek was joined in the effort by a well-known leader during the revolution, Bung Tomo, who came to West Sumatra for about a month at this time and also by the retired Sundanese army general, Didi Kartasasmita.

12. "Dasar Pedoman dan Program Bersama," in PAD, *Kini Tabir Dapat Dibuka*, pp. 57-58.

13. Ibid., pp. 43-44.

14. So stated by two CIA officials, involved with Indonesia at that time, Dean Almy and Joseph Burkholder Smith, (separate interviews with them, 1992).

15. Smith interview, 1992, and Smith, *Portrait of a Cold Warrior*, pp. 226-27, 235.

16. Ibid., pp. 226-27, 235.

17. Ibid., p. 225.

18. Ibid., pp. 228-29.

19. Interviews with Allison, 1960 and 1975.

20. There is also in our possession a letter from Mr. Sutan Mohd. Rasjid in Geneva, dated 10 Oct. 1958, and addressed to Roland Liem c/o the Chinese Permanent Mission to the UN in New York.

21. From Whitney, Office of the Special Assistant Intelligence London to Secretary of State, Roger Channel No. 2222, 2 Oct. 1957. The cable bears a penned notation that copy 002 is to go to Ulmer at CIA (756.D.00/10-257).

22. Ibid., No. 2275, 4 Oct. 1957 (756D.00/10-457). A penned notation says a copy was sent to CIA. This was presumably a copy of the letter carried to Sulawesi by Barlian and Husein, when they went to obtain Sumual's signature on the documents drawn up by the rebels in Padang after the Munas conference. Sumitro's letter to Sumual called for all regions to adhere to the principles of the Palembang Charter and observed that Sukarno's "tactical victory" at the Munas "should not permit Communists to increase [their] influence throughout Indonesia," but it did not incorporate so strong an anti-Communist tone as was to be conveyed to outside powers. It did, however, urge that "facilities and opportunities from overseas should be mobilized and created."

23. Ibid. These points are clearly consistent with the decisions reached at Palembang and in the later Padang meetings and differ only in their greater emphasis on the idea of an armed struggle and on their statement of the rebel need for weapons from abroad.

24. Roger Channel London to Secretary of State, 8 Oct. 1957. This, too, bears the notation that a copy was sent to Ulmer at CIA.

25. Cumming (Dulles) to Amembassy Jakarta, Roger Channel, 25 Oct. 1957 (756D.00/10-2557). Since transmission and classification (Secret) had been approved by Gordon Mein (director of the Office of Southwest Pacific Affairs), the latter was clearly knowledgeable of the cable's content.

26. Ibid. For Scott's roughly consistent version of his talks with Sumitro, see his letter to O. C. Morland in the Foreign Office, dated 25 Oct. 1957. (FO371/ 129516 PRO.).

27. Based on interviews with knowledgeable Indonesians between 1958 and 1972, with several corroborating follow-up discussions in 1991.

28. That John Foster Dulles was ultimately (by fall 1957) out in front of even his brother in the CIA is also clearly evident in the now-available record of his telephone calls.

29. That this sentiment reached down to the village level was evident in the survey of twenty-three Javanese and thirty Sumatran villages carried out during 1955-57 under the auspices of the University of Indonesia's Faculty of Economics and Cornell University's Modern Indonesia Project. It was also clear when one of the authors talked with inhabitants of several villages on Java, Sumatra, and Bali in 1954-55.

30. PAD, *Kini Tabir Dapat Dibuka*, p. 43 (note the slightly different language in Sumitro's report).

31. "Recommendation and Supporting Analysis of F.E.," 2 Oct. 1957 (Secret). Prepared [in the Department of State] by G. Mein, F. Underhill, and R. Bacon.

32. NIE: 65-67, *FRUS*, vol. 22, p. 430.

33. These figures derive or are extrapolated from John Legge, *Central Authority and Regional Autonomy in Indonesia* (Ithaca: Cornell University Press, 1961), pp. 148-50; Lev, *Transition to Guided Democracy*, n. 47, pp. 92-93, 96-97; Feith, *The Indonesian Elections of 1955*, esp. pp. 57-81. The only other provinces where the PKI won significant backing were North and South Sumatra, where it drew strength from Javanese plantation and oilfield workers. South Sumatra was the only area outside of Java where elections were held in 1957. In that election on Dec. 1 for its provincial legislature, the Masjumi gained 553,276 votes, but the PKI overtook the PNI as the second largest party, garnering 228,965 as against the PNI's 187,042, with the Nahdatul Ulama winning 113,888.

34. Memorandum from William Brown, US Embassy, Jakarta, "Growing Uneasi-

ness over Intentions of the Regions," 5 Nov. 1957 (756D.02/11-557).

35. For one of Allison's most comprehensive briefs urging the sale of arms, see Telegram: Allison to Department of State, 11 Oct. 1957, *FRUS*, vol. 22, pp. 475-80.

36. "Recommendation and Supporting Analysis by FE," Department of State, 2 Oct. 1957.

37. Interview with Colonel George Benson, Washington, D.C., 30 Dec. 1975.

38. Interview with General A.H. Nasution, Jakarta, 16 Jan. 1991.

39. Interview with Colonel Benson, Dec. 1975.

40. Ambassador Allison had already complained about this to Assistant Secretary Robertson in September 1957 and subsequently saw Washington as increasingly inclined to accept CIA reporting over that of his embassy. Interviews, 1960 and 1975.

41. The term Allison used in these interviews.

42. UN doc. A/PV 700 as quoted in *FRUS*, vol. 22, p. 483, n. 2.

43. This follows GMcTK's discussions in 1960 with Allison and his political counselor Gregory W. Hackler, who had participated in drafting the plan, and Allison's subsequent careful scrutiny of GMcTK's notes on this point. Allison later explained that the implication Sukarno was favorably disposed arose during talks with him in the presence of Congressmen D. S. Saund of California.

44. Quotes are from Allison's discussion with G.McT. Kahin in 1960, 1969, and 1975.

45. *FRUS*, vol. 22, pp. 487-88.

46. Allison, *Ambassador from the Prairie*, p. 330.

47. Interview with Allison, fall 1960.

48. The specific proposal voted on was for the Secretary General of the United Nations to assist the two parties to reach a political settlement. See Alastair Taylor, *Indonesian Independence and the United Nations*, p. 443.

49. Interview with Kenneth Young, New York, 19 May 1960. Young had previously served as director of the Department of State's Office of Philippine and Southeast Asian Affairs.

50. Washington's anxiety over the takeover of Dutch businesses and plantations was further reduced when it became clear during the second half of December that the takeovers had slowed down and were now channeled through and largely controlled by Prime Minister Djuanda's office, with army officers rather

than officials of SOBSI (the PKI's trade union association) administering them. By the end of December some 10,000 of 46,000 Dutch nationals had left for the Netherlands, but Dutch technical personnel and some administrators were being urged to stay on. Djuanda's government had said that the Dutch properties were not being nationalized, but it had not made clear whether compensation would be paid.

51. It had been Lubis, it will be remembered, who mounted the coups in late 1956 aimed at seizing Jakarta, ousting Nasution, and clipping Sukarno's wings. See chap. 2.

52. Opinion of Mohammad Natsir, former head of the Masjumi, interview Jakarta, 23 Jan. 1971. There were about 10,000 Bimanese residing in Jakarta in 1957.

53. *Peristiwa Tjikini* (Jakarta: Surungan, 1958). It is unclear what ties this group had with the anti-Communist Gebak organization in Sumatra, headed by Dahlan Djambek, or whether they were in fact branches of the same organization. According to Zulkifli Lubis, the organization on Java was headed by a Muslim from Surabaya, named, ironically, Aidit, and originally most anti-Communist politicians joined it. Lubis said that the GAK spread to Sumatra. Interview, Jakarta, 10 May 1991.

54. Telegram, Ambassador Jones to Secretary of State 3398, 2 May 1958 (756D. 00/5-258).

55. Saleh Ibrahim was generally believed to have joined Kartosuwirjo's Darul Islam army. In fact, he at this time fled to West Sumatra. (Interview with Ahmad Husein, 9 May 1991). Later, in Apr. 1958, he was one of a group flown out from there to Okinawa to get communications and intelligence training from American and Chinese officers. He returned to Aceh in 1959, where he helped in training rebel forces there, including Daud Beureuh's Darul Islam. (Interview with a fellow participant in the training. Padang, 14 Feb. 1991.) Under General Suharto's New Order, he again joined Zulkifli Lubis in Jakarta.

56. Interview with Zulkifli Lubis, Jakarta, 24 Feb. 1971. A senior Masjumi leader, Mohammad Natsir, widely known for his honesty and himself a friend of Lubis, recalls that Lubis acknowledged to him that, when these youths came to see him shortly before their assassination attempt, "I'm afraid I was not sufficiently explicit in expressing my disapproval." Interview, 23 Jan. 1971.

57. Interview, July 1992.

58. Interview with Colonel Ahmad Husein, Jakarta, June 1985. Earlier in South Sumatra Lubis had been assisted by Barlian and Nawawi.

59. According to the respected senior Masjumi leader, Mohamad Roem, Saleh Ibrahim, whom he referred to as "the chief agent of Lubis," was at the time using a car belonging to Samsi, an official of the Masjumi office, who, Roem stated, had received it as a gift from the senior Masjumi official (and former prime minister) Burhanuddin Harahap. Interview, Jakarta, Jan. 1959.

60. Powers, *The Man Who Kept the Secrets*, p. 337. The Cikini affair, it should be noted, was not the only assassination attempt against Sukarno.

61. United States Senate, Select Committee to Study Governmental Operations (Washington, D.C.: GPO, 1975).

62. Interview, Washington, D.C., 27 Dec. 1975. In this interview Cumming was highly circumspect in talking about Cikini, saying that he himself had found no evidence that the CIA had been involved, but that he believed that the Darul Islam had been. Earlier in our long (five-hour) discussion he had mentioned that during the first years of his tour in Indonesia he had found Darul Islam to be a "promising phenomenon" (GMcTK).

63. Sukarno's views on this matter were well known to his own inner circle. The quotations are from an interview with Moekarto Notowidigdo, a centrist from the PNI then serving as ambassador to the United States (Washington, D.C., 25 Aug. 1960) In the last interview I (GMcTK) had with Sukarno in mid-1963 he was still much concerned about the CIA's hostility toward him and queried me about various American individuals and one U.S. nongovernmental organization as to whether they were acting for the CIA. It should be noted that Sukarno regarded Ambassador Allison and his successor, Howard P. Jones, as separate from the CIA and acting autonomously from it. I then had the sense that Sukarno was no more clear than I whether State Department and CIA policies that impinged on Indonesia emanated from the same or different sources.

64. Interview with Allison, with notes of discussion subsequently checked by Allison.

65. Allison to Robertson, 27 Nov. 1957. *FRUS*, vol. 22, p. 517. See also Allison, *Ambassador from the Prairie*, p. 337.

66. Robertson to Allison, 7 Dec. 1957. *FRUS*, vol. 22, pp. 534-35. Emphasis in the original

67. Interview with Allison; see Allison, *Ambassador from the Prairie*, p. 334.

68. See Mein's memorandum to Assistant Secretary Walter Robertson of 12 Nov. 1957, *FRUS*, vol. 22, pp. 496-99.

69. Interview with Allison, Honolulu, 9 Dec. 1975.

70. Ibid. Although Mein and his deputy, Jim O'Sullivan, were informed of the operation, the Indonesian desk officer was not.

71. Allison to Undersecretary of State Herter, 20 Dec. 1957, in *FRUS*, vol. 22, p. 557. See also Allison, *Ambassador from the Prairie*, pp. 336-37. The deputy assistant secretary of state for Far Eastern affairs, Howard P. Jones, advised Dulles on Dec. 27, "Indonesia officials continue to show a readiness . . . to talk over outstanding issues with the Dutch providing these include West New Guinea." *FRUS*, vol. 22, p. 569.

72. Discussion with Allison, 9 Dec. 1975.

73. *FRUS*, vol. 22, p. 556, n. 2. That the Department of Defense was thinking along somewhat similar lines is evident in the letter of the deputy assistant secretary of defense, John Irwin, to the secretary of state, 26 Dec. 1957, ibid., pp. 566-67.

74. Discussion with Allison, Honolulu, 9 Dec. 1975.

75. Allison to Secretary of State, 3 Dec. 1957.

76. Interviews with Sutan Sjahrir and with Mohd. Roem, January-February 1959; also with Sjafruddin Prawiranegara (1971). The papers involved in the attacks, according to Roem, were *Bintang Timor, Merdeka, Suluh Indonesia*, and in particular, *Pemuda*. Natsir wrote a firm but friendly letter to Sukarno, but, despite the president's subsequent oral assurance to him that the press attacks would cease, they did so only briefly (copy of letter in the authors' possession).

77. Burhanuddin was a close acquaintance of Saleh Ibrahim, implicated in the assassination attempt.

78. Allison to State, 21 Dec. 1957; *FRUS*, vol. 22, p. 560.

79. Discussions of one of the writers with these three men in 1958, 1959, and 1963.

80. See Allison's cable of 30 Dec. 1957, in *FRUS*, vol. 22, p. 576. It is of course not very likely that, even with strong American encouragement, these political elements would have been successful.

81. Allison said he later learned about the extent of this covert activity only by accident when a high-ranking naval official, assuming that the ambassador would have been informed, discussed various aspects of it with him. Discussions with Allison, 1975.

Chapter 6

1. The above account was provided to the authors by Dean Almy, a CIA station officer then stationed in Medan, who subsequently held a senior position in the agency, and is consistent with information from other sources. All quotes are his.

2. This account is based on corroborating neutral Indonesian sources, who also note that efforts by one of Nasution's senior officers, Colonel Yani, to have the arms returned, were unavailing.

3. Keyes Beech, *Not Without the Americans* (Garden City, N.Y.: Doubleday, 1971), p. 270.

4. Based on extensive interviews with knowledgeable Indonesians, especially colonels Husein and Lubis (Jakarta, 9-10 May 1991). See also the account of U.S. Air Force Colonel L. Fletcher Prouty (then the Pentagon's liaison officer

with the CIA), *The Secret Team* (Englewood Cliffs, N.J.; Prentice-Hall, 1973) Brian Tooley and William Pinwell, *Oyster: The Story of Australian Secret Intelligence* (Port Melbourne: Heinemann Australia, 1989), p. 73. According to these authors, Prouty told them that "U.S. submarines supporting the rebellion used the Australian territory of Christmas Island." Ibid. See also Smith, *Portrait of a Cold Warrior*, p. 242. Submarines supplying the rebels on Sulawesi apparently came from or via Taiwan.

5. Separate, but corroborative, interviews with colonels Husein and Lubis, Jakarta, 9-10 May 1991, and with one of the soldiers sent out for training, Padang, Jan. 1991.

6. Interview with Colonel Husein, Jakarta, 9 May 1991.

7. Interviews with Lieutenant General Djatikusomo (Jakarta, 17 Feb. 1971), Colonel Achmad Husein(Jakarta, 9 May 1991), Colonel Zulkifli Lubis (Jakarta, 10 May 1991). For Malaya see also Roger Hilsman, *To Move a Nation* (Garden City, N.Y.: Doubleday, 1967), p. 369.

8. Interview, Singapore, 22 Jan. 1961.

9. Telephone Call to Mr Allen W. Dulles, Friday 29 Nov. 1957. 10.58 a.m. (J. F. Dulles Phone Calls, Dwight D. Eisenhower Library).

10. Robert B. Mahoney, Jr., *U.S. Responses to International Incidents and Crises, 1955-1975*, vol. 2, *Summaries of Incidents and Responses* (Arlington, Va.: Center for Naval Analysis, 1977), p. C-17.

11. *FRUS*, vol. 22, p. 533. When Dulles informed him of the possibility of elements of the Seventh Fleet being deployed to Singapore, the Dutch ambassador stated "it would be a move that would be greatly welcomed by his Government." Memorandum of Conversation with Ambassador van Roijen, 8 Dec. 1957 (Dwight D. Eisenhower Library).

12. On the internal situation in Singapore see John Drysdale, *Singapore: Struggle for Success* (Singapore: Times Books International, 1984); C.M. Turnbull, *A History of Singapore, 1819-1988* (Singapore/New York: Oxford University Press, 1989), esp. pp. 259-60. On the role of British MI5 and 6 and the CIA, see Tookey and Pinwell, *Oyster*, pp. 68-69 and Smith, *Portrait of a Cold Warrior*, p. 235.

13. Interview with George Bogaars, Singapore, 8 July 1985.

14. Mahoney, *U.S. Responses*, p. C-17.

15. Kementerian Penerangan, 14 Dec. 1957. I believe that the first scholar to note the importance of this archipelagic factor was Barry Desker in a 1974 seminar paper presented at Cornell University.

16. For date of protest see Department of State, Memorandum of Conversation, "Indonesian Territorial Waters" (with Ambassador Takeo Shimoda), 30 Dec.

1957 (756D.022/12-3057). For the British response, see "pertinent extracts from a message" addressed to CINCPAC by General Sir Francis Festing. C in C Far East Land Forces, Singapore, contained in "Memorandum for Assistant Secretary of State for Far Eastern Affairs" from the Office of the Chief of Naval Operations, dated 31 Dec. 1957 (756D.022/12-3157). The Australian and Japanese governments were also deeply concerned.

17. Chief of Naval Operations, Arleigh Burke, in notifying the deputy undersecretary of state, Robert Murphy, of the navy's opposition to the Indonesian declaration, observed that it "provides a basis for an unfriendly Indonesian government to block U.S. and other western ships from passing through these strategic waterways." Arleigh Burke to Robert Murphy, 27 Dec. 1957 (Nat. Archives).

18. For brief reference to the meeting with Macmillan, see *FRUS*, vol. 22, pp. 552-53.

19. H.P.J. to Sec'y. 6 Feb. 1958: "U.S. Assurances to British re Indo Policy and Rebellion." H.P. Jones collection, Hoover Institution on War, Revolution and Peace, Stanford University, Stanford, Calif., "Political Scene" file in Box 17. We were fortunate in gaining access to these documents soon after Ambassador Jones deposited them and before officials of Hoover decided they should be classified.

20. Organizational meeting, 23 Dec. 1957, Ambassador's Office File, Box 92 Howard P. Jones, Collection, Hoover Institution, Stanford University, Stanford, Calif.

21. See Memorandum dated 7 Jan. 1958 of discussion at the 350th Meeting of the National Security Council, Monday, 6 Jan. 1958. Sukarno was to visit India, Egypt, Yugoslavia, Syria, Pakistan, Ceylon (Sri Lanka), Burma, Thailand, and Japan.

22. Interview with Barlian, Jakarta, 23 Feb. 1971.

23. On 24 Dec. 1957, military and civilian leaders in both Central and South Kalimantan signed a charter establishing a council similar to those on Sumatra and Sulawesi. But the ties of the locally popular Colonel Hassan Basry with Nasution proved a deterrent to their taking further action (Jakarta to Secretary of State 1803, 26 Dec. 1957; Nasution, *Memenuhi Panggilan Tugas* 4: 34, 115), as was the council's reported loyalty to Idham Chalid, chairman of the traditional Islamic Nahdatul Ulama party and deputy premier, who was close to Sukarno and sought to be neutral. In addition, the military commander of Kalimantan was Javanese as were 50 percent of his troops, which provided a further brake on any precipitate action in support of regional rebellion. (Interviews with Nasution, Jakarta, 27 May 1971, and Zulkifli Lubis, Jakarta, 10 May 1991; see also Jakarta to Secretary of State 1803, 26 Dec. 1957. (756D.00/12-2657).

24. Interview with Barlian. There are conflicting reports as to whether it was Nasution or Husein who sabotaged hopes for a meeting on Bangka, but it could have

been either, as Husein would have been unwilling to have such a meeting if Simbolon at least were not there; and Nasution clearly would have wished to exclude both Simbolon and Lubis. Nasution notes in his account that after Cikini the government ceased all efforts at compromise, and concluded that this was also the attitude of the dissidents. *Memenuhi Panggilan Tugas* 4: 173.

25. Interview of Simbolon with *Time* correspondent James Bell, reported in Foreign Service Despatch 343, 24 Jan. 1958, "Recent Developments in Sumatra: *Time* Correspondent Interviews" (756D.00/1-2458). Simbolon in the same interview claimed he had been responsible for calling the rebel colonels together at Palembang at the time of the Munas conference.

26. Interview with Natsir, Jakarta, 31 May 1971.

27. Assaat in talks with Hatta had agreed to serve as an intermediary with the rebels to try and arrange for a compromise settlement. Interview with Assaat (with ex-PRRI military leaders present), Jakarta, 22 Feb. 1971.

28. Interviews with Natsir, 23 Jan. 1971; Sjafruddin, Jakarta, 21 Feb. 1971 and 1 March 1971.

29. Interview with Natsir, 23 Jan. 1971. The fact that an American from the Asia Foundation (regarded with some justification as then having ties with the U.S. government) arrived in Padang the day before the Sungai Dareh conference seemed to suggest American interest in its proceedings. Mohamad Roem states that this American, by name of Stuart, took the room in the Hotel Muara he had just vacated. Interview, Jakarta, Jan. 1959.

30. Simbolon denies that this issue was ever discussed at the meeting: "The idea of a separatist state had never entered the mind of those present. The struggle had been designed since the very beginning to be nation wide, embracing the whole territory of Indonesia." (Letter from Simbolon, dated 16 Aug. 1988). Barlian also stated that at Sungai Dareh "the others" not including himself, "wanted a counter government but not a separate state." Interview, 23 Feb. 1971. Mohamad Roem, who had close ties with and enjoyed the confidence of Natsir, Sjafruddin, and Burhanuddin, stated that Lubis was the strongest proponent for a separate state of Sumatra. Interview, Feb. 1959. A few fairly senior British officials stationed in both Malaya and British Borneo unofficially briefly floated the idea of Sumatra's joining Malaya.

31. "*Time* Correspondent Interviews," p. 4, as reported by the American Embassy in Foreign Service Despatch 343, 24 Jan. 1958.

32. Interviews with Sjafruddin and Natsir.

33. Interview with Sjafruddin, Jakarta, 21 May 1971. From the colonels' point of view there was a clear advantage in establishing a single council which could coordinate activities in the different regions. Formation of a unified command had been posited as early as the Palembang conference in Sept. 1957 (see chap. 5).

34. Interview with Zulkifli Lubis, Jakarta, 24 Feb. 1971. For Sumitro's more sanguine assessment of the conference and its results, see Sumitro, "Searchlight on Indonesia" (mimeo, Singapore, ca. Feb. 1959), pp. 10-11.

35. "*Time* Correspondent James Bell's Interviews," p. 3, as reported by U.S. Jakarta Embassy, 24 Jan. 1958.

36. *Pedoman*, 22 Jan. 1958. This statement was also quoted by Djuanda when reporting on the situation in Sumatra before parliament on 3 Feb. 1958, when he also stated that Nasution had received assurances of loyalty from Barlian. See also Telegram: Jakarta to Secretary of State 2252, 23 Jan. 1958.

37. Interview with Barlian, Jakarta, 23 Feb. 1971.

38. See chap. 3.

39. Colonel Ibnu Sutowo, whom Barlian succeeded, and Colonel Bambang Utojo, who had held the post from 1952-1955. Nasution, *Memenuhi Panggilan Tugas* 4: 190-91.

40. The Commander of Regiment VI, Lieutenant Colonel Worang, for example, "indicated that any pro-rebel move by Barlian would have been disavowed at least in Worang's regimental area, and probably by other officers as well." Alliband, "Upheaval in Sumatra," p. 178.

41. Interview with Sjafruddin, Jakarta, 21 Feb. 1971.

42. "*Time* correspondent interviews," p.4, as reported by American embassy, 24 Jan. 1958.

43. Copy of English translation of letter in our possession.

44. British Embassy to Foreign Office, dated 30 Jan. 1958 (FO371/135847). The embassy commented that if the Masjumi leaders really thought the letter would have this effect, "they seem to be out of touch with the temper of the present administration." It further commented that this, together with "the failure to arrange adequate publicity in advance" for the letter, "is symptomatic of the political weakness of the dissident elements."

45. Interview with Sjafruddin, Jakarta, 21 Feb. 1971.

46. See telephone call to Governor Herter, Sunday, 8 Dec. 1957, 10.16 a.m. (Dwight D. Eisenhower Library).

47. Exchange between F.S. Tomlinson and Mr. Freeland of the Foreign Office, 30 Dec. 1957, enclosed in material from J.G.W. Ramage to A.J. de la Mare, Esquire, Washington, D.C., in FO371/129516.

48. Central Intelligence Agency, "Memorandum: Probable Developments in Indonesia," 31 Jan. 1958, signed by Allen W. Dulles, Director of Central Intelligence (Dwight D. Eisenhower Library), 14 pages. The memorandum also went

to: Mr. Cutler, Mr. Robertson, General Erskine, Admiral Stump, Mr. Cumming, General Schow, Admiral Frost, General Lewis, and General Collins.

49. A Labour Front source was later to assure American officials that, although "Singapore Labour Front Government going through motions [to] placate Djakarta," it "sympathizes with central Sumatrans. Source added that government doing all it can to help dissidents, and would have permitted shipment several bren gun carriers to Sumatra some weeks ago if newspapers had not gotten wind of story and broken it in press." Telegram: Singapore to Secretary of State 1613, 3 Apr. 1958 (756D.00/4-358).

50. H.P. Jones's notes on 6 Feb. 1958, in his "History PRRI" p. 13, in container 64 Hoover Library.

51. Tooley and Pinwell, *Oyster*, p. 173. This study draws on recently declassified Australian government documents.

52. For the pressure regarding SEATO they exerted on the U.S., see telegram 3139, from Min. of External Affairs, Canberra to Office of Australian High Commissioner in London (enclosing Telegraph 3138 to Dulles, 4-5 Jan. 1958) (F0371/129528).

53. Mohamad Roem, interviews, Jan.-Feb. 1959. Roem went to Padang on 21 Jan. in response to a cable request from Natsir, and again on 30 Jan., accompanied by senior Masjumi leaders Prawoto Mangkusasmito and Fakih Usman.

54. Hatta's most prominent intermediary was Dr. Assaat, a distinguished nonparty leader who sought to arrange for a compromise agreement, but after failing to do so remained in Padang. Interview with Assaat, Jakarta, 22 Feb. 1971. Juir Mohammad of the Socialist party during early February met with Husein, Assaat, and Natsir. Interview, Jakarta, Jan. 1991. Ex-colonel Daan Jahja also visited Sumatra immediately before the break to try to persuade the rebels against it. He arrived in Padang around Feb. 6, where he saw Simbolon to tell him that he could not count on Barlian, flew to Pekanbaru, then back to Padang, returning to Jakarta on Feb. 8. Interview, Jakarta, 31 May 1971. Sjahrir and other PSI leaders sent emissaries to Sumatra to persuade Sumitro not to press for a break, but Sumitro appeared deliberately to avoid them. And subsequently, when Djohan Sjarusah and Subadio Sastrosatomo visited Sumitro in Singapore to present the party's views, Sumitro refused to accept their arguments. Interviews with Subadio Sastrosatomo and Sarbini, Jakarta, Feb. 1971.

55. Interview with Hatta, Jakarta, 12 Dec. 1958.

56. Interview with the Sultan of Yogyakarta, Hamengku Buwono IX, 13 Jan. 1959. He stated in the interview that "it would be a mistake to go so far as to completely break, because if the situation remained short of an actual break it would be difficult to get Javanese troops to fight in Sumatra." Ibid. Nasution contends that in the event "no *panglima* [commander] refused to contribute forces for the operations in Sumatra." Nasution, *Memenuhi Panggilan Tugas* 4: 212-13.

57. Telegram from USARMA to Sec. of State, No. CX -23, 27 Jan. 1958 (756D.00/1-2758). On Cikini, see chap. 5.

58. Telegram: Medan to Secretary of State, #24, 10 Feb. 1958 (756D.00/2-1058) reporting on conversations of a journalist with Simbolon and other military leaders at the end of January.

59. Interview with Barlian, Jakarta, 23 Feb. 1971. Husein was also now in the position of being nominal head of the military rebels with the prospect of heading the military side of any government they proclaimed.

60. See British reports of contacts, including Telegram No. 747, Singapore to Foreign Office, 30 Dec. 1957, reporting on conversation with two members of British Embassy Staff in Singapore with Sumitro, where he stated: "Soekarno was now inextricably involved with the Communists and in any case completely unreliable."

61. British Embassy, Jakarta to Foreign Office, Despatch No. 23 (1015/58), 20 Feb. 1958, p. 4.

62. There is no local press record of such a speech on this date, that we have been able to find. The only source is the Sumitro press release. Simbolon stated to one of the authors: "I honestly don't remember" whether he delivered the speech, but that the situation "must have been quite conducive to have made such [a] statement over Radio Padang." Letter, 16 Aug. 1985.

63. It is perhaps revealing that in his "Searchlight on Indonesia" (published a year later), pp. 11 and 12, Sumitro also credits Colonel Simbolon, rather than Husein, with issuing the ultimatum to the central government on 10 Feb.

64. *New York Times*, 5 Feb. 1958. See also Harvey, *Permesta*, p. 86.

65. Report by Ambassador Jones of his conversation with PM Djuanda in Telegram: Jakarta to Secretary of State 3300, 21 March 1958.

66. Roem's corroboratory account of this proposal and of the Masjumi leaders' reactions comes from one of the authors' interviews with him, Jan.-Feb. 1959.

67. Among these was Ismael Lengah, a former commander of the Banteng division. See *Waspada*, 11 Feb. 1958.

68. Makmum Salim, *Sedjarah Operasi2 Gabungan terhadup PRRI-Permesta* (Jakarta: Pusat Sedjarah Abri, 1971), pp. 13-14; Nopriyasman, "Gaduh di Ranah Minang: Suatu Studi tentang Pemberontakan PRRI di Sumatera Barat (1958-1961) [Turmoil in the Minang area: A study concerning the PRRI rebellion in West Sumatra (1958-1961)]" (Skripsi, Fakultas Sastra, University of Andalas, 1988), p. 51; Alliband, "Upheaval in Sumatra," p. 174. Husein himself insists that at this time "all the members of the Dewan Banteng were one" in support of the ultimatum and it was only when Hatta and Sjahrir would not go along that the local PSI members turned against it. (Interview, 9 May 1991.)

69. Telegram Jakarta to Secretary of State, 2474, 11 Feb. 1958 (756D.00/2-1158).

70. Mohammad Natsir noted that "all the military leaders" in Padang backed the ultimatum: "They were all so bellicose." Interview, Jakarta, 31 May 1971.

71. "Mukaddimah Piagam Perdjuangan" (5 pp.), mimeo, in our possession, dated 10 Feb. 1958.

72. "Piagam Perdjuangan: Menjelamatkan Negara" (3 pp.) mimeo, in our possession, signed Lt. Col. Ahmad Husein, Padang, 10 Feb. 1958. An abbreviated report was carried in *Waspada*, 12 Feb. 1958.

73. Office Memorandum to Mr. Robertson from John Gordon Mein, 14 Feb. 1958 (756D.00/2-1458); Telegram, Jakarta to Secretary of State, 2478, 11 Feb. 1958 (756D.00/2-1158).

74. British Embassy report, 14 Feb. 1958.

75. Gordon Mein reported that a statement by Nasution "tended to implicate the Central Sumatra regional movement in the assassination attempt on Sukarno last November since the Padang group is presently harboring Lt. [sic] Col. Lubis who has been named by Army Headquarters as the ringleader in the plot against the President." Mein Memorandun, 14 Feb. 1958.

76. "Keputusan 'Dewan Perdjuangan' tentang Pembentukan Pemerintah Revolusioner Republik Indonesia" (3 pp.), mimeo, in our possession, signed Lt. Col. Ahmad Husein, Padang, 15 Feb. 1958.

77. Permesta leader Warouw was named as minister of development, Saladin Sarumpait as minister of agriculture and minister of labor, Lieutenant Colonel Saleh Lahade as minister of information, and Muchtar Lintang as minister of religion. Also included in the government were the Sumatrans Mohammad Sjafei as minister of education and culture, and also minister of health; and Gani Usman (Ajah Gani) as minister of social affairs.

78. "Program Pemerintah Revolusioner Republik Indonesia" (6 pp.), mimeo, in our possession, signed by Mr. Sjafruddin Prawiranegara (as PRRI Prime Minister [Perdana Menteri P.R.R.I.]), Padang, 15 Feb. 1958.

79. Indonesia was to be made self-supporting in food staples, and the Dutch-owned interisland shipping company (KPM) was to be replaced by Indonesia's own merchant fleet. The government would take over various vital enterprises, utilizing foreign loans as capital. Religious freedom was to be guaranteed and fundamental rights, as set forth in the existing constitution, would be protected. Promotion of a democratic political system was also to entail improvements in the election laws, with the aim of attaining a simpler and healthier party system.

80. See "Instruksi Intern buat Saudara Tahir, Karim Loebis dan Z.J. Sahusilawane," signed by Perdana Menteri Sjafruddin Prawira Negara and Menteri Luar Negeri Maludin Simbolon, 28 Feb. 1958. (Doc. 5 of a PRRI Collection

of internal correspondence and memoranda among rebels in Sumatra and their representatives abroad. These documents are lodged in the ISEAS Library in Singapore and will be referred to by the number they are assigned in this collection.)

81. "Secretary Dulles' News Conference of February 11, 1958," PR 63 (756D. 00/2-1458) (Nat. Archives).

82. See, e.g., *Washington Post* (Keyes Beech), 17 Feb. 1958.

83. See FE (Robertson) to The Secretary, "Reactions to your February 11 Press Conference Statement on Indonesia," undated (756D.00/2-1258).

84. *Abadi* (editorial), 14 Feb. 1958.

85. D.F. MacDermott to Foreign Office, 14 Feb. 1958 (1015/58), FO 371/135848 (PRO).

86. *Hearings*, Part II, 26-28 Feb. 1958, p. 219.

87. *Pedoman*, 26 Feb. 1958. (*Pedoman* reflected the views of the Indonesian Socialist Party [PSI].)

Chapter 7

1. Interviews with Hatta, Jakarta, 12 Dec. 1958, 8 Jan. 1959.

2. Interviews with Mohamad Roem, Jan.-Feb. 1959. The British embassy report of the meeting between Hatta and Sukarno "received from a reliable source," read: "President Sukarno is alleged to have asked Dr. Hatta's advice on the bombing of Sumatra to which Dr. Hatta replied that any such bombing was bound to do lasting harm to inter-island relations. The President then asked Hatta if he would go to Central Sumatra 'in order to try to smooth things over.' Hatta replied that . . . he was not prepared to do Sukarno's dirty work and from then on the tone of the meeting deteriorated and . . . nothing came of it." Letter, 27 Feb. 1958.

3. Interview with Hatta, 12 Dec. 1958, and US ARMA to Sec. of State CX-46, 22 Feb. 1958 (756D.00/2-2258).

4. Roem, Interviews, Jan.-Feb. 1959.

5. Ibid., Noer, *Mohammad Hatta*, pp. 535-36, and interview with Hatta, 12 Dec. 1958.

6. Interview with Hatta, 12 Dec. 1958. Also British Embassy report, 20 Feb. 1958. Nasution writes that Sukarno's talks with Hatta were unsuccessful because Hatta refused to agree to the use of force. Nasution, *Memenuhi Panggilan Tugas* 4: 184.

7. Jones to Secretary of State, 3300, 21 March 1958.

8. Nasution, *Memenuhi Panggilan Tugas* 4: 179, 185. During this three-day tour from 23-26 Jan. he visited Tapanuli, East Sumatra, Aceh, and Tanjung Pinang.

9. Makmum Salim, *Sedjarah Operasi2 Gabungan terhadap PRRI-Permesta* (Jakarta: Pusat Sedjarah ABRI, 1971), pp. 17-18; see also Harvey, *Permesta*, p. 95; USARMA to Sec. of State CX-38, 18 Feb. 1958 (756D.00/2-1858).

10. With regard to Nasution's role, the British embassy reported to the Foreign Office: "During the past year the General has been something of an enigma. With a background of anti-communism, he has been hesitant rather than rough in his dealings with the dissident military commanders in the outer regions. During the past few months however, his patience with the regional commanders appears to have been wearing thin and since the Padang proclamation he has taken the lead in extreme action." Despatch 23, British Embassy to Foreign Office, 20 Feb. 1958 (FO 371/135848).

11. Nasution, *Memenuhi Panggilan Tugas* 4: 179.

12. Interview with Imran Manan, and Azmi, Padang, 12 Feb. 1991.

13. These statements are based on interviews with two of the returnees from Bandung, and several of the former students who had joined the rebels, Padang, Feb. 1991.

14. James Mossman, *Rebels in Paradise* (London: Cape, 1961), p. 64.

15. These included some emissaries from the political parties in Jakarta, who had been in West Sumatra at the time of the PRRI proclamation. Interview with Juir Mohamad, a member of the PSI who was among those detained, Jakarta, 14 Jan. 1991.

16. William Stevenson, *Birds' Nests in their Beards* (Boston: Houghton Mifflin, 1964), p. 144; Mossman, *Rebels*, p. 65.

17. Despatch No. 23 (1015/58), 20 Feb. 1958 (FO371/135848), British Embassy Jakarta to Foreign Office. USARMA to Sec. of State, CX-46, 22 Feb. 1958 (756D.00/2-2258). Husein in an interview stated he only had three battalions at the time of the government attacks. Interview, Jakarta, 22 Feb. 1971.

18. *New York Times*, 9 March 1958.

19. According to Hatta, during 1957 Nasution had "twice tried to mobilize an expeditionary force against West Sumatra, but in each case the military commanders in Java had refused to cooperate, saying that they would not participate in a situation where Indonesians fought Indonesians." Interview with Hatta, Jakarta, 12 Dec. 1958. Immediately before the Munas conference of Sept. 1957, East Java Comander Sarbini "was quite outspoken in his opposition to the use of force when this possibility was mentioned by Nasution" while "Colonel Sudirman, who formerly commanded East Java and subsequently the South Sulawesi operational command, informed his superiors that if a decision to use force were taken he would resign immediately and state publicly the rea-

son for his resignation." "Evaluation of the Possibilities of A Forceful Solution to Regional Question," Foreign Service Despatch 221, 22 Oct. 1957 (Nat. Archives 756D.00/10-2257). By 6 March 1958, Sarbini had still not released any troops for the Sumatra operations, but the Central Java commander Suharto (the future President Suharto), had released "about three battalions" which, according to the U.S. embassy were "heavily Communist infiltrated and led by a Communist Sundanese officer." Telegram: Jakarta to Sec. of State 2893, 6 March 1958 (756D.0013-658).

20. See, e.g., a British report of 20 Feb. 1958, which states: "the Central Government have no military transport aircraft which could carry troops direct from Djakarta to Padang, Bukittinggi or Macassar and return, and to mount an operation against Central Sumatra they would have to be either in full control of Palembang or base their forces in Medan. It would be possible to bomb Padang with the five operational twin-engined bombers which they at present possess, but the results of this would be violent and incalculable throughout the rest of Indonesia."

21. See above, chap. 3.

22. This was in fact a problem, Nasution writing that the Siliwangi and Brawijaya divisions were nailed down in facing the Darul Islam in West Java and South Sulawesi, so he had to rely principally on Diponegoro plus RPKAD while the other two divisions were only able to free one battalion each for him. Nasution, *Memenuhi Panggilan Tugas* 4: 182.

23. Ibid., pp. 200, 202. The full text appears from pp. 192-205.

24. Telephone Call: John Foster Dulles to Herter, 21 Feb. 1958, 5.06 p.m.

25. Telephone call from Secretary Dulles to Allen Dulles, 4 March 1958, 10.16. a.m.

26. Interview with General Nasution, Jakarta, 27 May 1971. The *New York Times*, March 1958, also reported that a navy spokesman in Singapore had stated that two United States destroyers, the *Eversole* and the *Shelton*, which were then in Singapore, would be available to help evacute U.S. citizens from Sumatra.

27. Cottrell was selected by Hugh S. Cumming to head the embassy during the period between Allison's recall and the arrival of Howard P. Jones as ambassador on 7 March 1958.

28. Interview with George Benson, U.S. military attaché in Jakarta during this period, Washington, D.C., 30 Dec. 1975.

29. Interview with Ahmad Husein, Jakarta, 9 May 1991.

30. Jakarta to British Foreign Office, 9 March 1958 (PRO). See also Nasution, *Memenuhi Panggilan Tugas* 4: 180.

31. See Jakarta to Foreign Office, 9 March 1958, p. 2 (PRO). (Emphasis is in the despatch.) About 800 people entered the Rumbai camp (Telegram, 12 March 1958).

32. *Straits Times*, Singapore, 13 March 1958, p. 1.

33. Interview with Zulkifli Lubis, Jakarta, 10 May 1991.

34. This is from the "Verbatim Text" of Dulles's remarks as conveyed to the American embassy in Jakarta, 14 March 1958. Several phrases were deleted in the text released to the press—this original being somewhat more explicit and sharper in tone.

35. Interview with Lieutenant General Djatikasumo, Jakarta, 17 Feb. 1971. The government's fear that the rebels would resort to such a scorched-earth policy was also emphasized by another senior government officer prominently involved in East Sumatran operations, General Rukmito Hendraningrat (later in charge of operations against Permesta). Interview, Jakarta, 27 May 1971.

36. Interview with Zulkifli Lubis and E.S. Pohan, Jakarta, 24 Feb. 1971.

37. Interview with Husein (with Simbolon, Sumual, et al, present), Jakarta, 22 Feb. 1971.

38. Interview with Nasution, Jakarta, 27 May 1971. An indication of Nasution's haste was that his deputies, Generals Yani and Rukmito, were obliged to borrow from the American military attaché two critical maps (from the U.S. survey series) of the Padang and Indragiri areas needed to plan their campaign. Interview with U.S. army Colonel (ret.) George Benson, Washington D.C., 5 Dec. 1991.

39. Interview with Nasution, Jakarta, 27 May 1971. Dulles acknowledged to the press just after the conference ended that Indonesia had been discussed at "closed sessions" of the SEATO meeting. The *New York Times*, 14 March 1958. The PRRI representative was Nun Pantauw. At the close of the SEATO conference Dulles revealed that the circumstances under which the United States would accord belligerent status to the PRRI were being considered by the State Department's legal adviser. See Tillman Durdin in the *New York Times*, 14 March 1958. For the British demarche see "Foreign Office Minute—Sir F. Hoyer Millar, 'Conversation with the Indonesian Ambassador,' 7 March 1958." FO371/135849. See also Millar's instructions from F.S. Tomlinson of 6 March 1958. FO 371/135849 (PRO).

40. Lieutenant General Djatikusumo, Nasution's deputy in charge of eastern Sumatra operations, states that the planes involved in these airdrops were from Taiwan, via Bangkok, which on their return flight to Taiwan stopped over in Singapore for refueling and for reattaching the Kuomintang (Nationalist China) insignia. Interview, Jakarta, 17 Feb. 1971.

41. Interview with General Nasution, 27 May 1971.

42. Interview with Lieutenant General Djatikusumo, Jakarta, 17 Feb. 1971. For a full enumeration of the government forces involved, see Nasution, *Memenuhi Panggilan Tugas* 4: 223, and Salim, *Sedjarah Operasi* 2, p. 21. See also Ambassador Jones, "History of the PRRI," p. 25, Hoover Library, Container No. 64.

43. See Nasution, *Memenuhi Panggilan Tugas* 4: 228, for a full listing of the weapons they found.

44. Interview with Ahmad Husein, 22 Feb. 1971. Ex-colonel Daan Jahja said there was only a squad of about 20 rebel troops at the airfield itself to guard the crates of weapons, not to defend the airstrip. Interview, 31 May 1971. One of the rebels' chief strategists, Zulkifli Lubis, states that the soldiers were prepared, but lacked fighting spirit. Interview with Zulkifli Lubis, Jakarta, 10 May 1971.

45. See Salim, *Sedjarah Operasi2*, pp. 23-25. The above account is also consistent with Ambassador Jones's chronological "History PRRI," located in the Hoover Library.

46. The above data on the destroyers, the *Bremerton*, and the destroyers' rendezvous with the *Ticonderoga* are based on the now-declassified Deck Logs of the *Bremerton*, *Ticonderoga*, and *Shelton* and on the U.S. Navy Historical Center's histories of the *Eversole* (DD-789) and *Bremerton* (CA-130). For help in interpretation of the Deck Logs we are indebted to John C. Reilly Jr., Head, Ships Histories Branch of the Naval Historical Center, Washington Navy Yard. Without the logs it would have been impossible to reconstruct this episode fully, for the *Eversole's* brief official history for this period says only that it and the *Shelton* were engaged "in a training exercise" in the area of the South China Sea "necessitated by critical world conditions in the area" and that they were in Singapore for "recreation." The official history of the *Bremerton* states only that it was in Singapore on a good-will "People to People" mission. The data on the aircraft carrier and its marines are also based on an interview with George Benson (U.S. Army, ret.), who at the time was U.S. Army Military Attaché in Jakarta. Washington, D.C., 30 Dec. 1975, and Ambassador Howard P. Jones, "Chronology Concerned Basically with the PRRI Rebellion," p. 24, originally lodged in container no. 64, Folder: "History, PRRI," Howard P. Jones Collection, Hoover Library of War, Revolution and Peace, Stanford University. In a secret message to the British Foreign Office in the early morning of 13 March Sir Robert Scott, Commissioner General for Southeast Asia, cabled that "United States naval forces, including a carrier and helicopters, are in the Singapore area. From our talks with the United States Admiral it is clear that in the event of acute danger to employees concentrated at Rumbai [in the Caltex area], these forces would be used to give some measure of protection to them and to attempt evacuation by helicopter." Cypher/OTP, Sir R. Scott, no. 164, 13 March 1958. The Singapore *Straits Times* and the *New York Times* (12 March 1958) make brief mention of the presence of the first two destroyers. The British report that the carrier had reached "the Singapore area" appears consistent with daily mileages recorded in the *Ticonderoga's* Deck Log Book. This shows that by midnight of 12/13 March it had steamed 1073 nautical miles from Subic and since it continued south until after noon on 13 March must have added at least half of the 362 miles covered that day (or 181 more). This total of some 1,250 nautical miles could have put it very close to Singapore before it reversed course. Speculation concerning the meaning of the aborting of the rendezvous between the *Ticonderoga* and the destroyers is from a letter of 14 Sept. 1992 from John C. Reilly.

47. Navy Message, 11 March 1958: CTF 75 to Secretary of State (756D.00/3-1158).

48. Ambassador Jones's "History, PRRI." See also *Abadi* (the Masjumi Party newspaper), 15 March 1958.

49. *Pedoman* (PSI newspaper), 15 March 1958.

50. "Pidato dari Komandan Operasi Sabang Merauke, Henry Siregar, berkenaan dengan peringatan ulang tahun pertama Operasi Sabang Merauke, tgl. 15 Maret 1959" (PRRI Doc. 14).

51. Nasution, *Memenuhi Panggilan Tugas* 4: 232, 236.

52. J.F.D. Telephone call to Allen Dulles, 27 Feb. 1958.

53. Geoffrey Slater and Jack Waterford, "Finger in the Pie," *Canberra Times*, 17 Feb. 1991. This article apparently provides the first public disclosure of previously classified Australian government documents relating to the 1958 SEATO conference.

54. Tookey and Pinwell, *Oyster*, p. 71.

55. Slater and Waterford, "Finger in the Pie."

56. Tookey and Pinwell, *Oyster*, p. 71.

57. Telegram from [Dulles] Manila to Sec. State: Dulte 8, 13 March 1958, "Eyes only Acting Secretary for President from Secretary" (Dwight D. Eisenhower Library).

58. Telegram from [Dulles] Taipei to Sec. State: Dulte 11, 14 March 1958 (756D.00/3-1458). Lloyd stated that his opposition to according the rebels belligerent status was that it risked "prompting the Russians to do the same" (presumably in behalf of rebels elsewhere). For this and Dulles's argument in parentheses above regarding belligerents' right to buy arms, see Casey's report in Slater and Waterford, "Finger in the Pie."

59. "Memorandum of Conversation with the President," 19 March 1958 (John Foster Dulles Papers, 1952-59: White House Memoranda Series, Box 6, White House—Meetings with the President 1/1-6/30/1958 [6].)

60. Jones, *The Possible Dream*, p. 116, and Memorandum: Walter Robertson [Assistant Secretary of State] to the Secretary, "Recognition of the Dissidents in Indonesia" (referring to a meeting in Dulles's office on 19 March), 26 March 1958 (Memo prepared 21 March). Jones's book refers to this meeting with Sukarno as being "a few weeks" after 14 March, when it should read "a few days." See also Jakarta to Secretary of State, 19 March 1958, sec. 3, p. 2.

61. Jakarta to Secretary of State, 20 March 1958, sec. 4, p. 1.

62. From Jakarta to Foreign Office, telegram 228, 22 March 1958. Sukendro added "that another aircraft carrying arms had also landed in Menado and that the name of the pilot and the number of this aircraft was known to the Central Government. Ships were also smuggling arms to other areas held by the dissidents." Ibid. According to a secret PRRI memo, "Efforts/Work Abroad from S.K." (presumably Sumitro) apparently written in late April 1958, (PRRI Doc. 116), 350,000 Straits dollars was paid for the plane. Some of the rebel leaders believed that Sumitro was overcharging for the purchases he made for the PRRI and pocketing a commission for himself (a charge frequently made in his purchase of jeeps in Singapore), so the amount charged for the plane may have been less.

63. Interview of one of the authors with John Griffin, Saigon, 26 Jan. 1961. Griffin was with AP in Indonesia in Jan., Feb., March, and Apr., 1958. It is worth noting that during this period the *New York Times* had little coverage of events in Sumatra, and in dealing with the rebellion tended to be strongly supportive of Washington's stance.

64. Smith, *Portrait of a Cold Warrior*, p. 246.

65. Interview with Kawilarang, 26 May 1971.

66. USARMA, Jakarta to Secretary of State, 14 March 1958 (National Archives, 756D.00/3-13548 HBS).

67. Harvey, *Permesta: Half a Rebellion*, p. 103.

68. NSC: Summaries 610F, 4 Apr. 1958, p.6. See also Kawilarang's brief and guarded account of his resignation in K.H. Ramadhan, *A.E. Kawilarang Untuk Sang Merah Putih* (Jakarta: Sinar Harapan, 1988), p. 292.

69. Pirngadie, *PRRI Affair*, p. 40.

70. Interviews, Daan Jahja, Jakarta, 30-31 May 1971.

71. Interview with Kawilarang, 26 May 1971. According to ex-colonel Daan Jahja, Kawilarang told him that he was disturbed at the low quality of troops he would have in Sumatra, and did not know what field commanders he could trust. Arrangements were made with the British for him to be flown by Catalina to Lake Singkarak in Central Sumatra, but at the last moment there was a mechanical problem with the plane; it could not take off and the British did not provide a replacement. Kawilarang seemed relieved to have the decision made for him and went back to the Minahasa. He had been close to Daan Jahja, and invited him — unsuccessfully — to become his chief of staff. Interviews with Daan Jahja, 30-31 May 1971.

72. J.F.D. telephone call to Admiral Burke, 28 March 1958. This call concerned primarily a U.S. Navy plane that Jakarta government forces' antiaircraft had sufficiently disabled so that it was forced down in the Philippines. (For a full account, see below.)

73. J.F.D. telephone call to Allen Dulles, 2 April 1958.

74. Jones had served concurrently as economic counselor in the U.S. Jakarta embassy and as head of the U.S. Economic Aid Mission there from mid-1954 to mid-1955 after which he had served as deputy assistant secretary of state for Far Eastern economic affairs until his appointment as ambassador to Indonesia. He had originally been slated to become ambassador to the Chinese Nationalist regime on Taiwan, where he had previously served as deputy chief of mission in the American embassy. Allison had received a telegram on Jan. 4 from the State Department requesting he prepare to leave Jakarta for Prague by Feb. 1. The reported reason was that he was "too favorably disposed to Indonesia in its dispute with the Netherlands over the West Irian issue." Jones chronology, p. 7.

75. Telegram from Jakarta to Secretary of State (No. 3312, 21 March 1958) (Nat. Archives, 756D.00/3-2158).

76. Interview with H. P. Jones, Jakarta, 21 July 1963.

77. Telegram: Jakarta to Secretary of State, 3565, 6 Apr. 1958 (546D.00/4-658).

78. Memorandum for the Secretary of Defense, from N.F. Twining, Chairman of Joint Chiefs of Staff, dated 7 Apr. 1958.

79. See Jones, *The Possible Dream*, p. 122.

80. Dulles to American Embassies Jakarta and Manila, 1 May 1958 (756D.00/4-1658). Ten MIG-17Fs had been purchased from Egypt and were due to arrive 10 May, with an additional thirty reported on 3 April to have been purchased in Poland and due to arrive in six months. Four destroyers, eight sub-chasers, and two submarines were reported to have been purchased in Poland with personnel to man them due "soon to leave for Poland." Mortars purchased in Yugoslavia were supposed to arrive in mid-May. Jones, "Chronology: Concerned Basically with PRRI Rebellion of 1958" (typescript), p.30, Howard P. Jones Collection, Box 17, Hoover Library.

81. Record of Howard P. Jones, "Secretary State/British Ambassador Discussion of What Actions to Take re. Indo and PRRI." Political Scene File, Box 17, Hoover Library.

82. Memorandum of discussion by S. Everett Gleason, April 15, 1958 of National Security Council, 362nd meeting, 14 Apr. 1958. (Eisenhower Library, Whitman File, NSC Records.

83. J.F.D. Telephone call to Allen Dulles, 15 Apr. 1958, 1.52 p.m.

84. Telephone call from Allen Dulles [to J.F.D.], 15 Apr. 1958, 2.40 p.m.

85. "Memorandum of Conversation with the President" 15 April 1958. Portions here italicized have been deleted [sanitized] in this document and come from Howard Jones's notes on the unexpurgated version of the "Eisenhower/Dulles Conversation Indo. April 15, 1958," taken when he had access to the unsanitized memorandum. Howard P. Jones Collection, at the Hoover Library of War Revolution and Peace, Stanford University.

86. "Memorandum of Conversation with the President," 15 Apr. 1958. It is noteworthy that, though members of the rebel group consistently deny making any mention of a "Sumatra state," this term occurs frequently in the U.S. documents.

87. Howard P. Jones's "Chronology: Concerned Basically with PRRI Rebellion of 1958," p. 34.

88. Colonel Sukendro, for instance, noted that American dropping of weapons to Nainggolan's troops in their uprising in Medan "has produced violent anti-American reaction among officers and troops of Regiment 2 which has been anti-Communist in orientation." Jones, "Chronology PRRI" (p. 32).

89. Interview with Mohammad Natsir, Jakarta, 23 Jan. 1971. He went on to explain: "But this factor did not affect the situation outside of Java and did not hurt us in terms of nationalism there" (i.e., in the areas outside of Java).

90. Nasution, *Memenuhi Panggilan Tugas* 4: 237.

91. Djuanda so informed Ambassador Jones on 21 March, "Chronicle B," p. 9 in Box 17, Jones's collection, Hoover Library.

92. On 13 April Lieutenant Colonel Sukardjo, a Jakarta intelligence officer, reported that both Major Johan, with his Bn. 141 near Padang Panjang and Major Iskandar, with his battalion 142 in the vicinity of Kerinci, had revolted against Husein, in addition to the earlier defection of Major Nurmathias. See USARMA to Secretary of State No. CX-108, 120545Z, 13 Apr. 1958. This report was erroneous, since neither Johan nor Iskandar did defect and Major Johan in fact became one of the most effective of the rebel commanders. The same report made mention that there was a "serious split between Masjumi and PSI members of Banteng Council," and that Husein had replaced leading PSI men with those from Masjumi.

93. Interview with Zulkifli Lubis, Jakarta, 10 May 1991.

94. Interview with Ahmad Husein, Jakarta, 9 May 1991. It is unclear whether the explosions that destroyed the planes were from antiaircraft fire as they were leaving Balikpapan or from timed explosives that had been placed on board. Nasution in his memoirs also notes that the PRRI were about to receive B-26 bombers from the U.S. and that he had information that it would also be sending the rebels a B-29. Nasution, *Memenuhi Panggilan Tugas* 4: 245, 257.

95. With respect to negotiation for the acquisition of two amphibious planes, see PRRI Doc. 116.

96. Interviews with former PRRI local officials, West Sumatra, Feb. 1991.

97. The planes also dropped napalm, but according to Ahmad Husein this was confined to the wooded hills between Padang and the port of Teluk Bayur, and caused no casualties. Interview, 9 May 1991.

98. Telegram, USARMA Jakarta to Sec. of State C123,230746Z, 23 Apr. 1958. In a letter of 18 May 1958 to E. Pohan, the PRRI's resident agent in Singapore, Sjafruddin wrote that "The voluntary forces, such as the student army, the university student corps, and the new and young troops in general were not so influenced by the feelings of panic and despair [as were many of Husein's regular troops]." Letter dated 18 May 1958, PRRI Doc. 16.

99. As Daan Jahja put it: "Actually Yani's troops were sitting ducks and could easily have been picked off by a small number of troops. They came ashore on rafts made of oil drums and had to get out in waist deep water." Interview with Daan Jahja, 30 May 1971. Mossman, who was in Padang during part of the landings, gives his account of them in *Rebels in Paradise*, pp.154-61, and he makes a similar point with regard to the parachute drops: "Slowly, helplessly, General Nasution's paratroops descended upon the valley. Most of them could have been killed before they even reached the ground, yet the rebels never fired a shot," ibid., p. 153. Reports differ as to whether Jakarta employed one or more planes. Effectiveness of the bombing was enhanced by the acquisition in Egypt of delayed action bombs, the Indonesian air attaché in Cairo, Colonel Budiardjo, managing to send out some of the fuses by diplomatic pouch. Interview with General Budiardjo, Jakarta, 22 May 1971. He states that these permitted increased accuracy and had "great psychological impact on the rebels."

100. Nasution, *Memenuhi Panggilan Tugas* 4: 241-43. For a full account of these operations, see also Salim, *Sedjarah Operasi2*, pp. 33-40.

101. See Harry H. Bell, "Political and Economic Pressures on Lt. Col. Barlian, Jakarta," Foreign Service Despatch 522, dated 16 Apr. 1958, p. 4.

102. Interview with Barlian, 23 Feb. 1971. Nasution, *Memenuhi Panggilan Tugas* 4: 190, 237.

103. Jakarta to Secretary of State, Telegram 4023, 3 May 1958 (756D.00/5-358). It was later reported that he was planning to sink two tankers to block Palembang harbor. US ARMA Jakarta to Secretary of State, CX-153, 9 May 1958 (756D.00/5-958). Husein's similar requisitioning from Caltex is described in a letter of 16 May 1990 to one of the authors from R.H. Hopper, who in 1958 was a senior Caltex officer stationed at its Sumatran field.

104. Interview with Sofyan Asnawi, Padang, 14 Feb. 1991, who was in Nawawi's headquarters when the government forces attacked. He was one of four emissaries from Colonel Djambek charged with trying to persuade Barlian to rally to the PRRI; see also Jakarta to Secretary of State 4023, 3 May 1958.

105. Jakarta to Secretary of State, Telegram 4023, 3 May 1958. Nasution, *Memenuhi Panggilan Tugas* 4: 237; USARMA Jakarta to Secretary of State, CX149, 6 May 1958, CX-153, 9 May 1958; and interview with Barlian, 23 Feb. 1971.

106. See Salim, *Sedjarah Operasi2*, pp. 42-43; also interview with Colonel Johan, Bandung, 26 Feb. 1994. For a certainly romanticized version of the defenses put up by the PRRI forces, particularly those commanded by Zadelberg and

Major Johan, see Sjafruddin's letter to Pohan, dated 18 May 1958, PRRI Doc. 16.

107. According to Colonel Sukendro, Yani was expecting to capture Bukittinggi on 28 April. USARMA to Secretary of State, C-130, 26 Apr. 1958.

108. JFD telephone call to Allen Dulles, 12.30 p.m., Thursday, 17 Apr. 1958.

Chapter 8

1. For an extensive account of Jusuf's actions and his role in Permesta, see Harvey, *Permesta*, pp. 45-47, 61, 64-65, 97-98, 155-56.

2. ALUSNA to Secretary of State 021007Z May (Navy Message), 2 May 1958 (756D.00/5-258).

3. USARMA Jakarta to Sec. of State, CX-158, 120620Z May (Army Message) 12 May 1958 (756D.00/5-258), reporting on a conversation between Jusuf and Major George Benson of 11 May. See also USARMA Jakarta to Sec. of State, CX-155, 10 May 1958 (756D.00/5-1058). This reported that the mission had been undertaken in response to an initiative from Warouw, but when they got there: "Instead of negotiating Warrouw [sic] attempted to talk officers from South Sulawesi to join rebel movement."

4. The terms "adventurers" and "soldiers of fortune" were then being employed by J.F. Dulles with respect to press reports that Americans were fighting on the side of the rebels. This was meant to distinguish them from members of the U.S. military forces who Dulles insisted were not involved.

5. USARMA Djakarta to Sec. of State CX-158, 120620Z May (Army Message), 12 May 1958, reporting on a conversation of Jusuf and Major Benson of 11 May.

6. Ambassador Jones to Secretary of State 4152, 10 May 1958 (756D.00/5-1058).

7. For coverage of these reports by Djuanda and Lieutenant Colonel Pirngadi (the army spokesman), see the Jakarta newspapers, *Abadi* (Masjumi) and *Pedoman* (PSI) for 2 May 1958, *Merdeka* for 3 May and 8 May, and *Suluh Indonesia* (PNI) for 2 May and 10 May. We are indebted to Benedict Anderson for having located and extracted these press reports. (All the newspapers are held in the Echols Collection of Corrnell University's Kroch Library.)

8. Jones to Secretary of State 4063, 6 May 1958 (756D.00/5-658), and Jones to Secretary of State 423, 15 May 1958 (FW756D.00/5-558).

9. Interview with General Nasution, Jakarta, 27 May 1971.

10. 358th Meeting, NSC, 13 March 1958, and 359th meeting, March 20, 1958. (Both memoranda of the discussion by S. Everett Gleason, deputy executive secretary of the NSC.)

11. USARMA to Sec. of State C-130, 26 Apr. 1958 (756D.00/4-2658).

12. With respect to British reconnaissance, see Slater and Waterford, "Finger in the Pie," *Canberra Times*, 17 Feb. 1991.

13. Memo of conversation with Mr. Allen W. Dulles, Friday, 28 March 1958, 11 a.m. (Dulles Papers, Box 8, Princeton Library), and Dulles's telephone call to Burke, 28 March 1958, 11.16 a.m.

14. Telephone call, 28 March 1958, 11.24 a.m.

15. For a full account of the incident in the Philippines, see Daniel Doeppers, "An Incident in the PRRI/Permesta Rebellion of 1958," *Indonesia* 14 (October 1972): 183-95.

16. Telephone call, 28 March, 5.12 p.m.

17. Nasution, *Memenuhi Panggilan Tugas* 4: 157, 245, and interview with General Nasution, Jakarta, 27 May 1971. According to him, Padang airfield was big enough to take B25s, B26s, and B29s. The Dutch had extended the runway at Padang during the revolution, because the Indian government refused them transit rights. Their Constellations thus had to fly via Mauritius, and needed to stop in Sumatra, if headwinds were strong, before landing in Djakarta.

18. Interview, 27 May 1971.

19. USARMA to Sec. of State, 26 Apr. 1958.

20. Harvey, *Permesta*, p. 107.

21. Jakarta to Secretary of State 3965, 30 Apr. 1958. H.P. Jones gives the total as six, with four bombers and two Mustangs. (Chronology, 1 May 1958 [p.38]), while Nasution puts it at eight.

22. Harvey, *Permesta*, p. 107.

23. Jakarta to Secretary of State 3834, 22 Apr. 1958.

24. USARMA C-122, 23 Apr. 1958 (756D.00/4-2558), and C-126, 25 Apr. 1958 (756D.00/4-2658). Two B-26s involved in this raid were supposed to have proceeded on to arrive in Padang the day before Jakarta's attack against that city. According to Husein, they had blown up after the raid on Balikpapan. See chap. 7.

25. Nasution, *Memenuhi Panggilan Tugas* 4: 257.

26. Ibid. and USARMA to Secretary of State CX-126, 25 Apr. 1958 (756D.00/4-2558). Statement by Sumual, one of the bluntest and most forthright—as well as militarily one of the ablest of the rebel commanders. He stated this in an interview (Jakarta, 22 Feb. 1971), witnessed by most of the principal senior ex-PRRI and Permesta leaders, including Achmad Husein, Maludin Simbolon, Saleh Lahade, and Daan Mogot, where he outlined rebel strategy for attacking

Java and blamed Washington for reneging on its commitment to provide the necessary air power.

27. Ambassador Jones' notes in "1958 Political Scene" folder, Box 17, Jones Collection, Hoover Library.

28. Sumual interview, 22 Feb. 1971.

29. USARMA to Sec. of State, CX-149, 6 May 1958.

30. Interviews with Lt. General Rukmito Hendraningrat (who in 1958 was in charge of the government's campaign to recover Sulawesi and adjacent islands), Jakarta, 27 May 1971. The ships at Dongala had just disembarked their troops when they were bombed. It was reported that on the 27-28 April raids six B-26 bombers and two F-51 fighters were used. CX-146, 5 May 1958 (756D.00/5-558). See also Harvey, *Permesta*, pp. 108, 107; USARMA CX-145, 3 May 1958 (756D.00/5-358); and interview with Des Alwi, Jakarta, 11 Jan. 1991.

31. Departemen Penerangan, "Judgement of the Court in the Case of Allen Lawrence Pope" (Jakarta, mimeo, 14 May 1960), p. 2. These ships were reported to be the Panamanian steamer *Flying Lark* and the Italian *Aquila*. The British tanker was the *San Faviano*. See *The Age* (Melbourne), 2-3 May 1958.

32. USARMA to Sec. of State, DTG 140627Z, 17 June 1958 (756D.00/6-1458).

33. Herter to Amembassy Paris, marked "for Cumming," 9 May 1958; USARMA to Sec. of State, CX-155, 10 May 1958 (756D.00/5-1058).

34. *Sydney Herald*, 9 May 1958; USARMA to Sec. of State CX-155, 10 May 1958.

35. USARMA to Sec. of State, CX-155, 10 May 1958.

36. Departemen Penerangan, "Judgement of the Court," p. 2.

37. On 3 May, when on a visit to Jakarta Rukmito requested aircover for his operations, Army headquarters promised that the air power centered on Sumatra would be shifted to East Indonesia at the end of the Sumatra actions, "probably next week." USARMA to Sec. of State CX-145, 3 May 1958. See Nasution, *Memenuhi Panggilan Tugas* 4: 273.

38. This operation was led by Lieutenant Colonel L. Huhnholz. Salim, *Sedjarah Operasi2*, pp. 102-104. According to Jusuf they also captured one of the rebels' B-26 aircraft.

39. USARMA to Secretary of State, CX 162, DTG160735Z, 17 May 1958 (756D. 00/5-1658). See also Nasution, *Memenuhi Panggilan Tugas* 4: 252, 257. According to Kawilarang "5 or 6, probably 5," of the rebel planes were destroyed on the ground in Manado by the government air force. Interview, Jakarta, 26 May 1971.

40. According to General Rukmito, Permesta then had only three Mustangs and two B-26s based there. Interview, Jakarta, 27 May 1971.

41. Telegrams 3587, 8 Apr. 1958; 3680, 12 Apr. 1958, Section 1; 3729, 15 Apr. 1958 (756D.00/4-858, 1258, 1558).

42. Memorandum of General N. F. Twining, chairman of the JCS, to the Secretary of Defense, 8 Apr. 1958.

43. "Memorandum for the Secretary of Defense," from Maxwell D. Taylor, dated 18 Apr. 1958 (756D.00/4-2158). See also "DOD attitude 'Ally with Nasution rather than send U.S. troops to prevent defeat of anti-Communist Dissident Elements,'" Telegram, 18 Apr. 1958.

44. Telephone call, J.F.D. to Allen Dulles, 23 Apr. 1958.

45. From Copenhagen to Secretary of State (signed Dulles), Dulte 15, 7 May 1958 (756D.00/5-758).

46. See, e.g., *Merdeka, Mimbar Indonesia, Pemuda, Sin Po*, and *Suluh Indonesia*.

47. This was evident in a survey made by Cornell University's Modern Indonesia Project during this period, which found considerably more coverage of Indonesia's regional rebellions in the *Ithaca Journal* than in the *New York Times*.

48. For Hilsman's assessment, see his *To Move a Nation* (Garden City, N.Y.: Doubleday, 1967), p. 84.

49. Telegram, Jakarta to Secretary of State, 4152, 10 May 1958, and 4116, 8 May 1958 (756D.00/5-1058, 858).

50. USARMA to Sec. of State CX-170, 25 May 1958 (756D.00/5-2558).

51. Telegram CINCPAC to Secretary of State, 080332Z, 8 May 1958 (756D.00/5-858). Admiral Stump later explained to one of the authors that the factor that finally decisively turned him in favor of Nasution was his own first meeting with General Gatot Subroto, Nasution's deputy chief of staff, where he first learned (rather belatedly) that Nasution and Gatot had played key roles in suppressing the Communist-led 1948 Madiun rebellion. Interview, New York, 9 Jan. 1960.

52. Jones, *Possible Dream*, p. 147.

53. Telegram (3300)Top Secret, Secretary Dulles to Amembassy Jakarta, 13 May 1958 (756D.00/5-1258, 6358).

54. Jakarta to Secretary of State 4230, 15 May 1958 (756D.00/5-1558).

55. Jakarta to Secretary of State 4234, 15 May 1958 (756D.00/5-1558).

56. Department of State 3343 to Amembassy Jakarta, 18 May 1958 (756D.00/5-1858).

57. Departemen Penerangan, "Judgement of the Court in the Case of Allan Lawrence Pope" (Official English translation of Document No. 43/P.T./Pid./ 1959) (Jakarta, mimeo, 14 May 1960), (copy in our possession), pp. 8-15; *New*

York Times, 2 Jan. 1960; see also Jones, *The Possible Dream*, p. 141. See Dep. Pen., "Judgement of the Court" and Trial transcript, 14 May 1960; *Washington Post*, 28 May 1958; see also L. Fletcher Prouty, *The Secret Team: The CIA and Its Allies in Control of the United States and the World* (Englewood Cliffs, N.J.: Prentice-Hall, 1973), pp. 324-27.

58. Jakarta to Secretary of State 4576, 5 June 1958 (756D.00/6-558).

59. See the *Manila Times*, 29 May 1958.

60. USARMA Jakarta to Secretary of State (CX-180), 2 June 1958 (756D.00/6-258).

61. British Embassy, Jakarta, letter from D.F. MacDermot to O.C. Morland, 2 June 1958.

62. Jones, *The Possible Dream*, p. 141.

63. Dep. Pen., "Judgement of the court in the case of Allen Lawrence Pope."

64. For information concerning the Camp Bruckner document, listing the eight persons involved, and the fact that Pope's TDY was for 120 days, we are indebted to the late Molly Bondan, the official government translator at the trial, and a person whose veracity was beyond reproach. L. Fletcher Prouty, a retired U.S. Air Force intelligence officer, states that among Pope's possessions was "a set of U.S. Air Force orders that proved beyond any doubt that he was an active U.S. Airforce pilot." *The Secret Team*, p. 324. If Prouty is correct, this evidence was not introduced in Pope's trial.

65. Memorandum for Brigadier General Chester V. Clifton, from Allen W. Dulles, Director, Central Intelligence Agency, 7 Apr. 1961 (National Archives) (Emphasis added). This report, in response to a request from President Kennedy, was sent to his aide, General Clifton. (A copy was sent to McGeorge Bundy, the president's special assistant for national security affairs, by Walter Elder, assistant to Director Allen Dulles.)

66. This account from Cindy Adams is cited approvingly by Ambassador Jones in his book, *The Possible Dream*, p. 142. Cindy Adams is the only person Sukarno authorized to write his biography. See her *Sukarno, An Autobiography as Told to Cindy Adams* (Indianapolis: Bobbs-Merrill, 1965), p. 271.

67. Interview with Lieutenant General Budiardjo (who drove the jeep), Jakarta, 22 May 1971.

68. Department of State Telegram to CINCPAC, To Admiral Stump from Robertson 3403, 23 May 1958, p. 2 (756D.00/5-2358).

69. Memorandum of Conversation, "Indonesian Situation," 20 May 1958 (756D.00/5-2058).

70. Cumming states he and Irwin spent about twelve days in Singapore — before, during, and after the Pope episode — where, after looking into the situation

they advised Washington to "stand down" the Singapore operation in support of the rebels and that within twenty-four hours of their recommendation Washington agreed. Interview with Ambassador Cumming, Washington, D.C., 27 Dec. 1975.

71. Circular 160 from Department of State, 7 June 1958. In response to Jones's urgings some of these measures—the licenses for the spare parts and action on diesel generators and continuation of work on the Sumatra highway—had been approved by Dulles on 17 May (without any announcement) as a quiet reward for the army's having just taken measures to stop an "anti-interventionist rally" directed against the United States, which had been scheduled for 16 May. Department of State to Amembassy Jakarta 3335, 17 May 1958 (756D.00/5-1658).

72. Memorandum for FE-Mr Robertson, signed John Foster Dulles, 23 May 1958.

73. Jakarta to Secretary of State 4576, 5 June 1958.

74. Jakarta to Secretary of State 4500, 31 May 1958 (756D.00/5-3158).

75. See Harvey, *Permesta*, p. 115. Sumual's proposal apparently resulted from pressure from Washington. In a letter dated 10 June 1958 to PRRI representatives abroad, Mr. St. Mohd Rasjid, the chief of their overseas representation, wrote: "Sumual's statement of 2 weeks ago urging reconciliation was at the instigation of the American side, and together with this America was pressuring Jakarta to negotiate with the P.R.R.I. because America still wants to see a unified Indonesia with a strong, but anti-Communist government." Rasjid Letter to Sdr.2 Perwakilan P.R.R.I. di Eropah, Geneve, 10 June 1958.(PRRI Doc.1).

76. USARMA to Sec. of State CX-217, 30 June 1958 (756D.00/6-3058). Also for the composition of the forces. General Rukmito Hendraningrat, Jakarta's commander, was able to marshal a total of sixteen battalions in this operation. Interview, 27 May 1971.

77. For details, see Harvey, *Permesta*, pp. 116-18.

78. Interview with Alex Kawilarang, Jakarta, 26 May 1971. According to Des Alwi, the CIA's mission to Minahasa totaled twelve men of whom seven were air force people (two of them Taiwanese pilots) and five artillery instructors. Frank Robertson, Far Eastern correspondent of the *London Daily Telegraph*, who visited Minahasa in early 1958, stated that the artillery in question consisted of recoilless rifles and antiaircraft guns. He recalled, that apart from CIA officers, the majority of the group were Taiwanese military officers and noncommissioned technical personnel, who served as an air ground maintenance crew. All of them wore civilian garb. (Separate interviews in Hong Kong, 2 Feb. 1961.)

79. U.S. Embassy, Seoul to Secretary of State, 2 Apr. 1958 (756D.00/4-258).

80. See Jones, *The Possible Dream*, p. 152, his Hoover Library folder "History PRRI," p. 39, and David Mozingo, *Chinese Policy Toward Indonesia 1949-*

1967 (Ithaca, N.Y.: Cornell University Press, 1976), p. 146. Mozingo states that "Chou En-lai reportedly reiterated the offer of volunteers in August."

81. Seoul to Sec. of State 855, 19 May 1958; see also CNO to Sec. of State 092041Z May (Navy Message) 9 May 1958; and COMNAVFORKOREA to Sec. of State 120342Z May (Army Message), 12 May 1958, and telegram Dulles to Amembassy Seoul, 24 May 1958 and U.S. Embassy Seoul to Secretary of State 877, 29 May 1958 (756D.00/5-1958, 958, 1258, 2358, 2958).

82. All quotes from Telegram from Seoul to Secretary of State, 880, 30 May 1958 (756D.00/5-3058).

83. INR (R. Gordon Arneson) to the Under Secretary, "Intelligence Note: Chinese Communist Offer of 'Volunteers' to Djakarta" (date unclear, poss. 14 May 1958). It will be recalled that this was a period of great and growing tension in the Formosa Straits between China and Taiwan (supported by the United States), with China assuming what appeared to be an increasingly belligerent stance. In 1953 Burma's U Nu government, after appealing in vain to the United States to halt its support to Nationalist China's (KMT) invaders in Burma had indeed brought the issue to the United Nations. Jones's concern is evident in his cable of 12 May to Robertson.

84. Dept. of State to Amembassy Taipei 762, 26 May 1958 (756D.00/5-2658). This was in criticism of statements by the ambassador and the assistant air force secretary "expressing doubt that GRC would attack Communist Chinese troops bound for Indonesia without prior consultation with us." Apparently Chiang had already assured the United States "that he would take no action pending further advice from us."

85. Dept. of State [Herter] to Amembassy Jakarta 3184 (copy to Taipei), 3 May 1958.

86. Dept. of State to Amembassy New Delhi 2653 (copy to Amembassy Jakarta 3309), 14 May 1958 (756D.001/5-1458), and USARMA Jakarta to Secretary of State CX-219, 1 July 1958 (756D.00/7-158): Jones to Secretary of State, 7 July, 10 July, 21 July 1958 (756D.00/7-758, 1058, 2158). There were also B-26 attacks on 15 June and 27 June (see Jakarta to Secretary of State, 1 July 1958 (756D.00/7-158). Not until 8 July did Acting Secretary Herter instruct the U.S. Ambassador to Taipei to discourage any further raids. Herter to Taipei, 8 July 1958 (756D.00/7-758).

87. Foreign Service Despatches from Amembassy Taipei to Dept. of State 704, 16 June 1958, and 786, 26 June 1958 (756D.00/7-1658).

88. Amembassy to Dept. of State, Despatch 28, 11 July 1958 (756D.00/7-1158). ("Other prominent Chinese believe that release of these persons can be effected only after rebel activity subsides and charges of Taiwan aid to the rebels recede into the background and an appropriate financial settlement is made with the security authorities"), and Amembassy to Washington, 28 Oct. 1958. (This is a retrospective report and it would appear that the order was promulgated at the beginning of October.)

89. Nick Joaquin, *The Aquinos of Tarlac* (unexpurgated edition: Manila: Solar Publishing Corporation, 1986), p. 268.

90. Interview with Colonel Husein, Jakarta, 9 May 1991.

91. Joaquin, *The Aquinos of Tarlac*, pp. 269-70.

92. Interviews of one of the authors with Diokno in Manila, April 1978. Diokno and Aquino, both jailed by Marcos, shared a cell for a long period and became close friends. Diokno asked that Aquino's role not be divulged until after his death—something Diokno feared might occur soon. Aquino's cover in Manado was as correspondent for the *Manila Times*.

93. See the *Manila Times* for mid-February through May 1958, and especially Feb. 14, 15, 22, April 1, May 1, 6, 10, 12, 13, 17, 28, 29, 1958. See also Vicente Barranco, "Fundamentals of Our Foreign Policy," *The Sunday Times Magazine*, 7 May 1961 and Leon O. Ty, "Should Serrano Tell All?" *Philippine Free Press*, 17 May 1958. See also Jones, *The Possible Dream*, p. 140. The Philippine press gave wide coverage to Jakarta's charge that Philippine troops, in company with some from Taiwan, had supported the rebels in their attack against and seizure of Morotai island (with its large airfield) and that Sumitro had given $170,000 to Vargas and an unnamed Philippine senator.

94. Telegram, Manila to Secretary of State 435, 28 July 1958 (756D.00/7-2858).

95. A rebel B-26 strafed Gorontalo on 15 June (Jakarta to Sec. of State 4752, 17 June 1958, also ALUSNA 17 June). The attack was officially "deplored" by Dulles, Telegram 19 June. Villages near Manado were bombed by a B-26 on 27 June, immediately after government forces had recaptured the town, and one of Jakarta's navy tankers was also bombed. Jakarta to Sec. of State 4946, 28 June 1958; USARMA to Sec. of State, CX-219, 1 July 1958 (756D.00/6-1758, 2858; /7-158). Though the Indonesian military believed these attacks were coming from outside Indonesia, they assured the Americans that they would not permit any publicity about them. Jakarta to Sec. of State 20, 1 July 1958. On 6 July, a four-engine bomber dropped oil and gas supplies at a village in north Central Sulawesi, 83, 7 July 1958; on 19 July, a B-26 bombed the coast near Manado, Jones to Secretary of State 323, 24 July 1958 (756D.00/7-158, 758, 2458).

96. Jakarta to Sec. of State 4752, 17 June 1958; 83, 7 July 1958; 143, 10 July 1958; 220, 15 July 1958; 323, 24 July 1958; and 301, 21 July 1958.

97. See Telegram: Dulles to Amembassy Jakarta, Deptel 3901, 27 June 1958; and Dulles to Amembassy Jakarta, Deptel 3911, 28 June 1958 (756D.00/6-2758, 2858).

98. On the reasons behind the invitation and for the Sultan's refusal, see Lev, *Transition to Guided Democracy*, pp. 148-49, and Telegram: Jakarta to Secretary of State 4928, 27 June 1958 (756D.00/6-2758). Lev notes that an ambiguous remark by the Sultan had led Djuanda and Sukarno to believe he would accept the post.

99. These were Sadjarwo, Prijono, Chaerul Saleh, and especially Hanafi, all of them, according to Lev, "on the radical left but non-Communist," as were the less controversial Tobing and Sudibjo. Lev, *Transition to Guided Democracy*, p. 149. Chaerul Saleh was one of the bitterest and most influential opponents of the PKI. Professor Prijono was certainly not regarded by Indonesian intellectuals as a Communist. He was moderately progressive, highly idealistic, but regarded as politically naive for having accepted the Stalin Peace Prize, without realizing the implications. This, of course, damned him in the eyes of most U.S. officials—though not Jones. Hanafi had a special personal relationship with Sukarno going back to the latter's period of exile by the Dutch to Bencoolen where as a young boy Hanafi became his protegé and was regarded as fiercely loyal to him. Sukarno explained this to Ambassador Jones, who so informed Washington in a cable of 21 July 1958, but apparently with little effect on existing prejudices there.

100. Sukarno brought in two new ministers, the historian and former minister of education (1953-55), Moh. Yamin, regarded by Washington (and a good many Indonesians) as a "longtime radical-nationalist ideologue," as minister without portfolio, together with former West Java army commander Colonel Suprajogi, the one change that U.S. officials applauded; ibid. See also Jakarta to Secretary of State 4928, 27 June 1958, which reports: "Addition of Col. Suprajogi puts a Nasution man in Cabinet and represents significant move by Army to exercise direct influence on Cabinet decisions."

101. Telegram: Department of State to Amembassy Jakarta 3930, 30 June 1958.

102. Memorandum: "Indonesia." Ass't Secretary Robertson to Dulles, 23 June 1958, p. 2 (756D.00/6-2358).

103. The British Embassy reported to London that, on 30 Sept., the chief of Indonesian air force intelligence finally decided to go public, causing "some dismay in the United States Embassy," he warned the populace that the rebel air force might well resume attacks from foreign bases. The rebels, he charged, "were now training pilots and air crew in foreign countries, including Formosa [Taiwan] and estimated that they were still in possession of sixteen aircraft, i.e. seven B-26, six P-51 (Mustangs), and three B-29," all then "grounded at an airbase in a foreign country."(British Embassy [1091/58] to Foreign Office, 5 Oct. 1958).

104. Jones to Secretary of State 744. 27 Aug. 1958, sect. 2.

105. Cable: Jones to Dulles, 27 June 1958.

106. At the beginning of August the American government resumed negotiations with the Indonesians on a Civil Aviation Agreement, and provided limited assistance to their Merchant Marine. It also withdrew American objections to a loan by the Export Import Bank of $12 million for delivery of three Lockheed Electras to the Indonesian airline Garuda, while also supporting other Export Import Bank financing for agricultural and power plants in Indonesia. See Telegram: Department of State to Amembassy Jakarta 244 (signed Dulles), 1 Aug. 1958 (756D.5-MSP/8-158).

107. For an indication of Herter's acknowledged confusion regarding Indonesia at this time, see his Memorandum for Dulles of 31 July 1958, wherein he notes "the wide divergence" among the papers prepared by Robertson's office and strongly urges Dulles to postpone a decision on Indonesia until after the secretary's return from Brazil (Dwight D. Eisenhower Library); and Robertson's strong insistence to Dulles that Herter's requested delay (until after the secretary's trip) was too long and that "we have to face up to the situation" in Indonesia with a decision taken the next day before Dulles's departure. Telephone call Robertson to Dulles, 31 July, 4.21 p.m. Robertson and Jones were old friends, and Robertson, despite a reputation for hawkishness on some Far Eastern matters, was considerably more supportive of Jones on Indonesia than Dulles or Herter. Discussions with Howard Jones, Ithaca, N.Y., 1969.

108. Herter (acting) to Amembassy, Jakarta, 20 Aug. 1958 (756D.00/8-2058).

109. Herter to Amembassy Jakarta, 21 Aug. 1958 (Roger Channel). The importance and sensitivity of this message can be seen not only in its content but the fact that it was sent by CIA back channel and both drafted and given its classification by the secretary of the Interagency Committee on Indonesia, Hugh S. Cumming, Jr.

110. This was the clear impression gained in an interview with him, Washington, 18 July 1960. Jakarta to Secretary of State 628, 18 Aug. 1958 (756D.5-MSP/8-1858). Alarmed at the speed and extent of the concessions being made, and reflecting the now-evident rift between the Pentagon and the Department of State in their approach to Indonesia, Dulles' deputy Herter cabled to Jakarta: "No repeat No authority has been given for any action which would give Indonesians reason hope for or expect massive U.S. military aid near future. On contrary, authority for limited package with phased deliveries was limit of decision made at top level here. As you know future policy and action re Indonesia dependent on effect achieved by these first steps in seeking work with Indonesians. You should inform General Vittrup that no more discussions Indonesian Army Navy or Air Force shopping list . . . should take place without further instructions. His sole mission at present relates to present $7 million package." (Department of State to Amembassy Jakarta 355, 18 Aug. 1958 (756D.5-MSP/8-1658). American alarm was in part a result of the reaction from European allies, particularly the Dutch who feared that the military equipment now being provided by the United States would be used by the Indonesian government not against the Communists but against Dutch-held West Irian. See Telegrams: Department of State to Amembassy The Hague, 247, 13 Aug. 1958; Department of State to Amembassy Jakarta 345, 16 Aug. 1958; Jakarta to Secretary of State 592, 14 Aug. 1958 (756D.56/8-1358; 756D.5-MSP/8-1458).

111. Jakarta to Secretary of State 872 (756D.00/9-558).

112. See Lev, *Transition to Guided Democracy*, for a full analysis.

113. Ibid., p.171.

114. The Indonesian Political Situation," 20 Oct. 1958, attachment to Despatch 323 Amembassy Jakarta to Department of State, 13 Nov. 1958, p. C.2 (FW756D. 00/11-1358).

115. Jones to Secretary of State, no. 1113, 29 Sept. 1958 (756D.00/9-2958).

Chapter 9

1. Amembassy, Jakarta to Washington 4685, 12 June 1958, p. 6.

2. According to Natsir, communication with Manado was infrequent as messages had to be relayed via Singapore. Interview with Natsir, Jakarta, 26 May 1971.

3. Letter to Sjafruddin from Rasjid in Geneva, 20 Nov. 1958, PRRI Doc. 40.

4. Harvey, *Permesta*, pp. 118-19.

5. Military Attaché's report for June, 1958 (FO371/135905/15803), and "Embassy Dispatch to Foreign Office—4 July, 1958" attached as Appendix "A" to the Military Attaché's Report. In early July the road from Padang to Bukittinggi was still reportedly unsafe except by military convoy.

6. Interviews in Situjuh Padang Kuning and in Bukittinggi, June 1985, and in Payakumbuh, Feb. 1991.The figure given by local informants was "about 143." See also *Tjoba Bandingkan* (Djawatan Penerangan Prop. Sum. Barat, 1958), which gives the figure killed at 148. It is not clear who ordered the killing, though local people say the order came down from the PRRI military leadership. Sometime before the government attack, the mostly non-Communist detainees held in the prison at Muara Labuh had been released and allowed to return home. Interview with Juir Mohammad, a prominent member of the PSI, Jakarta, Jan. 1991.

7. As of the end of 1958 the Sultan of Yogyakarta estimated that six battalions had been sent from Central Java. Interview, Jakarta, 13 Jan. 1959. There was a tendency for the PRRI to exaggerate the proportion of troops that were pro-Communist.

8. Interviews, Guguk, Payakumbuh, and Padang, Feb. 1991. Government forces had freed these prisoners after they landed.

9. Interviews and British military attaché's report of June 1958 (FO 371/135905). It will be recalled that many officials did not expect to be paid unless they went into the jungle.

10. Appendix A to British military attaché's report for June 1958.

11. FO371/144066. Kawilarang had been the most senior Minahasan officer in the TNI before being appointed military attaché in Washington and subsequently defecting to the rebels. He was the only rebel military leader who was not dishonorably discharged and was reported to have maintained contact with Nasution, though both men deny this was the case.

12. Letter from Rasjid to Sjafruddin, 20 Nov. 1958, PRRI Doc. 40 and see also letter from Rasjid to Sumitro, 17 Nov. 1958, PRRI Doc. 41. Rasjid described

himself to the British as "Representative for Europe and Ambassador at Large of the PRRI." Minutes dated 31 Oct. 1958 in FO371/135855.

13. Letter from Rasjid to Sjafruddin, 20 Nov. 1958. PRRI Doc. 40.

14. Letter from Agus Ramedhan to PRRI representatitives, 2 Dec. 1958 Paris (PRRI Doc. 38) and Ramedhan to PRRI European Representatives, 7 Dec. 1958, Paris. (PRRI Doc. 2).

15. Letter from Rasjid to the Secretary of State dated 8 Nov. 1958, enclosed in British Foreign Office Minutes, 24 Nov. 1958 by Miss J.C. Petrie, included in FO371/ 135856; and Jakarta to Secretary of State 1705, 21 Nov. 1958 (756D.00/11-2158).

16. Interview with Saafruddin Bahar, Jakarta, 3 May 1991, also with Imran Manan and Azmi, Padang, 12 Feb. 1991.

17. Interview with Mohammad Natsir, Jakarta, 23 Jan. 1971.

18. Interview with Saafruddin Bahar, also with Anwar, Z.A., Guguk, Payakumbuh, 16 Feb. 1991. The Murba was a small, but influential, nationalist Communist party bitterly opposed to the PKI.

19. PRRI Radio broadcast by Sjafruddin, 15 Feb. 1959 (PRRI Doc. 13).

20. See PRRI radio broadcasts of 15 Feb. 1959 by Sjafruddin (PRRI Docs. 13 and 113).

21. See letter to Sdr. TKL in Singapore from (183) in Geneva, 12 Dec. 1958. Many of the PRRI agents abroad communicated with each other by code, so it is sometimes difficult to identify the authors of the letters. TKL is Tahir Karim Lubis, a senior PRRI representative in Singapore, but it is unclear who 183 is, though he was evidently an agent stationed in Asia visiting Geneva and not Rasjid himself. The letter asks TKL to "explain to Tgk Abdul Rahman [the new Prime Minister of Malaya] that in the present stage of struggle [it is] better to try to free ourselves from Java first and to maintain ties with Sulawesi establishing a Federal State of Indonesia first, and at the second stage there is the possibility of establishing a state of Sumatra and joining with Malaya." PRRI Doc. 86.

22. PRRI Radio broadcasts of 28 May 1959 and May 1959, recording interviews with Colonel Dahlan Djambek (PRRI Doc 22 and 23). According to Djambek, the following leaders attended the meeting: Sjafruddin, Assaat, Moh. Sjafei, Colonel Maludin Simbolon, Suleiman, Mr. Burhanuddin Harahap, Moh. Natsir, and Colonel Ahmad Husein. They received supporting telegrams from Deputy Prime Minister, Colonel Warouw in Sulawesi, and Minister of Defense Sarumpait in Tapanuli; ibid. In the RPI constitution, "Undang-Undang Dasar Republik Persatuan Indonesia," (typescript, n. d.), pp. 9-10, 19, the component states (*negara-negara Bagian*) that were founding members of the RPI were listed as the State of the Islamic Republic of Aceh, Tapanuli/East Sumatra (North Sumatra); West Sumatra; Riau; Jambi; South Sumatra, North Sulawesi,

Islamic Republic of South Sulawesi, North Maluku, and South Maluku. "Undang-Undang Dasar, RPI," p. 62.

23. Interview with Sjafruddin, 21 May 1971. The constitution for the RPI runs to 113 typwritten pages, with a further forty-one pages of appendices made up of proclamation documents. Copy (typescript) in authors' possession. The date of the document is 8 Feb. 1960.

24. Interview of Simbolon with British Consul McKay, Medan, 20 Sept. 1961 (FO 371/15996).

25. Interview with Sjafruddin, 21 May 1971, and Zulkifli Lubis, 10 May 1991.

26. Morris, "Islam and Politics in Aceh," pp. 229-30. See also Foreign Service Despatch 683, Amembassy Jakarta to Department of State, 20 March 1959 (756D.521/3-2059).

27. Jakarta to Foreign Officer, 26 March, 29 May 1959. FO 371/144067. See also van Dijk, *Rebellion under the Banner of Islam*, pp. 334-35. Darul Islam soldiers would make up an auxiliary militia, the most qualified members of which would eventually be recruited into the Indonesian National Army. Morris, "Islam and Politics in Aceh," p. 232. On the negotiations see ibid., pp. 231-35. See also Amconsul Medan to Department of State, Despatch 113, 19 June 1959, and Despatch 19, 27 Aug. 1959.

28. According to Morris, about 75 percent of the active Darul Islam fighting forces transferred their allegiance from Daud Beureueh to the Revolutionary Council. Morris, "Islam and Politics in Aceh," p. 230. According to Dennis Bloodworth of the London *Observer*, then widely regarded as the most knowledgeable correspondent based on Singapore, a large quantity of U.S. arms was sent to Daud Beureueh's group at that time by ship from Pakistan. Interview, Singapore, 22 Jan. 1961.

29. See Jakarta to Foreign Office, 13 Oct. 1959, and 1 Jan. 1960; also van Dijk, *Rebellion under the Banner of Islam*, pp. 214-15.

30. Interviews with Hatta 8 Jan. and 10 Mar. and with Djuanda, 17 Mar. 1959. Both felt that under the 1945 constitution, Parliament would be much more responsible and, according to Hatta, the parties would be "more democratic and less oligarchic." For further details, see Lev, *Transition to Guided Democracy*, pp. 235-57, and Kahin, "Indonesia," in *Major Governments of Asia*, ed. Kahin, esp. pp. 662-65. On 6 March 1960, what remained of the existing parliamentary system was dealt a mortal blow when Sukarno dissolved parliament and soon afterward replaced it with an appointed body. The 1945 constitution had originally actually been in full effect only for two and a half months, until 15 Nov. 1945, when, under the leadership of a new prime minister, Sutan Sjahrir, it yielded de facto to a parliamentary system with members of the representative body appointed by Sukarno and Hatta, the condition of revolution making it impossible to hold elections.

31. In the opinion of Wilopo, the chairman of the Constituent Assembly, its efforts to find a sufficient consensus for passage of a new constitution foundered

primarily over the issue of the place of Islam in the state. Interview, 11 March 1959.

32. This account draws heavily on what is clearly the best and most comprehensive analysis of the return to the constitution of 1945 and the politics surrounding this move, in Lev, *Transition to Guided Democracy*, pp. 263-77.

33. Foreign Service Despatch 841, Amembassy Jakarta to Department of State, 5 Apr. 1959 (756D.00/4-559).

34. Interview with Mohammad Natsir, 31 May 1971.

35. For a retrospective account of the chaotic and corrupt overseas operations and the wide range of difficulties encountered in attempts to get supplies into Sumatra, see PRRI Doc. 112, unsigned from Kuala Lumpur, 22 June 1962, apparently written to Natsir.

36. Letter from Nukum Sanany in Singapore to Hasanuddin, 24 March 1959. PRRI Doc. 81.

37. Sumitro's lack of rapport with the civilian leadership on Sumatra may have been in part due to his earlier political affiliation with the PSI rather than the Masjumi and perhaps his Javanese background, as well as his wife's being Menadonese. After discussions with Rasjid, one of the PRRI overseas agents said that: "Rasjid said he was a socialist and follower of Sumit[ro] and Sjahrir but differs with Sumit[ro] because he [Rasjid] is religious and Sumitro is not religious and in fact is afraid of Islam." Letter from (113) in Hong Kong to Sdr. T., 7 Feb. 1959. Here Des Alwi is referred to as the "golden boy of Sumitro." PRRI Doc. 110.

38. Interviews with Dennis Bloodworth of the London *Observer*, 22 Jan. 1961, and Des Alwi, the PRRI/Permesta representative in Hong Kong, 2 Feb. 1961.

39. Interview with Natsir, 23 Jan. 1971.

40. Interview with General Djatikusumo, Jakarta, 17 Feb. 1971.

41. Hanna, *Sequel to Colonialism*, p. 184. This move was made even though at this time the British still retained control over defense and foreign policy. Further complicating the situation for the rebels on Sumatra was the fact that many of the supplies being carried there by motor boat or fishing vessel from ports in Malaya had to enter via territory controlled either by the Darul Islam in Aceh or by bandit gangs on the east coast, both of whom often confiscated much if not all of the imported arms.

42. Concerning this standing offer of the Soviets previously spurned by Jakarta for fear of undermining any prospect of military or economic assistance from the U.S., Ambassador Jones observed: "Convinced we were turning our back on them, the Indonesians finally took up that option and accepted aid from the Soviet government." Jones, *The Possible Dream*, p. 122. The NSC estimated that during 1957-58 Soviet Bloc nonmilitary aid commitments (credit for capi-

tal equipment, foodstuffs, and technicians) "mostly on easy credit terms," totaled $194 million, "with additional amounts offered and under discussion." It calculated total U.S. assistance (1950 through 30 June 1958)—nearly all provided prior to fiscal year 1957-58—at $276.9 million, of which $61.4 million was in grants, $118.8 million in credits, and $96.7 million in PL-480 (U.S. agricultural products) sales (sold for rupiah, 80 percent of which could be loaned to Indonesia for economic development). "Financial Appendix" to "U.S. Policy Towards Indonesia," NSC 5901, 16 Jan. 1959, pp. 30, 32 (Dwight D. Eisenhower Library).

43. The sole exception among U.S. allies was Belgium and the amount was inconsequential.

44. Memorandum: Indonesian Arms Procurement, From Richard K. Stuart to J. Gordon Mein, 8 Sept. 1959, pp. 3-4 (756D.561/9-859). Of these orders for 1958, $120,203,400 were with Poland, $45,179,600 with Czechoslovakia, and $20,925,900 with Yugoslavia. Orders with Switzerland totaled $4,090,900 and Belgium $1,321,700; ibid., p. 2. For the first half of 1959 orders with Poland ceased, but were $5,687,408 with Czechoslovakia and $25,375,800 with Yugoslavia. The State Department's tabulation listed no orders direct from the USSR itself until July-Aug. 1959, when they totaled $5,000,000; ibid., p. 2.

45. See below.

46. While the State Department registered no orders with Britain or West Germany during the first half of 1958, these totaled $28,961,200 and $35,747,800, respectively, during the second half of 1958 and first half of 1959.

47. National Security Council, Financial Appendix to NSE 5901, "US Policy Towards Indonesia," 16 Jan. 1959, p. 24. U.S. negotiators were authorized to accept terms of repayment in Indonesian rupiahs even so at only 15 percent of the dollar cost.

48. Department of State to Amembassy, Jakarta (No. 1401), 4 Feb. 1959, and Jakarta to Secretary of State 2515, 13 Feb. 1959 (756D.56/2-459, 756D.00 (W)-2-1259). See also Robertson to the Secretary [Herter] Through Dillon. Memo: "Additional Military Assistance to the Indonesian Army," 9 Jan. 1959; and Memorandum of Conversation: "Military Assistance to Indonesia," MalcolmBooker, Minister Australian Embassy and John Gordon Mein, Director of Southwest Pacific Affairs, 4 Feb. 1959 (756D.5-MSP 1-959, 2-459). As early as 8 Nov. 1958, the Indonesian ambassador to Washington had been assured that the military airplanes that his government had requested would be all or in part made available on "a government to government basis," thus bypassing normal sales channels. Memorandum: "Possible Sale of U.S. Government Surplus F-51 and B-25 Aircraft," From John Gordon Mein to Assistant Secretary Robertson, 8 Jan. 1959.

49. National Security Council, Financial Appendix to NSC 5901, "U.S. Policy towards Indonesia," 16 Jan. 1959, p. 22. Moreover, despite the fact that the costs for this equipment to the Jakarta government were insignificant they also

covered all necessary "repair and rehabilitation" of these items, their "packing, crating, handling, and transportation charges and the cost of training service."

50. Ibid., and Memorandum: "Possible Sale of U.S. Government Surplus F-51 and B-25 Aircraft," From John Gordon Mein to Assistant Secretary Robertson, 8 Jan. 1959, and uncaptioned note of 8 Apr. 1959, from "The Acting Secretary of State: to the Ambassador of the Republic of Indonesia." (756D.5622/2-959).

51. Memorandum: "Indonesian Arms Procurement; Updating RAS Memorandum of the Same Title dated July 15, 1959," from Richard K. Stuart to J. Gordon Mein, 8 Sept. 1959. (756D.561/9-859).

52. Ibid. See also State Department Office Memorandum, "Indonesian Arms Procurement," from John Lacey to J. Gordon Mein, 15 July 1959, p. 1 (756D.561/7-1559), which notes that the air force and the navy—in contrast to the army—were "in a position of heavy logistical dependence on the bloc."

53. Information from several reputable Indonesian sources, including interview with Professor Selo Soemardjan, 12 Jan. 1961.

54. This was Ambassador Jones's conclusion and was abundantly clear in Herter's performance in a private session at the Council on Foreign Relations concerned with Indonesia.

55. This proposal was drafted 16 Jan. and then submitted to the National Security Council for discussion.

56. Memorandum of Discussion at the 395th Meeting of the NSC, 29 Jan. 1959, p. 2.

57. NSC 5901, "U.S. Policy on Indonesia," 16 Jan. 1959.

58. The quote is from an interview with Nasution, 15 Jan. 1959.

59. Interview with Sukarno, Jakarta, early Apr. 1959.

60. Memorandum, "New Government in Indonesia" from Graham Parsons to the Secretary [Herter], 16 July 1959.

61. Memorandum, "Current Situation in Indonesia," from John Gordon Mein to Graham Parsons, assistant secretary of state for Far Eastern Affairs, 31 Dec. 1959. Parsons, previously deputy assistant secretary, had replaced Walter Robertson in June 1959.

62. The new law in some ways strengthened Sukarno's position vis-à-vis the army by providing for just one central war administrator (Sukarno) rather than three (the three chiefs of the defense services); and provided for three separate stages of emergency: civil emergency, military emergency, and state of war. Execution of the first category was primarily in the hands of the mostly civilian regional heads. Presidential Decision 315/1959, 16 Dec. 1959.

63. Interview with Kawilarang, Jakarta 26 May 1971.

64. A Minahasan from Tomohon, Timbuleng had since late 1950 been a member of a south Minahasan rebel group—Pasukan Pembela Keadilan (The Defenders of Justice Army)—becoming its commander in 1954. With some 2,000 of his men he joined Permesta only in March 1958. Harvey, *Permesta*, p. 160. According to some accounts, the arrest was ordered by Sumual.

65. Account based on Harvey's extensive treatment, *Permesta*, pp. 130-33.

66. More than 25,000 of these had been under Kawilarang and Somba's command, and a further 11,000 surrendered with Manguni and Saerang. See ibid., pp. 146-48. Other reports estimate the strength of the forces under Kawilarang, Somba, and Saerang at over 30,000, with about 1,200 under Sumual still in rebellion. See "memorandum by the Military Attaché on the situation up to 14 August 1961," in Jakarta to Foreign Office, 11 Sept. 1961 (FO371/159961). The fact that Kawilarang alone was not arrested nor detained lent some credence to the belief that Nasution had encouraged him to join the rebels with the expectation that, given his prestige, "he could contribute to ending the rebellion in Sulawesi or at least keep Nasution informed." The quotation is from an interview with Sjafruddin, 21 May 1971. It should, however, be reiterated that both Nasution and Kawilarang have denied that this was the case.

67. Interviews with Sjafruddin, Jakarta, 1 March 1971 and with Natsir, Jakarta, 31 May 1971.

68. See British Consulate, Medan to British Embassy, Jakarta, 20 Sept. 1961. According to Simbolon, he outlined to Husein the hopelessness of their position, and told him "that our only solution was to surrender on the best terms available. With this he agreed." Ibid.

69. Interview with Sjafruddin, Jakarta, 21 Feb. 1971.

70. "Memorandum by British Military Attaché August 14, 1961," and interview, West Sumatra, 6, 16, 20 Feb. 1991.

71. British Military Attaché (Colonel Boyle) memo, 14 Aug. 1961, FO 371/159961. Finding it impossible to accept the fact of surrender, Nainggolan was hospitalized with a mental breakdown. "To him it must have seemed that all that had gone before had been for nothing."British Consulate, Medan to British Embassy, Jakarta," 10 Aug. 1961 (FO 371/159961). Nainggolan was the son of a Toba Batak father and a Menadonese mother. His mother and sister had reportedly been murdered by Karo Bataks during the independence revolution. Although he recovered from the breakdown, Nainggolan was eventually to commit suicide.

72. Interviews with Natsir, Jakarta, 31 May 1971, and with Sjafruddin, 21 Feb. 1971.

73. Jakarta to Foreign Office, 25 Aug. 1961 (FO 371/159960). For the Ibnu Hadjar rebellion, see chap. 3. The rebellion in Maluku dated from 1950 and had been almost completely wiped out several years before the PRRI/Permesta rebellion had begun. In 1958, there were no more than a few small pockets of resistance left.

74. They had trekked north to this area for their surrender because it was then occupied by the government's Siliwangi division (composed mostly of soldiers from West Java) from whom they expected (with good reason) better treatment than from the units of the Central Java based Diponegoro division then occupying Central Sumatra. Interview with Sjafruddin, 21 May 1971.

75. Interview with Sjafruddin, 21 Feb. 1971, and Jakarta to Foreign office, 4 Sept. 1961 (FO371/159960).

76. Interview with Sjafruddin, 21 May 1971.

77. Harvey, *Permesta*, p. 149.

78. Letter from Natsir to Taher Karim Lubis, Padang Sidempuan, 15 Oct. 1961 (PPRI Doc. 6).

79. Interviews with Saafruddin Bahar, Jakarta, 3 May 1991 and Buchari Tamam, Padang, 6 May 1991.

80. Natsir's letter of 15 Oct. 1961 (he gives a date of 13 Sept.), and the above interviews, and interview, Sjamsul Bahar, Bukittinggi, June 1985. Several people attributed Djambek's death to a PKI leader in Payakumbuh named Gandi. In interviews with former PRRI followers in the Kamang area, several still believed that Djambek was never killed, because he would never have surrendered. They recalled a speech he had made in which he had sworn "that even if all the others surrendered he would continue to fight to the last drop of his blood." Interviews, Feb. 1991.

81. Interview with Sjafruddin, 1 Mar. 1971. Kawilarang was never arrested and Sumitro, out of the country when the surrenders took place, stayed comfortably abroad, mostly in Kuala Lumpur, until the late 1960s when President Suharto's intelligence chief, Ali Moertopo, arranged for his return as a free man to Jakarta.

82. Recall Robert Lovett's oral history interview cited in the Introduction and his characterization of the still-secret Lovett-Bruce memorandum.

83. Reliable figures on casualties—especially civilian—are difficult to find. Genberal Nasution gives a total of 10,150 killed on the government side—2,499 soldiers, 956 members of the OPR militia, 274 police, and 5,592 civilians. (He does not provide figures for the navy—where losses were heavy—or for the air force.) He lists 22,174 rebels as killed but does not indicate whether this includes civilians. Nasution, *Memenuhi Panggilan Tugas* 4: 383.

Conclusion and Epilogue

1. According to this concept, army officers should participate actively in government affairs but not seek a dominant position. The concept was expanded at

an army seminar in April 1965 into a doctrine, later known as *dwi fungsi* (dual function), declaring that the armed forces were both a military and a social-political force, and as the latter their activities covered "the ideological, political, social, economic, cultural, and religious fields." Crouch, *Army and Politics*, pp. 344-45.

2. A scholarly account of the Constituent Assembly's accomplishments and promise is finally available in the excellent study of Buyung Nasution (based on his doctoral dissertation at Leiden University), *The Aspiration for Constitutional Government in Indonesia: A Socio-legal Study of the Indonesian Konstituante 1956-1959* (Jakarta: Pustaka Sinar Harapan, 1992).

3. Martial law was administered by an army hierarchy under a Supreme War Administrator (a position held by Nasution) which paralleled civilian territorial administration down to the local level. See McVey, "Post Revolutionary Transformation, Part II," p. 151, and Lev, *Transition to Guided Democracy*, pp. 59-61.

4. Lev, *Transition to Guided Democracy*, p. 186. As previously noted, it was the Masjumi, PSI, Parkindo and IPKI that Nasution banned in many outer island regions in September 1958. See also ibid., p. 187.

5. He did on occasion, however, transfer officers because of their involvement in corruption, such as Ibnu Sutowo in 1958 and Suharto in 1959. Crouch, *Army and Politics*, p. 40.

6. The quote concerning Sukarno is from a retrospective CIA Intelligence Report produced in 1968, *Indonesia—1965: The Coup That Backfired* (Intelligence Report, Central Intelligence Agency, Dec. 1968), p. 190. (This is apparently the only CIA Indonesian political study ever made public at the agency's own initiative.)

7. Sukarno said that Britain's ascertainment of opinion regarding the Malaysia proposal through talks with local chieftains and headmen on the British colonial payroll reminded him of the Dutch action in 1948-9 in setting up their puppet states in eastern Indonesia. Interview, Bogor, 20 July 1963.

8. Interview with Nasution, Jakarta, 8 July 1963.

9. Jones, *The Possible Dream*, p. 360.

10. Ambassador Jones reported back: "He avoided like the plague any discussion of possible military takeover, even though this hovered in air throughout talk, and at no time did he pick up obvious hints of US support in time of crisis." Telegram, Jakarta (Jones) to Sec. State, 946, 6 March 1964.

11. Statement by Ambassador Howard P. Jones at the Chiefs of Mission Conference, Baguio, the Philippines, 10 March 1965 (typescript), pp. 17-18. (Hoover Institute Archives).

12 Jakarta (Francis Galbraith "For the Ambassador") to State, 21 Sept. 1965. (Howard P. Jones Collection, Hoover Institute Archives).

13. Declassified Documents Reference Service (R) 594H, Jakarta Telegram 605, 13 Feb. 1965.

14. Jones, *The Possible Dream*, p. 49.

15. Declassified Documents Reference Service (R), 600E, Jakarta Telegram 2623, 3 June 1965.

16. See Crouch, *Army and Politics*, pp. 106-7; Bunnell, "American Policy toward Indonesia," pp. 33-34.

17. CIA, *Indonesia—1965: The Coup That Backfired*, pp. 188-89.

18. Ibid., p. 194.

19. Membership of the forty-five member Revolutionary Council's Presidium as announced by Untung included fairly senior leaders of the PNI and Nahdatul Ulama parties and several smaller ones and three minor second or third level leaders from the PKI and twenty-two officers from the armed forces—including nine generals. The overwhelming majority of those designated as members of the Presidium had never heard of it before and were mystified as to why their names had been used.

20. CIA, *Indonesia—1965; The Coup That Backfired*, p. 71.

21. Robert Cribb, ed., *The Indonesian Killings of 1965-1966* (Melbourne: Center of Southeast Asian Studies, 1990), p. 3. For Sudomo's estimate of those killed, see Crouch, *Army and Politics*, p. 155. The estimate (for those jailed or sent to concentration camps) is cited by Amnesty International's Secretary General, Martin Ennals, as having been given by Admiral Sudomo. *New York Review of Books*, 9 Feb. 1978, p. 44.

22. Frederick Bunnell, "American 'Low Posture' Policy Toward Indonesia In The Months Leading To The 1965 'Coup,' "*Indonesia* 50 (October 1990), p. 30.

23. Crouch, Army and Politics, p. 104.

24. *The Coup Attempt of the "September 30 Movement" in Indonesia* (Jakarta, Pembimbing Masa 1968). In 1966 Nugroho had published a briefer account of the affair, *40 Hari Kegagalan G-30-S* (Staf Pertahanan-keamanan, Jakarta.)

25. Crouch, *Army and Politics*, p. 112.

26. CIA, *Indonesia—1965: The Coup That Backfired*, p. 311. Presumably this 318-page CIA study was prepared to help compensate for the weakness of the Nugroho-Saleh book.

27. For the fullest accounts see Gabriel Kolko, *Confronting the Third World: United States Foreign Policy, 1945-1980* (New York: Pantheon, 1988), especially pp. 179-83; and Bunnell, "American 'Low Posture' Policy," pp. 58-60. A careful scrutiny of the evidence can lead to no other conclusion but that, as

Bunnell states: "Though not a prime mover of those tragic events, the United States was, however, surely an important and willing accomplice." Bunnell, "American 'Low Posture' Policy," p. 60.

28. Amembassy to State, 5 Nov. 1965.

29. Kolko, *Confronting the Third World*, p. 181, and Bunnell in their studies of the available documents reach the same conclusion. Colby's evaluation was made in response to a question from one of the present authors at a symposium on Secrecy and U.S. Foreign Policy held at Tufts University, 26-27 Feb. 1988.

30. Bunnell, "American 'Low Posture' Policy," p. 60; n. 152, p. 59.

INDEX